S0-BLT-775

THE HOLY SPIRIT
IN THE NEW TESTAMENT

BY

HENRY BARCLAY SWETE

BAKER BOOK HOUSE
Grand Rapids, Michigan

ISBN: 0-8010-8078-9

Reproduced from the edition
issued in London
in 1910
by Macmillan and Company

Second printing, September 1976

PHOTOLITHOPRINTED BY CUSHING - MALLOY, INC.
ANN ARBOR, MICHIGAN, UNITED STATES OF AMERICA
1976

INTRODUCTION

HENRY Barclay Swete was born near Bristol, England, in 1835, the only child of his father's second marriage. His mother died a month after his birth, and when his father remarried some three years later, he brought in a stepmother whose rigid and unsympathetic character represented a repressing influence for the young boy. He was of a gentle and retiring disposition, almost to the point of bashfulness. Under these circumstances, even his great gifts of mind were not quickly discovered. His father was a clergyman of the Church of England of Irish origin, but his views were too staunchly Calvinistic to permit him to be ordained in Ireland. Thus he was led to move to England where he served in the pastoral ministry and for some years, including those of the early childhood of Henry, as headmaster of a school for boys. After studies carried out in Cambridge and a stage of a few years as curate to his father, H. B. Swete entered the teaching ministry at Cambridge and continued in this type of work until his 80th year, with the exception of some thirteen years in the pastoral ministry of a country parish between 1877 and 1890. His literary production is quite amazing in its variety. His earliest work appears to have been a discussion on the subject of Baptism entitled *Two Sides to Every Question: Or Nine Questions to the Baptists With an Examination of Their Reply*. This pamphlet of forty-four pages was published in 1860. Since that date there was an almost continuous flow of important contributions. For the sake of brevity, the list will be limited here to the main works and will be arranged according to topics.

Perhaps one of the areas for which H. B. Swete's name is best remembered is the edition of the LXX. This tremendous work accomplished at the request of the Cambridge University Press occupied a major part of his time and attention since 1885. The first volume appeared in 1887, the second in 1891, the third in 1894; and each of these passed during the lifetime of Swete through three editions, volumes one and three even through four editions. Swete further prepared as a companion volume *An Introduction to the Old Testament in Greek*, Cambridge University Press, 1900. A second edition of this work revised by R. R. Ottley was published in 1914. In addition to this, there were important excerpts on the Psalms and on the Psalms of Solomon which were published separately.

In the area of New Testament, H. B. Swete is noted particularly for his monumental commentaries on Mark (1898; 2nd edition, 1902) and on the Apocalypse of St. John) 1906; 2nd edition, 1907; 3rd edition, 1909). We should not forget, however, that he wrote two early commentaries on Thessalonians (1863) and on Galatians (1866). He also edited the commentary of Theodore of Mopsuestia on the Epistles of Paul (1880, 1882). He showed interest in the Apocryphal Gospel of St. Peter (1892, 1893) and produced small volumes on *Studies in the Teaching of Our Lord* (1903) and on *The Last Discourse and Prayer of Our Lord* (1913). In 1920 a brief work on *The Parables of the Kingdom* appeared posthumously.

Swete was always interested in the origins of Christian doctrine. This is apparent in a rather rare early book entitled *England Versus Rome: A Brief Handbook of the Roman Catholic Controversy for the Use of Members of the English Church* (1868). It is apparent also in a number of studies on the Apostles' Creed. A general volume dealing with Harnack's views was published in 1894. We also have a series of monographs relating in the main to the latter articles of the Creed: *The Appearances of Our Lord After the Passion* (1907); *The Ascended Christ* (1910); *The Holy Catholic Church* (1915); *The Forgiveness of Sins* (1916); *The Life of the World to Come* (1917). We might mention here also his very helpful introduction to the Fathers entitled *Patristic Study* (1902).

Among the doctrines of our faith, the doctrine of the Holy Spirit seemed to hold in a special way the attention of Dr. Swete. His earliest work of mature scholarship was entitled *On the Early History of the Doctrine of the Holy Spirit: With Especial Reference to the Controversies of the Fourth Century*, Cambridge: Deighton, Bell, 1873. Three years later he produced *On the History of the Doctrine of the Procession of the Holy Spirit, From the Apostolic Age to the the Death of Charlemagne*, Cambridge: Deighton, Bell, 1876. These two volumes have become quite rare, but the substance of his conclusions may be found in his article "Holy Ghost" in Smith and Wace, *Dictionary of Christian Biography* III (1882), 113-133. We should probably mention also his article "Holy Spirit" in *Hastings' Dictionary of the Bible* II (1899), 402-411. In 1909 he returned to this general theme in a major volume, *The Holy Spirit in the New Testament,* the volume presently reprinted. This line of work was carried out in a sequel published in 1912 under the title *The Holy Spirit in the Ancient Church. A Study of Christian Teaching in the Age of the Fathers.* H. B. Swete, as we understand, would have desired to carry on this study further through the history of the Church, but he himself did not have opportunity to do so. Professor Howard Watkin-Jones did carry on this line of study in part in his important contributions entitled *The Holy Spirit in the Mediaeval Church*, London: Epworth, 1922; and *The Holy Spirit from Arminius to Wesley,* London: Epworth, 1929. The Methodist affiliation of the author, as well as the names included in the title of the latter, indicate rather clearly an Arminian orientation in this sequel to Swete's labors. In the same context one might well mention the work of Professor G. F. Nuttall, *The Holy Spirit in Puritan Faith and Experience,* Oxford: B. Blackwell, 1946. Together these five volumes form a most impressive historical study of the doctrine of the Holy Spirit, and while there are areas that might deserve consideration which have not been treated therein, there is reason to be very grateful for the elaboration that has thus been made available.

Professor Swete was further influential as an editor. He was the founder of the *Journal of Theological Studies,* and he undertook for the theological faculties of Cambridge to edit three volumes of essays: *Essays on Some Theological Questions of the Day* (1905); *Essays on Some Biblical Questions of the Day* (1909); *Essays on the Early History of the Church and the Ministry* (1918). The last volume was prepared for the press by C. H. Turner, death in 1917 having prevented H. B. Swete from completing this project. A useful remembrance of him together with bibliographic indication is found in the little volume *Henry Barclay Swete,* London: Macmillan, 1918. Much of the information contained in the present preface has been drawn from it.

It is a matter of great pleasure that this important contribution of the great Cambridge professor should again be made available in print.

Roger Nicole

Gordon Divinity School

PREFACE

THIS book is not an attempt to demonstrate the truth of the Catholic doctrine of the Holy Spirit by an appeal to the New Testament, nor does it profess to make a formal contribution to the study of New Testament theology. Its purpose is rather to assist the reader in the effort to realize the position of the first Christian teachers and writers, when they speak of the Holy Spirit in connexion with the history of their times or out of their own experiences of the spiritual life.

In pursuing this aim I have not thought it necessary to spend many words upon the questions of literary and historical criticism which are raised by every book in the New Testament. The testimony which the writers bear to the belief or the experience of their age is but seldom, and in a relatively low degree, affected by questions of this kind. Whether the Miraculous Conception is a fact, as I believe, or a legend, as many now assume, the story shews the relation which, in the judgement of two representative Christian writers of the first century, the Holy Spirit held to the beginnings of our Lord's human life. Whether the fourth Gospel was written by the son of Zebedee or by some other early Evangelist, its estimate of the work of the Paraclete is equally valuable as an interpretation of the teaching of Christ upon this subject in the light of the subsequent history of the Apostolic Church. And whatever views may be held as to the historical character of certain narratives, or the date or authorship of certain books, the New Testament as a whole speaks with a voice too clear and full to be overpowered by the din of our critical controversies. In the following pages I ask the reader to listen to that voice, as it tells him what the presence and working of the Spirit of Christ meant to the first generation of believers.

In the first two parts of this book, which form a running commentary upon the New Testament references to the Holy Spirit, I have placed at the head of each chapter the Greek text of the passages discussed in it. In the commentary itself quotations are made in an English form, which departs from the Revised Version wherever it has seemed desirable to call attention to points of order or structure or exact meaning which could not be emphasized in a version intended for general use.

My best thanks are due to my friend Dr Bebb, Principal of St David's College, Lampeter, who in the midst of many engagements has found time to correct the sheets of this book; and to the compositors, readers, and officers of the University Press, to whose conscientious work I have owed much for many years.

I hope that I may be permitted to follow up this study of New Testament Pneumatology by a companion volume on the Pneumatology of the ancient Church in post-Apostolic times.

H. B. S.

CONTENTS

οὐχ ἕτερον μὲν ἐν νόμῳ καὶ προφήταις, ἕτερον δὲ ἐν εὐαγγελίοις καὶ ἀποστόλοις, ἀλλ’ ἕν ἐστι καὶ τὸ αὐτὸ πνεῦμα ἅγιον τὸ ἐν παλαιᾷ τε καὶ καινῇ διαθήκῃ τὰς θείας λαλῆσαν γραφάς.

CYRIL OF JERUSALEM.

FOREWORD.

An enquiry into the teaching of the New Testament on the being and functions of the Holy Spirit must begin with a brief retrospect. The New Testament tacitly assumes acquaintance with the Old Testament doctrine of the Spirit, and starts from it. Before the reader can follow the Apostolic writers in their advance upon the position of the Hebrew Canon, he must understand what that position was, and how it presented itself to the minds of devout Jews in the time of our Lord.

1. The doctrine of the Spirit is a prominent feature in the theology of the Old Testament. While the Son or Word of God scarcely appears in its pages, the Spirit of Jahveh or Elohim meets us in each of the three great sections of the Hebrew Bible.

The Hebrew *rûaḥ*[1], like the Greek πνεῦμα and the Latin *spiritus*, originally had a physiological and not a psychological value, denoting the human breath. But since the breath is the symbol of animal life, and in man is also the means of express-

[1] On *rûaḥ* see Brown-Driver-Briggs, *Hebrew and English Lexicon*, p. 924 *b*, ff.

ing emotion and thought, the word naturally passed into higher meanings, such as the principle of life as contrasted with the 'flesh' or material form; the seat of thought and desire, of the rational and moral nature of man. While *nephesh*[1] (*ψυχή*, *anima*) is predicated freely of irrational animals as well as of human beings, *rûaḥ* is rarely used except in reference to man or to God, in whose image man was made. No Hebrew writer speaks of the 'soul' of God[2], but of the Spirit of God more frequent mention is made than of the spirit of man. The Spirit of God is the vital power which belongs to the Divine Being, and is seen to be operative in the world and in men. It is the Divine Energy which is the origin of all created life, and especially of human existence and the faculties of human nature. To its action are ascribed gifts of bodily strength and physical courage, as well as mental and spiritual capacities. More particularly, it is regarded as the source of the gift of prophecy. The prophet is a *man of the Spirit*[3]; the Spirit of God falls upon him, fills his mind, and speaks by his mouth; he finds himself at times dominated by a spiritual force which comes from without and from above. Yet the prophets of the

Gen. i. 2, Job xxxiii. 4, Ps. xxxiii. 6.

Judg. xiii. 25, xiv. 6, 1 Sam. xi. 6; Gen. xli. 38, Exod. xxxi. 3, Num. xi. 17, Deut. xxxiv. 9. Hosea ix. 7, Num. xxiv. 2, 2 Sam. xxiii. 2, Mic. iii. 8.

[1] On *nephesh* and *rûaḥ* in relation to man see the remarks of Prof. Kautzsch (Hastings, *B. D.* v. 666 *b*): "As long as the Divine breath of life is outside man it can never be called *nephesh*...on the other hand the breath of life which has entered man's body ...may be called either *rûaḥ* or *nephesh*."

[2] Such passages as Lev. xxvi. 11, Isa. i. 14, xlii. 1, Jer. v. 9, where God speaks after the manner of men, are scarcely exceptions.

[3] אִישׁ הָרוּחַ, LXX. ἄνθρωπος ὁ πνευματοφόρος, Vulg. *vir spiritualis*.

Old Testament lay no exclusive claim to the possession of the Spirit. The nation of Israel as a whole had been under the Spirit's guidance from the time of the Exodus. [Isa. lxiii. 10 f., Hagg. ii. 5, Zech. iv. 6; Neh. ix. 20.] Even the individual Israelite, though not a prophet, might become conscious of the presence of a purifying, uplifting Power which he knew as the Spirit of God's holiness, the princely, supremely good Spirit which was working in the depths of his being. [Ps. li. 10 ff., cxliii. 10 ff.] He learnt to recognize in it a force which was present everywhere, on earth, in heaven, and in Sheol, searching out men's ways, throwing the light of God on the darkest recesses of their lives. [Ps. cxxxix. 7 ff.]

To this consciousness of the activity of the Divine Spirit in the life of Israel the Prophets added the expectation of a future outpouring of spiritual life which was to surpass all earlier gifts both in fulness and in extent. They foresaw a great revival of national vitality. The Spirit of God would breathe on a dead people and they would live. The Spirit would enter into their hearts and be in them a 'new spirit,' a spirit of penitence, obedience, and reconciliation with God. [Jer. xxxi. 31 ff., Ezek. xxxvi. 26 f., xxxvii. 9—14, xxxix. 29.] In those days the Spirit would be poured upon *all flesh*, i.e. on all sorts and conditions of men in Israel, without distinction of age or sex or rank. [Joel ii. 28 ff.] The desire of Moses the man of God that all the Lord's people might be prophets would at length receive its fulfilment. [Num. xi. 29.] This great outpouring of the Spirit would find its culminating point in the Messianic King, on whom the Spirit of Jahveh was to rest permanently as the spirit of [Isa. xi. 1 ff., lxi. 1 ff.]

wisdom and understanding, counsel and might, knowledge and holy fear; the ideal Prophet, who would be anointed by the Spirit to preach a gospel of liberation and healing, comfort and joy. Great as had been the energy of the Divine Spirit in their own experience, it was foreseen by the Prophets that the new Israel of the Messianic age would be inspired both in head and members with a fuller strength and a deeper wisdom, corresponding with the larger mission on which it was to be sent.

2. The student of the New Testament must not overlook the non-canonical Jewish literature of Palestine and Alexandria which was earlier than the Christian era[1].

In the Palestinian writings of this period the doctrine of the Holy Spirit is less prominent than in the Canon; the stream of tradition on this subject has grown sluggish and shallow. The rising angelology of Judaism seems to have checked the earlier belief in the presence and activity of the Divine Spirit. Thus the Book of Enoch, which has much to say about angelic beings, and speaks frequently of the 'Lord of the spirits,' mentions the Spirit of the Lord but once. Nevertheless the chief features in the Old Testament doctrine reappear in this group of non-canonical writings. They recognize the Spirit of God as the vitalizing power in creation, the author of prophecy, the source of the purity and sincerity which give insight

Enoch lxvii. 10.

Judith xvi. 14, Apoc. Baruch xxiii. 5, Sirach

[1] For a fuller treatment of this subject the reader may consult I. F. Wood, *The Spirit of God in Biblical Literature*, pp. 60—113.

and judgement; they repeat the promise of a great xlviii. 24,
outpouring of the Spirit on Israel in the Messianic Susanna 45.
age, and they see in the future Messiah the special Jubilees i. 23, Pss. of
organ of spiritual power and life. Solomon xvii. 42, xviii. 8.

The Alexandrian Jewish literature is far more fruitful in references to the Holy Spirit, but less faithful to the great lines of Old Testament teaching. Under Greek influences Hebrew theology was carried at Alexandria into new fields of thought where it blended with conceptions more or less foreign to it. Thus the Book of Wisdom magnifies the cosmic significance of the work of the Spirit: the *Spirit of the Lord has filled the world*; it *holds all things together*; it *is in all things*. It is practically identified with Wisdom; Wisdom is *a holy spirit of discipline*, a spirit intelligent, beneficent, philanthropic, all powerful, all seeing. This great gift is not limited to Israel—so the writer of Wisdom not obscurely hints. On the last point Philo is explicit; from his point of view the Spirit is 'the pure wisdom of which every man partakes'; if the worst of men have their better moments, they are indebted for these to this source of enlightenment. Even the prophetic *afflatus* is not confined to the Prophets of the Canon; Philo himself had many a time been conscious of a mysterious illumination which he could ascribe to nothing short of a Divine gift. On the other hand the Old Testament conception of prophecy is degraded by inspiration being regarded as an ἐνθουσιασμός, a possession which overmasters the prophet's reason, turning him into a mere instrument

Wisd. i. 7, vii. 21 ff., xi. 24—xii. 2.

De gigant. 5 f., 12.

De migr. Abrah. 7.

upon which the Spirit plays. Of the elevation of the moral and spiritual life of man by the immanent Spirit of God Philo seems to have no knowledge. He attributes to the Spirit an operation upon the intellect rather than upon the heart.

There is, however, little reason to suppose that any of the New Testament writers was indebted to Alexandrian theology for his view of the work of the Holy Spirit. The Epistle to the Hebrews, which shews some affinity to Alexandrian ideas, contributes less to the New Testament doctrine of the Spirit than any other New Testament book of the same length. If St Paul or St John owes anything to Philo, it is in the field of Christology that the debt has been incurred, and not in that of Pneumatology[1]. Nor, so far as we can judge, is the Palestinian literature responsible for the characteristic treatment of the Spirit which we find in the New Testament. This treatment is doubtless due in great part to the experience of the Apostolic Church, which was conscious of the new life of the Spirit, and describes the things which it had seen and heard and felt and known. But the experience of the primitive Church was but a continuation and enlargement of the experience of the Church of Israel which is expressed in the Old Testament. The New Testament doctrine of the Spirit begins where the Old Testament doctrine breaks off. The Holy Spirit of the

[1] Philo's use of παράκλητος is no exception; it anticipates to some extent the use of the word in 1 Jo. ii. 1, but not its application to the Spirit as distinct from the Logos.

Gospels and the Acts, of the Epistles and the Apocalypse, is still "God exerting power, especially life-giving power[1]"; the Spirit of God which moved on the face of the waters, which inspired the Prophets and the Psalmists, which guided Israel and dwelt in the hearts of those members of the nation who were Israelites indeed. But His presence under the New Covenant is manifested in new ways: in the Conception and Baptism, the life and ministry of Jesus Christ; in the regeneration and renewal of the members of Christ; in the common life and work of His mystical Body, the Universal Church.

3. The New Testament revelation of the Spirit is partly historical, partly didactic. We see the Spirit manifesting itself in the events of our Lord's life, and in the experience of believers after His ascension; and we also receive direct teaching upon the work of the Paraclete and upon the relation of Christians to Him. These aspects of the subject will be separately examined in the first and second parts of this book. In the third part an attempt will be made to collect the chief results, and thus to present the teaching of the Apostolic age as a whole.

Mentes nostras, Domine, Spiritus Paraclitus qui a te procedit illuminet et inducat in omnem, sicut tuus promisit Filius, ueritatem. Per Iesum Christum Dominum nostrum.

[1] See A. B. Davidson, *Old Testament Prophecy*, p. 370.

PART I.

THE HOLY SPIRIT IN THE HISTORY OF THE NEW TESTAMENT.

I. The Birth and Ministry of the Baptist.

II. The Conception and Early Life of Jesus.

III. The Baptism of Jesus.

IV. The Baptized Life and Ministry of the Christ.

V. The Pentecostal Outpouring of the Spirit.

VI. The Life of the early Palestinian Church.

VII. The Founding of the Gentile Churches.

γεννᾶται Χριστός; προτρέχει· βαπτίζεται; μαρτυρεῖ· πειράζεται; ἀνάγει· δυνάμεις ἐπιτελεῖ; συμπαρομαρτεῖ· ἀνέρχεται; διαδέχεται.

πνεῦμα τὸ...λαλοῦν, ἀποστέλλον, ἀφορίζον...διαιροῦν χαρίσματα, ποιοῦν ἀποστόλους, προφήτας, εὐαγγελιστάς, ποιμένας καὶ διδασκάλους.

Gregory of Nazianzus.

I.

THE BIRTH AND MINISTRY OF THE BAPTIST.

Ἔσται γὰρ μέγας ἐνώπιον Κυρίου, καὶ οἶνον καὶ σίκερα Lc. i. 15—
οὐ μὴ πίῃ, καὶ πνεύματος ἁγίου πλησθήσεται ἔτι ἐκ κοιλίας 17.
μητρὸς αὐτοῦ· καὶ πολλοὺς τῶν υἱῶν Ἰσραὴλ ἐπιστρέψει ἐπὶ Κύριον τὸν θεὸν αὐτῶν. καὶ αὐτὸς προελεύσεται ἐνώπιον αὐτοῦ ἐν πνεύματι καὶ δυνάμει Ἠλεία, ἐπιστρέψαι καρδίας πατέρων ἐπὶ τέκνα καὶ ἀπειθεῖς ἐν φρονήσει δικαίων, ἑτοιμάσαι Κυρίῳ λαὸν κατεσκευασμένον.

Καὶ Ζαχαρίας ὁ πατὴρ αὐτοῦ ἐπλήσθη πνεύματος ἁγίου Lc. i. 67,
καὶ ἐπροφήτευσεν λέγων...... 76, 77.

> Καὶ σὺ δέ, παιδίον, προφήτης Ὑψίστου κληθήσῃ,
> προπορεύσῃ γὰρ ἐνώπιον Κυρίου ἑτοιμάσαι ὁδοὺς αὐτοῦ,
> τοῦ δοῦναι γνῶσιν σωτηρίας τῷ λαῷ αὐτοῦ
> ἐν ἀφέσει ἁμαρτιῶν αὐτῶν.

Τὸ δὲ παιδίον ηὔξανε καὶ ἐκραταιοῦτο πνεύματι, καὶ ἦν ἐν ταῖς ἐρήμοις ἕως ἡμέρας ἀναδείξεως αὐτοῦ πρὸς τὸν Ἰσραήλ. Lc. i. 80.

Ἐγένετο ῥῆμα θεοῦ ἐπὶ Ἰωάνην τὸν Ζαχαρίου υἱὸν ἐν τῇ ἐρήμῳ. Lc. iii. 2.

Ἐγένετο Ἰωάνης ὁ βαπτίζων ἐν τῇ ἐρήμῳ κηρύσσων βάπτισμα μετανοίας εἰς ἄφεσιν ἁμαρτιῶν.	Παραγίνεται Ἰωάνης ὁ βαπτιστὴς κηρύσσων ἐν τῇ ἐρήμῳ τῆς Ἰουδαίας, λέγων Μετανοεῖτε· ἤγγικεν γὰρ ἡ βασιλεία τῶν οὐρανῶν.	Ἦλθεν εἰς πᾶσαν περίχωρον τοῦ Ἰορδάνου κηρύσσων βάπτισμα μετανοίας εἰς ἄφεσιν ἁμαρτιῶν.	Mc. i. 4, Mt. iii. 1, 2, Lc. iii. 3.

Part I. i.

Mal. iii. 1 (LXX.), iv. 4, 5 (LXX.= Heb. iii. 23, 24). Isa. xl. 3 (LXX.).

Ἰδοὺ ἐξαποστέλλω τὸν ἄγγελόν μου, καὶ ἐπιβλέψεται ὁδὸν πρὸ προσώπου μου...καὶ ἰδοὺ ἐγὼ ἀποστέλλω ὑμῖν Ἠλίαν τὸν Θεσβίτην...ὃς ἀποκαταστήσει καρδίαν πατρὸς πρὸς υἱόν.

Φωνὴ βοῶντος ἐν τῇ ἐρήμῳ Ἑτοιμάσατε τὴν ὁδὸν Κυρίου, εὐθείας ποιεῖτε τὰς τρίβους τοῦ θεοῦ ἡμῶν.

Lc. i. 3.

OUR first Gospel begins with the human descent and birth of Jesus Christ; our second, with the ministry of John the Baptist. St Luke, true to his principle of 'tracing the course of all things from the first,' starts from the parentage and infancy of John, and his narrative reveals the fact that the birth of the Baptist was accompanied by a manifestation of the Spirit unparalleled in the life of the Jewish people since the days of the Maccabees[1].

Lc. i. 5 f., 39.

1. The movement began in a priestly home in the hill country of Judaea, where the simple piety of the Old Testament was reflected in the lives of the aged priest Zacharias and his wife Elisabeth. Both were *righteous before God, walking in all the commandments and ordinances of the Lord blameless.* To these 'Israelites indeed' a heavenly messenger

Cf. Gen. vii. 1, xvii. 1.

[1] The Maccabean age recognized that prophets had ceased in Israel; cf. 1 Macc. iv. 46, ix. 27, xiv. 41; Ps. lxxiv. 9. Harnack (*Mission u. Ausbreitung*, I. p. 240 f., E. tr. I. p. 414 f.) condemns the notion that prophecy died out long before the Christian era, citing the case of Philo, the pre-Christian apocalyptic literature, and the references to false prophets in the Gospels. But admitting these exceptions, no outburst of prophecy such as St Luke records is known to have occurred before the eve of the Advent.

announced the coming birth of the Forerunner. The tidings were brought by Gabriel, the angel of Daniel's vision; and they came to Zacharias in the Temple, as he stood ministering at the altar of incense. The son that is to be born, so the angel said, *shall be great in the sight of the Lord, and wine and strong liquor shall he not drink, and with Holy Spirit shall he be filled*[1] *even from his mother's womb; and many of the sons of Israel shall he turn unto the Lord their God*[2], *and it is he who shall go before in His sight in the spirit and power of Elijah, to turn fathers' hearts to children and disobedient men to walk in just men's wisdom, to make ready for the Lord a people prepared.*

Part I. i.

Dan. viii. 16, ix. 21; Lc. i. 11, 19.

Lc. i. 15 ff.; cf. Num. vi. 3, Judg. xiii. 4, 7, 14.

In these words the keynote of the Baptist's life is struck. It is to be replete with the presence and workings of the Divine Spirit; in the power of the Spirit it is to fulfil its mission of bringing Israel back to God by recalling the age of the fathers, the manners and life of the Prophets, the Kings, the Judges, the Patriarchs. That it may do this it must follow the best lines of Old Testament piety. John must be a Nazirite all his days; a new Samson, fitted by lifelong abstinence for the great feats of strength that belong to the consecrated life. The

[1] The phrase 'to be filled with Holy Spirit' is peculiar to St Luke (Lc. i. 15, 41, 67, Acts ii. 4, iv. 8, 31, ix. 17, xiii. 9), but the idea is found in the Old Testament (Exod. xxviii. 3, xxxv. 31): cf. Schoettgen I. p. 255.

[2] For this association of the ministry of conversion with the Holy Spirit cf. Ps. li. 13: the immediate reference, as Lc. i. 17 shews, is to Mal. iv. 6.

Part I. i.

exhilaration that comes from strong drink is to be unknown to him; from his infancy he is to be filled with a spiritual power which will supersede the use of stimulants. If in this respect he is to resemble Samson, the work of his life is to be that of another and yet greater hero of the Old Testament, Elijah the Tishbite. The son of Zacharias and Elisabeth will be Malachi's revived Elijah; with Elijah's courage and force he will preach repentance in the days of Herod and Herodias, as Elijah had preached it to the northern kingdom in the reign of Ahab and Jezebel.

Cf. Acts ii. 13 ff., Eph. v. 18.

Mal. iv. 4 f. (LXX.). 1 Kings xix. 10, 14.

After the birth of John both the parents of the Baptist shared at times the gift of the Spirit which was to be the lifelong endowment of their son. On the occasion of Mary's visit to her kinswoman, Elisabeth was *filled with Holy Spirit*, and enabled to interpret Mary's tidings with such clearness of insight that she recognized her at once as the mother of the Messiah. Zacharias experienced a like inspiration when at the naming of his son he *prophesied*. His 'prophecy[1]' is an echo of the message which he had received from Gabriel and had at the time disbelieved, but was now able to grasp and express in even clearer terms:

Lc. i. 41.

Lc. i. 43 (ἡ μήτηρ τοῦ κυρίου μου).

Lc. i. 67.

Lc. i. 76 ff.

> *Yea, and thou, child, shalt be called 'Prophet of the Most High,'*

[1] So the *Benedictus* was called in the Gallican Liturgy, where it preceded the Eucharistic lessons, the prayer that followed being known as *collectio post prophetiam*.

For thou shalt go before in the sight of the Lord
to make ready his ways,
To give knowledge of salvation to his people
In remission of their sins.

The words carry us somewhat further than those of Gabriel, but do not go beyond the sphere of Old Testament teaching; the prophetic books of the Old Testament are full of a salvation in store for Israel, and even the reference to the remission of sins can be paralleled without difficulty. Zacharias speaks as any pious Israelite versed in the Psalms and prophetical books might have spoken in the Spirit.

Cf. Lc. i. 16 ff.

See (e.g.) Ex. xxxii. 32, xxxiv. 7, Numb. xiv. 17 ff., Ps. lxxxv. 2, Jer. xxxi. 34.

2. The child John fulfilled the promise of his birth. Men marvelled not only at the story of his birth, but also at the growing strength of his young life; *the hand of the Lord was with him*. The phrase again follows Old Testament lines, recalling scenes in the lives of Elijah and Elisha, whose feats of physical or spiritual strength are ascribed to 'the hand of Jahveh upon' them. In Ezekiel the inrush of prophetic inspiration[1] is repeatedly attributed to the same cause. The conception comes very near to the Old Testament view of the Spirit as the operative power of God, and in this sense the words are probably used by St Luke; but his choice of a preposition tempers the metaphor[2]. The Hand

Lc. i. 66 (χεὶρ Κυρίου ἦν μετ' αὐτοῦ). 1 Kings xviii. 46, 2 Kings iii. 15. Ezek. i. 3, iii. 14, 22, viii. 1, xxxvii. 1, xl. 1.

[1] Cf. Brown-Driver-Briggs, p. 390 *a*: יָד is used here "of [the] grasp of [Jahveh]'s hand in prophetic inspiration."

[2] St Luke uses μετά again in this phrase (Acts xi. 21); ἐπί is employed, but in another sense, Acts xiii. 11.

of God was 'with' the son of Zacharias; the childhood of John was not swept by great gusts of Divine *afflatus*, but rather it was guided and upheld by a Presence which made it both sweeter and stronger than childhood commonly is. The same thought is expressed more distinctly when it
Lc. i. 80. is added that *the child grew and waxed strong in spirit.* The spiritual faculties of his nature gained strength day by day, keeping pace with his physical growth. 'Spirit' is here the spiritual side of human life, in contrast with the animal or the merely intellectual. But the progressive strengthening of the spiritual life in man implies the action of the Spirit of God[1]; it is not normal or automatic, like growth to physical maturity. The future Baptist was no ordinary boy; in him the development of body and spirit proceeded *pari passu.* In the sunshine of the Divine favour, under the quickening breeze of the Divine Spirit, the lad's powers of spiritual perception and activity ripened daily, even as his body was braced and matured by the air of the Judaean highlands where he had his home.

Meanwhile John was not wholly ignorant of his destiny; he could not have lived as a *nazir* without being aware that some special calling was upon him. By the time that he had reached maturity both his parents were probably dead[2], and the youth,

[1] The process is described in Eph. iii. 16 ἵνα δῷ ὑμῖν...δυνάμει κραταιωθῆναι (comp. St Luke's ἐκραταιοῦτο) διὰ τοῦ πνεύματος αὐτοῦ εἰς τὸν ἔσω ἄνθρωπον.

[2] Both were of advanced age at the time of his birth (Lc. i. 7).

left alone in the world, chose the life of an anchorite; *he was in the deserts.* Not far from his home the Essenes had their settlements, above the shores of the Dead Sea[1], over Engedi and Masada; and it has been hastily concluded that in early life John identified himself with this Jewish sect. But, as Bishop Lightfoot points out, "the rule of his life was *isolation*; the principle of theirs, *community*[2]." An Essene, then, he did not become, though like others of his time he may have been influenced by the asceticism of the Essenes[3]. Nor is it probable that his first move took him into the immediate neighbourhood of their resorts; the wilderness into which he retired at first was, it may be supposed, the uninhabited country beyond the suburbs of his native town. There he remained *till the day of his shewing*[4] *unto Israel,* preparing himself by an ascetic life and a devout silence for the call to active work[5].

Part I. i.

[1] Pliny *H. N.* v. 17 "ab occidente litore Esseni fugiunt."

[2] *Colossians*[1], p. 161.

[3] For an instance of a recluse who was not an Essene see Joseph. *vit.* 2 πυθόμενός τινα Βάννουν ὄνομα κατὰ τὴν ἐρημίαν διατρίβειν, ἐσθῆτι μὲν ἀπὸ δένδρων χρώμενον, κτλ.

[4] ἀναδείξεως: cf. Lc. x. 1, Acts i. 24, and Godet's remark (*Saint Luc*[3] I. p. 159): "le mot...désigne proprement l'installation d'un employé dans sa charge, sa présentation officielle."

[5] The story has points of resemblance to that of Samuel's early life; see 1 Sam. i. 5, 11; iii. 19—iv. 1. Cf. Loisy, *Les Evangiles Synoptiques*, p. 315: "le rédacteur de cette notice...parait être souvenu du jeune Samuel grandissant dans la retraite du sanctuaire, jusqu'à ce que sa réputation de prophète se répande dans tout Israel."

Lc. iii. 2 (*ἐγένετο ῥῆμα θεοῦ ἐπὶ Ἰωάνην*). 1 Kings xvii. 2.

3. The call came to John as it had come to the old prophets, in 'a word of God' which addressed itself directly to his consciousness. St Luke uses once more a well-worn phrase from the Old Testament[1]. As 'the word' had come to Elijah, so it came to his successor; John knew that he had heard in his spirit the Voice of God speaking to him, and that he stood in the Divine Presence, a servant called to do the bidding of the God of Israel. This word reached him through the Spirit, which had filled him from the beginning; but it was a new movement of the Spirit, and one which at once gave John a place in the great line of the ancient prophets. From that day all Israel knew that it had a prophet again. It was indeed a notable day in the life of the nation, and St Luke marks it by an elaborate effort to fix the date of the year in which it fell.

Lc. iii. 1.

We enter now on ground which is common to the three Synoptists. But St Luke still has a source of information which neither the Second nor the First Gospel has used. *There came John the Baptizer in the wilderness* is all that St Mark has to tell; St Matthew adds that the wilderness was that of Judaea. St Luke is more precise: *he came into all the circuit of the Jordan.* The call drew him forth from the solitudes of the Judaean highlands: he descended into the valley through which the Jordan drops into the Dead Sea. His purpose may have been twofold. In the first place, the Jordan valley

Mc. i. 4 (*reading ὁ βαπτίζων*). Mt. iii. 1. Lc. iii. 3.

[1] LXX. *passim*: ἐγένετο ῥῆμα Κυρίου ἐπί...

was in direct communication with Jerusalem; thither people could flock to hear from his mouth the word of God. But further, the Jordan supplied the water necessary for a great baptismal rite. The 'word' which came to him had sent him not only to preach repentance but to baptize any who repented[1]. He had no doubt as to the reality of his mission, yet he was conscious of its limitations. He could preach *a baptism of repentance unto remission of sins*, but had no authority to remit. He could baptize with water, but not with the Spirit. Himself full of the Spirit up to the measure of his capacity, he could not bestow the Spirit upon other men; his baptism was a bare recognition of a change of purpose which would purify and spiritualize life. For more than this the Baptist pointed to another, mightier than himself, for whom his mission was preparatory. In this propaedeutic purpose there lay the deeper aim of his ministry, which seems to have been revealed to him with a force of a second 'word of God.' It was not till his preaching of repentance had raised expectations which he was unable to fulfil that he began to speak of one who should come after him and baptize with the Holy Spirit. The same Voice which sent John to baptize with water guided him to the Person who possessed the fountain of the

Part I. i.

Mc., Lc. (βάπτισμα μετανοίας εἰς ἄφεσιν ἁμαρτιῶν).

Lc. iii. 15.

Cf. Jo. i. 33.

[1] Jo. i. 33 ὁ πέμψας με βαπτίζειν ἐν ὕδατι. The prophets had associated lustrations with the Messianic times; e.g. Jer. xxxiii. 8, Ezek. xxxvi. 25, Zech. xiii. 1. Such passages may have prepared John for this further commission, and the nation to accept his baptism.

Part I. i. Spirit. Thus the ministry of repentance grew into
Jo. i. 7 f. a witness concerning the Light. The Spirit led the Baptist on from one step to another until his whole task was fulfilled, and he could welcome the waning
Jo. iii. 30. of his own reputation in the rising glory of the Christ.

The Synoptists, or the primitive tradition which is behind the Synoptic Gospels, saw in the ministry of John the Baptist a fulfilment of ancient prophecy.
Mc. i. 2, Mt. xi. 10, Lc. vii. 27. In the words of the second Isaiah (xl. 1) he was *the voice of one that crieth, Prepare ye in the wilderness the way of the Lord, make straight in the desert a high way for our God.* Malachi (iii. 1) had written of him, *Behold, I send my messenger, and he shall prepare the way before me*[1]. According to the fourth
Jo. i. 23. Gospel the Baptist quoted the former passage in reference to himself, and the latter is applied to him in the *Benedictus* and even in the message of Gabriel to Zacharias. The new Prophet was conscious that he gave effect to the expectations of his predecessors[2] by preparing the way of the Christ. The Spirit which moved them to write moved John to act, and through his mission there was given to their words a fulfilment larger and greater than any that they could have imagined.

4. The conception of the Spirit which appears

[1] The quotations are not exact, agreeing neither with LXX. nor M.T.; possibly they were taken from a catena of prophetic testimonies (see *St Mark*, ad loc.).

[2] On this see 1 Pet. i. 10 ff. with Dr Hort's notes on the whole passage.

in these records of the early life and the ministry of John the Baptist is in accord both with the place of John in the order of events and with the Jewish-Christian origin of the records. It is also essentially of a piece with the teaching of the Old Testament. John was in fact what Jesus was supposed to be, 'a prophet as one of the prophets,' a true successor of the old Hebrew prophets, not so much of the prophets of the canon as of the non-literary seers who began with Samuel and culminated in Elijah and Elisha. In some respects he even recalled the earlier type of Old Testament heroes represented by Samson and the Judges. The Holy Spirit with which he was filled was not the new spirit of Christ and the Christian Church, but the spirit which gave to the saints of the Old Testament the strength and wisdom which was theirs; the spirit of Nazirite consecration, of absolute courage and loyalty to God, of utter self-abnegation; the spirit and power of Elijah, the Prophet-preacher of northern Israel. John was a prophet and more than a prophet; he rose to a level of moral grandeur never attained by the greatest of his predecessors; yet it was not given to him to enter the Kingdom of Heaven, or to taste the good things which were prepared for the members of Christ. He stood on the border of the promised land and from his Pisgah saw it with his eyes; he beheld the Spirit descend on the Christ and knew that this was the greater Baptist, who should baptize with the Holy Ghost. But he himself was not thus baptized, and, full as he was of the Spirit,

Part I. i. there were mysteries in the spiritual life which he could not have understood. The Spirit was in John the Baptist as it was in the ancient Psalmists and Prophets, not as afterwards it dwelt in the Apostles and prophets of the New Testament, not as it now dwells in all believers; and it is among the evidences of the substantial truth of the Gospel records that the last of the prophets of Israel is represented as inspired by the Spirit of the Old Covenant, and not as he would have been depicted by the imagination of men who had tasted of the Pentecostal gift.

On the other hand the Spirit in the Baptist prepared the way of the Lord with greater directness and plainness of speech than in any of the prophets of the Old Testament. Even the Synoptists represent John as preaching the near approach
Mt. iii. 2 (ἤγγικεν). of the Kingdom of Heaven; creating expectations
of the imminent coming of the Messiah, and thus
Lc. iii. 18 (παρακαλῶν εὐηγγελίζετο τὸν λαόν). 'proclaiming a gospel to the people,' i.e. to Israel.
In the fourth Gospel Jesus is declared by him to
be *the Son of God, the Lamb of God*, the Bride-
Jo. i. 29, 34, 36, iii. 29. groom of Israel, whose fame must grow while His
forerunner waned. Thus the ministry of the Baptist
was a link between the old order and the new, and
when Jesus began to teach He took up the thread
Mc. i. 14 f. which John had been compelled to drop. In the
Baptist the prophetic Spirit uttered its last testimony to Him that was to come, completing the witness of the Old Testament at the moment when the Christ was ready to enter upon His work.

II.

THE CONCEPTION AND EARLY LIFE OF JESUS.

Καὶ εἰσελθὼν πρὸς αὐτὴν εἶπεν Χαῖρε, κεχαριτωμένη· Lc. i. 28—
ὁ κύριος μετὰ σοῦ...μὴ φοβοῦ, Μαριάμ, εὗρες γὰρ χάριν παρὰ 36.
τῷ θεῷ· καὶ ἰδοὺ συλλήμψῃ ἐν γαστρὶ καὶ τέξῃ υἱόν, καὶ
καλέσεις τὸ ὄνομα αὐτοῦ Ἰησοῦν. οὗτος ἔσται μέγας, καὶ
υἱὸς Ὑψίστου κληθήσεται· καὶ δώσει αὐτῷ Κύριος ὁ θεὸς
τὸν θρόνον Δαυείδ... πνεῦμα ἅγιον ἐπελεύσεται ἐπὶ σέ,
καὶ δύναμις Ὑψίστου ἐπισκιάσει σοι· διὸ καὶ τὸ γεννώμενον
ἅγιον κληθήσεται, υἱὸς θεοῦ...ὅτι οὐκ ἀδυνατήσει παρὰ τοῦ
θεοῦ πᾶν ῥῆμα.

Καὶ ἐπλήσθη πνεύματος ἁγίου ἡ Ἐλεισάβετ...καὶ Lc.i.41,46.
εἶπεν Μαριάμ Μεγαλύνει ἡ ψυχή μου τὸν κύριον κτλ.

Μνηστευθείσης τῆς μητρὸς αὐτοῦ Μαρίας τῷ Ἰωσήφ, Mt. i. 18.
πρὶν ἢ συνελθεῖν αὐτοὺς εὑρέθη ἐν γαστρὶ ἔχουσα ἐκ
πνεύματος ἁγίου.

Ἰωσήφ, υἱὸς Δαυείδ, μὴ φοβηθῇς παραλαβεῖν Μαρίαν Mt. i. 20,
τὴν γυναῖκά σου· τὸ γὰρ ἐν αὐτῇ γεννηθὲν ἐκ πνεύ- 21.
ματός ἐστιν ἁγίου. τέξεται δὲ υἱόν, καὶ καλέσεις τὸ ὄνομα
αὐτοῦ Ἰησοῦν· αὐτὸς γὰρ σώσει τὸν λαὸν αὐτοῦ ἀπὸ τῶν
ἁμαρτιῶν αὐτῶν.

Ἄνθρωπος ἦν ἐν Ἰερουσαλὴμ ᾧ ὄνομα Συμεών...προσ- Lc. ii. 25—
δεχόμενος παράκλησιν τοῦ Ἰσραήλ, καὶ πνεῦμα ἦν ἅγιον 27.
ἐπ' αὐτόν· καὶ ἦν αὐτῷ κεχρηματισμένον ὑπὸ τοῦ
πνεύματος τοῦ ἁγίου μὴ ἰδεῖν θάνατον πρὶν ἢ ἂν ἴδῃ τὸν
χριστὸν Κυρίου. καὶ ἦλθεν ἐν τῷ πνεύματι εἰς τὸ ἱερόν
κτλ.

Καὶ ἦν Ἅννα προφῆτις...καὶ ἐλάλει περὶ αὐτοῦ πᾶσιν Lc. ii. 36,
τοῖς προσδεχομένοις λύτρωσιν Ἰερουσαλήμ. 38.

Part I. ii.

Lc. ii. 40. *Τὸ δὲ παιδίον ηὔξανεν καὶ ἐκραταιοῦτο πληρούμενον σοφίᾳ, καὶ χάρις θεοῦ ἦν ἐπ' αὐτό.*

Lc. ii. 42—52. *Ὑπέμεινεν Ἰησοῦς ὁ παῖς ἐν Ἰερουσαλήμ...εὗρον αὐτὸν ἐν τῷ ἱερῷ καθεζόμενον ἐν μέσῳ τῶν διδασκάλων, καὶ ἀκούοντα αὐτῶν καὶ ἐπερωτῶντα αὐτούς. ἐξίσταντο δὲ πάντες οἱ ἀκούοντες αὐτοῦ ἐπὶ τῇ συνέσει καὶ ταῖς ἀποκρίσεσιν αὐτοῦ...καὶ εἶπεν πρὸς αὐτούς Τί ὅτι ἐζητεῖτέ με; οὐκ ᾔδειτε ὅτι ἐν τοῖς τοῦ πατρός μου δεῖ εἶναί με; καὶ ἡ μήτηρ αὐτοῦ διετήρει πάντα τὰ ῥήματα ἐν τῇ καρδίᾳ αὐτῆς. καὶ Ἰησοῦς προέκοπτεν τῇ σοφίᾳ καὶ ἡλικίᾳ καὶ χάριτι παρὰ θεῷ καὶ ἀνθρώποις.*

---

1. THE third Gospel draws both a parallel and a contrast between the entrance into the world of the Forerunner and that of the Christ. Each is heralded by an annunciation, and in each case it is the archangel Gabriel to whom the message is entrusted. Moreover there is a strong general similarity between the opening words of the message to Zacharias and the message to Mary, which can be seen at a glance when they are printed side by side :

Lc. i. 13, 15, 30 f.

Fear not, Zacharias,	*Fear not, Mary,*
because thy supplication was heard,	*for thou didst find favour with God,*
and thy wife Elisabeth	*and behold thou shalt conceive in thy womb,*
shall bear a son to thee,	*and bear a son,*
and thou shalt call his name John.	*and shalt call his name Jesus.*
...For he shall be great[1]*...*	*He shall be great*[2]*...*

But as each message proceeds to unfold the greatness of the son who is to be born, a wide difference appears. John is to be a great Nazirite, a great prophet and preacher of repentance; Jesus *shall be called Son of the Most High, and the Lord God*[1] *shall give him the throne of David his father, and he shall reign over the house of Jacob for ever; and of his reign there shall be no end.* Moreover, a pledge of this higher destiny is given in the greater wonder of the Lord's birth. The Virgin's question, *How shall this be?* is answered, *There shall come upon thee Holy Spirit and the Most High's power shall overshadow thee; wherefore also that which is to be born shall be called holy*[2], *son of God*[3]. For John the Forerunner it suffices that he shall be full of the Spirit from his mother's womb, whereas Jesus is to be conceived by the power of the Spirit in the womb, and for that reason (διό) is to bear titles such as could not be given to John.

Lc. i. 32 υἱὸς Ὑψίστου κληθήσεται, cf. i. 76 προφήτης Ὑψίστου κληθήσῃ.

Lc. i. 34 f.

Lc. i. 15, 31 (ἐκ κοιλίας, ἐν γαστρί).

At first sight Mary's question, *How shall this be?*. appears to be the exact counterpart of Zacharias's, *How shall I know this?* But while the latter was due to unbelief[4], the former, as the sequel shews, was called forth by the struggle to believe, and accordingly it was answered not by a rebuke but by the removal of the difficulty. The Angel explains that the ordinary operation of a natural law is in Mary's case to be superseded by the direct

Lc. i. 34 (cf. 18 f.).

Lc. i. 20.

[1] κύριος ὁ θεός, i.e. Jahveh, the God of Israel.

[2] Dr Nestle points out (*Exp. Times*, Aug. 1908) that ἅγιος is sometimes equivalent to Ναζειραῖος. But Jesus was not a Nazirite, nor in any danger of being so regarded; cf. Mt. xi. 18 f.

[3] As to the soundness of the text of Lc. i. 34 f. see the remarks of Bp Chase in *Cambridge Theological Essays*, p. 409.

[4] See Lc. i. 20, οὐκ ἐπίστευσας: i. 45, ἡ πιστεύσασα.

Part I. ii.

work of the Spirit of God. It is to be observed that, as elsewhere in the first chapter of St Luke, the answer is expressed in terms of the Old Testament. A 'holy spirit,' a breath of the Divine Spirit, shall fall upon Mary with an illapse sudden and irresistible; the verb used to describe the illapse (ἐπέρχεσθαι) is employed by the LXX. for the descent of a whirlwind, for the stirring of the mind by a fit of passion, for the refreshing breeze that springs up after a long spell of breathless heat[1]. A 'power of the Most High' shall cast its shadow over her, even as the cloud of the Shekinah overshadowed the Tabernacle[2], working silently yet surely, with the gentleness of perfect strength.

The miracle of the Holy Conception is not altogether without parallel in the history of revelation. Physical effects are not infrequently ascribed by the writers of the Old Testament to the agency of the Gen. i. 2, vi. 3. Spirit. The Spirit of God is represented as the cosmic force which operated upon the primaeval chaos; and as the vital energy which maintains the physical life in man[3]. Remarkable displays of bodily Cf. Judg. xiv. 6, 19. strength are ascribed to the action upon men of the Spirit of Jahveh. The Old Testament, moreover, Gen. xvii. 17. has its marvellous births, such as that of Isaac, with

[1] Isa. xxviii. 18 καταιγὶς φερομένη ἐὰν ἐπέλθῃ. Num. v. 14 [ἐὰν] ἐπέλθῃ αὐτῷ πνεῦμα ζηλώσεως. Isa. xxxii. 15 ἕως ἂν ἐπέλθῃ (so codd. ℵA) ἐφ' ὑμᾶς πνεῦμα ἀφ' ὑψηλοῦ.

[2] Exod. xl. 35 LXX. ἐπεσκίαζεν (שָׁכַן) ἐπ' αὐτὴν ἡ νεφέλη.

[3] This is at least a possible view of Gen. vi. 3: see Driver *ad loc.*

which indeed a comparison is suggested by the last words of Gabriel's answer, *Nothing from God shall be impossible*[1]. Isaac, according to St Paul, was 'born after the Spirit[2],' i.e. by a special operation (Gal. iv. 29.) of Divine power. The analogy is incomplete, but to this extent it is sound; in the conception of our Lord, as in Isaac's case, we have an intervention of Divine 'power' which supplies the place of 'nature' in producing a physical result. In neither instance, however, is the result produced without the spiritual effort implied in the concurrence of the mother with the Divine Will. *By faith even Sarah herself* (Heb. xi. 11.) *received power to conceive seed...since she counted him faithful who had promised*; and precisely the same obedient faith is shewn in Mary's, *Behold the* (Lc. i. 38.) *handmaid of the Lord; be it done to me according to thy word.* In each case moral strength was imparted first, as the condition upon which physical power followed; *by faith* Mary, no less than Sarah, *received power*[3].

One vast difference distinguishes the Conception of our Lord from other miraculous conceptions. It not only implied moral and spiritual power in the mother, but it gave an unexampled character to the child. The Holy Spirit sanctified the flesh on which it wrought. Of the Child of Mary while yet unborn

[1] In Gen. xviii. 14 cod. D (the Cotton MS.) reads, as St Luke seems to have read, παρὰ τοῦ θεοῦ (מֵיְהוָֹה).

[2] Cf. Du Bose, *Gospel according to St Paul*, p. 119 f.

[3] This was seen by the earliest constructive theologian of the Church: see Irenaeus, iii. 22, 4; v. 19. 1.

Part I. ii.

Lc. i. 35. Cf. Mc. i. 24, Jo. vi. 69; Acts iii. 14, 1 Jo. ii. 20, Apoc. iii. 7.

(τὸ γεννώμενον)[1], it is said that He shall be known as *holy*, even as *son of God*. His unique conception, without human paternity, means that He is to hold this unique position in human history. The words must be understood not as revealing the Divine nature of our Lord as it was taught by St Paul and St John and dogmatically by the post-Apostolic Church, but with reference to their context and to the beliefs of the Jewish-Christian circle in which they were handed down. The Angel's words base the sanctity and Divine sonship of Mary's child not on His preexistence but on His conception by the Divine Spirit[2]. This does not exclude other and deeper reasons for His claim to the titles attributed to Him, but it certainly makes the Holy Conception one reason and the most obvious. Must not that Child be[3] holy and son of God who had no earthly father, whose mother was overshadowed by the Power of the Most High? Paternity is not, of course, ascribed to the Holy Spirit by this process of thought[4], for the Holy Spirit is not hypostatized in

[1] With τὸ γεννώμενον cf. Jud. xiii. 8, LXX. τῷ παιδίῳ τῷ τικτομένῳ.

[2] διὸ καὶ τὸ γεννώμενον ἅγιον κληθήσεται.

[3] κληθήσεται must not be pressed: 'shall have a right to the title' is perhaps the nearest rendering: cf. 1 Jo. iii. 1 ἵνα... κληθῶμεν· καὶ ἐσμέν.

[4] On this point see Pearson *ad loc.*: "because the Holy Ghost did not beget him by any communication of his essence, therefore he is not the father of him": compare his note in reference to Tertullian *de carne* 18 and Hilary *trin.* ii. 26. The maternity ascribed to the Holy Spirit in the Hebrew Gospel

Part I. ii.

the early narratives of St Luke. God, working by His Spirit, is the Father of the humanity of Jesus, in the sense that its origination from the substance of the Virgin Mother was a Divine act. The result of this Divine intervention is to be seen in the human life of the Lord; in His sinlessness, His entire consecration, His sense of the Fatherhood of God, from the dawn of consciousness to His last breath. The entail of sin was broken at last, and one born of a woman was, even as man, holy and a son of God.

2. When we turn to our other New Testament authority for the Miraculous Conception, the opening chapter of St Matthew's Gospel, the whole setting of the narrative is found to be different. No comparison is instituted here between John and Jesus; the first Gospel does not concern itself with the Forerunner until the time comes when he begins actively to prepare the way of his Successor. St Matthew's interest lies wholly in presenting Jesus as the predestined King of Israel. This is the purpose of the pedigree which precedes and of the story of the Magi which follows his reference to the Conception, and it is kept well in view in the account of the Conception itself.

Mt. i. 18–25.

In St Matthew the annunciation is made to Joseph, and it follows in point of time the annunciation made in St Luke to Mary, for it represents the

(Orig. *in Joann.* t. ii. 12 ἡ μήτηρ μου, τὸ ἅγιον πνεῦμα) refers to the Baptism and was perhaps suggested by the usual gender of רוּחַ.

Part I. ii.

Conception as an accomplished fact[1]. An angel (who is not said to have been Gabriel) is sent to Joseph to assist him in forming a right judgement upon a fact already known to him. Joseph is accosted as a *son of David*, and the title may have served to remind him that Mary's child, if acknowledged by him, could claim a place in the royal line.

Mt. i. 20 f.

But a higher destiny in fact awaits this child. *That which was begotten in her is of Holy Spirit; and she shall bear a son, and thou shalt call his name Jesus, for he it is who shall save his people from their sins.* This whole occurrence, the Evangelist

Mt. i. 22 (τοῦτο δὲ ὅλον γέγονεν ἵνα).

comments, was intended to fulfil the word of Jahveh spoken by the prophet Isaiah:

Isa. vii. 14.

> *Behold the virgin shall be with child and bear a son,*
> *And they shall call his name Emmanuel.*

St Luke makes no allusion to this prophecy; to St Matthew, with his keener eye for Old Testament anticipations of the Gospel history, it seemed to be a verbal prediction of the circumstances of the miraculous conception. But it was more than this. The words were spoken to Ahaz, King of Judah, at a crisis when the enemies of Judah were conspiring to dethrone the House of David; the birth of the virgin's son, whatever the exact reference may have been, was to be a sign that God was with His people and with the royal line. Such a sign, but with a larger and deeper meaning, was given to Israel by the Conception and Birth of Jesus. His very name

[1] Matt. i. 20 τὸ ἐν αὐτῇ γεννηθέν. Contrast St Luke's τὸ γεννώμενον.

pointed Him out as a living pledge of God's Presence with Israel; as Himself a Deliverer sent to save Israel from enemies worse than Rezin and Pekah, a Christ-King come to reign over the people of the Lord.

All this is peculiar to St Matthew, and it is in accordance with the special purpose of the first Gospel. But the two records, though covering different ground, and approaching the subject from different points of view, are absolutely one in ascribing the Conception of Mary's Son to a Divine act. Twice in Mt. i. 18—21 we are told that Mary conceived ἐκ πνεύματος ἁγίου[1]—*of, from, Holy Spirit.* The prepositional clause represents, even more clearly than the words of St Luke, that the Spirit was the source of the vitalizing energy which gave life to the embryo in Mary's womb. It is at least possible that the writer of the first Gospel borrowed this mode of speaking from the use of his own Church; certainly it is found in the old Creed of the Roman Church[2].

It does not belong to the present enquiry to consider the credibility of the Gospel narratives of the Conception. The narratives are in any case a true part of the first and third Gospels as we have

[1] Cf. Jo. iii. 6 τὸ γεγεννημένον ἐκ τοῦ πνεύματος.

[2] The Roman Creed of the second century used the same preposition in reference to both the Spirit and the mother (τὸν γεννηθέντα ἐκ πνεύματος ἁγίου καὶ Μαρίας τῆς παρθένου, *qui natus est de Spiritu sancto et Maria uirgine*). Compare Mt. i. 16 ἐξ ἧς ἐγεννήθη with *v.* 20 τὸ ἐν αὐτῇ γεννηθὲν ἐκ πνεύματός ἐστιν ἁγίου, and Ignatius, *Eph.* 18 ἐκ σπέρματος μὲν Δαβίδ, πνεύματος δὲ ἁγίου

Part I. ii. received them, and they form a most important feature in the history of the work of the Holy Spirit as it is given in the New Testament. In this act the Spirit is seen presiding over the beginnings of a new creation. As in the beginning of cosmic life, as in the first quickening of the higher life in man, so at the outset of the new order which the Incarnation inaugurated, it belonged to the Divine Spirit to set in motion the great process which was to follow. The first and third Gospels, in tracing this new departure in human history to a unique operation of Holy Spirit, are in line with the Biblical accounts of the Spirit's action in the creation of the world and of man[1]. In the new world, in the New Man, as in the old, life begins with the Breath of God[2].

3. The birth of our Lord is not represented by the canonical Gospels as in itself miraculous or attended by any special signs of Divine power[3]. The miracle lay in the Conception and not in the birth of Jesus; birth followed under ordinary conditions. It was however preceded and followed by

Lc. i. 41. another outburst of prophecy. Elisabeth was *filled with Holy Spirit* when the Virgin visited her, and the Virgin herself, if she answered Elisabeth with

[1] Gen. i. 2 (P), ii. 7 (J).

[2] This thought may lie in the background of Lc. iii. 38 τοῦ Ἀδὰμ τοῦ θεοῦ. Cf. 1 Cor. xv. 45 f.

[3] The Apocryphal Gospels on the other hand insist upon a miraculous *birth*; cf. *Protev. Jacobi* 18 f. παρθένος ἐγέννησεν, ὃ οὐ χωρεῖ ἡ φύσις. Objection has been taken not altogether without reason to the use of the term 'Virgin-Birth' on the ground that it admits of this interpretation.

Part I. ii.

the *impromptu* ode attributed to her in the Greek text of Luke i. 46, was certainly under the same influence. In Latin texts, however, 'Elisabeth' is widely read for 'Mary,' and there is reason to suspect that neither name stood in the earliest copies, in which case it has been held that 'Elisabeth' and not 'Mary' must be supplied. On the other hand there is much force in the reply that the words *All generations shall count me blessed* are more suitable to the mother of the Christ than to the mother of the Forerunner[1]. In either case the *Magnificat* must be regarded as an inspired song, and a witness to the spiritual activity which prevailed in the circle to which both Elisabeth and Mary belonged[2]. This activity, according to the third Gospel, continued after the birth of our Lord, and was extended to a group of devout Jews who, in St Luke's words, were *expecting consolation for Israel*, and *a deliverance of Jerusalem*, at the coming of the King Messiah. To this little band of faithful men and women, the true successors of those whom the ancient prophets comforted in the days of the Babylonian exile, the Holy Spirit spoke by Symeon of Jerusalem and Hannah of the tribe of Asher. Hannah's psalm of praise when she saw the Infant in the Temple is lost, but Symeon's has, like

Lc. i. 48.

Lc. ii. 25, 38 (προσδεχόμενος παράκλησιν τοῦ Ἰσραήλ ...τοῖς προσδεχομένοις λύτρωσιν Ἰερουσαλήμ). Cf. Isa. xl. 1 (παρακαλεῖτε παρακαλεῖτε τὸν λαόν μου...: λαλήσατε εἰς τὴν καρδίαν Ἰερουσαλήμ).

Lc. ii. 38 (ἀνθωμολογεῖτο τῷ θεῷ).

[1] The arguments urged on either side may be seen in the notes of Prof. Burkitt and the Bishop of Salisbury appended to the introduction to Dr Burn's *Niceta* (pp. cliii f., clv ff.); see also Prof. Burkitt's remarks in *J. T. S.* VII. p. 225 f.

[2] It is assumed that the Song is what it is represented to be, and not a Jewish-Christian hymn put into the mouth of Mary or Elisabeth, or the work of the Evangelist himself.

Part I. ii. *Benedictus* and *Magnificat*, passed from St Luke's Gospel into the daily offices of the Church, in which it has been sung since the fourth century[1]. Hannah was known as 'a prophetess'; whether Symeon had a reputation of this kind does not appear, but he was
Lc. ii. 25 f. to all intents a prophet; *Holy Spirit was on him*; he was conscious of having received an oracular intimation (ἦν αὐτῷ κεχρηματισμένον) from the Holy Spirit that he should live to see the Anointed of the Lord[2]; it was the Spirit that moved him to enter the Precinct at the moment of the Presentation; the Spirit breathes in every word of the *Nunc Dimittis*, and his words to Mary are a formal prediction in
Lc. ii. 34 f. the manner of the Old Testament Prophets.

4. Of the infancy of Jesus after the return to Nazareth, the canonical Gospels, exercising a wise reserve, have nothing to tell[3]. The two notices of His childhood in St Luke, though they do not mention the Holy Spirit, are sufficient evidence of the Spirit's continued action upon His opening life.
Lc. ii. 40. The first relates to His early years at Nazareth: *the child grew and waxed strong, being* ever more and more *filled*[4] *with wisdom, and God's favour was upon*

[1] See *Apostolic Constitutions*, vii. 49.

[2] In Lc. ii. 25, 26 the transition from the anarthrous πνεῦμα ἅγιον to τὸ πν. τὸ ἅγιον deserves notice. With τὸν χριστὸν Κυρίου cf. 1 Regn. xxiv. 7, 11, xxvi. 9, Ps. ii. 3, LXX.; χριστὸς κύριος appears in Lam. iv. 20, Ps. Sol. xvii. 36.

[3] The portents and precocious sayings attributed to the child-Christ in the Gospels of the Infancy present a contrast to this reserve which has often been pointed out, but they exhibit no true sign of spiritual life.

[4] πληρούμενον not πεπληρωμένον or πληρωθέν; the filling, like

it. Again the Evangelist mentally compares the Messiah with His Forerunner; the first words of his account are identical with those which he had used of the childhood of the Baptist[1]. But more is said of the Child of Mary than of the child of Elisabeth; in the former the strengthening of the spiritual nature by the Divine Spirit[2] was shewn by a growing fulness of wisdom: the wisdom of a child, it is true—for when He was a child He "spake as a child, thought as a child, reasoned as a child"—but of a child without childish faults and follies, whose words and thoughts and judgements, while they were such as became His age[3], fulfilled the ideal of childhood, so that at each stage in His growth nothing was wanting to complete the development of mind and character proper to that stage. And the Divine favour was upon the Child, whether we understand by χάρις θεοῦ the complacency with which God must regard a sinless life in child or man, or the 'grace' with which He enriches nature in His elect[4].

Part I. ii.

So the Child grew into the Boy and the Boy into the Man, the intellectual and spiritual growth keeping pace with the physical. *Jesus advanced* Lc. ii. 52.

the physical growth, was progressive. Contrast Rom. xv. 14, Phil. i. 11, Col. ii. 10, and compare Eph. v. 18.

[1] Lc. i. 80, ii. 40 both begin: τὸ δὲ παιδίον ηὔξανε[ν], καὶ ἐκραταιοῦτο.

[2] Doubtless πνεύματι is to be supplied in ii. 40 (cf. i. 80).

[3] Cf. Iren. ii. 22. 4 "in infantibus infans, in parvulis parvulus."

[4] See Du Bose, *Gospel in the Gospels*, p. 30. But the use of χάρις in i. 30, ii. 32 points to the former sense.

Part I. ii.

continually[1] *in wisdom and stature and favour with God and men.* If the ascetic and strenuous youth of John reminded the Evangelist of Samson, Jesus recalls to his memory the gentler Samuel, whose mother's song has suggested much of the *Magnificat.* The Son of Mary at Nazareth, as the son of

Cf. 1 Sam. ii. 21, 26.

Hannah at Ramah, became the favourite of His fellow-townsmen, while He was increasingly conscious of the abiding favour of God.

5. One glimpse of His boyhood was given to the Rabbis at Jerusalem. At the age of twelve He was again taken to the Temple. No Symeon or Hannah was there to greet Him on this occasion; but it did not need the utterance of a prophet now to point

Lc. ii. 43 (ὁ παῖς, no longer τὸ παιδίον as in *v.* 40).

Him out. The Boy was distinguished from other boys by spiritual gifts which in the atmosphere of the Temple manifested themselves to all that heard. Even the masters of Israel were for the moment

Lc. ii. 47 (ἐξίσταντο ἐπὶ τῇ συνέσει..αὐτοῦ).

lifted above the level of their solemn trifling by the marvel of His intelligence[2] as it was revealed by His answers. There was no attempt on His part to take, with the precocity of premature knowledge, the place of the teacher; He was content to ask for information, but His questions and the answers which He

[1] προέκοπτεν: cf. 2 Macc. viii. 8 κατὰ μικρὸν εἰς προκοπὴν ἐρχόμενον. Gal. i. 14 προέκοπτον ἐν τῷ Ἰουδαϊσμῷ. 2 Tim. ii. 16; iii. 13 (where προκόπτειν is followed by ἐπὶ πλεῖον, ἐπὶ τὸ χεῖρον).

[2] On σύνεσις see Lightfoot on Col. i. 9: "σύνεσις 'intelligence' is critical: apprehends the bearings of things"; it may thus imply "a tentative, partial, approach to σοφία." In the Boy Jesus σοφία was already present (ii. 40, 52), but glimpses of it only were caught by those who heard Him in the Temple.

gave when questions were put to Him by the Rabbis disclosed an 'apprehension of the bearings of things,' a grasp of spiritual truth, which in one so young amazed even experienced teachers. Both His questions and His answers have perished. But one utterance[1] survives, and it is a revelation of the deepest secret of the Boy's heart. To His parents, distressed by His disappearance and disposed to resent it, His only answer was, *Why was it that you* Lc. ii. 49. *sought me? Knew you not that in the house of my Father I needs must be?* The consciousness of a unique relation to God, and an over-mastering enthusiasm for the spiritual and eternal, had begun to overshadow all earthly interests. Yet, as the sequel shews, they were not suffered to interfere with the obligations of human life, and the next eighteen years are summed up in the amazing words, *He was* Lc. ii. 51. *subject to them*[2]. Thus the Spirit in the Boy is seen at once illuminating thought and prompting to duty; opening the mind to the mysteries of God, and at the same time urging the regular discharge of the responsibilities of an obscure and monotonous life.

[1] Cf. Lc. ii. 50 τὸ ῥῆμα ὃ ἐλάλησεν αὐτοῖς.

[2] Ἦν ὑποτασσόμενος expresses the attitude of His entire life at Nazareth during these years of growth.

III.

THE BAPTISM OF JESUS.

<table>
<tr><td>Mc. i. 9—11.
Mt. iii. 13—17.
Lc. iii. 21, 22.
Jo. i. 32 f.
Ev. sec. Hebraeos.
Ev. Ebionit.</td><td>Καὶ ἐγένετο ἐν ἐκείναις ταῖς ἡμέραις ἦλθεν Ἰησοῦς ἀπὸ Ναζαρὲτ τῆς Γαλιλαίας καὶ ἐβαπτίσθη εἰς τὸν Ἰορδάνην ὑπὸ Ἰωάνου.</td><td>Τότε παραγίνεται ὁ Ἰησοῦς ἀπὸ τῆς Γαλιλαίας ἐπὶ τὸν Ἰορδάνην πρὸς τὸν Ἰωάνην τοῦ βαπτισθῆναι ὑπ' αὐτοῦ. ὁ δὲ διεκώλυεν αὐτὸν λέγων Ἐγὼ χρείαν ἔχω ὑπὸ σοῦ βαπτισθῆναι, καὶ σὺ ἔρχῃ πρὸς μέ; ἀποκριθεὶς δὲ ὁ Ἰησοῦς εἶπεν αὐτῷ Ἄφες ἄρτι· οὕτω γὰρ πρέπον ἐστὶν ἡμῖν πληρῶσαι πᾶσαν δικαιοσύνην. τότε ἀφίησιν αὐτόν.</td><td>Ἐγένετο δὲ ἐν τῷ βαπτισθῆναι ἅπαντα τὸν λαὸν</td></tr>
<tr><td></td><td>καὶ εὐθὺς ἀναβαίνων ἐκ τοῦ ὕδατος εἶδεν σχιζομένους τοὺς οὐρανοὺς καὶ τὸ πνεῦμα ὡς περιστερὰν καταβαῖνον εἰς αὐτόν·</td><td>βαπτισθεὶς δὲ ὁ Ἰησοῦς εὐθὺς ἀνέβη ἀπὸ τοῦ ὕδατος· καὶ ἰδοὺ ἠνεῴχθησαν οἱ οὐρανοί, καὶ εἶδεν πνεῦμα θεοῦ καταβαῖνον ὡσεὶ περιστεράν, ἐρχόμενον ἐπ' αὐτόν·</td><td>καὶ Ἰησοῦ βαπτισθέντος καὶ προσευχομένου ἀνεῳχθῆναι τὸν οὐρανόν, καὶ καταβῆναι τὸ πνεῦμα τὸ ἅγιον σωματικῷ εἴδει ὡς περιστερὰν ἐπ' αὐτόν, καὶ φωνὴν ἐξ οὐρανοῦ γενέσθαι Σὺ εἶ ὁ υἱός μου, ὁ ἀγαπητός· ἐν σοὶ εὐδόκησα.</td></tr>
<tr><td></td><td>καὶ φωνὴ ἐγένετο ἐκ τῶν οὐρανῶν Σὺ εἶ ὁ υἱός μου, ὁ ἀγαπητός· ἐν σοὶ εὐδόκησα.</td><td>καὶ ἰδοὺ φωνὴ ἐκ τῶν οὐρανῶν λέγουσα Οὗτός ἐστιν ὁ υἱός μου, ὁ ἀγαπητός, ἐν ᾧ εὐδόκησα.</td><td></td></tr>
</table>

Part I. iii.

Ecce mater Domini et fratres eius dicebant ei: Ioannes baptista baptizat in remissionem peccatorum: eamus et baptizemur ab eo. dixit autem eis: Quid peccaui ut uadam et baptizer ab eo? nisi forte hoc ipsum quod dixi ignorantia est.

Τοῦ λαοῦ βαπτισθέντος ἦλθε καὶ Ἰησοῦς καὶ ἐβαπτίσθη ὑπὸ τοῦ Ἰωάννου.

καὶ ἐμαρτύρησεν Ἰωάνης λέγων ὅτι Τεθέαμαι τὸ πνεῦμα καταβαῖνον ὡς περιστερὰν ἐξ οὐρανοῦ, καὶ ἔμεινεν ἐπ' αὐτόν· κἀγὼ οὐκ ᾔδειν αὐτόν, ἀλλ' ὁ πέμψας με βαπτίζειν ἐν ὕδατι ἐκεῖνός μοι εἶπεν Ἐφ' ὃν ἂν ἴδῃς τὸ πνεῦμα καταβαῖνον καὶ μένον ἐπ' αὐτόν, οὗτός ἐστιν ὁ βαπτίζων ἐν πνεύματι ἁγίῳ.

factum est autem, cum ascendisset Dominus de aqua, descendit fons omnis Spiritus sancti et requieuit super eum et dixit illi: Fili mi, in omnibus prophetis exspectabam te, ut uenires et requiescerem in te. tu es enim requies mea, tu es filius meus primogenitus, qui regnas in aeternum.

καὶ ὡς ἀνῆλθεν ἀπὸ τοῦ ὕδατος ἠνοίγησαν οἱ οὐρανοί, καὶ εἶδεν τὸ πνεῦμα τὸ ἅγιον ἐν εἴδει περιστερᾶς κατελθούσης καὶ εἰσελθούσης εἰς αὐτόν. καὶ φωνὴ ἐγένετο ἐκ τοῦ οὐρανοῦ λέγουσα Σύ μου εἶ ὁ υἱός, ὁ ἀγαπητός· ἐν σοὶ εὐδόκησα· καὶ πάλιν Ἐγὼ σήμερον γεγέννηκά σε. καὶ εὐθὺς περιέλαμψε τὸν τόπον φῶς μέγα. ὃ ἰδὼν ὁ Ἰωάννης λέγει αὐτῷ Σὺ τίς εἶ, κύριε; καὶ πάλιν φωνὴ ἐξ οὐρανοῦ πρὸς αὐτόν Οὗτός ἐστιν ὁ υἱός μου, ὁ ἀγαπητός, ἐφ' ὃν εὐδόκησα.

Part I. iii.

THE Holy Spirit, by which the Sacred Humanity was conceived, working upon it during the years of immaturity, had brought it at length to the fullness of its powers. The preparation was long, extending far beyond the attainment of manhood, for the manhood of Jesus was to be at its best and strongest before He entered on His short public
Lc. iii. 23. ministry. *When he began* (ἀρχόμενος), *he was about*[1] *thirty years of age.* There does not appear to have been any formal or technical reason for the choice of the thirtieth year; it may have been in early times the superior limit of the term of Levitical service[2], but if so, the limit had been pushed further back, first perhaps to twenty-five, and then to twenty years. On the other hand the Rabbis did not enter upon their office before forty[3], and this was, according to Irenaeus[4], the *magistri aetas perfecta.* The Lord was subject to no such restrictions, and when He knew in His spirit that the time had come to take up His public work, He came forward to do so. It was no conventional rule that guided Him, but the Holy Spirit working in the sphere of His human consciousness[5].

[1] For ὡς, ὡσεί in St Luke see Lc. ix. 28, xxii. 59, Acts i. 15, x. 3, xix. 7, 34.

[2] See Numb. iv. 3 (Heb.), and cf. viii. 24. The LXX. gives 25 in both passages. In 1 Chron. xxiii. 24, 27 David is said to have made 20 the age at which the Levite began to minister; but cf. xxiii. 3 and Dr Barnes *ad l.*

[3] See Schoettgen, I. 269.

[4] Iren. ii. 22—4 ff. Cf. *J. T. S.* IX. p. 53 ff.

[5] See Ellicott, *Historical Lectures*, p. 105. A widely different view of the Lord's action in seeking baptism is given in the strange

1. The tidings reached Nazareth that the prophet John had begun to preach repentance in the valley of the Jordan, and that Judaea and Jerusalem were flocking to him. Jesus recognized the call, and set forth for the Jordan, with the purpose, as our first Gospel says, of seeking baptism from John. We may imagine Him as crossing the Esdraelon valley from Nazareth, then following the course of the Jordan past Scythopolis (Bethshean), and finally reaching the outskirts of the crowd of pilgrims which marked the presence of the Baptist; the spot may have been either at the north end of the Jordan valley, at Bethany or Aenon, or perhaps at the traditional locality near Jericho where the Jordan is preparing to empty itself into the Dead Sea[1].

Part I. iii.

Mc. i. 9.

Mt. iii. 13 (τοῦ βαπτισθῆναι ὑπ' αὐτοῦ).

Jo. i. 28, iii. 23.

John, it appears, had entered on the second stage of his ministry, in which he spoke plainly of a greater Successor. *There comes* (he had said) *he that is stronger than I after me, the strap of whose shoes I am not fit to stoop and unloose. I baptized you with water, but he shall baptize you with Holy Spirit. And with fire*, St Matthew and St Luke add[2], but the words are perhaps due to recollections of the Pentecost, or a reference to the *unquenchable fire* which is mentioned in the context; if they are genuine, the Baptist may have had in mind Malachi iii. 2 f.

Mc. i. 7 f., Mt. iii. 11, Lc. iii. 16; cf. Jo. i. 26 f.

Mt. iii. 12, Lc. iii. 17.

tale for which the Gospel according to the Hebrews appears to have been responsible (Hieron. *c. Pelag.* iii. 2, see p. 39, col. 2).

[1] See Sanday, *Sacred Sites*, p. 33 ff.; the ford near Jericho is shewn in plate xxii. of the same work. Cf. also *Enc. Bibl.* 'John the Baptist' (2499 *a*).

[2] καὶ πυρί is omitted, however, in Acts i. 5.

or Isa. iv. 4. The point is not important; what is material is the Baptist's explicit claim for his Successor that He has the power to baptize *with* (or '*in*') *Holy Spirit*[1]. The fourth Gospel explains that John knew this by express revelation; the same Divine Voice which bade him baptize in the Jordan, spoke of another who should baptize with the Holy Spirit. Spiritual baptism was the promised blessing of the Messianic age, and it was the prerogative of the Messiah to bestow it. (Ezek. xxxvi. 25 ff.; Joel ii. 28 ff.)

It was at this moment that the Messiah Himself came to seek the baptism of water. (Jo. i. 33.) John, according to the fourth Gospel, did not recognize his kinsman; nor is there any improbability in this, if we remember that the Baptist had been in the wilderness through the greater part of our Lord's life at Nazareth. He may indeed never have met Jesus hitherto. On the other hand, the first Gospel represents the Baptist as not merely recognizing Jesus but seeking to prevent Him from submitting to baptism: (Mt. iii. 14 (διεκώλυεν αὐτόν).) *John would have hindered him, saying, I have need to be baptized of thee, and dost thou* (σύ) *come to me?* The Lord's answer—His second recorded utterance —was, (Mt. iii. 15.) *Let it be so now, for after this manner it is becoming for us to fulfil all righteousness.* Such sayings cannot be attributed to the imagination of the legend-maker; they bear the stamp of originality. John shrinks with characteristic humility from exercising his office on one who could give the baptism of the Spirit. Jesus, without disclaiming the power

[1] Mc. πνεύματι ἁγίῳ: Mt., Lc., Jo., ἐν πν. ἁγίῳ.

attributed to Him, puts the objection on one side as irrelevant in present circumstances; it was appropriate to His present earthly life that He should omit no act of homage that man can pay to the ordinance of God. Upon this John ceases to oppose; Jesus follows the crowd to the place of baptism, and is baptized in the Jordan[1], perhaps last of all, or when the crowd had dispersed[2].

2. The Baptism itself was not marked by any special manifestation, for the early addition to the canonical narrative which states that the water was illuminated by fire, or by a great light that seemed to rise from it[3], is probably no more than a legend of second century growth. It was an act of humble submission on the part of our Lord, and not of self-glorification. But it was immediately followed by a fresh illapse of the Spirit upon the newly-baptized. The work of righteousness performed, Jesus at once ascended from the water. As He went up He

[1] Mc. *εἰς τὸν Ἰορδάνην*. *Ἐν τῷ Ἰορδάνῃ* occurs in Mt. iii. 6, Mc. i. 5, but not in reference to the Baptism of Jesus.

[2] So Lc. (*ἐν τῷ βαπτισθῆναι ἅπαντα τὸν λαόν*. Cf. Plummer *ad loc.* "cum baptizatus esset omnis populus (cod. Brix.); not ...cum baptizaretur (cod. Am.)."

[3] See Justin *Dial.* 88 *κατελθόντος τοῦ Ἰησοῦ ἐπὶ τὸ ὕδωρ καὶ πῦρ ἀνήφθη ἐν τῷ Ἰορδάνῃ*: the story found a place also in one form of the *Praedicatio Pauli.* With it may be compared the incident which follows the Baptism in the Ebionite Gospel (*καὶ εὐθὺς περιέλαμψε τὸν τόπον φῶς μέγα*: cf. the addition to Mt. iii. 15 in the O. L. cod. a ("et cum baptizaretur lumen magnum circumfulsit de aqua ita ut timerent omnes qui aduenerant").

Part I. iii. prayed[1], and while He prayed there came to Him a
Jo. i. 32, 34 (τεθέαμαι, ἑώρακα). vision, which was shared, as the fourth Gospel tells us, by the Baptist. The heavens seemed to be torn asunder (σχιζομένους Mc.), like a veil rent in twain[2], and from the sanctuary within the veil there floated down a dove, or that which had the appearance of a dove[3]. With the vision there came a voice which in the Lord's consciousness if not in the Baptist's
Mc. i. 11. shaped itself into the words, *Thou art my Son, the Beloved; in thee I am well pleased*, or, in St
Mt. iii. 17. Matthew's later form[4], *This is my Son...in whom I am well pleased*; another tradition, preserved in the
Lc. iii. 22. 'Western' text of St Luke, substitutes for the last words, *I this day have begotten thee*[5]. The fourth Gospel does not mention the Voice, for it gives the Baptist's account; the third Gospel seems (perhaps only seems) to materialize the vision of the dove[6].

[1] Mc. εὐθὺς ἀναβαίνων...εἶδεν, Mt. εὐθὺς ἀνέβη...καὶ εἶδεν, Lc. Ἰησοῦ καὶ προσευχομένου.

[2] The same word is used of the rending of the Temple veil in Mc. xv. 38.

[3] All the Evangelists insert ὡσεί, or ὡς.

[4] Cf. H. J. C. Knight, *Temptation of our Lord*, p. 19, and note: "According to the earlier records the Voice addressed Him and no other." "St Matthew's record of the Voice presents it as men reasoned and dwelt upon it."

[5] Ps. ii. 7; cf. Acts xiii. 33 where the words are quoted with reference to the Resurrection. The Ebionite Gospel, it will be observed, seeks to combine the two traditions: "*there came a Voice...saying, 'In thee I am well pleased,' and again, 'I this day have begotten thee.'*" On John's exclaiming, *Who art thou, Lord?* this Voice speaks a third time and returns to the form first used.

[6] ἐγένετο...καταβῆναι τὸ πνεῦμα τὸ ἅγιον σωματικῷ εἴδει ὡς

But the four Gospels agree that the dove was but a symbol of the Holy Spirit, and that it was the Spirit and not the dove which descended and abode on the Christ[1]. The dove was the visible sign which drew attention to the illapse of the invisible Spirit; the Spirit was not in the dove, even as afterwards on the Pentecost it was not in the wind or the fire.

3. So much is plain. But it is not so easy to correlate the descent of the Spirit upon Jesus immediately after His baptism with the previous activities of the Spirit in His Conception and His early life. The baptismal descent admits of more than one interpretation. To the Ebionite Christian the Baptism of the Lord was the moment at which He received His Messianic sonship; to certain Christian Gnostics, the descent of the Spirit was the descent of the Christ upon the man Jesus. The Catholic Church, on the other hand, held that from the moment of His Conception Jesus was the Son of God, who as man was in all things guided and controlled by the Spirit of God[2]. But if so, what room was there for a fresh consecration, a new flooding of His human life with the Holy Spirit? What explanation is to be given, not of the

περιστεράν. But *σωματικὸν εἶδος* is not necessarily a material form: rather it is the semblance of that which is material, as the *ὡς* which follows suggests.

[1] Mt. *πνεῦμα θεοῦ καταβαῖνον...ἐρχόμενον*, Mc. *τὸ πνεῦμα καταβαῖνον*, Lc. *καταβῆναι τὸ πνεῦμα*, Jo. *τὸ πνεῦμα καταβαῖνον...ἔμενεν ἐπ' αὐτόν*. No evangelist says *εἶδεν περιστερὰν καταβαίνουσαν*.

[2] Cf. e.g. Iren. iii. 10, 11.

Part I. iii. Baptism itself, for that is sufficiently explained by our Lord's answer to John, but of the great illapse of the Spirit which followed it? This question has been anticipated by St Luke, the historian of the

Lc. iii. 23 (ἀρχόμενος). Holy Conception. The Baptism marked a new beginning in the life of our Lord. As His Conception was the beginning of His human existence, so was the Baptism of His ministry. The Messiah was about to enter on His official life, and at this new ἀρχή, this inception of His Messianic work, He must receive a new outpouring of the Spirit. As He had been conceived by the Spirit, so He must now be anointed by the Spirit for His supreme office as the Prophet, the Priest, the King of the Israel of God.

Yet the Baptism, it is plain, was not a public inauguration, nor did the vision and the voice which followed it serve the purpose of bearing witness to the nation that the Messiah had come. The crowds who were baptized on the same occasion saw and heard nothing, even if they were present at His baptism; there was no manifestation which addressed

Jo. i. 34. itself to the outward eye or ear. John indeed bore witness to the vision which he had seen, and the Lord carried away with Him from the Jordan a consciousness of the Father's testimony which was a constant

Jo. v. 37. source of inward strength: *the Father who sent me,* He exclaims, *he hath borne witness concerning me.*

1 Jo. v. 6 ff. To believers also for all time the Spirit and the Water of the Baptism are among the abiding evidences of the Messiahship of Jesus. But it is inconceivable

that the purpose of the Baptism and the Descent of the Spirit was to impress the Jewish people generally with the conviction that the Christ was among them. As it is described in the Gospels, no scene could have been less likely to produce such an effect; any who may have witnessed it saw nothing but a peasant from Galilee receiving amongst hundreds of other Jews the baptism of repentance; if they saw the dove, there would be nothing to connect it with the Holy Spirit; if they heard the voice they doubtless said, as another crowd on a similar occasion, *that it* had *thundered.* The Baptism was an inauguration of the Ministry only in the sense that it invested Jesus with new powers and a new mission. It was the spiritual, invisible, but effectual anointing of the Christ *with Holy Spirit and power* for His unique work: not for the Ministry only but for the whole term of the Messianic office, which is not even now completed but continues to the end of the present age. The Spirit came at the Baptism to abide upon Jesus as the Christ, and to be in Him the source of illumination and strength for those whom He in His turn should baptize. This vital point in the interpretation of the history comes to light in the fourth Gospel, where the Baptist witnesses, *I have beheld the Spirit descending as a dove out of heaven, and it abode upon him...He who sent me to baptize in water, he said to me, Upon whomsoever thou shalt see the Spirit descending and abiding upon him, this is he that baptizes in Holy Spirit.* The independent witness of the Gospel according to the

Jo. xii. 29.

Acts x. 38.

Jo. i. 32 f.

Part I. iii. Hebrews[1] is almost more striking: *it came to pass that when the Lord had ascended from the water, the whole fountain of Holy Spirit descended and rested on him*[2], *and said to him, My Son, in all the prophets I looked for thee that thou mightest come and I might rest in thee; for thou art my Rest, thou art my Son, my First-born, who art king for evermore.* There may be some confusion of thought in this early Jewish-Christian view of the Baptism, but in its insistence on the completeness and permanence[3] of the endowment of the Christ-King it is a noble comment on the words reported by St John. In one respect, however, it falls far behind them, for it makes no direct reference to the chief purpose of the Messianic Anointing. The chrism of the Spirit was received by our Lord not only with reference to His own needs, but that He might bestow it on all believers. The *whole fountain of the Spirit* is henceforth His, to shower upon His future Church. St John works out this point in his
1 Jo. ii. 20, 27. first Epistle: *you have an anointing* (χρίσμα) *from the Holy...the anointing which you received from him abides in you*[4]*...his anointing teaches you concerning all things.* But the thought is not limited to
2 Cor. i. 21 f. St John. St Paul speaks in similar language: *it is*

[1] Cited by Jerome (on Isa. xi. 2); see p. 39, col. 2.

[2] Cf. Isa. xi. 2 (LXX. ἀναπαύσεται ἐπ' αὐτὸν πνεῦμα τοῦ θεοῦ).

[3] Contrast Jo. i. 32 f. with Gen. vi. 3 LXX. οὐ μὴ καταμείνῃ τὸ πνεῦμά μου ἐν τοῖς ἀνθρώποις τούτοις εἰς τὸν αἰῶνα.

[4] μένει (or ? μενεῖ) ἐν ὑμῖν. Cf. Jo. i. 32 ἔμεινεν ἐπ' αὐτόν. The spiritual chrism abides in the χριστοί, as it abode in the Χριστός.

God...that anointed us, who also sealed us and gave the earnest of the Spirit in our hearts. The chrism which followed baptism in the ancient Church bore witness to the belief that every Christian receives from the Head of the Church the same Divine Unction that descended on the Christ[1]. Part I. iii.

[1] Cf. Tertullian *de bapt.* 7 perungimur benedicta unctione... unde Christus dicitur a chrismate, quod est unctio; Cyril of Jerusalem, *catech. myst.* iii. 1 ὑμῖν ὁμοίως ἀναβεβηκόσιν ἐκ τῆς κολυμβήθρας ἐδόθη χρίσμα, τὸ ἀντίτυπον οὗ ἐχρίσθη Χριστός.

IV.

THE BAPTIZED LIFE AND MINISTRY OF THE CHRIST.

Mc. i. 12, 13. Mt. iv. 1—11. Lc. iv. 1—13.	Καὶ εὐθὺς τὸ πνεῦμα αὐτὸν ἐκβάλλει εἰς τὴν ἔρημον· καὶ ἦν ἐν τῇ ἐρήμῳ τεσσεράκοντα ἡμέρας πειραζόμενος ὑπὸ τοῦ σατανᾶ. καὶ ἦν μετὰ τῶν θηρίων· καὶ οἱ ἄγγελοι διηκόνουν αὐτῷ.	Τότε ὁ Ἰησοῦς ἀνήχθη εἰς τὴν ἔρημον ὑπὸ τοῦ πνεύματος, πειρασθῆναι ὑπὸ τοῦ διαβόλου...καὶ ἰδοὺ ἄγγελοι προσῆλθον καὶ διηκόνουν αὐτῷ.	Ἰησοῦς δὲ πλήρης πνεύματος ἁγίου ὑπέστρεψεν ἀπὸ τοῦ Ἰορδάνου, καὶ ἤγετο ἐν τῷ πνεύματι ἐν τῇ ἐρήμῳ ἡμέρας τεσσεράκοντα πειραζόμενος ὑπὸ τοῦ διαβόλου, κτλ.

Lc. iv. 14—19 (cf. Mt. xii. 18). Καὶ ὑπέστρεψεν ὁ Ἰησοῦς ἐν τῇ δυνάμει τοῦ πνεύματος εἰς τὴν Γαλιλαίαν...καὶ ἦλθεν εἰς Ναζαρά...καὶ ...εὗρεν τὸν τόπον οὗ ἦν γεγραμμένον

Πνεῦμα Κυρίου ἐπ' ἐμέ,
οὗ εἵνεκεν ἔχρισέν με εὐαγγελίσασθαι πτωχοῖς,
ἀπέσταλκέν με κηρύξαι αἰχμαλώτοις ἄφεσιν καὶ τυφλοῖς ἀνάβλεψιν,
ἀποστεῖλαι τεθραυσμένους ἐν ἀφέσει,
κηρύξαι ἐνιαυτὸν Κυρίου δεκτόν.

Mt. xii. 28. Lc. xi. 20.	Ἐν πνεύματι θεοῦ ἐγὼ ἐκβάλλω τὰ δαιμόνια.	Ἐν δακτύλῳ θεοῦ ἐγὼ ἐκβάλλω τὰ δαιμόνια.

Lc. x. 21. Ἐν αὐτῇ τῇ ὥρᾳ ἠγαλλιάσατο τῷ πνεύματι τῷ ἁγίῳ καὶ εἶπεν Ἐξομολογοῦμαί σοι, πάτερ κτλ.

Ev. sec. Hebr. Ἄρτι ἔλαβέ με ὁ μήτηρ μου τὸ ἅγιον πνεῦμα ἐν μιᾷ τῶν τριχῶν μου, καὶ ἀπήνεγκέ με εἰς τὸ ὄρος τὸ μέγα Θαβώρ.

Part I. iv.

1. "THE Baptism," it has been said, "marks the point of complete apprehension by the Lord's human mind of the fulness of all that He was, and the function which it was His to fill in the divinely ordered life of the world[1]." It was also the occasion of His investment with the spiritual powers which enabled Him to fill it. These new powers were presently to be brought into exercise and tested to the uttermost by the public Ministry and the Passion. But before the Ministry began, there came an interval of preparatory discipline which was spent in solitude. *Immediately* after the vision and the Voice *the Spirit* Mc. i. 12.
urges him to go *forth into the wilderness.* So the Mt. iv. 1. Lc. iv. 1.
second Gospel, after its vivid manner; the first says less graphically but to the same effect, *Then was Jesus led up into the wilderness by the Spirit*, and the third likewise. In both statements the nature of the Spirit's action on the newly anointed Christ is clearly seen; it is a pressure exerted upon His spirit, a strong lead given to His mind and will. Under either aspect it seems to have been a new experience in the human life of Jesus; the fervour and exaltation which it implies are in marked contrast with the quiet years at Nazareth, while they accord well with the new *rôle* which had been initiated by the Baptism. The 'wilderness,' whether it is to be identified with the traditional *Quarantania* on the west of the Jordan, or with the Moabite or Judaean highlands, offered conditions which lent themselves to the purposes of a Prophet preparing for a great ministry; and in

[1] H. J. C. Knight, *Temptation of our Lord*, p. 13.

Part I. iv.

Lc. i. 80; cf. 1 Kings xvii. 3, xix. 4.

Mc. i. 13.

betaking Himself thither the Lord was following the example of His forerunner, and His forerunner's archetype Elijah. But it was not for meditation or ecstatic communion only that Jesus now threw Himself into the heart of a solitude where *he was with the wild beasts*. In the mind of the Divine Spirit, and of His human spirit as it identified itself with the Spirit of God, His retreat had a further aim; He was led thither *to be tempted by the Devil*. The juxtaposition of the two invisible agents, and their joint participation in a great crisis, is startling: the Spirit of God and the Evil Spirit appear in the same scene, the Devil tempting, the Divine Spirit leading the way to the place of temptation. The wilderness becomes a battlefield on which the supreme forces of good and evil converge; a decisive battle is to be fought there, and the leaders on both sides are at one in this that they welcome the opportunity and seek the same trysting-place.

Mt. iv. 1 (πειρασθῆ-ναι).

The Temptation may be regarded as a necessary factor in the experience of our Lord's human life. Proclaimed by the Father's Voice His Son, the Beloved, the object of the Divine complacency, He was called as Son to learn obedience by the things which He suffered; and without the sharpest suffering of temptation He could not have been perfected. The immortal words of the son of Sirach were supremely true of the one sinless Servant of God: "My son, if thou comest to serve the Lord, prepare thy soul for temptation." But the Temptation of our Lord was not only a personal discipline needful

Heb. v. 8f.

Sirach ii. 1 (τέκνον, εἰ προσέρχῃ δουλεύειν Κυρίῳ θεῷ,

Part I. iv.

(ἑτοίμασον τὴν ψυχήν σου εἰς πειρασμόν).

for the perfecting of His own humanity[1]; it was a first step in the fulfilment of His official work, and the necessary foundation of all that followed. The Temptation holds an essential place in the salvation of mankind. Even if it be held that the Fall is a legend and the first Adam a mythical character, the fact of human sin remains, and sin is a moral defeat which must be reversed if men are to be saved. Moreover, it must be reversed by Man and in Man, as it was sustained by and in Man. Mere sinlessness, unless it were tested by temptation, would not be such a victory; the Second Man must not only be without sin; He must have encountered Sin and overcome it. Further, there was an obvious necessity that the first great victory should be won before the Lord's official life began. The work of that life was to expel the powers of evil which had gained the upper hand in the world, and He who would do this must first repel an attack made by them upon Himself. *No one can enter into the house of the strong and spoil his goods, unless he first bind the strong; and then he will spoil his house.* The issue of the Temptation was the binding of Satan by the Christ, and the first consequences of this binding are seen in the spoiling of Satan's house which began in the towns and villages of Galilee, and is in process to this day wherever Christ works through His Church. But the impulse, the guidance which led to both the binding and the spoiling is to be ascribed, according to the synoptic Gospels,

Mc. iii. 27.

[1] See Westcott's notes on Heb. v. 8 f.

Part I. iv.

to the Spirit by which Jesus was anointed to the Christ-life.

2. Though the Gospels are silent upon the matter[1], it cannot be doubted that the Spirit which urged the Lord to the conflict with Satan strengthened Him for it and carried Him through. Even the quasi-apocalyptic symbolism of the story, as it stands in the first and third Gospels[2], reveals indications of an extraordinary elevation of spirit which argues some special action of the Spirit of God, such as the power to live by the food of the divine word, to overleap the horizon which bounds vision[3], to transport oneself into conditions or surroundings other than those which exist in actual experience. When from these signs of an abnormal spiritual life we turn to the three acts of the great drama, the Spirit makes its presence yet more evident. It is seen in the insight which discerns the subtle danger that underlies an apparently innocent exercise of Messianic power; in the strength of will which resists the impatience that grasps at an end without regard to the means by which the end is reached; in the humility which, though fully conscious of a unique relation to God, refuses while in the flesh to transcend the limitations of mortal weakness. In

[1] Unless Lc. iv. 1 (ἤγετο ἐν τῷ πνεύματι ἐν τῇ ἐρήμῳ ἡμέρας τεσσεράκοντα πειραζόμενος) is thought to extend the guidance to the forty days.

[2] See Sanday, *Outlines of the Life of Christ*, p. 43; *Life of Christ in recent research*, pp. 27 f., 110.

[3] See H. J. C. Knight, *op. cit.*, pp. 86 f., 110 f.

all this we may reverently recognize the hand of the Spirit of God upholding and guiding the humanity of our Lord, and giving promise to us of a like support and direction in our own temptations. For if He *has been in all points tempted similarly* to ourselves[1] Heb. iv. 15. it is reasonable to infer, as the writer to the Hebrews has done, that we are assured of His full sympathy and powerful succour in our time of need. One profound difference separates Him from ourselves; in Him there was no uncontrolled desire which *when* Jas. i. 15. *it has conceived brings forth sin*; the suggestions of evil came only from without. But they came in the most subtle and persuasive forms, appealing to the noblest instincts and the highest aims; to resist them, we may believe, cost Him even more than resistance to temptation costs other men. Yet the strength by which He resisted was not other than that by which we ourselves may conquer. If the human spirit of our Lord detected the true nature of the suggestions which were made to it and repelled them, it did so in the power of the Holy Spirit, and not simply by the force of a sinless human will.

3. The temptation being completed and the Tempter having *departed for a season*[2], Jesus re- Lc. iv. 13 (ἄχρι καιροῦ).
turned to Galilee. The return, as it appears from St Luke, began immediately after the Baptism, but

[1] The words χωρὶς ἁμαρτίας which follow πεπειρασμένον κατὰ πάντα καθ' ὁμοιότητα indicate the one exception to the ὁμοιότης of His case and ours; see Westcott's note.

[2] For traces of later temptations see Lc. xxii. 53, Jo. xiv. 30. These were doubtless met in the same strength.

Part I. iv. had been interrupted by the Divine impulse which led Him into the wilderness[1]. Now it is resumed, for the wilderness has no further claim upon Him, whereas Galilee is calling for His ministry. The Spirit is with Him still, but in a new way; not now urging Him to a life of solitude, but on the contrary impelling Him to public work; not merely arming Him for spiritual conflicts (though these had not ceased, or at best were but suspended), but endowing Him with the power of strenuous action. The same Spirit which in the wilderness overcame the Evil One now equipped Him for the public ministry[2].

Lc. iv. 14. *Jesus returned in the power of the Spirit into Galilee.* St Luke, to whom we owe this fresh reference to the Spirit, evidently means his readers to understand that it covers the whole of the Lord's ministerial life, for he brings into close connexion with it the discourse in the synagogue at Nazareth, which belongs, as we gather from St Mark, to a later period, but is appropriate here as striking the keynote of the entire ministry. (Lc. iv. 16 ff.; cf. Mc. vi. 1 (note).) The text of the discourse is the classical passage in the Second Isaiah where the Prophet of the Exile speaks in glowing words of the greatness of his commission. (Isa. lxi. 1 ff.) *The Spirit of the Lord is upon*

[1] Cf. Lc. iv. 1 Ἰησοῦς δὲ πλήρης πνεύματος ἁγίου ὑπέστρεψεν ἀπὸ τοῦ Ἰορδάνου, καὶ ἤγετο κτλ., with *v.* 14 καὶ ὑπέστρεψεν ὁ Ἰησοῦς ἐν τῇ δυνάμει τοῦ πνεύματος εἰς τὴν Γαλιλαίαν.

[2] The Galilean ministry did not formally begin till after the imprisonment of John (Mc. i. 14, Mt. iv. 12). But ministerial work began after the return from the Jordan, with only a few days' interval (Jo. ii. 1).

me[1]*; because*[2] *the Lord hath anointed me to preach good tidings unto the meek; he hath sent me to bind up the brokenhearted, to proclaim liberty to the captives, and the opening of the prison to them that are bound; to proclaim the acceptable year of the Lord*[3]. Jesus, having read thus far, folded up the roll of Isaiah and began, *To-day has this scripture been fulfilled in your ears.* Lc. iv. 21. Another Prophet of the captivity, another Evangelist of the poor, the crushed, and the prisoner, another Preacher of a year of grace is here this day; and He also has been anointed by the Spirit for His work. Thus the Lord Himself traces to the Messianic Anointing which He had received the whole of the illuminating, remedial, liberating work of the years between the Baptism and the Passion. The consciousness of that great outpouring of the Spirit was the strength of His preaching, of His marvellous works, and of His personal life.

(*a*) The preaching of our Lord was *in the power of the Spirit. A new teaching*, the crowds exclaimed; Mc. i. 27. but its novelty lay not so much in the substance of what He taught as in the spiritual force with which His message was delivered. *He taught them as one having authority and not as their scribes.* Mt. vii. 29. The Scribes taught *in the oldness of the letter*; if they went beyond what had been said by earlier Rabbis, it

[1] Cf. Isa. xlii. 1 ff., quoted in Mt. xii. 18 ff.

[2] Heb. יַעַן, LXX. and Lc. οὗ εἵνεκεν. The purpose of the Spirit's descent is indicated.

[3] So the passage stands in the R.V. of Isaiah. St Luke's quotation partly follows the LXX., partly interprets.

Part I. iv.

was but to set up a stronger 'fence' round the Law, and to add one more burden to a weight which already was grievous to be borne. On the other hand, the words of Jesus came to His own generation as they come to men still, with the freshness of
Jo. vi. 63. the breath of heaven; they *are spirit and are life.* Whether He taught the multitudes in parables, or delivered the new law of liberty to His disciples, or gave commandment to His chosen Apostles, the Spirit of God, it was plain, spoke by His lips. The word of the Lord did not come to Him at intervals, as it came to the prophets of old; all that He said was said in the Spirit. It was the consciousness of this perfect inspiration that moved Him on the eve
Mc. xiii. 31. of His Passion to say with full conviction, *The heaven and the earth shall pass, but my words shall not pass.* Spoken by human lips and in the terms of human life, all His words were spoken in the power of the Spirit of God.

(*b*) The 'signs' which attended the Ministry of Jesus[1] are attributed by our Lord Himself to the Holy Spirit. To ascribe them to the unclean spirit
Mc. iii. 29f.: cf. Mt. xii. 32. Beelzebul was a worse sin than to speak evil of the Son of Man; it was to blaspheme the Spirit of God.
Lc. xi. 20. *With the finger of God I cast out the demon-spirits,* He said to the Pharisees, using a metaphor which the Pentateuch and the Psalms apply to the Divine

[1] No miracle was wrought by the Lord before His baptism; the ἀρχὴ τῶν σημείων (Jo. ii. 11) followed almost immediately after the return in the power of the Spirit.

Spirit[1], and which the writer of the first Gospel actually interprets in this way[2]. When in the fourth Gospel Jesus says, *The Father abiding in me doeth his works*, He asserts the same principle, and extends it to all the acts of His Ministry; for it is by the Spirit that God abides in humanity. This truth was grasped after the Pentecost by those who had witnessed the miracles, e.g. by St Peter when he tells Cornelius how *God anointed* Jesus *with Holy Spirit and power, who went through* the land *doing good and healing all who were being overpowered*[3] *by the Devil; for God was with him.* The miracles were signs of the Presence of God with Jesus, of the Spirit that dwelt in Him[4], which was stronger than the power of evil and could set its victims free.

Part I. iv.

Jo. xiv. 10, cf. 1 Jo. iv. 13.

Acts x. 38 f.

(*c*) Lastly, in the personal life of the Lord, as it is revealed in His Ministry, the Holy Spirit is seen to inspire every movement of thought and will. One who lived under the scrutiny of all eyes and yet could challenge His worst enemy to convict

Jo. viii. 29, 46.

[1] See Exod. viii. 19, xxxi. 18, Deut. ix. 10, Ps. viii. 3 (cf. xxxiii. 6).

[2] In Mt. xii. 28 ἐν πνεύματι θεοῦ takes the place of Lc.'s (xi. 20) ἐν δακτύλῳ θεοῦ.

[3] καταδυναστευομένους, 'under his despotic sway': a strong contrast to the terms which describe the power exercised over men by the Divine Spirit (cf. e.g. Rom. viii. 14 πνεύματι θεοῦ ἄγονται, Gal. v. 16 πνεύματι περιπατεῖτε).

[4] The ninth anathema of Cyril condemns only such an undue insistence upon this intervention of the Spirit in the miracles of Christ as might seem to imply that they were wrought by a power which was not essentially His own.

Part I. iv.

Him of sin, and even dare to appeal to the Searcher of hearts, must indeed have been conscious of being in perfect harmony with the Spirit of God. The Gospels do not stop to point out what is proclaimed aloud by the whole history. Yet on one unique occasion the place of the Holy Spirit in the daily life of the Lord is recognized by St Luke, to whom, it will be remembered, we owe more than one of the references which the Gospels make to the Spirit in His relation to Jesus Christ[1]. *In that hour*, he writes—the hour of hope and promise when the Seventy returned with a report of the power they had exercised over unclean spirits—*Jesus exulted in the Holy*[2] *Spirit.* It was perhaps the only occasion of this kind in the days of His flesh. The Lord's human heart bounded within Him as He saw the Divine counsels fulfilling themselves through the feeble efforts of His simplest disciples. It was human joy, but not merely human; this great throb of exultation came to Him 'in the Holy Spirit': through the power which the Spirit gave Him in that hour of transcending human thought, and seeing present things in the light of their eternal issues[3].

Lc. x. 21 (ἠγαλλιάσατο ἐν τῷ πνεύματι τῷ ἁγίῳ).

4. The Ministry was followed and consummated by the Passion. If the Spirit led our Lord into the

[1] See Salmon, *Human Element in the Gospels*, p. 298 f.

[2] On the reading τῷ ἁγίῳ see Salmon *l. c.* It has the support of ℵBCDKL etc.

[3] This 'exultation in the Holy Spirit' is followed both in Mt. (xi. 25—30) and Lc. (x. 21 f.) by a self-revelation which is the most remarkable in the Synoptic teaching of our Lord.

wilderness for His first great conflict and victory, it is not overbold to believe that it led Him also to the last struggle with evil, and to the final triumph. This fact surely lies only just below the surface of the mysterious words which describe His conduct at certain moments in the long way to the Cross. His repeated predictions of the Passion: His stern rebuke of Peter, when by dissuading the Lord from the Cross he shewed that he 'minded not the things of God but the things of men'; the set face, the vehemence of manner which, as St Peter long afterwards remembered, startled and alarmed the Twelve as they followed in His steps; the prayer which rose thrice from the olive trees in Gethsemane with its burden, *Not what I will but what Thou wilt*: the last act by which the Lord dismissed His human spirit and completed the sacrifice of His life—all these are indications not only of a conflict more severe and far more sustained than the Temptation in the wilderness, but of a strength and a conquest in which the Spirit of God cooperated with the sinless spirit of the Son of Man. It does not need any verbal statement on the part of the Evangelists to assure us of this: the fact is self-evident from a consideration of the whole history of our Lord's life. *Through an eternal spirit*, as the writer to the Hebrews says, *He offered Himself to God.* The Sacrifice of the Cross was consummated by the act of our Lord's own human spirit, which was so penetrated and elevated by the Spirit of God that it lived in the eternal and invisible, and was able to 'endure the cross, despising shame.'

Part I. iv.

Mt. xvi. 23 (οὐ φρονεῖς τὰ τοῦ θεοῦ ἀλλὰ τὰ τῶν ἀνθρώπων). Lc. ix. 51, Mc. x. 32.

Mc. xiv. 36. Mt. xxvii. 50 (ἀφῆκεν τὸ πνεῦμα); cf. Jo. x. 17 f.

Heb. ix. 14.

Heb. xii. 2.

Part I. iv.

5. The Resurrection, the life of the Forty Days, the Ascension, and the Ascended life are all intimately bound up with the anointing of our Lord's humanity with the Holy Spirit. One striking incident, peculiar to St John, which shews us the risen Manhood breathing forth the Spirit on the Apostles and their company, will be considered in the second part of this book, in connexion with the Lord's teaching upon that occasion. But the Gospels do not lead us far into the mystery of the post-Resurrection life; what the New Testament has to teach about it will come into fuller view when we examine the witness of the Acts, the Epistles, and the Apocalypse.

Jo. xx. 22.

V.

THE PENTECOSTAL OUTPOURING OF THE SPIRIT.

Ἐντειλάμενος τοῖς ἀποστόλοις διὰ πνεύματος ἁγίου οὓς ἐξελέξατο ἀνελήμφθη. Acts i. 2.

Ἰωάνης μὲν ἐβάπτισεν ὕδατι, ὑμεῖς δὲ ἐν πνεύματι βαπτισθήσεσθε ἁγίῳ οὐ μετὰ πολλὰς ταύτας ἡμέρας (cf. xi. 16). Acts i. 5.

Λήμψεσθε δύναμιν ἐπελθόντος τοῦ ἁγίου πνεύματος ἐφ' ὑμᾶς, καὶ ἔσεσθέ μου μάρτυρες. Acts i. 8.

Ἔδει πληρωθῆναι τὴν γραφὴν ἣν προεῖπε τὸ πνεῦμα τὸ ἅγιον διὰ στόματος Δαυείδ. Acts i. 16 (cf. iv. 25).

Ἐν τῷ συνπληροῦσθαι τὴν ἡμέραν τῆς πεντηκοστῆς ἦσαν πάντες ὁμοῦ ἐπὶ τὸ αὐτό, καὶ ἐγένετο ἄφνω ἐκ τοῦ οὐρανοῦ ἦχος ὥσπερ φερομένης πνοῆς βιαίας, καὶ ἐπλήρωσεν ὅλον τὸν οἶκον οὗ ἦσαν καθήμενοι· καὶ ὤφθησαν αὐτοῖς διαμεριζόμεναι γλῶσσαι ὡσεὶ πυρός, καὶ ἐκάθισεν ἐφ' ἕνα ἕκαστον αὐτῶν, καὶ ἐπλήσθησαν πάντες πνεύματος ἁγίου, καὶ ἤρξαντο λαλεῖν ἑτέραις γλώσσαις καθὼς τὸ πνεῦμα ἐδίδου ἀποφθέγγεσθαι αὐτοῖς. Acts ii. 1 (cf. xi. 15).

Οὐ γὰρ ὡς ὑμεῖς ὑπολαμβάνετε οὗτοι μεθύουσιν...ἀλλὰ τοῦτό ἐστιν τὸ εἰρημένον διὰ τοῦ προφήτου Ἰωήλ Acts ii. 15 ff.

Καὶ ἔσται ἐν ταῖς ἐσχάταις ἡμέραις (λέγει ὁ θεός)
ἐκχεῶ ἀπὸ τοῦ πνεύματός μου ἐπὶ πᾶσαν σάρκα,
καὶ προφητεύσουσιν οἱ υἱοὶ ὑμῶν καὶ αἱ θυγατέρες ὑμῶν·
καὶ οἱ νεανίσκοι ὑμῶν ὁράσεις ὄψονται,
καὶ οἱ πρεσβύτεροι ὑμῶν ἐνυπνίοις ἐνυπνιασθήσονται·
καί γε ἐπὶ τοὺς δούλους μου καὶ ἐπὶ τὰς δούλας μου
ἐν ταῖς ἡμέραις ἐκείναις ἐκχεῶ ἀπὸ τοῦ πνεύματός μου,
καὶ προφητεύσουσιν.

Part I. v.

Acts ii. 33. Τῇ δεξιᾷ οὖν τοῦ θεοῦ ὑψωθεὶς τήν τε ἐπαγγελίαν τοῦ πνεύματος τοῦ ἁγίου λαβὼν παρὰ τοῦ πατρός, ἐξέχεεν τοῦτο ὃ ὑμεῖς καὶ βλέπετε καὶ ἀκούετε.

Acts ii. 38. Μετανοήσατε, καὶ βαπτισθήτω ἕκαστος ὑμῶν ἐν τῷ ὀνόματι Ἰησοῦ Χριστοῦ εἰς ἄφεσιν τῶν ἁμαρτιῶν ὑμῶν, καὶ λήμψεσθε τὴν δωρεὰν τοῦ ἁγίου πνεύματος· ὑμῖν γάρ ἐστιν ἡ ἐπαγγελία καὶ τοῖς τέκνοις ὑμῶν, καὶ πᾶσι τοῖς εἰς μακρὰν ὅσους ἂν προσκαλέσηται Κύριος ὁ θεὸς ἡμῶν.

If St Luke's 'former treatise' gave prominence to the work of the Holy Spirit in the days of the Son of Man, its sequel, the Acts, is wholly occupied with the work of the Spirit in the life of the Church during the thirty years that followed the Lord's departure[1].

1. The Book of the Acts takes up the thread of the story just before the point at which the Gospel had dropped it. It begins with a brief summary of the Forty Days, adding a fuller account of the Ascension. These introductory verses (i. 1—12) mark the transition from the earthly Ministry of the Lord (*ὧν ἤρξατο Ἰησοῦς ποιεῖν τε καὶ διδάσκειν*) to the Ministry of the Spirit which was to follow His Ascension. The earthly Ministry
Lc. iv. 14. had been from the first *in the power of the Spirit*, as the Gospel has taught us; and the Acts opens

[1] St Luke's special interest in the relation of the Spirit to the Incarnate Life may be due to his intimate knowledge of the work of the Spirit in the Apostolic Church. Looking back, and interpreting the Lord's life in the light of the Pentecost, he was able to see that the baptism of the Church with the Spirit was anticipated by the events that prepared for the Advent and accompanied it.

with an intimation that this continued to the end; the last injunctions to the Apostles were given, it is noted, *through Holy Spirit*[1]; the Messianic inspiration was upon the Risen Christ as it had been upon the Christ of the Ministry, and was perhaps enhanced by the more spiritual conditions of the Resurrection life[2].

Part I. v.

Acts i. 2.

In these interviews before the Ascension the Lord's mind seems to have recalled the days of His own Baptism and Anointing by the Holy Spirit. He knew that a like event was about to occur in the history of the Church; her baptism with the Spirit was at hand. The Eleven were charged not to leave Jerusalem but to wait there for the fulfilment of the Father's promise; *for John indeed baptized with water, but ye shall be baptized*[3] *in Holy Spirit not many days hence*[4]. As to the time of the

Acts i. 5; cf. Lc. xxiv. 48.

[1] The position of διὰ πνεύματος ἁγίου between τοῖς ἀποστόλοις and οὓς ἐξελέξατο has led some interpreters to connect the words with ἐξελέξατο rather than with ἐντειλάμενος. But, as Blass says, this is all but impossible.

[2] Cf. Hastings' *D. C. G.* I. 736 *b* f.: [the remark in Acts i. 2] "seems to suggest that with the Resurrection the dispensation of the Holy Spirit began, and that the disciples were conscious, as they listened to the new and final charge of the Lord, that they were in contact, as they never had been before, with the powers of the world to come."

[3] Augustine (*ep.* 265) mentions only to condemn some Latin texts which read μέλλετε βαπτίζειν or βαπτίσετε. To baptize with the Spirit was the function of the Master, not of the disciples, except ministerially.

[4] The Bezan text adds, but not convincingly, ἕως τῆς πεντηκοστῆς. It belonged to the discipline of waiting that neither the exact day nor a time-limit should be named.

establishment of the Messianic Kingdom He had nothing to say; it was in the Father's hands. It was enough for them to know what directly concerned their own immediate future, and the discharge of their duty in it. (Acts i. 8; cf. xi. 15 f.) *Ye shall receive power when the Holy Spirit has come upon you*[1], *and ye shall be my witnesses both in Jerusalem and in all Judaea and Samaria and unto the end of the earth.* As the Lord's own Baptism had been followed by His Ministry in Galilee, so the Baptism of the Church was to be preparatory to a world-wide ministry: a ministry not, like His own, creative of a new order, but one of simple testimony; yet only to be fulfilled in the power of the Spirit of God[2].

2. During the days of waiting that followed the Ascension this mysterious prophecy of an approaching Baptism of the Spirit must have been much in (Acts i. 14.) the thoughts and prayers of the Eleven and their company. They could not form any conception of the manner in which the promise would fulfil itself in their experience. We can overhear their questionings as they discussed the Lord's words: *What* (Cf. Jo. xvi. 18.) *was this that he said to us?...we cannot tell what he said.* But the historian is not concerned with their anticipations, and the only reference to the Spirit between the Ascension and the Pentecost occurs in St Peter's speech upon the election of a new Apostle in the room of Judas. The Apostle finds the fate of Judas foreshadowed in Pss. lxix. 23 ff., cix. 8; the

[1] For this use of ἐπέρχεσθαι see p. 26.

[2] Cf. Jo. xv. 27.

traitor's end was a necessary fulfilment of those passages: *there must needs have been fulfilled the scripture which the Holy Spirit spoke beforehand by the mouth*[1] *of David concerning Judas.* In this view of the functions of prophecy there is nothing new; it was common to devout Jews of St Peter's time. But it is new to find one of the Eleven interpreting the Psalms as prophetic of events in the life of Jesus; that he could do so even before the coming of the Spirit seems to be due to the impression left upon his mind by the teaching of the risen Lord. In the sequel we shall see to what purpose the same Apostle uses this new key to the understanding of the Psalms and the Prophets when the Spirit of Christ has opened his mind yet further to see the ultimate purpose of Old Testament prophecy.

Part I. v.

Acts i. 16.

See Lc. xxiv. 44 f.

3. At length, *not many days* after the Ascension, yet doubtless after an interval which seemed long to the waiting Church, the Spirit came and baptized the Apostles and their company. St Luke connects the event with the Day of Pentecost, the festival of the wheat-harvest which fell on the fiftieth day after the waving of the Paschal barley sheaf. But there is an ambiguity in his words which leaves the reader in doubt whether it occurred on the day itself or just before the day. St Luke's phrase ἐν τῷ συνπληροῦσθαι τὴν ἡμέραν τῆς πεντηκοστῆς means, as the margin of the English R.V. says, *when the day of*

Acts ii. 1.

[1] Διὰ στόματος is frequent in St Luke when he is quoting documents or speeches which were originally Hebrew or Aramaic (Lc. i. 70, Acts iii. 18, 21, iv. 25).

Part I. v.

Pentecost was being fulfilled; but it is a question of interpretation whether this signifies 'while the day was in progress,' or 'when it was close at hand' or 'had almost come[1].' Whichever view may be accepted, the coming of the Spirit is associated with

Lev. xxiii. 15 ff.

the harvest festival of the Jewish year, when the firstfruits of the earth were offered, and men gave thanks for the ingathering. It is easy to see the appropriateness of such a day for the coming of the Divine Gift which is the firstfruits of the spiritual harvest. Among the later Jews the Pentecost was kept as the anniversary of the giving of the Law[2], and it has been pointed out that the Holy Spirit

Jas. i. 25, Rom. viii. 2; cf. 2 Cor. iii. 3.

came to write on men's hearts *the perfect law of liberty, the law of the Spirit of life*. The New Testament, however, does not encourage the belief that the selection of the Pentecost was due to either of these associations, and it is more than doubtful whether the second was in vogue within the Apostolic age. One reason for the choice of the day, however, appears from the history itself. The Pentecost was the next great festival after the Passover, and it

[1] Lc. ix. 51 ἐν τῷ συμπληροῦσθαι τὰς ἡμέρας τῆς ἀναλήμψεως αὐτοῦ is perhaps in favour of (1): the *days of* (to) *the assumption* are regarded as a period approaching completion. Compare also Acts xxi. 27 ἔμελλον οἱ ἑπτὰ ἡμέραι συντελεῖσθαι. The D text removes the ambiguity by the singular paraphrase ἐγένετο ἐν ταῖς ἡμέραις ἐκείναις τοῦ συμπλ. τὴν ἡμέραν τῆς πεντ. The Church of the second and third centuries gave the name of 'Pentecost' to the whole period between Easter and Whitsuntide (Tert. *de bapt.* 19), but τὴν ἡμέραν limits us here to the day of the feast.

[2] Cf. Edersheim, *Temple*, p. 225.

Part I. v.

was only on great festivals that a concourse of worshippers from the Dispersion could be expected to assemble at Jerusalem. If the coming of the Spirit was to be made known through the Jewish world, the Pentecost offered the next opportunity. It is interesting to remember that the Pentecost fell on the same day of the week as the day of the Passover-sheaf, i.e. Nisan 16. Thus if the Crucifixion took place on Nisan 14, as St John seems to imply, and that day was a Friday, the Pentecost as well as the Resurrection fell upon the first day of the week, and Sunday commemorates both the Lord's victory over death and the Spirit's entrance upon its work of giving life. The weekly Lord's Day is also the day of the Spirit of Christ.

The believers in Jerusalem—a few days before the Pentecost they were about a hundred and twenty, but the number may have been swelled by pilgrims from Galilee as the festival drew on—were *all together in the same place* on the day of the Spirit's coming. The hour was before 9 a.m. Was the place the Court of the Women in the Temple precinct? Or was it the large upper room where they had met day by day during the interval of waiting, and which had probably been the scene of the Last Supper? There is something to be said in favour of the Temple, i.e. either the court, or one of the chambers which opened into it[1]. On the other hand Christian tradition from the fourth century has

Acts ii. 1.

Acts ii. 15.

Acts i. 13, 15: cf. Mc. xiv. 15.

[1] See the reasons for this view given by Bp Chase, *Credibility of the Acts*, p. 30 ff.

regarded the Cenaculum as the place of the Descent[1], and this tradition is recommended by other considerations as well as by its antiquity. Not to press the fitness of a coincidence which brings the Paraclete to the Apostles on the very spot where they had received the promise of His coming, and where they had first seen the Risen Christ, it is distinctly more probable that the illapse occurred while they were assembled in a private house than in a room attached to the most public place of resort in Jerusalem, with the crowds close at hand which were already pouring into the Temple enclosure to celebrate the Feast. No event of the seven weeks which ended on the day of Pentecost seems more clearly to demand closed doors and the privacy of the 'upper room.'

While the brethren were assembled, and perhaps engaged in their morning act of common prayer[2], *there came suddenly from heaven a loud sound*[3] *as of the rushing of*[4] *a mighty*[5] *wind.* The great gale

[1] See Sanday, *Sacred Sites*, p. 83 ff. (where some interesting references are given to Christian writers from Cyril of Jerusalem onwards), and plates xlix., l.

[2] Cf. Acts i. 14, ii. 42.

[3] Ἦχος, not *φωνή* as in Jo. iii. 8. For ἦχος cf. Lc. xxi. 25, Heb. xii. 19.

[4] So R.V. admirably renders *φερομένης*. Φέρεσθαι is the normal verb for the rushing of the wind (cf. e.g. Jer. xviii. 14), or for the rapid movement of objects which it carries along (Acts xv. 29, WH. mg.; 2 Pet. i. 21).

[5] Βίαιος, *βία* are almost technical in this connexion. See Exod. xiv. 21 *ἐν ἀνέμῳ νότῳ βιαίῳ*, Ps. (xlvii.) xlviii. 8, *ἐν πνεύματι βιαίῳ συντρίψεις πλοῖα*, Acts xxvii. 41 *ἡ δὲ πρύμνα ἐλύετο ὑπὸ τῆς βίας*.

seemed to enter and fill the chamber, and not simply to pursue its course without. The Spirit "was not in the wind," as it was not in the dove of the Baptism; but the wind represented the strength of the Divine Breath which had come to fill first the House of God, and then to sweep over the face of the earth with life-giving power, as in the beginning when it was borne over the waters of the chaos. The roar of the wind appealed to the ear, but it was accompanied or immediately followed by an appeal to the eye. *There appeared to them tongues parting asunder* (διαμεριζόμεναι) *as of fire, and* the fire *sat on each one of them.* The idea presented is that of great jets of flame breaking up into smaller scintillations, one of which rested upon the head of each of the assembled brethren. The whole was a vision, as St Luke is careful to explain[1], but a vision that corresponded to a great spiritual fact which at the same moment accomplished itself in the experience of all who were present. If, as St Matthew relates, the Baptist had said that the Christ should baptize in *Holy Spirit and fire*, his words would at once be recalled by those who had been his disciples. But apart from the Baptist's saying the tongues of fire would readily be understood to proclaim the Presence of God, awakening memories of such Old Testament incidents as the Burning Bush, the consumption of the sacrifice on Mount Carmel, the revelation to Elijah in the cave on Horeb,

Part I. v.

1 Kings xix. 11.

Gen. i. 2 (πνεῦμα θεοῦ ἐπεφέρετο).

Acts ii. 3.

Mt. iii. 11.

Exod. iii. 2. 1 Kings xviii. 38, xix. 12.

[1] His words are, ὤφθησαν γλῶσσαι ὡσεὶ πυρός.

Part I. v. Ezek. i. 4. the vision of Ezekiel by the river Chebar[1]. Yet there was a new feature in the fire of Pentecost, for which the Old Testament had no precedent, the distribution of the tongues of flame, and the settling of one of them on each individual in the assembly[2]. The distribution of the sacred fire evidently pointed to the truth that the Paraclete had come to dwell not only with the society as a whole, nor only with the officers of the society, but with all its members. As for the tongue-like form of the flames, events led to their being interpreted as emblems of new powers of utterance bestowed upon believers by the Spirit
Acts ii. 4. of Christ. *They were all filled with Holy Spirit*[3], *and began to speak with other* (ἑτέραις) *tongues*[4], *according as the Spirit gave them to utter* (ἀποφθέγγεσθαι). This power, whatever it was, was an immediate proof, both to themselves and to all Jerusalem, that they were under the influence of a new force, which they knew to be the promised Paraclete.

There is no historical statement in the New Testament which is more difficult to interpret than St Luke's account of the Pentecostal gift of tongues. It is scarcely possible, without abandoning the

[1] In the last two cases the fire follows or is accompanied by wind.

[2] With διαμεριζόμεναι compare Heb. ii. 4 πνεύματος ἁγίου μερισμοῖς; and with ἐκάθισεν ἐφ' ἕνα ἕκαστον, 1 Cor. xii. 4 ff. διαιρέσεις δὲ χαρισμάτων εἰσίν...ἑκάστῳ δὲ δίδοται ἡ φανέρωσις.

[3] See p. 13, note 1.

[4] Cf. 1 Cor. xiv. 21 (Isa. xxviii. 11). 'Mc.' xvi. 18 has γλώσσαις λαλήσουσιν καιναῖς, but καιναῖς is omitted by good MSS. (C*LΔΨ).

natural meaning of the words, to escape from the conclusion that the historian represents the gift as meeting the needs of a polyglott multitude. But to what extent was the multitude polyglott? Could not every one in the crowd, whether Jew or proselyte, have understood either a dialect of Aramaic or the colloquial Greek which was spoken everywhere in the basin of the Mediterranean[1]? Are we to understand that the newly baptized brotherhood found themselves able with quickened powers of utterance to use either Aramaic or Greek, so that they could reach the whole of the pilgrims both from East and West? In what language was St Peter's long speech delivered, or was it delivered first in one language, and then in another? It is clear that the difficulties of the narrative are not altogether removed by supposing, as the Christian student has the right to suppose, that a unique miracle was wrought to signalize the coming of the Paraclete. To regard the gift of tongues, as many of the Fathers of the Church did, as having answered the wider purpose of qualifying the Apostles and other early missionaries for their work of evangelizing the world is scarcely possible. It is one of the clearest signs of a Divine preparation of the world for the Gospel that the command to preach it everywhere came at a time when one language gave access to almost every nation in the Roman world. The various peoples to whom the missionaries of the Cross were sent were scarcely more polyglott than the crowds present

[1] This point is well put in Hastings' *D. B.* IV. 795.

Part I. v.

at Jerusalem on the day of Pentecost, nor is there any evidence that the gift of tongues, so far as it continued in exercise, was actually used for the purpose of preaching to the heathen. Thus the purpose of the miracle, if it is to be regarded in that light, was not to lighten the labour of the Christian missionary, but to call attention at the first outset to the advent of the Paraclete, to demonstrate the reality of the heavenly gift, and to symbolize the vanishing of racial distinctions before the progress of a catholic Church. Whatever may be the true explanation of the Pentecostal gift of tongues regarded as a historical fact, its spiritual significance is best understood when it is placed in the light of such considerations as these.

Acts ii. 5 ff.

4. At the sound of the roaring wind[1], the crowd gathered quickly round the brethren who meantime seem to have entered the Temple Court. When they heard themselves addressed in their several tongues by these men of Galilee their first feeling was one of perplexed amazement, which in some of the baser sort presently gave place to ribaldry: *they are filled*, some shouted, *with sweet wine*[2]. While to the devout the utterances of the brethren were revelations of *the mighty works of God*, those who had no spiritual capacity heard nothing but the confused

Acts ii. 7 (ἐθαύμαζον). Acts ii. 13 (διαχλευάζοντες... Γλεύκους μεμεστωμένοι εἰσίν).

[1] γενομένης...τῆς φωνῆς ταύτης: A.V. "when this was noised abroad," as if φωνῆς were φήμης; cf. Vulg. "facta...hac voce." The φωνή seems to be that of the ἦχος πνοῆς φερομένης (*v.* 2).

[2] Γλεῦκος is properly the juice fresh from the grape (Vulg. *musto*). The word suggests that the speakers professed to be reminded of the shouts and songs and revelry of the vintage.

noise which might come from half-intoxicated revellers. St Peter, ever ready to act, and now prompted by the Spirit, accepted the challenge and poured out a flood of inspired eloquence. 'There was another explanation to be given of the miracle they had witnessed, and it could be found in the book of the prophet Joel. The last days foreseen by the prophet had come at last, the gift of the Spirit was no longer limited to a few chosen servants of God; henceforth it was for *all the Lord's people*, for young and old, for women as well as for men, for the servant as well as for the master. *Your sons and your daughters shall prophesy, your old men shall dream dreams, your young men shall see visions; and also upon the servants and upon the handmaids in those days will I pour out my Spirit.* So Joel had foretold, and that day they had witnessed the beginning of this great effusion of spiritual power and life, the dawn of *the great and glorious*[1] *day of the Lord* when all who called on the name of the God of Israel should be saved.'

Part I. v.

Acts ii. 14 (ἀπεφθέγξατο; cf. *v.* 4 (ἀποφθέγγεσθαι).

Joel ii. 28 ff. = iii. 1 ff. (Heb.).

Numb. xi. 29.

Acts ii. 17 f.

Acts ii. 20.

Neither the Prophet nor the Apostle who quoted him could have seen all that was implied in this prophecy, or how it would work itself out in the history of the Church. In the thought of both, *all flesh* seems to have borne the narrow sense 'all Israelites and all proselytes to the religion of Israel from among the Gentiles.' Yet the Apostle can already see further than the pre-Christian prophet;

[1] ἐπιφανῆ, Heb. נוֹרָא, 'aweful': the whole phrase occurs again in Mal. iii. 23 = iv. 4 (Heb. and LXX.).

Part I. v. 'afterwards' becomes in his interpretation *in the last days*[1], and by these he understands the Messianic age, which he recognizes as already begun. The discourse of St Peter, as reported by St Luke[2], is a witness to the reality of the spiritual crisis through which the speaker had passed. It is evident that if it truly represents the substance of what St Peter said, as there is good reason to suppose that it does, the Apostle had 'received power' from some new source. The Peter of the Day of Pentecost is a new man, far other than the Peter of the Passover; his words
Acts ii. 23 f., 36. shew not only the freedom of speech (παρρησία) which was characteristic of this Apostle, but a blending of courage, wisdom, and skill which we do not associate with him as he appears in the Gospels, and an insight into the work of the Messiah and the nature of His Kingdom such as even to the last day of the Lord's stay upon earth was certainly beyond his
Cf. Acts i. 6. reach[3]. And in courage and general understanding of the new situation Peter was not alone; the whole company of believers was filled with the same spirit;
Acts ii. 14 (σταθεὶς δὲ ὁ Πέτρος σὺν τοῖς ἕνδεκα). the rest of the Twelve stood up with him, identifying themselves with his words. From that day forward a new strength, which was not their own, marked all

[1] Acts ii. 17 ἐν ταῖς ἐσχάταις ἡμέραις. In Joel ii. 28 (= iii. 1) the Heb. is simply אַחֲרֵי־כֵן (LXX. μετὰ ταῦτα).

[2] On the trustworthiness of the reports of St Peter's speeches in the Acts see Bp Chase's third Hulsean Lecture (*Credibility*, p. 122 ff.).

[3] The question in Acts i. 6 is attributed to the Eleven, but Peter is doubtless their spokesman; the voice is the voice of Simon son of John.

the sayings and deeds of the Apostolic Church. It is in this great change of mental and spiritual attitude rather than in the external signs of wind and fire or in strange powers of utterance that we recognize the supreme miracle of the day of Pentecost.

Acts iv. 13, 19, 31, v. 29 f., 41 f.

After his quotation from Joel, St Peter twice again refers to the coming of the Spirit, and each of these references increases our sense of his grasp of the significance of that great event. In the first place he boldly connects it with the Ascension of Jesus Christ. *Having been by the right hand of God lifted up, and having received from the Father the promise of the Holy Spirit, he poured forth*[1] *this which ye both see and hear.* The visible and audible manifestations of Pentecost were the lowest links in a chain which reached from heaven to earth; the furthest streams of a river which was welling out from the Throne of God. They indicated the presence of the Spirit in the Church, but the presence of the Spirit was the fulfilment of a Divine promise that could not find its accomplishment until the Son of Man had been glorified. If this was in the Apostle's mind, whence could he have learnt it except from the last discourse of the Lord, which the Spirit of Christ brought back to his memory and enabled him for the first time to understand? He now saw that the Pentecostal outpouring was direct evidence that Jesus was with the Father; it was the ripe fruit of the Passion and the Resurrection

Acts ii. 33.

Cf. Apoc. xxii. 1.

Cf. Jo. xiv. 26.

[1] Ἐξέχεεν is Joel's word (ii. 28, LXX. ἐκχεῶ). Cf. Acts x. 45, Rom. v. 5, Tit. iii. 6.

Part I. v. consummated and crowned by His Ascension into heaven. This great gift had come from the hands of the exalted Christ; He had poured it out, and the invisible act had been proclaimed by visible and audible tokens.

But the Apostle goes further. All who heard him, Jews or proselytes, might themselves experience the power of the Spirit. *Repent, and let each one of you be baptized in the name of Jesus Christ unto remission of your sins, and you shall receive the gift of the Holy Spirit; for to you is the promise and to your children*[1], *and to all who are afar, as many as the Lord our God shall call to himself*[2]. St Peter sees that to Israelites and proselytes the only conditions necessary for their participation in the Spirit are repentance and faith expressed by the receiving of baptism in the name of Jesus Christ. The baptized would in all cases obtain the promised gift. But his words must not be made to bear a meaning which could not as yet have been present to his mind. It is clear from the subsequent chapters of the Acts that years passed before he realized that baptism with its attendant gifts of remission and the Spirit could be given to the uncircumcised Gentile. The Pentecostal outpouring of the Spirit did not at once illuminate every corner of the understanding, or solve problems for which a solution could be gained by experience; but it had already thrown a

Acts ii. 38 f.

See Acts x., xi.

[1] Cf. Ps. Sol. viii. 39 ἡμῖν καὶ τοῖς τέκνοις ἡμῶν ἡ εὐδοκία εἰς τὸν αἰῶνα.

[2] See Joel ii. 32; Isa. lvii. 19.

broad path of light across the darkness, and the day of a fuller knowledge had dawned.

5. St Luke does not say that the three thousand who were baptized that day received the gift of the Spirit immediately, or that they spake with tongues as the original company of believers had done when the Spirit came to them. Yet his account of the life upon which they entered shews that they were at once animated by a new spirit which was a greater and more permanent manifestation of the Spirit of Christ.

The Pentecostal outpouring of the Holy Spirit was far more than a miraculous display of spiritual power, intended to arrest attention and invite enquiry into the new faith. It was the beginning of a new era: an advent of the Spirit, as the Incarnation was the advent of the Son. Not as though either the Son or the Spirit had been absent from the world before the Advent. Each coming was a new manifestation, and the beginning of a new mission. *God sent forth his Son*, and when the mission of the Son had been fulfilled, He *sent forth the Spirit of his Son* to take up the work under new conditions. The Pentecost inaugurated this second Divine Mission. But the mission was greater and more far-reaching than the wonders of the Pentecost might suggest. The Spirit was to find *a still more excellent way* of revealing His presence and power than by the rushing wind and self-distributing tongues of fire, or the seeing of visions, the dreaming of dreams, the gift of tongues and

Gal. iv. 4, 6.

1 Cor. xii. 31.

Part I. v.

Acts ii. 42—47.

prophecy. The closing verses of the second chapter of the Acts, with their picture of the simple, joyful, strenuous life of the newly baptized in the days that followed the Pentecost, reveal even more than the miracles of the Pentecost itself the nature of the Power which had come to dwell with the Church.

VI.

THE LIFE OF THE EARLY PALESTINIAN CHURCH.

Τότε Πέτρος πλησθεὶς πνεύματος ἁγίου εἶπεν πρὸς αὐτούς Acts iv. 8.
Ἄρχοντες τοῦ λαοῦ καὶ πρεσβύτεροι κτλ.

Καὶ δεηθέντων αὐτῶν ἐσαλεύθη ὁ τόπος ἐν ᾧ ἦσαν Acts iv.
συνηγμένοι, καὶ ἐπλήσθησαν ἅπαντες τοῦ ἁγίου πνεύματος, 31 ff.
καὶ ἐλάλουν τὸν λόγον τοῦ θεοῦ μετὰ παρρησίας. τοῦ δὲ
πλήθους τῶν πιστευσάντων ἦν καρδία καὶ ψυχὴ μία...καὶ
δυνάμει μεγάλῃ ἀπεδίδουν τὸ μαρτύριον οἱ ἀπόστολοι τοῦ
κυρίου Ἰησοῦ τῆς ἀναστάσεως, χάρις τε μεγάλη ἦν ἐπὶ
πάντας αὐτούς.

Ἰωσὴφ δὲ ὁ ἐπικληθεὶς Βαρνάβας ἀπὸ τῶν ἀποστόλων, Acts iv. 36.
ὅ ἐστιν μεθερμηνευόμενον Υἱὸς παρακλήσεως κτλ.

Διὰ τί ἐπλήρωσεν ὁ σατανᾶς τὴν καρδίαν σου ψεύσασθαί Acts v. 3 f.,
σε τὸ πνεῦμα τὸ ἅγιον;...οὐκ ἐψεύσω ἀνθρώποις ἀλλὰ τῷ 9.
θεῷ...τί ὅτι συνεφωνήθη ὑμῖν πειράσαι τὸ πνεῦμα Κυρίου;

Καὶ ἡμεῖς ἐσμὲν μάρτυρες τῶν ῥημάτων τούτων, καὶ τὸ Acts v. 32.
πνεῦμα τὸ ἅγιον ὃ ἔδωκεν ὁ θεὸς τοῖς πειθαρχοῦσιν αὐτῷ.

Ἐπισκέψασθε δέ, ἀδελφοί, ἄνδρας ἐξ ὑμῶν μαρτυρουμένους Acts vi. 3 ff.
ἑπτά, πλήρεις πνεύματος καὶ σοφίας...καὶ ἐξελέξαντο Στέ- Acts vi. 5.
φανον, ἄνδρα πλήρη πίστεως καὶ πνεύματος ἁγίου...Στέφανος Acts vi. 8.
δὲ πλήρης χάριτος καὶ δυνάμεως ἐποίει τέρατα καὶ σημεῖα
μεγάλα ἐν τῷ λαῷ...καὶ οὐκ ἴσχυον ἀντιστῆναι τῇ σοφίᾳ καὶ Acts vi. 10.
τῷ πνεύματι ᾧ ἐλάλει.

Ὑμεῖς ἀεὶ τῷ πνεύματι τῷ ἁγίῳ ἀντιπίπτετε· ὡς οἱ Acts vii.
πατέρες ὑμῶν καὶ ὑμεῖς. 51.

Part I. vi.

Acts vii. 55. Ὑπάρχων δὲ πλήρης πνεύματος ἁγίου, ἀτενίσας εἰς τὸν οὐρανὸν εἶδεν δόξαν θεοῦ καὶ Ἰησοῦν ἑστῶτα ἐκ δεξιῶν τοῦ θεοῦ.

Acts viii. 15—20. Προσηύξαντο περὶ αὐτῶν ὅπως λάβωσιν πνεῦμα ἅγιον· οὐδέπω γὰρ ἦν ἐπ' οὐδενὶ αὐτῶν ἐπιπεπτωκός, μόνον δὲ βεβαπτισμένοι ὑπῆρχον εἰς τὸ ὄνομα τοῦ κυρίου Ἰησοῦ. τότε ἐπετίθεσαν τὰς χεῖρας ἐπ' αὐτούς, καὶ ἐλάμβανον πνεῦμα ἅγιον. ἰδὼν δὲ ὁ Σίμων ὅτι διὰ τῆς ἐπιθέσεως τῶν χειρῶν τῶν ἀποστόλων δίδοται τὸ πνεῦμα, προσήνεγκεν αὐτοῖς χρήματα λέγων Δότε κἀμοὶ τὴν ἐξουσίαν ταύτην, ἵνα ᾧ ἐὰν ἐπιθῶ τὰς χεῖρας λαμβάνῃ πνεῦμα ἅγιον. Πέτρος δὲ εἶπεν πρὸς αὐτόν Τὸ ἀργύριόν σου σὺν σοὶ εἴη εἰς ἀπώλειαν, ὅτι τὴν δωρεὰν τοῦ θεοῦ ἐνόμισας διὰ χρημάτων κτᾶσθαι.

Acts viii. 29, 39. Εἶπεν δὲ τὸ πνεῦμα τῷ Φιλίππῳ κτλ.

Πνεῦμα Κυρίου ἥρπασεν τὸν Φίλιππον.

Acts ix. 17. Ἀπῆλθεν δὲ Ἀνανίας καὶ εἰσῆλθεν εἰς τὴν οἰκίαν, καὶ ἐπιθεὶς ἐπ' αὐτὸν τὰς χεῖρας εἶπεν Σαοὺλ ἀδελφέ, ὁ κύριος ἀπέσταλκέν με...ὅπως ἀναβλέψῃς καὶ πλησθῇς πνεύματος ἁγίου.

Acts ix. 31. Ἡ μὲν οὖν ἐκκλησία καθ' ὅλης τῆς Ἰουδαίας καὶ Γαλιλαίας καὶ Σαμαρίας...πορευομένη τῷ φόβῳ τοῦ κυρίου καὶ τῇ παρακλήσει τοῦ ἁγίου πνεύματος ἐπληθύνετο.

Acts x. 19, 34, 38, 44—47 (cf. xi. 15 ff.). Τοῦ δὲ Πέτρου διενθυμουμένου περὶ τοῦ ὁράματος εἶπεν τὸ πνεῦμα...ἀνοίξας δὲ Πέτρος τὸ στόμα εἶπεν...ἔχρισεν αὐτὸν ὁ θεὸς πνεύματι ἁγίῳ καὶ δυνάμει...ἔτι λαλοῦντος τοῦ Πέτρου...ἐπέπεσε τὸ πνεῦμα τὸ ἅγιον ἐπὶ πάντας τοὺς ἀκούοντας τὸν λόγον. καὶ ἐξέστησαν οἱ ἐκ περιτομῆς...ὅτι καὶ ἐπὶ τὰ ἔθνη ἡ δωρεὰ τοῦ πνεύματος τοῦ ἁγίου ἐκκέχυται· ἤκουον γὰρ αὐτῶν λαλούντων γλώσσαις καὶ μεγαλυνόντων τὸν θεόν. τότε ἀπεκρίθη Πέτρος Μήτι τὸ ὕδωρ δύναται κωλῦσαί τις τοῦ μὴ βαπτισθῆναι τούτους οἵτινες τὸ πνεῦμα τὸ ἅγιον ἔλαβον ὡς καὶ ἡμεῖς;

Acts xi. 27 (cf. xxi. 4, 10). Κατῆλθον ἀπὸ Ἱερουσαλὴμ προφῆται εἰς Ἀντιόχειαν· ἀναστὰς δὲ εἷς ἐξ αὐτῶν ὀνόματι Ἄγαβος ἐσήμαινεν διὰ τοῦ πνεύματος κτλ.

Acts xv. 28. Ἔδοξεν γὰρ τῷ πνεύματι τῷ ἁγίῳ καὶ ἡμῖν.

Part I. vi.

THE Day of Pentecost was the beginning of a Divine economy which is to continue to the end of the present age. The Paraclete had come to stay. While the tokens of His coming, the wind and fire, were momentary, and certain of His gifts ceased or were suspended after a few generations, His own presence in the Christian brotherhood was, from the Pentecost, permanent and assured. Yet the manifestations of the Spirit were variable, and have varied in fact, according to the requirements of periods, Churches, and individuals. In the Acts we learn how the Spirit revealed itself in the experience of the Apostolic age. The Book falls into two nearly equal parts, of which the first shews us the Paraclete at work in the Churches of Palestine, while the second relates the extension of His mission to the Gentiles.

Jo. xiv. 16.
Cf. 1 Cor. xiii. 8.

1. The Apostles in the power of the Spirit rose at once to their new duties. They shewed themselves capable of teaching and ruling the Church, and representing their Master in the face of the world. They instructed the newly baptized, wrought signs and wonders in Jerusalem, proclaimed the Resurrection of Jesus and the hope which it held forth to mankind; through their preaching multitudes of men and women were added to the Church; even among the Jewish priesthood the faith gained a crowd of adherents[1]. We cannot err in attributing

Acts ii. 42 f., iii. 6 ff., v. 12 ff.
Acts iv. 4, 32.
Acts v. 14.
Acts vi. 7 (πολὺς ὄχλος τῶν ἱερέων ὑπήκουον τῇ πίστει).

[1] Secret adherents, perhaps, like the Sanhedrists Nicodemus and Joseph; under a Sadducean high-priesthood they could scarcely have professed their faith openly, at least in great numbers.

Part I. vi. to the Spirit of Christ this great accession of strength. Moreover, these new powers were found to endure the test of suffering. Quite early in the course of the history we see Peter and John standing before Acts iv. 5 f. the Sanhedrin, which was still led by Annas and Caiaphas. A few weeks before the situation would have filled them with alarm. Now the Apostles are fearless, and speak with as much freedom[1] and conviction as if they were addressing a Temple crowd. It was borne in upon the assembly that these Acts iv. 13. disciples were animated by the same spirit which had characterized the Master; they had been with Him so long that they had caught His manner, and inherited the independence, the directness, the incisiveness of His spirit. But, in truth, their boldness was not due so much to their having been long in the company of Jesus, as to His presence in them by the Spirit. Peter, as St Luke explains, Acts iv. 8. was *filled with Holy Spirit*; the Lord was fulfilling to him the promise to His disciples that when they stood before rulers and kings for His Mc. xiii. 11. sake, it should be 'given them in that hour what they should speak.' Even as they stood before the Council they could scarcely have failed to recall these words of Christ, or to attribute their courage to its true source. But if they did, no doubt could have been left when on their return to their own

[1] Their *φόβος τῶν Ἰουδαίων* (Jo. xx. 19) had given place to *παρρησία*. This setting loose of the tongue in the service of Christ and the Gospel is one of the normal signs of the Spirit's working; cf. e.g. Ps. li. 13—15.

company, as they prayed for strength to persist in their witness to Jesus Christ, *the place in which they were gathered together was shaken, and they were all filled with the Holy Spirit and continued to speak the word of God with boldness.* As the wind and fire had assured them of the original coming of the Paraclete, so the earthquake[1] spoke of His continued presence in their midst, under new and threatening conditions, and of His irresistible might. The Sanhedrin itself was powerless in the grip of the spiritual force which had begun to shake heaven and earth.

Acts iv. 31.

Heb. xii. 26 f.

For the presence and power of the Spirit were felt not by the Apostles only, but by the whole Church. Reference has been made to the new life which filled the Christian Society even in the days that immediately followed the Pentecost. The sudden addition of three thousand members to the little community might easily have overtaxed its strength. The peace of the young Church might have been at once imperilled by the conflict of interests certain to arise in so large a *clientèle* of untaught members; many who joined it in the excitement of Pentecost might have been expected to fall away when they realized the demands which their new faith made upon them. But none of these things happened; on the contrary the newly baptized *persevered in the teaching of the Apostles and the*

Acts ii. 42.

[1] The earthquake is a frequent symbol in the O.T. of the presence and power of God. See Exod. xix. 18, 1 Kings xix. 11, Pss. xcvi. 9, cxiv. 7, Joel iii. 16.

Part I. vi. *fellowship* of the body, *in the Breaking of the Bread and the Prayers*[1]; they readily accepted the discipline of the Christian life. Believers were known in those early days for their joyous, single-hearted piety, Acts ii. 46 f. and earned the good will of the whole population. The brotherhood was marked by a unity of purpose such that it seemed to be moved by a common life, Acts iv. 32. and to have one heart and one soul.

2. This early manifestation of the Spirit provoked after a time a counter-manifestation of evil. The first outbreak of evil in the Church of Jerusalem arose out of an excess of zeal which in itself Acts ii. 44. was good. From the first this Church had lived a common life, whether because it was fired by the example of the Essenes, or (as is more probable) in imitation of the first disciples of the Lord during the days of the Ministry. It would seem as if with the fresh illapse of spiritual power recorded in Acts iv. 31, the first enthusiasm for this life revived, and Acts iv. 32 ff. believers who still owned property in lands or houses began to strip themselves of it and devote the proceeds to the good of the community. Among Acts iv. 36 f. those who did so was one Joseph, a Hellenistic Levite from Cyprus, to whom the Apostles, following the example of the Master, had given the descriptive surname Barnabas, interpreted by St Luke as *Son of Paraclesis*[2]. The act of Joseph Barnabas was

[1] Ταῖς προσευχαῖς: "in templo maxime" (Blass).

[2] The meaning of Barnabas is not certain, see Dalman, *Gramm. d. Aramaisch*, p. 142, and Deissmann, *Bible Studies*, p. 307 ff. The gift of παράκλησις is connected with the Holy Spirit (Acts ix. 31), and with the office of the prophet (1 Cor. xiv. 3).

the simple outcome of the inner life of the spirit of unselfish love. But there were some whose motives were less pure, and two of the converts, a man and his wife, agreed upon a plan which seemed to promise them a high place in the esteem of their fellow-believers without a corresponding sacrifice. The man presented part of the price of the land which he had sold as if it had been the whole, and his wife, when questioned, told the same tale. This insincerity, worthy of the Pharisaic 'hypocrites,' met with a punishment that once for all vindicated in the eyes of the Church the awefulness of the gift which it had received. Ananias had suffered Satan to fill a heart which ought to have been full of the Spirit of God. He and his wife had, at the suggestion of the evil spirit, attempted to *deceive the Holy Spirit, to lie not to men*, to Peter and John or to the whole brotherhood, *but to God*[1]. They had dared to *tempt the Spirit of the Lord*, to put to the trial His power to detect and to punish. It was a *sin unto death*, although it may be hoped that the loss of temporal life did not in this instance carry with it the infinite penalty of the second death. But in any case the impression produced was great and salutary: *great fear came upon the whole Church and upon all that heard these things*. It was felt on all hands that if the coming of the Spirit had transfigured and in a sense deified human life, it had also invested it

Part I. vi.

Acts v. 9 (συνεφωνήθη ὑμῖν).

Acts v. 3 f.

Acts v. 9 (πειράσαι τὸ πνεῦμα Κυρίου).

1 Jo. v. 6. Cf. 1 Cor. v. 5, xi. 30 ff.

Acts v. 11.

[1] Ψεύσασθαι τὸ πνεῦμα τὸ ἅγιον...οὐκ ἐψεύσω ἀνθρώποις ἀλλὰ τῷ θεῷ. Blass: "ψεύδεσθαί τινα *fallere*...Ἐψεύσω c. dat. ut λέγειν etc. τινί."

Part I. vi. with a sacredness which could not be violated without incurring the severest penalties. *He that is near me*, the Lord is reported to have said, *is near the fire*[1]; but after the Pentecost the Church had the fire not near only but within her, and there was a peril in the possession as well as infinite gain.

3. A second trouble, which arose within the Church perhaps shortly afterwards, ended more happily. The internal peace of the Church, hitherto
Acts vi. 1. unbroken, was threatened by a feeling of jealousy on the part of the Hellenists towards their Aramaic-speaking brethren. Before a rupture could occur the Apostles intervened, and the matter which gave rise to complaint was placed in the hands of seven persons chosen by the whole body and appointed by the Twelve with prayer and laying on of hands. In selecting the Seven the Church was charged by the Apostles to see that they were not only men of
Acts vi. 3. approved life (*μαρτυρουμένους*), but *full of spirit and wisdom*. This provision is the more noteworthy because the duties of the Seven were not directly spiritual; it was their part to "serve tables," i.e. to provide for the daily meals of the needy members
Acts vi. 2, 4. of the community, leaving the Apostles free for *the* work of *prayer and the service of the word*[2]. Yet

[1] Ὁ ἐγγύς μου ἐγγὺς τοῦ πυρός (cited by Didymus on Ps. lxxxviii. 8). The second half of the saying is less often quoted but is necessary to its completeness: ὁ δὲ μακρὰν ἀπ' ἐμοῦ μακρὰν ἀπὸ τῆς βασιλείας. There is danger either way, but most danger in distance from Christ.

[2] Τῇ διακονίᾳ τοῦ λόγου, as contrasted with the διακονία τῶν τραπεζῶν (*v.* 2).

even in this lower office the Seven had need of a full measure of the wisdom which comes from the Spirit of God. It was realized that as Bezalel and Oholiab needed to be filled with the Spirit when they undertook the building of the Tabernacle, so even the more secular duties of the Christian worker called for His inspiration, especially when they had to do with the building of the Church.

Part I. vi.

Exod. xxxi. 1—11, xxxv. 30 ff.

None of the Seven seems to have so entirely and immediately answered to this requirement as did Stephen. He is described as *full of faith and Holy Spirit, full of grace and power*. When he spoke in the synagogue, men *were powerless to withstand the wisdom and the spirit with which he spoke*; when he was brought before the Sanhedrin, his face was *as the face of angel*. In the last scene he is still *full of Holy Spirit* as in the first; *gazing into heaven* in a spiritual ecstasy he *saw God's glory, and Jesus standing on the right hand of God*; his dying prayers are echoes of the prayers of the Lord upon the cross. Nowhere in the history of the Apostolic Church is there a more suggestive picture of the character which is inspired by the Spirit of Christ—a character at once strong and tender, forceful and spiritual. Towards the end of his defence Stephen spoke with a severity which perhaps exceeded the bounds of prudence: *Stiffnecked and uncircumcised in hearts and ears, you always resist the Holy Spirit; as your fathers did, so do you*. It is scarcely surprising that they would hear no more. But with the uncompromising sternness of the Hebrew prophets

Acts vi. 5, 8, 10, 15.

Acts vii. 55.

Acts vii. 51.

Part I. vi.

he united the spirit of love, and fell asleep with the prayer, *Lord, lay not this sin to their charge.* Yet until he was brought into notice by the necessity of providing for the administration of the daily dole, Stephen had been but one of the rank and file of the Jerusalem Church, and there were doubtless others who in like circumstances would have exhibited not less conspicuously the power of the Spirit of Christ.

Acts vii. 60.

4. Another of the Seven, Philip by name, approved himself as an evangelist or itinerant preacher of the word. Driven from Jerusalem by the great persecution which followed the martyrdom of Stephen[1], Philip found a refuge at *the city of Samaria*—Sebaste seems to be meant[2]—and set himself to witness there to the Lord Jesus. Signs of the Spirit's presence at once appeared; the crowds who thronged the streets gave heed with one accord to his preaching; miracles were wrought; the word was received with joy; men and women flocked to baptism. Yet there was no effusion of the Spirit on the baptized, such as Philip had perhaps expected to follow. Something was wanting which Philip could not supply, and the Apostles Peter and John, who were still in Jerusalem, came down to inspect and confirm Philip's work. As it belonged to the Apostles to lay their

Acts viii. 4 f.

Cf. Acts i. 8 (καὶ Σαμαρίᾳ).

Acts viii. 6 (οἱ ὄχλοι).

Acts vi. 6.

[1] For the time neither the 'service of tables' nor the 'service of the word' could be carried on at Jerusalem; the Church there was broken up, only the Apostles remaining at their posts (Acts viii. 1).

[2] Reading τὴν πόλιν with ℵBA.

hands with prayer on the Seven, so now these two Apostles *prayed for* Philip's converts *that they might receive Holy Spirit, and laid their hands on them,* and the simple ceremony[1] was accompanied by the Heavenly Gift; one after another[2] *they received Holy Spirit.* So the admission of the Samaritan converts to the full privileges of the Church was ratified, and another step was taken towards the pouring out of the Spirit *upon all flesh.*

Part I. vi.

Acts viii. 15 ff.

Joel ii. 28.

At Samaria as at Jerusalem the Spirit's coming was attested by signs which could not be misunderstood. Even Simon the sorcerer *saw that through laying on of the Apostles' hands the Spirit was being given.* But his unspiritual mind misinterpreted the fact. He supposed that these two men who had come from Jerusalem possessed a magical power unknown to himself, and he made overtures to them to sell him their secret. But the laying on of hands and the prayer which accompanied it possessed no magical efficacy which could be bought or sold. *Thy silver go with thee to destruction,* is the white-hot answer of Peter, *because thou thoughtest to purchase for thyself with money that which is the gift of God.* Yet if the Apostolic laying on of hands was a merely symbolical act which possessed no magical

Acts viii. 20.

[1] On the Biblical references to 'laying on of hands' see the writer's article in Hastings' *D. B.* III. 184 f., and cf. *Enc. Bibl.* 1956.

[2] Ἐλάμβανον, not ἔλαβον. Dr Hort explains this imperfect differently, *Ecclesia*, p. 55: "that is, shewed a succession of signs of the Spirit." But ἐλάμβανον corresponds to ἐπετίθεσαν: as each in turn received the imposition of hands he received also the gift of the Spirit.

Part I. vi. virtue, it was a ministry with which God was pleased to connect spiritual gifts. Whether it had been employed from the day of Pentecost itself, or whether it had its beginning with the new departure by which the work of the Church was extended to Samaria, there is no evidence to shew. We know only that it was

Acts xix. 6. used afterwards by St Paul, at least on one notable occasion, and that then also it conveyed the Holy Spirit; and that the writer to the Hebrews seems to

Heb. vi. 2. give it a place, after *the teaching of baptisms*, among *the first principles of Christ.* It is a natural if not a necessary inference that the Laying on of Hands became the ordinary complement of Baptism both in the Jewish and the Gentile churches of the Apostolic age, and was the means of imparting to the baptized certain spiritual gifts over and above the new birth by which they passed at their baptism into the life of faith.

To return to Philip. As the book proceeds, he is more than once associated with the operations of the Holy Spirit. After his return to Jerusalem an angel directs him to go southwards along the road to

Acts viii. 26. Gaza. *It is desert*, the historian says; and whether he means the city or the road to it[1], the words suggest that the purpose of the mission was not easy to grasp. But Philip obeyed, and presently a chariot was heard approaching from behind. At once a voice within him which he recognized as the voice of the Spirit bade him join the chariot. He went,

[1] The authorities for these divergent views are given by Dr Knowling, *ad loc.*

Part I. vi.

and the result was the conversion and baptism of the Ethiopian Eunuch. In Philip's interview with the Eunuch we observe the same skill in interpreting the Old Testament which marked the Apostles after the coming of the Spirit. The passage which the Eunuch was reading happened to be Isaiah liii., and Philip without hesitation *beginning from this scripture proclaimed to him the gospel of Jesus*. [Acts viii. 35 (εὐηγγελίσατο αὐτῷ τὸν Ἰησοῦν).] It may be that the Christian interpretation of this prophecy was already familiar to Philip, for our Lord had applied the passage to Himself [Lc. xxii. 37.]; but it is not quoted elsewhere in the Acts, and the meaning of Isa. liii. may have been suggested by the same Spirit that had bidden Philip to join the Eunuch. As soon as the Eunuch had received baptism Philip found himself under the control of the Holy Spirit carried to Azotus, the Ashdod of the Old Testament, and thence northward through Philistia and the Sharon, till he reached the great Hellenistic city, Caesarea by the sea. The historian represents this sudden change of route as a rapture: *the Spirit of the Lord caught away Philip, and the Eunuch saw him no more*[1]. [Acts viii. 39.] Like much else in the Acts that relates to and emanates from the Palestinian Church, the language is cast in an Old Testament mould. *The Spirit of Jahveh*, Obadiah said to Elijah, *shall carry thee whither I know not* [1 Kings xviii. 12.]; and when at length Elijah *went up by a whirlwind*, the

[1] The 'Western' reading, πνεῦμα ἅγιον ἐπέπεσεν ἐπὶ τὸν εὐνοῦχον, ἄγγελος δὲ Κυρίου ἥρπασεν τὸν Φίλιππον, seems to be a correction based on viii. 26, x. 44.

Part I. vi. sons of the prophets urged that search should be
2 Kings ii. 16; cf. Bel 36. made for him *lest peradventure the Spirit of Jahveh hath taken him up and cast him upon some mountain or into some valley.* Translated into prose, the words of St Luke may be taken to mean that Philip was urged by an impulse which came from the Holy Spirit to leave the Eunuch immediately after his baptism; when the Ethiopian looked round to thank his unknown benefactor, Philip was already out of sight. The 'rapture' could scarcely have been a mere ecstacy[1]; for the next verse shews us Philip arrived at Azotus and pressing on from thence to new scenes of work.

At Caesarea Philip seems to have taken up his abode. His work of 'serving tables' at Jerusalem may have come to an end with the dispersion
Acts xxi. 8; cf. Eph. iv. 11. of the Church, and events had shewn that he possessed the special gifts of a Christian teacher. A great field lay before him in the half-heathen city which was the seat of the Roman Procurator and the centre in Southern Palestine of Greek culture. Here Jews and Greeks were mingled in proportions scarcely to be found elsewhere in Palestine[2]; and Philip, if he was a Hellenist, as is probable, was well suited to do evangelistic work both among the Jews of the city and their proselytes. Our interest in Philip's Caesarean residence lies in a fact which

[1] Such as is described in 2 Cor. xii. 2 ff. (ἁρπαγέντα...ἡρπάγη).

[2] In Vespasian's time there were 20,000 Jews at Caesarea in the midst of a much larger number of heathen. See Schürer, *Jewish People*, E. tr. II. 1, p. 86 f.

comes to light in the second half of the Acts. Twenty years or more after his arrival at Caesarea his house in that city was for some days the resting-place of St Paul on the last journey of the Apostle to Jerusalem[1]. Philip by this time had four daughters, who followed the single life (*παρθένοι*)[2], and were prophetesses. The Spirit of the Lord rested on the children as it had rested on the father, but after a different manner; to him was given the work of an evangelist, to them the gift of prophecy. Already in this Christian household at Caesarea it was shewn that the same Spirit distributes His gifts to every member of Christ severally as He wills.

Part I. vi.

Acts xxi. 9.

Cf. 1 Cor. xii. 4, 11.

5. With the conversion of St Paul we are not directly concerned, for it was effected not by the Spirit of Christ but by the Lord in person. But the work of the Spirit finds a place in the sequel. Three days after the vision Ananias was sent to lay his hands on Saul, that he might *recover sight, and be filled with Holy Spirit.* Thereupon *there fell at once from* Saul's *eyes as it were scales,* and he *recovered sight, and arose and was baptized.* Here the laying on of hands precedes baptism, and is given by a disciple who, so far as we know, held no office in the Church, but was specially commissioned by the Lord and thus for the moment possessed a

Acts ix. 17 f.

[1] Was it a community of interests between the Evangelist of Caesarea and the Apostle of the Gentiles that led St Paul to linger in the house of Philip with Jerusalem so near?

[2] Cf. 1 Cor. vii. 34 ἡ παρθένος μεριμνᾷ τὰ τοῦ κυρίου.

Part I. vi. quasi-Apostolic authority[1]. In the case of Saul, again, it is not clear whether the gift of the Spirit preceded, accompanied, or followed baptism; nor is it necessary to distinguish the stages of an illumination which was practically a single act. It is important, however, to observe that even in his unique experience the visible signs of the invisible Gift are not superseded. He who had 'seen the Lord,' and been changed by the sight, needed nevertheless the ministry of the disciple; he must receive baptism and the laying on of hands like any other convert who had been brought to the faith by the preaching of an Evangelist or an Apostle.

Cf. 1 Cor. ix. 1.

6. By this time every part of Palestine had its Christian congregations; and the chapter which describes the conversion of the Apostle of the Gentiles contains a glowing account of the Palestinian Church as a whole. *The church throughout all Judaea and Galilee and Samaria had peace, being edified; and walking in the fear of the Lord and in the comfort of the Holy Spirit was multiplied.* So the Revised Version translates Acts ix. 31, but there is some ambiguity in the Greek. Dr Hort would render the second part of the verse, "*and walking by the fear of the Lord and by the invocation of the Holy Spirit* (probably the invoking His guidance as Paraclete to the Ecclesia) *was multiplied*[2]," while

Acts ix. 31.

[1] Acts ix. 17 ὁ κύριος ἀπέσταλκέν με, Ἰησοῦς ὁ ὀφθείς σοι.

[2] Hort, *Ecclesia*, p. 55. The meaning thus given to παράκλησις seems to be without example in LXX. or N.T. Moreover the attitude of the primitive Church towards the Spirit was rather one

others would punctuate the sentence differently: *being edified and walking in the fear of the Lord; and by the comfort of the Holy Spirit was multiplied.* The vital question is as to the meaning of παράκλησις τοῦ ἁγίου πνεύματος. Coming to the Acts from the reading of the Fourth Gospel, we are tempted to connect it with Παράκλητος; but it may be doubted whether that title of the Holy Spirit was known to St Luke. It seems still more precarious to give to παράκλησις here only in the N.T. the sense of ἐπίκλησις, 'invocation.' 'Exhortation' it can scarcely mean here, but 'encouragement,' 'comfort[1],' suits the context well; of this the harassed Church had need, and this the Holy Spirit, now that outward peace was restored, and His voice could again be heard, was able to impart. Fear of God and comfort of the Spirit characterized the religious life of the Church in those early days—the fear of the Old Testament tempered by the freedom and joy of the New. No real antinomy was felt to exist between the two: the sense of awe that guards the Christian life from sin, and the sense of peace and gladness that comes from the Spirit of Christ, are complementary and not mutually exclusive principles.

7 A new and far wider field was opened by the

of joyful welcome than of invocation; the cry *Veni, Creator Spiritus* belongs to a later age, when the Spirit was sought and perhaps expected, but not regarded as a Guest Who had already come, and come to abide.

[1] As in Acts xv. 31.

Part I. vi. baptism of Cornelius and his friends at Caesarea. If Philip was in that city at the time, it is significant that Peter was summoned from Joppa. The crisis was such as to demand the presence of an Apostle and the leader of the Apostolic College; for upon the decision which was to be taken the future of the Church depended. The keys of the Kingdom had been committed to St Peter, and it now fell to his lot to determine whether the doors of the Kingdom should be thrown open to the uncircumcised Gentile or shut against him. But the question was in fact answered

Acts x. 19. for him by the Holy Spirit. It was the Spirit who in the first instance bade him go with the messengers of Cornelius: *go with them, nothing doubting, for I have sent them.* When he arrived and delivered his message, it was the Spirit who determined his course of action by falling on all the uncircumcised and as

Acts x. 38. yet unbaptized hearers. As the Lord Jesus had been *anointed with Holy Spirit and with power*, as the ascended Christ had baptized the circumcised believers at Jerusalem with the Spirit on the day of Pentecost, so now He sent the same Spirit on this

Acts x. 44; xi. 15. company of Gentiles; *while Peter yet spoke...the Holy Spirit fell* on them as on Peter himself and the rest *at the beginning.* Could any doubt remain that these men who had been baptized with the Spirit might be baptized with water in the name of

Acts xi. 17. the Lord? *If God gave them the like gift as He did unto* Jewish believers, *who* was Peter or any human minister that he *could withstand God?* A second Pentecost had proclaimed the admissibility of Gentiles to Christian baptism[1], and thus laid the foundation of a Catholic Church.

8. While all believers, whether Jews or Gentiles, received the Spirit, some received Him as the Spirit of prophecy and 'prophesied,' or became 'prophets.' Such were Judas and Silas and Agabus, and others Acts xi. 28,
whose names are not given. At first, as might xv. 32.
have been expected, Jerusalem was the centre of prophetic activity, from which prophets, singly or in bands, went forth to visit other churches, as occasion arose. But the gift of prophecy was not limited to the mother Church; prophets are found ministering in the Church at Antioch and after- Acts xiii. 1.
wards at Tyre and Caesarea, and, as we shall see, Acts xxi. 4, 9; cf.
the order flourished also in the Pauline Churches. xx. 23.
The gift of tongues, which on the Day of Pentecost was the characteristic possession of those who had received the Spirit, seems to have fallen into disuse in the Palestinian churches[2] as the years went on and prophecy took its place. Of all the 'spiritual gifts' prophecy was the noblest and the most enduring, and for Jewish Christians it had the advantage of appearing in the light of a revival of

[1] Cf. Acts x. 45 καὶ ἐπὶ τὰ ἔθνη ἡ δωρεὰ τοῦ πνεύματος τοῦ ἁγίου ἐκκέχυται; xi. 15 ἐπέπεσεν τὸ πνεῦμα τὸ ἅγιον ἐπ' αὐτοὺς ὥσπερ καὶ ἐφ' ἡμᾶς ἐν ἀρχῇ.

[2] At least it is mentioned in this connexion only in Acts x. 46, on occasion of the 'second Pentecost' of the Gentile Church. On the other hand prophecy, though not named in Acts ii. except in the quotation from Joel, appears in Acts xi. 27, xiii. 1, xv. 32, xxi. 9 f.

Part I. vi. the Old Testament gift which had so long been in suspense.

9. One more reference to the Spirit in the early history of the Church of Jerusalem may be noticed here. The conference of Apostles and local Elders, held at Jerusalem to consider the position of the new Gentile Churches, felt itself at liberty to claim the presence of the Holy Spirit as Assessor. The decree which gives the decision of the conference

Acts xv. 28. begins, *It seemed good to the Holy Spirit and to us.* The Paraclete who was with believers individually was assuredly also with the Church in her corporate capacity. This claim must not be taken as one of infallibility or finality—some of the defects of the decree were afterwards modified or abandoned—but rather as a recognition of the fulfilment of the Lord's promise that the other Advocate should abide with them; that where two or three were met together in His name, there He by His Spirit would be in the midst of them. At the end of the letter of the conference the 'Western' text of the Acts adds words[1] which extend the Divine Presence to the non-official members of the new Churches: *Fare ye well, borne on your course in the Holy Spirit.* This has been condemned as a Montanist gloss, but it does not exceed the sober truth as it revealed itself to the Apostolic age. There is an inspiration which belongs to all believers in virtue of the indwelling of the Spirit in the whole Body of Christ.

[1] D reads: εὖ πράξατε, φερόμενοι (D^{lat} *ferentes*, Irenaeus iii. 14 *ambulantes*, Tertullian *de pud.* 12 *uectantes uos*) ἐν τῷ ἁγίῳ πνεύματι.

VII.

THE FOUNDING OF THE GENTILE CHURCHES.

Ἦσαν δὲ ἐν Ἀντιοχείᾳ κατὰ τὴν οὖσαν ἐκκλησίαν Acts xiii.
προφῆται καὶ διδάσκαλοι, ὅ τε Βαρνάβας καὶ Συμεὼν ὁ 1 ff.
καλούμενος Νίγερ, καὶ Λούκιος ὁ Κυρηναῖος, Μαναήν τε Ἡρῴδου τοῦ τετραάρχου σύντροφος καὶ Σαῦλος. Λειτουργούντων δὲ αὐτῶν τῷ κυρίῳ καὶ νηστευόντων εἶπεν τὸ πνεῦμα τὸ ἅγιον Ἀφορίσατε δή μοι τὸν Βαρνάβαν καὶ Σαῦλον εἰς τὸ ἔργον ὃ προσκέκλημαι αὐτούς. τότε νηστεύσαντες καὶ προσευξάμενοι καὶ ἐπιθέντες τὰς χεῖρας αὐτοῖς ἀπέλυσαν. αὐτοὶ μὲν οὖν ἐκπεμφθέντες ὑπὸ τοῦ ἁγίου πνεύματος κατῆλθον εἰς Σελευκίαν.

Οἵ τε μαθηταὶ ἐπληροῦντο χαρᾶς καὶ πνεύματος ἁγίου. Acts xiii.
Ὁ καρδιογνώστης θεὸς ἐμαρτύρησεν αὐτοῖς, δοὺς τὸ 52.
πνεῦμα τὸ ἅγιον καθὼς καὶ ἡμῖν. Acts xv. 8.

Διῆλθον δὲ τὴν Φρυγίαν καὶ Γαλατικὴν χώραν, κωλυ- Acts xvi.
θέντες ὑπὸ τοῦ ἁγίου πνεύματος λαλῆσαι τὸν λόγον ἐν τῇ 6 f.
Ἀσίᾳ· ἐλθόντες δὲ κατὰ τὴν Μυσίαν ἐπείραζον εἰς τὴν Βιθυνίαν πορευθῆναι, καὶ οὐκ εἴασεν αὐτοὺς τὸ πνεῦμα Ἰησοῦ.

Ἐγένετο δὲ...Παῦλον...ἐλθεῖν εἰς Ἔφεσον καὶ εὑρεῖν Acts xix. 1
τινὰς μαθητάς, εἶπέν τε πρὸς αὐτούς Εἰ πνεῦμα ἅγιον —6.
ἐλάβετε πιστεύσαντες; οἱ δὲ πρὸς αὐτόν Ἀλλ' οὐδ' εἰ πνεῦμα ἅγιόν ἐστιν ἠκούσαμεν. εἶπέν τε Εἰς τί οὖν ἐβαπτίσθητε; οἱ δὲ εἶπαν Εἰς τὸ Ἰωάνου βάπτισμα...ἀκούσαντες δὲ ἐβαπτίσθησαν εἰς τὸ ὄνομα τοῦ κυρίου Ἰησοῦ· καὶ ἐπιθέντος αὐτοῖς τοῦ Παύλου χεῖρας ἦλθε τὸ πνεῦμα τὸ ἅγιον ἐπ' αὐτούς, ἐλάλουν τε γλώσσαις καὶ ἐπροφήτευον.

Τὸ πνεῦμα τὸ ἅγιον κατὰ πόλιν διαμαρτύρεταί μοι λέγον ὅτι δεσμὰ καὶ θλίψεις με μένουσιν.

Acts xx. 23. Acts xx. 28.

Προσέχετε ἑαυτοῖς καὶ παντὶ τῷ ποιμνίῳ ἐν ᾧ ὑμᾶς τὸ πνεῦμα τὸ ἅγιον ἔθετο ἐπισκόπους.

Acts xxi. 4.

Τῷ Παύλῳ ἔλεγον διὰ τοῦ πνεύματος μὴ ἐπιβαίνειν εἰς Ἰεροσόλυμα.

Acts xxi. 10 f.

Κατῆλθέν τις ἀπὸ τῆς Ἰουδαίας προφήτης ὀνόματι Ἄγαβος, καὶ . . δήσας ἑαυτοῦ τοὺς πόδας καὶ τὰς χεῖρας εἶπεν Τάδε λέγει τὸ πνεῦμα τὸ ἅγιον Τὸν ἄνδρα οὗ ἐστὶν ἡ ζώνη αὕτη οὕτως δήσουσιν ἐν Ἰερουσαλὴμ οἱ Ἰουδαῖοι.

---

1. THE dispersion of the Jerusalem Church which followed the death of Stephen carried some of its Greek-speaking members as far as Antioch in Syria. (Acts vi. 5.) A proselyte from Antioch had been among the Seven, and now through the labours of these scattered disciples a congregation of Christian Hellenists arose on the banks of the Orontes. When the tidings of this new beginning reached the mother Church Barnabas was sent down, as Peter and John had been sent to Samaria, and this 'son of Paraclesis,' (Acts iv. 36: cf. xi. 23 f. (παρεκάλει).) being *a good man and full of Holy Spirit and faith,* strengthened and developed the new church, which grew so rapidly that it attracted the notice of the Greek citizens of Antioch, and their ready wit found for its members the nickname of 'Christians[1].' Before long the Church at Antioch was second only to the Jerusalem Church in importance and perhaps in numbers, (Acts xi. 26 (ὄχλον ἱκανόν).) and it was what the

[1] The termination in -ανός is Latin, but it is not unusual in the Greek of the period; cf. Ἡρῳδιανός, Ἀσιανός.

Jerusalem Church could not be, a purely Greek-speaking body. Part I. vii.

It was in the Church of Antioch that the movement began for evangelizing the Greek lands to the West. In the spring of A.D. 47[1], a solemn 'liturgy[2]' with fasting was being conducted in the congregation at Antioch by a group of prophets and teachers, men recognized as possessing special gifts of the Holy Spirit, among whom were Barnabas and Saul. It may have been that they were seeking light as to the next step which was to be taken. As the liturgy proceeded, the Spirit spoke by one of the prophets, perhaps Simeon Niger or Lucius of Cyrene or Manaen, *Separate me[3] Barnabas and Saul for the work to which I have called them.* The voice was the voice of a prophet, but all knew that it was the Spirit that had spoken, and hastened to fulfil the command. There was a further service of fasting and prayer, and then the two were 'separated[4],' i.e. consecrated to the service of the Holy Spirit by the Acts xiii. 1 ff.

[1] According to Mr C. H. Turner's chronology of St Paul's life (Hastings, *D. B.* I. 421).

[2] λειτουργούντων δὲ αὐτῶν τῷ κυρίῳ. The Breaking of the Bread may be intended or included, although the Eucharist was not yet technically called ἡ λειτουργία.

[3] ἀφορίσατε δή μοι. Cf. Rom. i. 1 ἀφωρισμένος εἰς εὐαγγέλιον θεοῦ. The LXX. uses this verb in reference to (1) Israel (Lev. xx. 26), and (2) Levi (Num. viii. 11). Δή places the command in the light of an answer to the prayers of the Church. 'You have sought guidance; here it is.'

[4] By an act of the Church through the Prophets and Teachers. In the Divine purpose the separation was made long before; cf. Gal. i. 15 ὁ ἀφορίσας με ἐκ κοιλίας μητρός μου.

Part I. vii.

laying on of the hands of the other prophets and teachers, and so dismissed. But it was felt that they had received their mission not from the Church, but directly from its Divine Guide; they were *sent out by the Holy Spirit.* (Acts xiii. 4.)

Thus the missions of the Church to heathen lands were set on foot by an act of the Spirit. As His illapse upon Cornelius and his party had affirmed the principle of admitting Gentiles to the Church, so His voice by the mouth of the Antiochian prophets sent the still hesitating Hellenistic teachers to the heathen West. From Antioch the way lay open to Asia Minor, and from Asia Minor to Europe and the whole basin of the Mediterranean. On the day when Barnabas and Saul went down to Seleucia to set sail for Cyprus[1], the evangelization of the Roman Empire began; and it began under the guidance of the Spirit of Christ.

2. The preaching of Barnabas and Saul (or Paul, for St Luke uses his Roman name now that he has entered on an Imperial mission[2]) was followed by an effusion of the Spirit not less abundant or less fruitful than that which had attended the preaching of the older Apostles. At Pisidian Antioch, the first place in Asia Minor where converts were made, *the disciples were con-* (Acts xiii. 52.)

[1] It does not appear that the missionaries were directed to Seleucia and thence to Cyprus by the Holy Spirit. Early associations would lead Barnabas thither (Acts iv. 36); besides, Cyprus was the natural stepping-stone between Syria and the West.

[2] See Ramsay, *St Paul the Traveller*, p. 358.

tinually filled (ἐπληροῦντο) *with joy and Holy Spirit.* The occasion was one for depression, for persecution had begun, and the missionaries had left. But joy and spiritual exultation, it is evident from the letters of St Paul, were normal effects of the Spirit's presence, and independent of external circumstances; indeed they might be heightened by pressure from without. So it proved at Pisidian Antioch, and the same general results followed wherever the missionaries went; the same feature of primitive Christian life repeated itself in every city where the Church was planted.

Part I. vii.

3. Further, the Spirit by whom St Paul was sent forth at the first is seen afterwards controlling and directing his way. This is specially clear in the course of events by which he was led to pass from Asia Minor to Europe. It is unnecessary to enter here into the geographical puzzle connected with Acts xvi. 6, 7. Whatever may be intended by *the Phrygian and Galatic region* (τὴν Φρυγίαν καὶ Γαλατικὴν χώραν), it is evident that at a certain point in their second journey the missionaries resolved to carry their work to the western sea-coast, but before they could fulfil their purpose they were prohibited by a Divine Voice within them or in the mouth of a prophet: they were *forbidden by the Holy Spirit to preach the word in Asia*[1]. Nothing could

Acts xvi. 6 f.

[1] Cod. D represents the prohibition as ultimately removed by the same authority; in Acts xix. 1 it adds: εἶπεν αὐτῷ τὸ πνεῦμα ὑποστρέφειν εἰς τὴν Ἀσίαν. Cf. xx. 3 where D inserts, εἶπεν δὲ τὸ πνεῦμα αὐτῷ ὑποστρέφειν διὰ τῆς Μακεδονίας.

Part I. vii.

have been more natural than the desire to advance from Phrygia to the coast; a great road called them thither, and such a centre of life as Ephesus offered an unrivalled field for the preaching of the Gospel. But they were checked by a force which was not merely distinguishable from their own will, but opposed to it. The same thing happened at a further stage in their journey. When, unable to go westward, they turned to the North with the intention of entering Bithynia, *the Spirit of Jesus suffered them not.* Neither Asia nor Bithynia was to be evangelized on the present occasion: some other call was more urgent. It is remarkable that in both cases the guidance was negative only, keeping the missionaries from a false move but not pointing out whither they should go. The actual step forward was determined by circumstances or, as in the latter instance, by a dream. It was no part of the Spirit's work to supersede the reason or the judgement; but rather to leave them free to work upon the facts. In this method of procedure by *the Spirit of Jesus* we have the counterpart of the method of Jesus Himself, whose teaching usually indicated the direction in which His disciples should go without dictating a definite line of conduct.

Acts xvi. 10 (συνβιβάζοντες).

4. When at length St Paul found himself at liberty to begin work at Ephesus, one of his earliest experiences proved the reality of the Pentecostal gift. Apollos who had been there before him and *taught the things concerning Jesus*, knew *only the baptism of John*, and though a fervent believer had

Acts xviii. 25.

not received the baptism of the Spirit. Apollos was now at Corinth, but the Apostle found at Ephesus a band of disciples who, if they had not been under the instruction of the Alexandrian teacher, occupied nearly the same position. Observing in these men no signs of the Spirit's working, he asked whether they had received the Spirit when they came to faith (πιστεύσαντες). Their answer was a frank confession that they had not even heard of any gift of the Spirit (ἀλλ' οὐδ' εἰ πνεῦμα ἅγιόν ἐστιν ἠκούσαμεν). Upon this they were instructed and baptized into Christ. The Apostle then laid his hands on them, as Peter and John on the Samaritans, and with the same result; *the Holy Spirit came upon them* with signs following; *they both spoke with tongues and prophesied.*

Part I. vii. — Acts xix. 1 ff.

Acts xix. 6.

It would be precarious to gather that St Paul everywhere as a matter of course laid his hands on the baptized. The case of these twelve disciples of the Baptist was exceptional, and this solemn confirmation of their baptism may have been exceptional likewise. Nevertheless, since St Paul did not usually baptize his converts but left the ministry of baptism in the hands of those to whom it belonged, probably his companions in travel, it is not improbable that it was his practice to follow up *the washing of regeneration* with the imposition of his own hands on all occasions when this was possible. It is at least significant that we find him following the example of the older Apostles in the use of so characteristic a rite, and with the same consequences. The facts create a

Part I. vii.

presumption that the laying on of hands after baptism by an Apostle was a recognized custom of the whole Church and one which it had pleased God to honour with special gifts of the Spirit of Christ.

5. The men on whom St Paul laid his hands at Acts xix. 6. Ephesus 'prophesied.' Prophecy was held in high honour by St Paul, and the Christian Prophets are placed by him in the second rank of the charismatic ministry, the Apostles only taking precedence of 1 Cor. xii. 28. Eph. ii. 20, iv. 11. them. In the Pauline churches the prophet counted for more than the pastor or teacher; he was the mouthpiece of the Spirit; as the Holy Spirit in the old time had spoken to Israel by the mouth of Acts i. 16, xxviii. 25. David or Isaiah[2], so now He spoke by these men in Gentile cities and in the midst of congregations largely composed of Gentile converts. The coming of the Spirit had restored to the Church the gift of prophecy, and the prophets, in whom it was manifested, took rank in the Church above the local bishops and deacons to whom were committed the lower gifts of government and service.

6. Yet the local ministries were not undervalued in the churches founded by St Paul, nor was their relation to the Spirit overlooked. Presbyters were appointed in every city where a Christian society had been planted, and were taught to regard Acts xx. 17, 28. themselves as having received their appointment from the Holy Spirit. The office was committed to them with prayer and the laying on of hands, perhaps preceded by an exercise of the prophetic gift. But beyond this, those who held it were assured that they

possessed a *charisma*, a special gift which if not equal in dignity to that of the prophet, qualified them to fulfil their own special work in the Body of Christ. It was realized that the One Spirit of Jesus Christ supplied the needs of all the members of the Church, *distributing to each one severally* such a measure of grace as his office or his condition of life required.

Part I. vii.

Cf. 1 Tim. i. 18, iv. 14, 2 Tim. i. 6 f.

Cf. 1 Cor. xii. 11.

How widely and in how many ways the Paraclete made His power felt in the Gentile Churches will be evident when we consider the teaching of the Pauline Epistles. But from the second part of the Acts alone it is clear that His Mission was no less world-wide than the destiny of the Christian Society. Contrary to the expectation of the Apostles, the Spirit was poured upon all the baptized without distinction. St Peter was on sure ground when he pressed this point upon the attention of the Apostles and Elders assembled at Jerusalem to consider the claims of the Gentile converts. *God, who knows the heart, bore witness to them, giving them the Holy Spirit even as He did to us, and made no difference between us and them, cleansing their hearts by faith.* This fact disposed finally of the attempt to convert the Church of God into a Jewish sect. It was the common possession by Jew and Gentile of the same Spirit which saved the principle of catholicity.

Acts xv. 8 f.

PART II.

THE HOLY SPIRIT IN THE TEACHING OF THE NEW TESTAMENT.

πολλῆς προσοχῆς ἀναγινώσκοντες τὰ θεῖα δεόμεθα, ἵνα μὴ προπετέστερον εἴπωμέν τινα ἢ νομίσωμεν περὶ αὐτῶν. καὶ προσέχων τῇ τῶν θείων ἀναγνώσει μετὰ πιστῆς καὶ θεῷ ἀρεσκούσης προλήψεως κροῦε τὰ κεκλεισμένα αὐτῆς, καὶ ἀνοιγήσεταί σοι ὑπὸ τοῦ θυρωροῦ περὶ οὗ εἶπεν ὁ Ἰησοῦς Τούτῳ ὁ θυρωρὸς ἀνοίγει.

ORIGEN

I.

THE SYNOPTIC TEACHING OF OUR LORD.

Εὗρεν τὸν τόπον οὗ ἦν γεγραμμένον Lc. iv. 17
Πνεῦμα Κυρίου ἐπ' ἐμέ, —21.
οὗ εἵνεκεν ἔχρισέν με......
ἤρξατο δὲ λέγειν πρὸς αὐτοὺς ὅτι Σήμερον πεπλήρωται ἡ γραφὴ αὕτη ἐν τοῖς ὠσὶν ὑμῶν.

	Εἰ δὲ ἐν πνεύματι θεοῦ ἐγὼ ἐκβάλλω τὰ δαιμόνια...	Εἰ δὲ ἐν δακτύλῳ θεοῦ ἐγὼ ἐκβάλλω τὰ δαιμόνια...	Mt. xii. 28. Lc. xi. 20.
Πάντα ἀφεθήσεται τοῖς υἱοῖς τῶν ἀνθρώπων, τὰ ἁμαρτήματα καὶ αἱ βλασφημίαι ὅσα ἐὰν βλασφημήσωσιν· ὃς δ' ἂν βλασφημήσῃ εἰς τὸ πνεῦμα τὸ ἅγιον οὐκ ἔχει ἄφεσιν εἰς	Πᾶσα ἁμαρτία καὶ βλασφημία ἀφεθήσεται τοῖς ἀνθρώποις, ἡ δὲ τοῦ πνεύματος βλασφημία οὐκ ἀφεθήσεται. καὶ ὃς ἐὰν εἴπῃ λόγον κατὰ τοῦ υἱοῦ τοῦ ἀνθρώπου, ἀφεθήσεται αὐτῷ· ὃς δ' ἂν εἴπῃ κατὰ τοῦ πνεύματος τοῦ ἁγίου, οὐκ ἀφεθήσεται αὐτῷ οὔτε ἐν τούτῳ τῷ αἰῶνι	Πᾶς ὃς ἐρεῖ λόγον εἰς τὸν υἱὸν τοῦ ἀνθρώπου ἀφεθήσεται αὐτῷ· τῷ δὲ εἰς τὸ ἅγιον πνεῦμα βλασφημήσαντι οὐκ ἀφεθήσεται.	Mc. iii. 28 ff. Mt. xii. 31 f. Lc. xii. 10.

Part II. i.	τὸν αἰῶνα, ἀλλὰ ἔνοχός ἐστιν αἰωνίου ἁμαρτήματος. ὅτι ἔλεγον Πνεῦμα ἀκάθαρτον ἔχει.	οὔτε ἐν τῷ μέλλοντι.	
Mt. vii. 11. Lc. xi. 13.		Εἰ οὖν ὑμεῖς πονηροὶ ὄντες οἴδατε δόματα ἀγαθὰ διδόναι τοῖς τέκνοις ὑμῶν, πόσῳ μᾶλλον ὁ πατὴρ ὑμῶν ὁ ἐν τοῖς οὐρανοῖς δώσει ἀγαθὰ τοῖς αἰτοῦσιν αὐτόν.	Εἰ οὖν ὑμεῖς πονηροὶ ὑπάρχοντες οἴδατε δόματα ἀγαθὰ διδόναι τοῖς τέκνοις ὑμῶν, πόσῳ μᾶλλον ὁ πατὴρ ὁ ἐξ οὐρανοῦ δώσει πνεῦμα ἅγιον τοῖς αἰτοῦσιν αὐτόν.
Mc. xii. 36. Mt. xxii. 43 f. Lc. xx. 42.	Αὐτὸς Δαυεὶδ εἶπεν ἐν τῷ πνεύματι τῷ ἁγίῳ κτλ.	Πῶς οὖν Δαυεὶδ ἐν πνεύματι καλεῖ αὐτὸν κύριον, λέγων κτλ.	Αὐτὸς γὰρ Δαυεὶδ λέγει ἐν βίβλῳ Ψαλμῶν κτλ.
Mc. xiii. 11. Mt. x. 20. Lc. xii. 12; cf. Lc. xxi. 14 f.	Οὐ γάρ ἐστε ὑμεῖς οἱ λαλοῦντες ἀλλὰ τὸ πνεῦμα τὸ ἅγιον.	Οὐ γὰρ ὑμεῖς ἐστὲ οἱ λαλοῦντες ἀλλὰ τὸ πνεῦμα τοῦ πατρὸς ὑμῶν τὸ λαλοῦν ἐν ὑμῖν.	Τὸ γὰρ ἅγιον πνεῦμα διδάξει ὑμᾶς ἐν αὐτῇ τῇ ὥρᾳ ἃ δεῖ εἰπεῖν.

Mt. xxviii. 19. Μαθητεύσατε πάντα τὰ ἔθνη, βαπτίζοντες αὐτοὺς εἰς τὸ ὄνομα τοῦ πατρὸς καὶ τοῦ υἱοῦ καὶ τοῦ ἁγίου πνεύματος.

Lc. xxiv. 48 f.; cf. Acts i. 5, 8. Ἰδοὺ ἐγὼ ἐξαποστέλλω τὴν ἐπαγγελίαν τοῦ πατρός μου ἐφ' ὑμᾶς· ὑμεῖς δὲ καθίσατε ἐν τῇ πόλει ἕως οὗ ἐνδύσησθε ἐξ ὕψους δύναμιν.

THE Synoptic recollections of our Lord's teaching upon the Holy Spirit are few, but perhaps as many as the scope of the first three Gospels might lead us to expect. It is even possible that they are fairly representative of His Galilean teaching on this subject, for the early Ministry was not the occasion or Galilee the place for a full revelation of the work of the Spirit in the new order which was to follow His Passion and Resurrection.

Part II. i.

1. It is convenient to begin, as St Luke begins, with the announcement in the synagogue at Nazareth. Though the incident belongs to a later stage in the Ministry[1], the words spoken at Nazareth disclose the consciousness of a unique relation to the Spirit which is presupposed by all that Jesus taught about Him.

The Spirit of the Lord is upon me, because the Lord hath anointed me to bring good tidings unto the meek. So begins the lesson which Jesus read out of the roll of the Book of Isaiah. The words have been taken by some interpreters of Isaiah as spoken by the prophet in reference to himself, while others regard them as put by him into the mouth of the Servant of the Lord. In either case their meaning was not exhausted by the experience of the past; *to-day*, the Lord proceeded, *has this scripture been fulfilled in your ears.* That day they had heard the voice of the true Christ of God.

Lc. iv. 18 (Isa. lxi. 1).

Lc. iv. 21.

The Christ takes His stand upon the words of the Old Testament. The Spirit by which He had been anointed was none other than the Spirit of the God of Israel, the Spirit that spake by the prophets of Israel. He accepts the character of the Lord's Anointed which had belonged to the prophets, the priests, and the kings of Israel. More than this, His description of His Messianic work is drawn upon the old lines; He has been anointed to

[1] See p. 56 f., where the facts are considered in connexion with the history of the Ministry.

Part II. i. proclaim a new Jubilee[1], an acceptable year of the Lord in which captives and prisoners shall be released and the poor shall come again into their own. But as the mission on which he is sent goes deeper into the heart of things than that of the Old Testament priest or prophet, so the anointing He has received is no mere formal appointment to an office, or even a special gift of prophetic power, but the flooding of His whole humanity with the light and power of the Divine Spirit. He is conscious of a plenitude of spiritual gifts which constitutes at last a fulfilment of the earlier hopes and experiences. The Messianic outpouring of the Spirit has begun in His person; He has received from the Father the
1 Jo. ii. 20, 26 f. unction which He will hereafter give to the Church. But for the present He does not actually call Himself the Christ; He claims only to have fulfilled the *rôle* of the Servant of the Lord. 'The Lord hath anointed me to bring good tidings' is a sufficient basis for the ministry of preaching and healing with which His work began.

Mc. ii. 10. 2. Early in the ministry at Capernaum the Christ interpreted His mission to *proclaim release to the captives* as an authority to remit sins. But as time went on, while expanding His offer of remission in a general way, He had occasion to limit it in one
Mc. iii. 29. direction. *Whosoever shall blaspheme*, He taught, *against the Holy Spirit has no remission for ever, but*

[1] Delitzsch *ad loc.*: "קָרָא דְרוֹר is the expression used in the Law to indicate the proclamation of freedom which the year of Jubilee brought with it."

is guilty of an eternal sin. 'All acts of sin shall be remitted to men on earth except one; for the man who has blasphemed the Holy Spirit there can be no remission either here or in the next age; such a man is in the grip of a sin from which there is no discharge.' The words are followed in St Mark by one of that Evangelist's rare notes of explanation: *because they said, 'It is an unclean spirit that he has.'* That some superhuman power wrought in Jesus was not to be denied in the face of His words and deeds. Rabbis who had come down from Jerusalem and had seen and heard for themselves could not resist the general belief that He worked by a power greater than that of man. But the question remained whether the power that inspired Him was good or evil, from above or from below, and they ventured to adopt the latter view and even to spread a report that He 'had Beelzebul,' i.e. was in collusion with the arch-demon. This was to characterize the Spirit by which He wrought as in the highest degree impure and diabolical, although it was clear that unclean spirits could not be cast out by one of themselves or by any power but the Holy Spirit of God. What these men had said and taught others to believe was therefore blasphemy of the most deadly kind, and, if deliberate, was past forgiveness. The man who was capable of calling good evil, of painting the Source of holiness in the colours of Hell, was beyond repentance and therefore beyond forgiveness; his sin must pass with him unremitted into the next aeon, to which the earthly mission of the Saviour did not extend.

Part II. i

Mc. iii. 28 f.

Mc. iii. 30.

Part II. i.

The first and third Gospels contrast this *blasphemy against the Spirit* with blasphemy against the Son of Man: *whosoever shall speak a word against the Son of Man, it shall be forgiven him; but whosoever shall speak against the Holy Spirit it shall not be forgiven him.* There is reason for supposing that this form of the saying may be a doublet of the Marcan form[1]. But the thought is dormant in St Mark; for if blasphemy against the Spirit is the sole exception to the sins which are within reach of forgiveness, blasphemy against Jesus which does not involve a conscious antagonism to His Spirit may be remitted. In any case the Marcan saying invests the work of the Holy Spirit with the inviolable sanctity that belongs to the Divine.

Mt. xii. 32, Lc. xii. 10.

3. In the course of the same conversation there is some direct teaching upon the subject of the casting out of unclean spirits. *If I by the Spirit of God cast out the demons, then is the Kingdom of God come upon you.* The presence of the Divine Spirit marks the advent of the Divine Kingdom, and its presence is known by the dispersion of the forces of evil. Our Lord here not only accepts the Old Testament doctrine of the Spirit of God but to some extent He seems to sanction the popular belief in the existence and activity of evil spirits. 'Demons' appear to enter into His scheme of the spiritual world, and their workings to be as real as those of the Spirit of God. Readers of the Gospel must of course be careful not to attribute to our Lord

Mt. xii. 28. Lc. xi. 20.

[1] See Driver in Hastings, *D. B.* IV. p. 588 f.; W. C. Allen, *St Matthew*, p. 136 f.

allusions to Jewish ideas which may be due to the Evangelists or their sources, and such are perhaps the greater part of the Synoptic references to the 'demons[1].' Even when Jesus is represented as addressing an evil spirit in the act of expelling it[2], it may be argued that He accommodates Himself to the prevalent belief, or that He personifies a mental disease, as on one occasion He rebuked the rage of a storm upon the Lake[3]; or that His words have been coloured by the media through which they have reached us. But it is otherwise with the passage before us. The whole argument turns on the reality of the kingdom and forces of Satan; it recognizes the existence of spiritual powers working under a chief and working against the Kingdom of God. There was thus much of solid truth in the demonology of Babylon, Persia, and Greece, and in that of His Jewish contemporaries, and our Lord endorses this truth without setting the seal of His authority to the mythical forms in which it was expressed[4]. It is worthy of note, for example, that He seems tacitly to set aside the name 'Beelzebul[5]' and to substitute the Old Testament term 'Satan,' even while He assumes the existence of such a

[1] Cf. e.g. Mc. i. 23, 26, 27, iii. 11, v. 2, 18, vi. 7, vii. 25; and the corresponding passages in Mt. and Lc.

[2] E.g. Mc. i. 25, ix. 25.

[3] Mc. iv. 39 εἶπεν τῇ θαλάσσῃ Σιώπα, πεφίμωσο (cf. i. 25 ἐπετίμησεν αὐτῷ ὁ Ἰ. λέγων Φιμώθητι).

[4] See the bibliography given in Hastings, *D. C. G.* I. 438 *b*.

[5] So Mc.; Mt. and Lc. are less careful to make this distinction.

Part II. i. being. Later Jewish developments are accepted only so far as they were legitimate inferences from the teaching of the Canon.

4. If the Spirit of God is the expeller of the evil forces which harass and defile human life, He is also the source in man of all spiritual good. This complementary view of the Spirit's work is

Lc. xi. 1 ff. the next to appear in the teaching of Jesus. He had been praying, and when He ceased, the Twelve asked to be taught to pray. The Lord's Prayer is given them, and a discourse on prayer follows. The Lord's Prayer begins with the recognition of the Fatherhood of God, and on this foundation the Lord builds an assurance of the efficacy of prayer.

Lc. xi. 11 ff. *Who among you that is a father will give his son a snake for a fish, or a scorpion for an egg? If then ye, evil as ye are, know how to give your children gifts that are good, how much more shall the Father who is of heaven give Holy Spirit to those who ask him?*

Mt. vii. 9 ff. The words occur also, but with a somewhat different context[1], in the Sermon on the Mount, where for *Holy Spirit* the first Gospel simply repeats *good things* from the protasis of the sentence. The simpler form is probably the earlier, and St Luke's *Holy Spirit*[2] will in that case be an interpretation in the light of the Pentecostal gift.

It should be added that in the Lucan recension of the Lord's Prayer, for *Thy Kingdom come* at

[1] After the Prayer, but not immediately after it.

[2] Cod. D gives even in Lc. ἀγαθὸν δόμα, and Cod. L mediates with πνεῦμα ἀγαθόν.

least one cursive MS., confirmed by several Fathers, reads, *Thy Holy Spirit come and cleanse us* (ἐλθάτω τὸ πνεῦμά σου τὸ ἅγιον καὶ καθαρισάτω ἡμᾶς)[1]. This is clearly a gloss, and one which does not belong to the first age; but it expresses the great truth that the Kingdom of God as an inward power is identical with the working of the Spirit of God[2], and it is valuable as an ancient interpretation of the clause. Part II. i.

5. Of the special gift of inspiration, the Spirit of prophecy, the Synoptic Christ speaks more than once. When He quotes Ps. cx., His formula is that of the pious Jew of His own time. *David himself said in the Holy Spirit*[3], *The Lord said unto my Lord*, or as St Matthew turns the words, *How then does David in spirit* (under inspiration) *call him Lord?* Almost the precise form of citation which St Mark puts into the mouth of Christ is to be found in the Talmud[4]. Our Lord, by adopting it, does not affirm the attribution of this particular Psalm to David, nor does He endorse the particular Mc. xii. 36. Mt. xxii. 43.

[1] So Ev. 710 (Gregory). Gregory of Nyssa *de orat. dom.* 3 says ὁ τὴν βασιλείαν ἐλθεῖν ἀξιῶν τὴν τοῦ ἁγίου πνεύματος συμμαχίαν ἐπιβοᾶται...ἐλθέτω, φησί, τὸ ἅγιον πνεῦμά σου ἐφ' ἡμᾶς καὶ καθαρισάτω ἡμᾶς. See WH., *Notes on select readings*, p. 60; Chase, *The Lord's Prayer in the Early Church*, p. 25 ff.; Resch, *Agrapha*, p. 398. In some texts ἐλθέτω τὸ ἅγιον πνεῦμα κτλ. seems to have been a substitute for ἁγιασθήτω τὸ ὄνομά σου.

[2] Cf. Greg. Nyss. as cited. Maximus, depending perhaps on Gregory, says more expressly: ἡ βασιλεία σου, τουτέστι τὸ πνεῦμα τὸ ἅγιον.

[3] St Luke has simply, Δαυεὶδ λέγει ἐν βίβλῳ Ψαλμῶν.

[4] See W. C. Allen on St Matthew *l. c.*

Part II. i. view of inspiration which was prevalent among the scribes. But He accepts the general principle that the Holy Spirit spoke by the prophets and psalmists, i.e. that their minds, as they prophesied, were raised above their natural level by a Divine gift.

With this acceptance of the inspiration of the Psalmist we may compare the Lord's promise of a like inspiration to His followers in certain circumstances connected with their future mission. *When they lead you* to judgement, *delivering you over* to the courts, *be not anxious beforehand what ye shall speak, but whatever shall be given you in that hour, this speak ye; for ye are not the speakers, but the Holy Spirit* speaks by you. This is not a general promise of inspiration, nor does it affirm the inspiration of the writers of the New Testament; it does not even predict the rise of an order of New Testament prophets. But it guarantees to Christian confessors, in the moment of need, the presence of an Advocate within who will speak by their mouth as truly as he spoke by the mouth of David or Isaiah. We have here the germ of the doctrine of the 'other Paraclete' or Advocate which is developed in the fourth Gospel. Though the advocacy here promised is limited to rare occasions if not to the first age, it represents the Spirit as fulfilling in the disciples after the departure of Jesus the office which Jesus Himself would have undertaken had He been still with them. This promise belongs to the apocalyptic discourse on the Mount of Olives which closely precedes the Passion (Mc.), for the position

Mc. xiii. 11 (cf. Mt. x. 19 f., Lc. xii. 11 f.).

which it holds in St Matthew and at its first appearance in St Luke can scarcely be original. Such a promise would naturally have been reserved for the eve of the Master's departure; in Galilee it would have been neither necessary nor indeed intelligible. Part II. i.

6. Alone of the three Synoptists St Matthew has preserved the Lord's great commission to His Church, *Go, disciple all the nations, baptizing them into the name of the Father and the Son and the Holy Spirit.* The words stand in all known MSS. and versions of the first Gospel, and from the second century at least[1] they have supplied the recognized form of Christian Baptism. Yet reasons have lately been produced[2] for hesitating to accept them as they are found in our present text. It has been urged that Eusebius frequently quotes the passage in the form *Go make disciples of all the nations,* either omitting all that follows or adding simply *in my name.* As in one place he expressly comments on the last three words, they must either have existed in some form of the text known to him, or have been strongly impressed on his own mind when he wrote. But that he was not acquainted with or did not accept the longer reading is put out of the question by the fact that he quotes it elsewhere as genuine. The evidence has been examined at length by the present Bishop of Ely[3], and few who have read his Mt. xxviii. 19.

[1] The words occur first as a formula in the Didache.

[2] By Mr F. C. Conybeare in the *Hibbert Journal* for Oct. 1902, and Prof. K. Lake in his Inaugural Lecture at Leiden in 1904.

[3] In *J. T. S.* VI. p. 481 ff.

investigation will disagree with his finding that the whole evidence "establishes without a shadow of doubt or uncertainty the genuineness of Matt. xxviii. 19."

It is less easy to interpret this great text than to defend its genuineness. As to its purpose, it can scarcely have been meant or at first understood to prescribe a form of words for use in the ministration of Christian Baptism, although our familiarity with this employment of the words may tempt us to take this view. All the baptisms recorded in the Acts[1] seem to have been administered simply in the name of Jesus Christ, and the same practice is implied in the Epistles[2]. We must look elsewhere for the original intention of the words.

The Father, the Son, and the Holy Spirit are named separately in our Lord's Synoptic teaching, and the Father and the Son or the Father and the Spirit are correlated in His more private or mystical instructions[3]. But until we reach this last command Jesus does not proceed to bring together into one category the Father, the Son, and the Spirit. To do this was to gather up the lines of all His earlier theological teaching; to crown all that He had taught concerning these Three Persons by presenting Them as at once a Triad and a Unity. But further—and here we begin to see the true purpose of His words—He associates this Divine Trinity with the

[1] Acts ii. 38, viii. 16, x. 48, xix. 5.

[2] Rom. vi. 3, 1 Cor. i. 13, Gal. iii. 27.

[3] E.g. in Mt. x. 20, xi. 27, Mc. xiii. 32.

life of each of His disciples and of His whole Ecclesia to the end of time, for every disciple is to be baptized into[1] the name of the Three. *Into the name* is a form of words which still needs further investigation, but part at least of its meaning can be grasped. Had the words run simply 'into the Father and the Son and the Holy Spirit' they might have been interpreted as implying merely the incorporation of believers by Christ's Baptism into the fellowship of the Holy Trinity. But *into the name* seems to suggest the further thought of 'proprietorship[2].' The baptized person is not only brought into union with the Three, but he is devoted to Their service, living thenceforth a consecrated life. Part II. i.

Whether this is in the words or not, they certainly carry the Synoptic doctrine of the Spirit far beyond the point hitherto reached. For the Spirit is now seen to be not merely God in action, but God in relation to God, and we approach a mystery which belongs to the Divine Life itself. Yet this great step is taken in the interests not of scientific but of practical theology. The very sentence in which the first glimpse is given of a mysterious threeness in the inner Life of God, turns our attention to the bearing of this revelation upon the life of

[1] So upon the whole it is best to translate εἰς here, as R.V. Though there are in the N.T. "very clear examples of εἰς encroaching on the domain of ἐν" (J. H. Moulton, *Prolegomena*, p. 62 f.), this is not one of them: cf. e.g. 1 Cor. x. 2 εἰς τὸν Μωυσῆν ἐβαπτίσαντο, xii. 13 εἰς ἓν σῶμα ἐβαπτίσθημεν, where ἐν τῷ Μωυσεῖ, ἐν ἑνὶ σώματι would modify or obscure the sense.

[2] See Deissmann, *Bible Studies* (E. tr.), pp. 146 ff., 196 f.

man. We are permitted to see the essential unity of the Father, the Son, and the Holy Spirit only in order that we may know ourselves to stand by virtue of our baptism into Christ in a vital relation to the Three. With the Father and the Son, the Holy Spirit claims our baptized life as His own. But what this means could be understood only when the Spirit had come; the Acts and Epistles are a running comment upon it. It is a life rather than a creed, a new relation to God rather than a new theology[1] that our Lord contemplates in the most theological, the most mystical of all His instructions.

7. St Luke represents our Lord as having in another of His last teachings foretold the Pente-
Lc. xxiv. 48 f. costal outpouring of the Holy Spirit. *Behold, I send forth the Promise of my Father upon you; but as for you, sit ye still in the city till ye have been clad with power from the height.* The words are
Acts i. 4, 8. repeated in substance at the beginning of Acts. Both passages contain the remarkable phrase 'the Promise of the Father,' the Acts adding, *which ye heard from me*; and in both the context shews that the Promise is the Gift of the Holy Spirit to be poured out on the Church after the Ascension. *The Promise of the Father* has been interpreted as the outpouring of the Spirit promised to Israel through the prophets—such prophecies as are to be found in Isaiah and Ezekiel, in Joel and Zechariah; but the mention of 'the Father' points rather to a promise

[1] Yet Basil has right when he says (*epp.* ii. 125) δεῖ...πιστευειν ὡς βαπτιζόμεθα.

made by Jesus Himself, and this interpretation is confirmed by the added words in Acts. No such promise given by the Son in His Father's name can be found in the Synoptic Gospels[1], and we are driven to the conclusion that the reference is to the last discourse which is recorded only by St John. On the night before His Passion the Lord had said, *I will pray the Father and he shall give you another Advocate: the Father will send* him *in my name: I will send* him *from the Father.* All was then in the future, and, as it might have seemed, a future yet distant, certainly difficult to realize. But much had occurred since that discourse was spoken: the Passion, the Resurrection, the life of the forty days; it was now the eve of the Ascension; the Pentecost was near at hand. With the coming of the Spirit full in view, the future is changed into a present: 'behold, I am sending it forth[2]'; the mission of the Spirit is as good as begun; the fulfilment of the Promise is imminent and potentially come. The note of this great coming event is 'power': power clothing the Eleven, an illapse of spiritual energy which will invest them and transfigure their lives in the sight of the world. These 'babes[3]' of the Ministry will be the strong men of the new order to be initiated by the Pentecost. As the Christ went forth to His work in Galilee *in the power of the Spirit*[4], so His disciples would know

Part II. i.

Jo. xiv. 16, 26.

[1] If we except Lc. xi. 13, on which see above, p. 120.

[2] ἐγὼ ἐξαποστέλλω. Contrast ἐγὼ πέμψω in Jo. xv. 26.

[3] νήπιοι (Lc. x. 20).

[4] Lc. iv. 14; cf. i. 17, 35; iv. 36, v. 7.

Part II. i. by their new sense of spiritual power that they had been baptized with the Promise of the Father and prepared for the service that lay before them in the world. Their way would lead, as His had led, through temptation and suffering to death; but not to failure or defeat. Henceforth there would be no wholesale desertion of the Master, no misunderstanding of the great purpose of His mission. The power of the Christ would rest upon them, and be perfected in their weakness. (2 Cor. xii. 9 f.)

II.

THE JOHANNINE TEACHING OF OUR LORD (i).

Ἀμὴν ἀμὴν λέγω σοι Ἐὰν μή τις γεννηθῇ ἄνωθεν, οὐ Jo. iii. 3, 5.
δύναται ἰδεῖν τὴν βασιλείαν τοῦ θεοῦ...ἀμὴν ἀμὴν λέγω σοι
Ἐὰν μή τις γεννηθῇ ἐξ ὕδατος καὶ πνεύματος, οὐ δύναται
εἰσελθεῖν εἰς τὴν βασιλείαν τοῦ θεοῦ.

Τὸ γεγεννημένον ἐκ τῆς σαρκὸς σάρξ ἐστιν, καὶ τὸ γεγεν- Jo. iii. 6 ff.
νημένον ἐκ τοῦ πνεύματος πνεῦμά ἐστιν. μὴ θαυμάσῃς ὅτι
εἶπόν σοι Δεῖ ὑμᾶς γεννηθῆναι ἄνωθεν. τὸ πνεῦμα ὅπου
θέλει πνεῖ καὶ τὴν φωνὴν αὐτοῦ ἀκούεις, ἀλλ' οὐκ οἶδας
πόθεν ἔρχεται καὶ ποῦ ὑπάγει· οὕτως ἐστὶν πᾶς ὁ γεγεν-
νημένος ἐκ τοῦ πνεύματος.

Ὃν γὰρ ἀπέστειλεν ὁ θεὸς τὰ ῥήματα τοῦ θεοῦ λαλεῖ· οὐ Jo. iii. 34.
γὰρ ἐκ μέτρου δίδωσιν τὸ πνεῦμα.

Εἰ ᾔδεις τὴν δωρεὰν τοῦ θεοῦ καὶ τίς ἐστὶν ὁ λέγων σοι Jo. iv. 10.
Δός μοι πεῖν, σὺ ἂν ᾔτησας αὐτὸν καὶ ἔδωκεν ἄν σοι ὕδωρ
ζῶν.

Ὃς δ' ἂν πίῃ ἐκ τοῦ ὕδατος οὗ ἐγὼ δώσω αὐτῷ, οὐ μὴ Jo. iv. 13 f.
διψήσει εἰς τὸν αἰῶνα, ἀλλὰ τὸ ὕδωρ ὃ δώσω αὐτῷ γενήσεται
ἐν αὐτῷ πηγὴ ὕδατος ἁλλομένου εἰς ζωὴν αἰώνιον.

Ἔρχεται ὥρα καὶ νῦν ἐστίν, ὅτε οἱ ἀληθινοὶ προσκυνηταὶ Jo. iv. 23 f.
προσκυνήσουσιν τῷ πατρὶ ἐν πνεύματι καὶ ἀληθείᾳ· καὶ γὰρ
ὁ πατὴρ τοιούτους ζητεῖ τοὺς προσκυνοῦντας αὐτόν. πνεῦμα
ὁ θεός, καὶ τοὺς προσκυνοῦντας αὐτὸν ἐν πνεύματι καὶ ἀληθείᾳ δεῖ προσκυνεῖν.

Τὸ πνεῦμά ἐστιν τὸ ζωοποιοῦν· ἡ σὰρξ οὐκ ὠφελεῖ οὐδέν. Jo. vi. 63.
τὰ ῥήματα ἃ ἐγὼ λελάληκα ὑμῖν πνεῦμά ἐστιν καὶ ζωή ἐστιν.

Jo. vii. 37 ff. Ἐάν τις διψᾷ ἐρχέσθω πρός με καὶ πινέτω. ὁ πιστεύων εἰς ἐμέ, καθὼς εἶπεν ἡ γραφή, ποταμοὶ ἐκ τῆς κοιλίας αὐτοῦ ῥεύσουσιν ὕδατος ζῶντος. τοῦτο δὲ εἶπεν περὶ τοῦ πνεύματος οὗ ἔμελλον λαμβάνειν οἱ πιστεύσαντες εἰς αὐτόν· οὔπω γὰρ ἦν πνεῦμα, ὅτι Ἰησοῦς οὔπω ἐδοξάσθη.

Jo. x. 3. Τούτῳ ὁ θυρωρὸς ἀνοίγει.

THE Fourth Gospel is 'spiritual' in a sense deeper than that which Clement of Alexandria attached to the word[1]. It deals more intimately than the Synoptic Gospels with the things of the Spirit, carrying its readers further into the inner life of man; and it yields fuller anticipations of the work of the Spirit of God in the Christian Church. How much the present form of the teaching owes to the inspired thought[2] or the personal ideals of the writer, or how much to his experience of post-Pentecostal times, it is not easy to determine. In this chapter and the next it will be assumed that the discourses attributed to our Lord are at least in substance His. To assign to the Evangelist more than the *rôle* of an interpreter is to over-estimate his genius or his inspiration, and to limit unduly the scope of Christ's mission as a Revealer of religious truth.

Jo. iii. 1—11. 1. The first of the great series of discourses which is a chief feature of St John's Gospel is an instruction upon the work of the Spirit as the re-

[1] *Ap.* Eus. *H. E.* vi. 14 τὸν μέντοι Ἰωάννην ἔσχατον συνιδόντα ὅτι τὰ σωματικὰ ἐν τοῖς εὐαγγελίοις δεδήλωται...πνευματικὸν ποιῆσαι εὐαγγέλιον (i.e., a mystical book as contrasted with a mere narrative).

[2] Eus. *l. c.* Ἰωάννην...πνεύματι θεοφορηθέντα.

Part II. ii.

generative principle in human life. Our Lord is visited at night by a Pharisee whose position as a member of the Sanhedrin forbids him to come openly by day. Nicodemus has convinced himself that Jesus is a *teacher come from God*, since the signs that He works shew that God is with Him; and *the teacher of Israel*, the accredited Rabbi, places himself at the feet of the Teacher authorized by Heaven. Jesus at once accepts the position and begins His teaching. But the teaching was not such as Nicodemus could at once receive, nor is it easy for the reader, though he may recognize the truth of what is taught, to see its connexion with the circumstances. Yet the connexion if not obvious is real and deep. Nicodemus is conscious only of an intellectual want; he knows himself to be in need of further instruction, but has not realized that there is a prior need. Spiritual life is the first necessity for one who would be a disciple of the New Kingdom[1]. And spiritual life must begin with spiritual birth. *Unless one has been born from above*[2] *he cannot see the Kingdom of God.* Without a Divine birth there is in man, as he now is, no capacity for discerning spiritual truth even if it is taught by a Teacher sent from God. When Nicodemus exclaims against the impossibility of a second birth, as he understands it—*can* a man *enter into his mother's womb a second time, and* so *be born?* —the Lord repeats His great saying with slight

Jo. iii. 2, 10 (ἀπὸ θεοῦ ἐλήλυθας διδάσκαλος ...σὺ εἶ ὁ διδάσκαλος τοῦ Ἰσραήλ).

[1] See Wendt, *Teaching of Jesus* (E. tr.) I. p. 246.

[2] For this sense of ἄνωθεν see Jo. iii. 31, xix. 11. Bp Westcott (*St John*, I. 136, ed. 1908) supports in an additional note the R.V. rendering *anew*.

Part II. ii. amplifications: *unless one has been born of water and Spirit he cannot enter into the Kingdom of God.* The birth from above is not of flesh[1] but of Spirit, and it admits not only to a sight of the Divine Kingdom but to a place in it.

Here, as in the other great Baptismal saying of Matt. xxviii. 19, the existing text has recently been attacked. It has been maintained[2] that the reference to *water* in *v.* 5, although it is now to be found in all MSS. and versions, had no place in the Fourth Gospel as it came from the writer. Justin, it is said, could not have failed to quote John iii. 5 in the fuller form if he had read it so, for the mention of water would have suited his argument, in which he speaks of regeneration in Baptism; yet he is content to write "Unless ye have been born anew ye shall in no wise enter into the Kingdom of heaven." This inference is thought to receive some support from textual considerations. Wendt with more probability suggests[3] that the mention of water is due to the Evangelist's presentation of the saying and had no place in its original form[4]; but in the absence of any evidence it is safer to adhere to the text which has documentary support.

[1] "Natural generation is only a feeble image of the supernatural generation" (Prof. Denney in Hastings' *D. C. G.* I. 890 *a*).

[2] By Prof. Lake, *Inaugural Lecture*: cf. Burkitt, *Ev. da Mepharreshe* II. p. 309 f.

[3] *Teaching of Jesus*, I. p. 91 f.

[4] As καὶ πυρί in Mt. iii. 11 is possibly due to St Matthew or to the Logia.

Yet though the reference to water must, in the present state of our knowledge, keep its place in verse 5, its omission in the true text of verse 8 shews that it is of secondary importance, the primary and essential source of the new birth being the Divine. Water[1] is the outward visible sign which attends the inward spiritual grace. The grace which is the real efficient is 'Spirit'—evidently the power of the Spirit of God, since the birth is "*from above.*" The Spirit is the generative power in the sphere of the spiritual life. Spiritual life comes from the Spirit and not from the flesh; it does not descend from father to son in the way of natural generation, but is imparted to each individual by a spiritual birth.

The Lord does not wait for any further question on the part of Nicodemus, but at once proceeds to work out His doctrine of the spiritual birth. Why is it necessary? Because 'flesh' and 'spirit' belong to different and indeed opposite categories, and the one cannot produce the other: flesh can only generate flesh; a spiritual nature, possessing spiritual capacities and born to a spiritual life, can only be generated by spirit. *That which has been born of the flesh is flesh, and that which has been born of the Spirit is spirit. Wonder not that I said to thee, You[2] must be born from above.* The strangeness of Jo. iii. 6 f.

[1] "As Nicodemus heard the words, *water* carried with it a reference to John's baptism" (Westcott). To the readers of the Gospel it would point to the 'washing of regeneration' (Tit. iii. 6), in which "the baptism of water was no longer separated from, but united with, the baptism of the spirit."

[2] Ὑμᾶς, i.e. τοὺς γεγεννημένους ἐκ τῆς σαρκός.

Part II. ii. this demand disappears when the law that like produces like is borne in mind. Human nature cannot rise above itself; to mount up to God and to things above men must receive a new principle of life from above, from God[1]. Nor ought a difficulty to be found in the mysteriousness of a spiritual birth.

Jo. iii. 8. *The spirit* of the wind *blows where it wills, and its voice thou hearest, but dost not know whence it comes and where it goes; so is every one who has been born of the Spirit* of God. You cannot restrict the action of the Divine Breath, or prescribe its course, any more than you can dictate to the winds of heaven. That the wind is at work we know by the familiar sounds of breeze or gale, but its origin and its destination are hidden from us. Such is the manner of the Spirit's working in him who has been born from above; there is the same mystery surrounding it, the same ignorance on man's part of the laws by which it is governed, the same certainty that its existence and its presence are matters of fact, since its effects fall within our range of observation, even within the cognizance of the senses; the Spirit's voice is heard in human utterances and the Spirit's power felt in human actions, though the Spirit itself is inaudible and invisible.

Nicodemus is still unconvinced, *How can these things come to pass?* A second birth is to this *teacher of Israel* unthinkable, although the conception is not wholly wanting in the scriptures of the Old Testament. In His reply, however, Jesus does

Ps. li. 10, Ezek. xxxvi. 26f.

[1] Cf. Jo. i. 13 ἐκ θεοῦ ἐγεννήθησαν.

not refer to the Old Testament; there is evidence Part II. ii.
nearer at hand in the personal experience of the Lord and His disciples. *That which we know we* Jo. iii. 11.
speak and that which we have seen we bear witness to. Conceived by the Spirit, baptized by the Spirit, full of the power of the Spirit, He knew Himself to be continually stirred by the Spirit's breath, and His experience must be shared by all who enter the Kingdom of God. In this there was nothing which belonged to the sphere of supra-mundane things: to be born from above, to hear the voice of the Spirit, to know the mystery of His presence and working in the inner life, are earthly things (ἐπίγεια[1]) and not Jo. iii. 12.
heavenly, belonging to the experience of man's present state and not to a remote and as yet incomprehensible future. The spiritual birth is from above, but it takes place on earth and belongs to the facts of daily life.

2. The concluding verses of ch. iii. are in form Jo. iii. 31—36.
a continuation of the Baptist's words in *vv.* 27—30, but probably consist of remarks by the Evangelist himself based on recollections partly of the Baptist's teaching, partly of our Lord's. A reference to the Holy Spirit in *v.* 34 may therefore be considered here, though it cannot definitely be assigned to Christ Himself.

The Evangelist takes up the words of Jesus in *v.* 11, and carries them further. Jesus *bears witness* Jo. iii. 32 ff.
to that which he has seen and which he heard...The man who has received his witness thereby sets his seal

[1] See Westcott's note *ad loc.*

Part II. ii.

to the doctrine *that God is true. For he whom God sent speaks God's words, for not by measure does he give the Spirit.* To accept the witness of Jesus is to accept the witness of God, for Jesus was sent by God and speaks in His name. So far the connexion is clear. But what relation does the last clause bear to this? and what is its precise meaning? Who is it that gives the Spirit, and to whom does he give it? Are we to understand that the Father gives the Spirit to the Son[1], or that the Son gives the Spirit to men? In the former case the thought will run: 'the Son cannot but speak the Father's words, seeing He has received an unlimited supply of the Divine Spirit.' In the latter it seems to be: 'that the Son speaks the words of God is evident from the unlimited power that He possesses of imparting the Spirit.' Against the second interpretation it may be urged that it anticipates the Pentecostal effusion, and is moreover perhaps less in accord with the words which follow in *v.* 35[2]. On the whole it seems best to supply ὁ θεός as the nominative, and to paraphrase: 'God gives[3] His Spirit to men ungrudgingly[4]; there is no limit to His bounty but that which comes from the incapacity of the recipient, and He who is sent of God is not thus limited; in His case the Divine current of light and power flows unchecked by human sin.'

[1] Codd. AC²D etc. supply ὁ θεός.

[2] Ὁ πατὴρ ἀγαπᾷ τὸν υἱόν, καὶ πάντα δέδωκεν ἐν τῇ χειρὶ αὐτοῦ.

[3] Δίδωσιν, not ἔδωκεν or δέδωκεν.

[4] Cf. Jas. i. 5 τοῦ διδόντος θεοῦ πᾶσιν ἁπλῶς, καὶ μὴ ὀνειδίζοντος.

Thus there is an implied contrast between Jesus and all other religious teachers[1], whose supply of the Spirit is bounded by their imperfect correspondence with His holy inspirations. Jesus alone speaks without limit to His power to teach, since the spiritual life realizes itself in Him to the full measure of the Divine gift. Part II. ii.

3. The conversation with the Samaritan woman in some respects offers a marked contrast to the conversation with Nicodemus. In Nicodemus the Lord meets the higher culture of His age; in the other case, He talks with a peasant, who was not even a Jew, and His manner of speaking is adapted to the circumstances. But on both occasions His subject is the same. With the untaught woman the conversation turns on the familiar well; the Spirit is not mentioned by name; yet it is impossible not to recognize in the living water of which He speaks to her the same inflow of new life of which Nicodemus had heard. Himself the gift of God, Jesus offers to give that which men cannot draw for themselves from the sources of material and intellectual well-being. *Whosoever shall have drunk of the water which I shall give him, shall not thirst for ever, but the water which I shall give him shall become within him a spring of water leaping up into eternal life.* Jo. iv. 7—26. Jo. iv. 14.

[1] Cf. the interesting fragment of Origen (*fragm.* 48, *ap.* Brooke, II. p. 263): εἰ γὰρ καὶ ἄνδρες σοφοὶ θεὸν ἐσχηκότες ἐλάλησαν τὰ τοῦ θεοῦ ῥήματα, ἀλλ' οὖν ἐκ μέρους εἶχον τὸ πνεῦμα τοῦ θεοῦ. He continues however: ὁ δέ γε σωτήρ, ἀποσταλεὶς ἐπὶ τῷ τὰ ῥήματα τοῦ θεοῦ λαλεῖν, οὐκ ἐκ μέρους δίδωσι τὸ πνεῦμα.

Part II. ii. Here is the same conception of a new life entering into men and rising to its source in God[1]. But there is progress in the teaching, for the water of life is now seen to be the gift of Jesus, and its vitality appears not only in the depths of the spirit where none but the man himself can be conscious of its presence, but in the overflow that rises, strong and sparkling, into the light of day. The water in Jacob's well lay still and dead far below the surface: the water of the Spirit, also stored below the surface, cannot rest there but must force its way upwards, a perennial spring beautifying and transfiguring the present life, and rising by leaps and bounds into a life that belongs to the coming age (*ἁλλόμενον εἰς ζωὴν αἰώνιον*). Eternal life, one of the watchwords of the Fourth Gospel, is connected in ch. iii. with faith in Jesus; in ch. vi. it is seen to come from eating His flesh and drinking His blood; in ch. x. and ch. xvii. it is represented as His direct gift. Here it is viewed as the result of the life of the Spirit in man, the issue and consummation of spiritual life, differing from it not in kind but only in permanence and in maturity.

As the Lord's conversation with the woman at the well advances, He drops the metaphor and applies what has been said to the circumstances of

Jo. iv. 21 ff. this Samaritan woman. The Samaritans, like the Jews, attached the highest importance to their local sanctuary[2]; and they did so with less reason, for the

[1] "As it comes down out of heaven, it returns thither" (Westcott).

[2] Ἐν τῷ ὄρει τούτῳ, i.e. on Gerizim, as contrasted with Zion, cf. *v.* 20.

Jew, with whom the Lord here identifies Himself Part II. ii.
(ἡμεῖς, *v.* 22), could claim a Divine revelation and worshipped a Deity of whom he had some certain knowledge (προσκυνοῦμεν ὃ οἴδαμεν), for the Messianic deliverance (ἡ σωτηρία) was to proceed from the bosom of the Jewish people (ἐκ τῶν Ἰουδαίων). But the controversy was not of lasting significance, for the times of Messiah were approaching or rather were already come, and under Messiah worship must cease to be localized, because it would be seen to be a spiritual reality. *The hour comes and is now* Jo. iv. 23.
here[1] *when the genuine worshippers shall worship the Father in spirit and truth; for the Father seeks such as his worshippers. God is spirit, and his worshippers must needs worship in spirit and truth.* Worship must be spiritual, since God is a purely spiritual Being. There is no express mention here of the Holy Spirit, but the spiritual worship which is claimed demands a spiritual force which is not innate in man; to worship in spirit and truth is possible only through the Spirit of God. The Spirit of God is *the Spirit of the truth* (Jo. xiv. 19), nay, *is the truth* (1 Jo. v. 6). Reality in worship as in all other spiritual acts can only be of the Spirit of the truth, and without reality worship is not acceptable to a God who Himself is the absolute Truth. Thus this saying of Christ prepares the way for later teaching in the New Testament which has to do with the relation of the Holy Spirit to Prayer. But the Samaritan woman was not ready

[1] Cf. Jo. v. 25, xvi. 32.

Part II. ii. for more than the elementary doctrine that a spiritual God demands a worship which is spiritual and therefore true to its conception and its end.

Jo. vi. 51—63. 4. The discourse in ch. vi. at first sight contrasts strongly with the teaching of chh. iii. and iv. To the audience in the Capernaum synagogue the Lord offers His own flesh and blood as the food

Jo. vi. 54f. and drink of eternal life; *he that eateth my flesh and drinketh my blood hath an eternal life...for my flesh is true food and my blood is true drink.* True[1] food, true[1] drink, doubtless in the sense that it corresponds to the true life; as the life of the body is the visible and temporary expression of man's true life, so is bodily food of the food of the higher life. Such an analogy was not difficult to understand; the difficulty lay in the food of the higher life being identified with the flesh and blood of Jesus. This saying was as hard to receive as Nicodemus had found the earlier saying about the new birth, and for the same reason; it was interpreted by those who heard it on the basis of a shallow materialism. In the synagogue the Lord left His words unexplained, but to His disciples in private He gave a clue to its true interpretation.

Jo. vi. 62. *What then if ye behold the Son of Man ascending where he was before?* Suppose they were to see the Christ who had come down from heaven (vi. 41, 51) going up again in human form: would not this be a yet greater stumblingblock? For how could flesh and blood dwell with God? or how could the

[1] ἀληθής.

flesh and blood which had ascended to heaven be Part II. ii.
the food of men on earth? Yet in fact the Ascension would render this possible, because it would spiritualize the flesh and blood of the Son of Man;
when He had ascended men would be able to touch Jo. xx. 17.
Him and even to feed upon Him, as they could not do before the Passion and Resurrection had been
crowned by the Ascension. For *the spirit is that* Jo. vi. 63.
which gives life, the flesh (as flesh) *profits nothing*[1]. *My utterances are spirit, and* (being spirit) *they are life*. Flesh in itself is but dead matter; spirit alone vivifies. Christ's words about eating His flesh and drinking His blood were no 'hard saying' (σκληρός ἐστιν ὁ λόγος), no dry and lifeless formula, but *spirit and life*, possessing a spiritual content, and therefore a vivifying power. It is Christ's flesh, His manhood, full of the Spirit and in its risen and glorified state wholly spiritualized, which is offered as the food of men. As the food is spiritual, so must also be the eating. This is not to take from the reality either of the gift or of the act by which it is appropriated[2]; on the contrary, the spiritual is alone real in the deepest sense of the word. The Body and Blood of Christ are through the Spirit verily and indeed taken and

[1] The Curetonian Syriac has, "or the body (? ἦ ἡ σάρξ) hath nothing profited"; the Sinaitic Syriac paraphrases: "He is the Spirit that giveth life to the body; but ye say, The body nothing profiteth." See Burkitt, *Ev. da Mepharreshe* I. p. 461, II. p. 314.

[2] Prof. Denney (Hastings, *D. C. G.* I. p. 741 *b*) rightly observes: "there is no depreciation of the Sacrament here and no exaltation of the words of Jesus as opposed to it."

Part II. ii. received by the faithful according to His word, and His word proves itself in their lives to be 'spirit and life.'

Here as in iv. 23 the Holy Spirit is not mentioned or immediately in view, yet here as there the whole teaching presupposes the action of the Spirit. It is the Spirit in the humanity of our Lord which is life-giving[1], and it is the Spirit that mediates the process by which in the Eucharist or otherwise the life-giving humanity is conveyed to believers and becomes to them the food of eternal life. The ancient Church expressed her sense of this operation of the Spirit in the Mysteries by invoking its presence both upon the elements and the communicants[2]. All this may have been rightly evolved from our Lord's teaching, although His words enunciate only the principle that spirit is the quickening power in life.

5. In the autumn that followed the discourse at Capernaum Jesus was at Jerusalem during the
Jo. vii. 8f., 14. Feast of Tabernacles. He was purposely late in arriving, and did not shew Himself in the Temple precincts before the middle of the Tabernacles week. Then, prophet-like, He suddenly appeared in the Temple, and began to teach. The teaching turned upon His own mission and the attitude of the Jews towards it, to which attention had been directed by

[1] Cf. Gore, *Body of Christ*, pp. 26 ff., 76 ff.

[2] Cf. e.g. the invocation in the Byzantine Liturgy of the ninth century (Brightman, p. 329): σοῦ δεόμεθα...ἐλθεῖν τὸ πνεῦμά σου τὸ πανάγιον ἐφ' ἡμᾶς καὶ ἐπὶ τὰ προκείμενα δῶρα ταῦτα.

the circumstances. When *the last day, the great day of the Feast,* arrived, the Lord made a final appeal to the crowds who filled the courts. He *stood and cried,* His position and the raising of His voice marking the importance of what He had to say[1]. *If any one thirsts,* He said, *let him come unto me and drink. He that believes on me, as said the Scripture, there shall flow out of his belly rivers of living water.* The reader will recognize at once the affinity of this saying to the promise given to the Samaritan woman (iv. 14). But it has its own special character, connecting it with the circumstances. It was *the last day* of the Feast, probably the seventh, for the eighth was not strictly included in the Festival[2]. On each of the seven days water was drawn by a priest at the Pool of Siloam, and brought amid the blowing of trumpets into the Temple-precinct, where it was received by other priests chanting Isa. xii. 3, *With joy shall ye draw water out of the wells of salvation,* and was eventually poured out at the altar of burnt-offering. This ceremony was emphasized on the seventh day by the water being carried round the altar in procession seven times. The occasion lent itself to fresh and public teaching upon the Water of Life. Jesus, Himself the mystical Siloam, the Sent of God[3], invites any

Jo. vii. 37 ff.

[1] *ἱστήκει...καὶ ἔκραζεν.* Κράζειν is used of our Lord elsewhere only in Jo. vii. 28, xii. 44, and Mt. xxvii. 50.

[2] See *Enc. Bibl.* 488 *b*, note; Zahn, *St John*, p. 388. Westcott (*St John*, I. 276 f.) adheres to the view that the eighth day is meant.

[3] Cf. Jo. ix. 7 Σιλωάμ, ὃ ἑρμηνεύεται Ἀπεσταλμένος.

Part II. ii. who will to come and draw from Him the living water. He who did so, He adds, should not only quench his own thirst but become a fountain of life to his fellows; not only would the Water that the Christ gave him spring up within him into life eternal, but he should be as a rock, out of whose cavity rivers of the water of life would flow forth for the refreshment of men. We are reminded of the miracles of Exod. xvii. and Numb. xx.; the 'Scripture' to which the Lord refers is doubtless the general sense of many passages which describe these scenes or spiritualize the conception of flowing waters, such as Pss. lxxviii. 16, cv. 41, Zech. xiv. 8, Isa. xliii. 19, 20[1]. What the water of life signified Jesus did not explain, perhaps because the symbol was generally understood; in the Talmud[2] the conception of the Holy Spirit as water drawn from a well is found more than once. Thus the
Jo. vii. 39. Evangelist's editorial note, *But this he spake concerning the Spirit*, may represent the impression which was made by the Lord's words on His hearers at the time. He adds from his later experience: *which they were about to receive who believed upon him*; for there was as yet no Spirit,

[1] LXX. *ἐξήγαγεν ὕδωρ ἐκ πέτρας καὶ κατήγαγεν ὡς ποταμοὺς ὕδατα...ἐπορεύθησαν ἐν ἀνύδροις ποταμοί...ἐξελεύσεται ὕδωρ ζῶν ἐξ Ἰερουσαλήμ...ἔδωκα ἐν τῇ ἐρήμῳ ὕδωρ καὶ ποταμοὺς ἐν τῇ ἀνύδρῳ, ποτίσαι τὸ γένος μου τὸ ἐκλεκτόν.*

[2] *Pesikta Rabbathi* c. i.; Jerusalem Talmud, *Sukkah* v. 1; *Midrash Rabbah*, Genesis, c. lxx. The references have been supplied by the kindness of Mr I. Abrahams, Reader in Talmudic at Cambridge.

because Jesus was not yet glorified. The MSS. and versions have made more than one attempt to qualify the last words, reading either, *The Holy Spirit was not yet upon them*[1], or *was not yet given*[2]. Both our English versions adopt the latter expedient though they are careful by the use of italics to warn the English reader that *given* does not stand in the best text. But no addition is necessary even in a version if 'Spirit' is understood to mean an effusion or gift or dispensation of the Spirit, as it often does[3]. When Jesus spoke there was as yet no spiritual force in the world such as was brought into it at the Pentecost and afterwards swept like a great tidal wave over the face of the earth. And the reason for this was that Jesus was still in the flesh, *was not yet glorified*; He had not yet been seen to ascend up whither He was before the Incarnation (vi. 62), He was not yet with the Father (xvi. 7, xx. 17); and there could not be a spiritual Presence until the Presence in the flesh had been withdrawn and until the work of the Son of Man had been crowned by His exaltation to the right hand of God. Hence the Lord at the Tabernacles spoke of the great outflow of the living water as yet future (ῥεύσουσιν); hence the Evangelist's comment *which they were about to receive* (ἔμελλον λαμβάνειν). St John looks back from days when the Pentecost

Part II. ii.

[1] So cod. D (+ ἐπ' αὐτοῖς).

[2] So cod. B (+ διδόμενον).

[3] The nearest parallel is Acts xix. 3 οὐδ' εἰ πνεῦμα ἅγιόν ἐστιν ἠκούσαμεν.

Part II. ii. was long past and 'there was Spirit' to those when the great outpouring was but a dim and unrealized hope.

It is not surprising that as there fell upon the ears of the crowd this great promise of overflowing spiritual life about to be drawn from the person of the speaker, voices were heard to say, *This is truly the*
Jo. vii. 40 f., 46. *Prophet! This is the Christ!*, or that the members of the Temple guard who had been sent to arrest Jesus returned empty-handed with the report *Never spake any man after this fashion.* To others the words may have seemed exorbitant or blasphemous. But the whole history of the Church and of the world from the Pentecost to the present time bears witness to their absolute truth.

Jo. x. 3. 6. It may be that in the deep thought of our Lord the Holy Spirit is the 'porter' of the fold, who opens the door to the true Shepherd of the sheep, closing it against thieves and robbers. But the details of a parable cannot be safely pressed. Moreover, as Westcott rightly says, if the Holy Spirit is intended, it is the Spirit acting through the appointed ministry. The visible 'porter' is the Bishop or Priest to whom has been committed the care of souls in any place (Mc. xiii. 34), and to whom belongs the duty of keeping watch. Nevertheless, if his vigilance is effective, and his judgement sound, this is due to the quickening and guidance of the Spirit of Christ, who by his hands opens and shuts the door of the fold.

III.

THE JOHANNINE TEACHING OF OUR LORD (ii).

Ἐὰν ἀγαπᾶτέ με, τὰς ἐντολάς μου τηρήσετε· κἀγὼ Jo. xiv. 15 ff.
ἐρωτήσω τὸν πατέρα καὶ ἄλλον παράκλητον δώσει ὑμῖν ἵνα
ᾖ μεθ' ὑμῶν εἰς τὸν αἰῶνα, τὸ πνεῦμα τῆς ἀληθείας, ὃ ὁ
κόσμος οὐ δύναται λαβεῖν, ὅτι οὐ θεωρεῖ αὐτὸ οὐδὲ γινώσκει·
ὑμεῖς γινώσκετε αὐτό, ὅτι παρ' ὑμῖν μένει καὶ μεθ' ὑμῶν
ἔσται. οὐκ ἀφήσω ὑμᾶς ὀρφανούς· ἔρχομαι πρὸς ὑμᾶς.

Ταῦτα λελάληκα ὑμῖν παρ' ὑμῖν μένων· ὁ δὲ παράκλητος, Jo. xiv. 26.
τὸ πνεῦμα τὸ ἅγιον ὃ πέμψει ὁ πατὴρ ἐν τῷ ὀνόματί μου,
ἐκεῖνος ὑμᾶς διδάξει πάντα, καὶ ὑπομνήσει ὑμᾶς πάντα ἃ
εἶπον ὑμῖν ἐγώ.

Ὅταν ἔλθῃ ὁ παράκλητος ὃν ἐγὼ πέμψω ὑμῖν παρὰ τοῦ Jo. xv. 26.
πατρός, τὸ πνεῦμα τῆς ἀληθείας ὃ παρὰ τοῦ πατρὸς ἐκπορεύεται, ἐκεῖνος μαρτυρήσει περὶ ἐμοῦ· καὶ ὑμεῖς δὲ μαρτυρεῖτε, ὅτι ἀπ' ἀρχῆς μετ' ἐμοῦ ἐστέ.

Ἀλλ' ἐγὼ τὴν ἀλήθειαν λέγω ὑμῖν Συμφέρει ὑμῖν ἵνα ἐγὼ Jo. xvi. 7 ff.
ἀπέλθω. ἐὰν γὰρ μὴ ἀπέλθω, ὁ παράκλητος οὐ μὴ ἔλθῃ
πρὸς ὑμᾶς· ἐὰν δὲ πορευθῶ, πέμψω αὐτὸν πρὸς ὑμᾶς. καὶ
ἐλθὼν ἐκεῖνος ἐλέγξει τὸν κόσμον περὶ ἁμαρτίας καὶ περὶ
δικαιοσύνης καὶ περὶ κρίσεως· περὶ ἁμαρτίας μέν, ὅτι οὐ
πιστεύουσιν εἰς ἐμέ· περὶ δικαιοσύνης δέ, ὅτι πρὸς τὸν
πατέρα ὑπάγω καὶ οὐκέτι θεωρεῖτέ με· περὶ δὲ κρίσεως, ὅτι
ὁ ἄρχων τοῦ κόσμου τούτου κέκριται. ἔτι πολλὰ ἔχω ὑμῖν
λέγειν, ἀλλ' οὐ δύνασθε βαστάζειν ἄρτι. ὅταν δὲ ἔλθῃ
ἐκεῖνος, τὸ πνεῦμα τῆς ἀληθείας, ὁδηγήσει ὑμᾶς εἰς τὴν
ἀλήθειαν πᾶσαν· οὐ γὰρ λαλήσει ἀφ' ἑαυτοῦ, ἀλλ' ὅσα
ἀκούει λαλήσει καὶ τὰ ἐρχόμενα ἀναγγελεῖ ὑμῖν. πάντα

Part II. iii. ὅσα ἔχει ὁ πατὴρ ἐμά ἐστιν· διὰ τοῦτο εἶπον ὅτι ἐκ τοῦ ἐμοῦ λαμβάνει καὶ ἀναγγελεῖ ὑμῖν. μικρὸν καὶ οὐκέτι θεωρεῖτέ με, καὶ πάλιν μικρὸν καὶ ὄψεσθέ με.

Jo. xx. 22. Καὶ τοῦτο εἰπὼν ἐνεφύσησεν, καὶ λέγει αὐτοῖς Λάβετε πνεῦμα ἅγιον· ἄν τινων ἀφῆτε τὰς ἁμαρτίας, ἀφέωνται αὐτοῖς· ἄν τινων κρατῆτε, κεκράτηνται.

THE Fourth Gospel in its earlier chapters reveals the Holy Spirit as the author of the spiritual life in men, and our Lord as the giver of the Spirit to those who will come to Him for the gift. In the latter part of the book, which contains the private instructions given to the disciples on the night before the Passion and after the Resurrection, the Holy Spirit is regarded in another light; the relation in which the Spirit will stand to the Christian brotherhood, the offices which it is to fulfil towards the future Church represented by the company assembled in the upper room, come here into view. The subject of the teaching on the Spirit in John iii.—vii. is the Giver of Life; the subject of the later teaching in John xiv.—xx. is the Paraclete. The first concerns the individual, the second the Body of Christ.

Jo. xiv. 16 ff. 1. The doctrine of the Paraclete implies the withdrawal of Jesus from the world, and was therefore naturally withheld till the eve of the Crucifixion. It is not until the note *I am going to the Father* has been sounded that it is needful or even possible to add, *The Father will give you another Paraclete.* The word παράκλητος passed into Aramaic[1] together-

Jo. xiv. 2 (πορεύομαι), 3 (ὑπάγω), 12 (πρὸς τὸν πατέρα πορεύομαι),

[1] In the form פרקליטא. Cf. Abbott, *Johannine Vocabulary*,

ther with its opposite κατήγορος; and it may have Part II. iii.
been used by our Lord in His intercourse with 16 (ἄλλον
His disciples in reference to Himself; indeed this παράκλη-
seems to be almost implied in His reference to τον δώσω ὑμῖν). Cf. 1 Jo. ii.
the Spirit without explanation as ἄλλος παράκλητος. 1.
There can be little doubt that whether applied to Jesus or to the Spirit it means 'Advocate' rather than 'Comforter[1].' The Spirit is the *other Advocate* who takes up the *rôle* of the Son of Man and carries on certain functions which the Lord discharges towards His Church. The first and most obvious of the functions of an advocate is to defend those whose cause he undertakes from the charges laid against them by their accusers. The Lord had thus defended His disciples while He was upon earth[2], and He had foretold that the Spirit of their Father would defend them after His departure[3]. Not that He has ceased to be their Advocate since His
departure, for, as St John teaches in his first Epistle, 1 Jo. ii. 1.
He fulfils this office where He is *with the Father*, protecting sinners against the Arch-enemy who 'accuses
the brethren before God day and night.' Mean- Apoc. xii.
while the Spirit, whose sphere of work is on earth[4], 10.

1720 *k*; Zahn, comm. on St John, p. 554. For κατήγορος, κατήγωρ (קטיגור) see Apoc. xii. 10, note.

[1] It is used in this latter sense by Aquila and Theodotion in Job xvi. 2, where they write παράκλητοι for παρακλήτορες (LXX.). But St John's use of the word in his first Epistle weighs heavily against the admission of the active sense in the Gospel.

[2] Cf. e.g. Mc. ii. 18 ff., 24 ff.

[3] Cf. Mt. x. 20, Mc. xiii. 11; see p. 122 f.

[4] An ἐπίγειον (Jo. iii. 12); see p. 135.

Part II. iii. silences the earthly adversaries of the Church through the victory of faith which overcomes the world. The *Acta martyrum*, the whole history of the Church, and the lives of countless believers who have no place in history, bear witness to the fulfilment of this office of the Paraclete-Spirit in the Body of Christ[1].

But the work of the 'other Paraclete' was not
limited to defence in an age of persecution. The
Jo. xiv. 16. Lord's promise is: *I will ask the Father, and he
shall give you another Advocate that he may be with
you for ever.* The Father had already given them
an Advocate who had taught, guarded, protected,
Jo. xvii. 12. kept them from evil; but His abode in the flesh was
limited, and now drawing to an end. The Son of
Man could not remain to the end of time; permanence was possible only for a purely spiritual
Power. Such a Power was now to be sent, even
Jo. xiv. 6. the Spirit of the truth[2]. *I am the Truth*, Jesus
had just said; and the work of the Incarnate Truth
on earth was to be taken up by the Spirit of the
truth and carried forward as long as the present
order should endure. The unbelieving world would
indeed be wholly unconscious of this invisible Presence:
Jo. xiv. 17. *which the world cannot receive, for it beholds*

[1] Compare the memorable words of the Viennese letter in Eus. *H. E.* v. 1, where it is said of the martyr Vettius Epagathus: ἀνελήμφθη καὶ αὐτὸς εἰς τὸν κλῆρον τῶν μαρτύρων, παράκλητος Χριστιανῶν χρηματίσας, ἔχων δὲ τὸν Παράκλητον ἐν αὑτῷ τὸ πνεῦμα πλεῖον τοῦ Ζαχαρίου.

[2] On this title of the Spirit see Hort, *The Way, The Truth, and the Life*, p. 57.

it not nor yet knows it[1]; there is nothing which strikes the vision or appeals to the natural understanding; to the former being pure spirit it cannot shew itself; the latter is closed against it by lack of spiritual sympathy. But the Spirit is not sent to the world, at least in the character of Paraclete; the mission of the Paraclete is to the disciples of Jesus who have already learnt to apprehend spiritual things through fellowship with the Lord; *you know it* (the Spirit), *for it dwells with you* (παρ' ὑμῖν) *and shall be*[2] *in you* (ἐν ὑμῖν)[3]. If with Westcott and Hort we read *And is in you*, the sense must be that even during the earthly life of Jesus the Spirit was already in their midst in the person of the Christ. But the documentary evidence for the future is scarcely inferior, and it accords with the series of futures which precedes (τηρήσετε, ἐρωτήσω, δώσει)[4]. 'It dwells with you,' describes the experience which was just about to end; 'it shall be in you,' that which was about to begin. Between the two there would be but the briefest interval; the going would be followed almost immediately by a coming. *I will not leave you bereaved*[5], *I am coming to you*[6]. *Yet a little and the*

Part II. iii.

Jo. xiv. 18 f.

[1] On θεωρεῖν and γινώσκειν in St John see Abbott, *Johannine Vocabulary*, 1593, 1625.

[2] Codd. ℵA read ἔσται, codd. BD* ἐστίν.

[3] Cf. μεθ' ὑμῶν (*v.* 16). Fellowship (μετά), presence (παρά), immanence (ἐν), are three relations in which the Spirit stands to the members of Christ's Body: see Westcott's note *ad loc.*

[4] Cf. Zahn, comm. on St John, p. 558.

[5] 'Ορφανούς: cf. 1 Thess. ii. 17 ἀπορφανισθέντες ἀφ' ὑμῶν.

[6] With this ἔρχομαι contrast the πορεύομαι of *v.* 12, and cf. *v.* 28 ὑπάγω καὶ ἔρχομαι.

Part II. iii. *world beholds me no more, but you behold me*[1]*; for I live, and ye shall live*[2]. The ascended Christ would be visible to His disciples in the Spirit; the spiritual life into which He should then have wholly passed would find its counterpart in the life of the Spirit which after the Pentecost would be theirs as it was
Jo. xiv. 20. His. *In that day you* (ὑμεῖς) *shall know that I am in my Father and you in me and I in you.* In the coming life of the Spirit they, if not the world, would realize more and more (γνώσεσθε) the perfect union of the Father and the Son and their own union with the Incarnate Son through His Spirit in them and their life in Him.

Jo. xiv. 25 ff. 2. In *vv.* 25 ff. the Lord returns to the future which lay before the disciples. The 'other Paraclete' is to be not only a perpetual Presence in their midst, but a perpetual Teacher. The teaching of Jesus in the flesh was now at an end; these were among His last words; the voice that spake as never man spake was not to be heard again. Was the teaching itself to cease? His answer is reassuring. *These things I have spoken to you while dwelling with you; but the Paraclete, the Holy Spirit which the Father will send in my name, he shall teach you all things and remind you of all things that I said to you.* The 'other Paraclete' is to carry on the Lord's office of teaching. Again he is identified with the Spirit, now

[1] Ὑμεῖς δὲ θεωρεῖτέ με, cf. *v.* 17 ὑμεῖς γινώσκετε αὐτό.

[2] Or, *ye behold me, for I live; and ye shall live;* or again as A.V., R.V., *ye behold* (*see*) *me; because I live, ye shall live also.* The Greek is ambiguous, as often in St John.

called the Holy Spirit (τὸ πνεῦμα τὸ ἅγιον), perhaps to proclaim His oneness with the Spirit who spake by the Prophets. Christ's *Spirit of the Truth*, the Paraclete of the future Church, was not a new Spirit but the Divine Spirit itself, invested with a new mission, sent by the Father in the name of Jesus, as Jesus Himself came in the name of His Father and not in His own (Jo. v. 43). What is the exact sense of the phrase 'in the name' is a point perhaps as yet imperfectly explored; but apart from the general question light may be gained here by comparing the missions of the Spirit and the Son. The Son came to represent, to interpret, to glorify the Father; and since the Son Himself was but partly understood even by His own, the Spirit was sent to reveal the Son. Neither the person of the Lord nor His work was intelligible to those who saw and heard Him, until the Spirit illuminated both. In the Spirit Christ came again, a Christ transfigured and glorified. As a teacher the Paraclete would extend the scope of our Lord's earthly ministry without abandoning any part of the ground that Christ had occupied. *He will teach you all things*, not universal knowledge, but all that belongs to the sphere of spiritual truth[1]; nothing that is essential to the knowledge of God or to the guidance of life shall be wanting. But as His teaching will be in Christ's name, it will

[1] Or more exactly περὶ πάντων "in connexion with the new results of thought and observation" (Westcott on 1 Jo. ii. 27). Ὑμᾶς, not the Apostles only but believers in general; οἴδατε πάντες (πάντα) is St John's comment in the Epistle (ib. *v.* 20).

Part II. iii. follow in the lines of Christ's teaching; '*He will remind you of all* that I taught.' The larger light of the Apostolic age would be in fact a reminiscence, a reawakening of the light kindled in Galilee and Jerusalem by Jesus Christ. Even the words spoken by Him would in many cases be brought back to the memories of those who heard them, or if not the words, at least their substance[1]. The survival of so large an amount of these personal recollections in the four Gospels may reasonably be claimed as a fulfilment of this promise. But the 'reminding' went of course much further than a mere recovery of the Lord's sayings; it enabled those who had been present to live through the Ministry again with a new appreciation of its meaning; logion and parable, question and answer, command and promise returned to them in new lights, and formed, it cannot be doubted, the basis of the Apostles' own teaching, and ultimately the nucleus of that great stream of Christian tradition which has moulded Christian belief and practice from their time to our own.

Jo. xv. 26 f. 3. The third passage in the last Discourse in which our Lord speaks of the Paraclete carries us a step further. *When the Paraclete shall have come, whom I will send to you from the Father, the Spirit of the truth which goes forth from the Father, he shall bear witness concerning me; and you also bear witness, because from the beginning*[2] *you are with me.* Here the double title *the Paraclete, the Spirit of*

[1] Cf. e.g. Jo. ii. 22, xii. 16.

[2] I.e. of the Ministry; cf. Mc. i. 1, Lc. i. 2, Jo. vi. 64, xvi. 4.

Truth is repeated from xiv. 16, but instead of the clause *which the Father shall send in my name*, added in xiv. 26, we now have the words *whom I* (ἐγώ) *will send to you from the Father...which goes forth from the Father*. The Paraclete, Christ teaches, is to be sent *from the Father* (παρὰ τοῦ πατρός) even as He Himself was[1]; and whenever the Spirit goes forth[2], it goes forth *from the Father*, as sent by Him. But in the approaching mission of the Paraclete Spirit, the immediate Sender of the Spirit will be the Incarnate Son, in whose name the Paraclete is to be sent and of whose own mission His coming is to be fruit and sequel. And the Paraclete being sent from the Father by the Son will bear witness of the Son who sent Him; being the Spirit of the Truth[3], He must needs bear His testimony to the truth. The testimony of the Spirit will

[1] Cf. Jo. i. 14, vi. 46, vii. 29, xvi. 27, xvii. 8.

[2] The present (ἐκπορεύεται), as contrasted with ἔλθῃ, πέμψω, μαρτυρήσει, states the law of the Spirit's life. Ἐκπορεύεσθαι is usually followed by ἐκ or ἀπό (Mt. xv. 18, Mc. vii. 15, 20 f., x. 46, Eph. iv. 29, Apoc. ix. 18, xi. 5, xix. 15, xxii. 1), and in the Constantinopolitan Creed παρά is silently changed into ἐκ (cf. Hort, *Two Dissertations*, p. 86), partly perhaps with a reference to 1 Cor. ii. 12 (τὸ ἐκ τοῦ θεοῦ), partly because ἐκ expresses more definitely the source from which the Spirit has His being; cf. Westcott's note *ad loc.*

[3] See on this title of the Spirit Dr Hort's *Hulsean Lectures*, pp. 57—59: "He goes forth, Christ teaches, from the Father, the God who is true, and bears witness to Christ as the Truth...the voice of the Spirit will be heard only in the interpretation of truth, and especially of the Truth...the truth given in Christ will need from age to age His expounding to unlock its stores."

Part II. iii. be given in the words, the actions, the lives of men. But it will not supersede human testimony, or be indistinguishable from it; the Spirit is not a substitute for the labour or the personality of the disciple, but a cooperating force: '*and ye, too* (the Lord adds), *bear witness*[1],' as those who are qualified to speak of Me in virtue of an experience which goes back to the beginning of the Ministry. Experience by itself could not have qualified the Eleven to bear their witness before the world, nor could the Spirit have supplied the lack of experience. The life in Galilee was crowned by the Gift of Pentecost, without which its lessons would have been barren of results, but on the other hand the Gift of Pentecost would have yielded widely different results if it had not fallen on
Acts iv. 13. men who *were with Jesus* and could testify to what they had seen and heard[2]. Nor was this collaboration of the human witness with the Divine limited to the first age; it extends to the whole life of the Church, which is a continuous joint-testimony of *the*
Apoc. xxii. 17. *Spirit and the Bride.*

4. The Lord has now said enough to make it clear that His departure will be no unmixed loss to
Jo. xvi. 7 ff. His disciples, nay, will be on the whole a gain. *I tell you the truth: it is profitable for you that I* (ἐγὼ) *go away. For if I go not away* (ἀπέλθω), *the Paraclete will not come* (ἔλθῃ) *unto you; but if I take my*

[1] Μαρτυρεῖτε is probably indicative, answering to ἐστέ.

[2] Acts iv. 13; cf. Acts i. 8, ii. 32, iii. 15, x. 39, 41, xiii. 31. In Acts v. 32 the order is reversed: ἡμεῖς ἐσμὲν μάρτυρες καὶ τὸ πνεῦμα τὸ ἅγιον.

Part II. iii.

journey hence (πορευθῶ) *I will send him unto you.* The mission of the Spirit could not begin till the mission of the Son was ended; Jesus could not come in the Spirit till He had ceased to live in the flesh. The Lord's final victory over death, and the spiritualizing of His humanity which began at the Resurrection and culminated in His return to the Father at the Ascension, were the necessary conditions of the sending of His Spirit to the Church. Furthermore, the gift of the Spirit could be claimed by Him for men only when He had taken His place as the Advocate of men in the Presence of God[1].

All this was realized, if not at the time yet afterwards, when the Spirit had come. But though the departure of the Lord might be necessary, the question remained what the Church could gain by exchanging the visible presence of Jesus for the invisible fellowship of His Spirit. This question is answered, so far as it could be answered before the Pentecost, by a revelation of the work which the Spirit was coming to do upon the world. *When* Jo. xvi. 8 ff.
he has come, he (ἐκεῖνος, i.e. the Paraclete) *shall convict* (ἐλέγξει) *the world in respect of sin, and of righteousness and of judgement. In respect of sin, in that they believe not on me; in respect of righteousness, in that I go my way to the Father and ye no more behold me; in respect of judgement, in that the ruler of this world has been judged.*

The conviction of the world by the Spirit is to be

[1] Cf. Jo. xvi. 7, Acts ii. 33, 1 Jo. ii. 1.

Part II. iii. threefold. (*a*) *He shall convict*[1] *the world in respect of sin,* bringing it home to men's consciences, detecting
Jo. viii. 46. and laying bare their guilt. *Which of you,* the Lord had asked, *convicts me of sin?* and no answer had been returned. But if the world could not convict Him, His Spirit could and should convict the world. That was perhaps no hard task, for heathen satirists did the same effectively enough in the century that followed the Ascension. But the Lord specifies a particular act which was the last that the world seemed capable of recognizing as a sin. The Spirit was to reveal the sinfulness of refusing to believe on Jesus; the men who had witnessed His signs and heard His words unmoved, who had shouted *Crucify him* and without remorse reviled Him as He hung on the Cross, the same men, when the light of the Spirit was turned upon their conduct, would discover in it the most damning of all sins, a rejection of the Only-begotten Son of
Acts ii. 37. God[2], and cry out in their distress, *What shall we do?*

Further, (*b*) the Spirit *shall convict the world in respect of righteousness.* What 'righteousness' meant had been shewn in the earthly life of Jesus; His

[1] The meaning of ἐλέγχειν in this place has been investigated by Hare, *Mission of the Comforter*, note L, and more briefly by Trench, *Syn. N. T.* Whatever its obscurity in Philo (Hastings, *D. C. G.* I. 891 *a*), in St John (iii. 20, viii. 46, xvi. 8) it is uniformly 'to convict,' i.e. to bring to light the true character of a man or his conduct; or 'to convince,' to bring home a truth which has been rejected or ignored. As Westcott says, it "involves the conception of authoritative examination, of unquestionable proof, of decisive judgement."

[2] Cf. Jo. iii. 18 ff.

death completed the revelation, by displaying a sinless humanity tested by the severest suffering and passing through it and through death itself without reproof. Yet the spectacle made no impression on His own generation; the world remained unconvinced even by the Cross. Jesus passed out of sight; He went to the Father; even the disciples 'beheld Him no more'; nothing was left but the promise that His invisible Spirit should work in the hearts of men. But it was this very transition from the visible to the invisible, from the flesh to the Spirit, which led friends as well as enemies to realize for the first time the grandeur of the life which had failed to make any adequate impression so long as it was before their eyes. Then for the first time the vision of a sinless humanity burst upon the world with the results that we know, changing both the conception which men had formed of the Person of Jesus, and the standards of human conduct. The same Power which convinced the world of its sin convinced it also of the righteousness of Him whom it had refused, not only in the sense that His innocence was established and His sinlessness admitted, but that the perfect life of Jesus henceforth filled a place in men's thoughts such as no other noble and heroic life has ever filled. For here, it was recognized at last, is the one perfect model of human righteousness, which God has accepted and crowned by admitting it into His presence[1]; this is the Righteous

[1] Cf. the second of the Ascension Day morning Psalms (Ps. xv.).

Part II. iii. one[1] who is with the Father, and through whom men may attain to the righteousness of God.

Lastly, (*c*) the Spirit *shall convict the world in respect of judgement.* For now that Sin and Righteousness have stood face to face in the world, and Righteousness has triumphed over Sin and Death and is at the right hand of God, there must come a time when the long war between these irreconcileable forces shall end in a final separation. A crisis is at hand, and even now is going forward in human history[2]; it began with the judgement which was passed on the ruler of this world by the life and death of Jesus, a judgement which is still in force and fruitful in results[3]. The Spirit brings this fact home to the minds of men, and they live henceforth as those who know that since the Resurrection the issues of the great struggle are determined, and every day is bringing nearer the final victory of righteousness and the final doom of sin.

Thus the Paraclete Spirit by His coming was to shift the whole standpoint of human opinion with reference to the vital questions of Sin and Righteousness and the conflict between them. And He was to do this, not for the Church only or even chiefly—for the Lord had already decided these fundamental points for His own—but for 'the world.' The effect

[1] Cf. Acts iii. 14, xxii. 14, Jas. v. 6, 1 Pet. iii. 18, 1 Jo. ii. 1, 29, iii. 7.

[2] Cf. Jo. xii. 31.

[3] Κέκριται, 'has been and still stands judged.' Cf. the new fragment of the Appendix to St Mark: πεπλήρωται ὁ ὅρος τῶν ἐτῶν τῆς ἐξουσίας τοῦ σατανᾶ.

of His conviction of the world is to be seen to-day in the changed attitude of modern thought and practice when it is compared with that of Graeco-Roman society in the time of our Lord. The modern world is far from being under the control of the Spirit of Christ, but pagan as it may remain in heart it has been convinced of certain great ethical truths, and can never return to the worst vices or the heartless selfishness of the older heathendom.

5. The discourse now passes from the Spirit's work upon the world to His more direct action upon the disciples of Christ. *I have yet many things to say unto you, but you cannot bear them now. But when he* (ἐκεῖνος) *shall have come, the Spirit of the truth, he shall guide you into all the truth; for he shall not speak from himself, but whatsoever things he hears he shall speak, and the things that are coming he shall declare to you. He shall glorify me, for he shall take from that which is mine and declare it to you. All things whatsoever the Father has are mine; for this cause I said that he* (the Paraclete) *takes of that which is mine and shall declare it to you.*

Jo. xvi. 12 ff.

The Samaritan Woman knew that when Messiah came He would declare all things[1]. But at the end of His life there were many things which Jesus had yet to say, and could not say even then to the Eleven, because of their incapacity to support the

[1] Jo. iv. 15 οἶδα ὅτι Μεσσίας ἔρχεται...ὅταν ἔλθῃ, ἐκεῖνος ἀναγγελεῖ ἡμῖν ἅπαντα. Cf. xvi. 13 ὅταν δὲ ἔλθῃ ἐκεῖνος (i.e. ὁ Παράκλητος)...τὰ ἐρχόμενα ἀναγγελεῖ ὑμῖν.

Part II. iii.

Jo. xvi. 25.

Jo. xvi. 22 (οὐ δύνασθε βαστάζειν ἄρτι).

Jo. xiv. 6, xvi. 13.

burden of fuller teaching. Even in what He had said He had spoken as it were *in proverbs* (ἐν παροιμίαις)[1], not in plain, direct, speech (παρρησίᾳ); under more explicit or more direct teaching the disciples would have broken down, as men do on whose shoulders a weight is laid which is too heavy for them to bear. The time was coming when He would teach them all He had to teach, telling them of the Father with unfettered speech. But this He could do only through the Spirit of the truth, to whom it belongs to guide the spirits of men into the truth as a whole (εἰς πᾶσαν τὴν ἀλήθειαν). If Jesus is the Way (ἡ ὁδός), the Spirit is the Guide (ὁ ὁδηγός)[2] who leads into it, i.e. into the truth in its completeness as it is in Jesus[3]. As the Son did not speak 'from Himself' (Jo. vii. 16 ff.), i.e. was not the Source of His own teaching, but spoke what He had received from the Father, so the Spirit will not speak from Himself as from a separate store of knowledge but will declare what He hears in that inner Life which is full of the voices of God[4]: He is to be the Witness of the

[1] See Abbott, *Johannine Vocabulary*, 1721 *a—d*, especially *d*: "Jn prefers to say that Jesus taught by '*proverbs*,' i.e. by truths of general import, whereas the Paraclete was to teach truths of particular import, appealing to the experience of the individual."

[2] With this use of ὁδηγεῖν (ὁδηγός) cf. Mt. xv. 14, xxiii. 16, 24, Acts viii. 31. The verb is frequent in the Psalms of the Septuagint, e.g. Ps. xxiv. (xxv.) 5 ὁδήγησόν με (הַדְרִיכֵנִי) ἐπὶ τὴν ἀλήθειάν σου καὶ δίδαξόν με—a passage which may be in view in Jo. xvi. 13.

[3] Cf. Eph. iv. 21, with Westcott's note *ad loc.*

[4] Cf. 1 Cor. ii. 10.

truth, but He is not its source, which is the Eternal Father. His teaching will therefore be essentially one with the teaching of Christ, since its Source is the same. But He will carry forward the revelation of Christ and complete it. *He will declare the coming things:* the things of that great and untried life which was about to open before the Church at the Pentecost and to reach its perfection at the Second Coming; the things of the new age, the dispensation of the Spirit; and, less distinctly seen, the things of the more distant future when God shall be all in all. Thus, while this promise includes the revelations of the Christian Prophets, it covers also the whole process of unfolding before the Christian Society in the Apostolic writings, in the work of her Bishops and Doctors, and in the experience of life, the ideals, the polity, and the prospects of the Body of Christ.

Part II. iii.

Jo. xvi. 13.

Another side of the Spirit's work of guidance remains to be stated. *He shall glorify me* (ἐμέ, emphatic[1]). Even to the world He will hold up the sinlessness, the righteousness of Jesus. But the glorification will be carried further in those who are 'led of the Spirit.' How? Not by shedding upon the Person and work of the Lord any new glory from without, but simply by revealing that which is and always has been His. All that a Paul or a John has said under the teaching of the Spirit about the glory of Christ is but a disclosure of that which is His essential character, His inalienable possession.

Jo. xvi. 14.

[1] Cf. ἐγώ in Jo. xv. 26.

Part II. iii. They have brought much to light, but they have added nothing to the glory which He had with the Father before the world was. The Spirit in glorifying the Son takes of that which is the Son's and declares it. That is all, but how much it is! For that which is the Son's comprises all that is the
Jo. xvii. 10. Father's; *all things that are mine,* the Lord says in His great concluding prayer, *are thine, and the things that are thine are mine,* the difference being this only, that the things which are His are so by the Father's gift. The intercommunion and interchange are absolute. The Only-begotten interprets the Father; the Spirit interprets the Son, and the Father in the Son. Thus the revelation of God is completed by the coming of the Spirit. The Lord's departure was not to be a withdrawal of the manifested glory of God, but a further stage in the manifestation. *A little while*—so this long exposi-
Jo. xvi. 16, 22. tion of the work of the Paraclete ends—*a little while and ye no more behold me* (θεωρεῖτε), *and again a little while and ye shall see* (ὄψεσθε) *me... again I shall see* (ὄψομαι) *you.* The visible form of the Son of Man was passing away, but the true and unending vision of His glory was on the point to begin. The disciples would see Him again and be seen by Him, but in the Spirit; and the joy of a spiritual vision none could take from them.

6. Almost the last words of the departing Lord were of this 'Other Paraclete' in whose coming He
Acts i. 3. would Himself return. When He *shewed himself alive after his passion,* His first interview with the

Eleven dealt with the same topic, but from another point of view. The gift of the Spirit was now no longer a hope but a fact. Part II. iii.

The Lord, standing in the midst of His disciples on Easter night, brought them the firstfruits of His victory. *Peace be to you! As my Father has commissioned* (ἀπέσταλκεν)[1] *me, I also send* (πέμπω) *you*[2]. Then, breathing on them, He added, *Take Holy Spirit; if ye remit the sins of any, they have been remitted; if ye retain the sins of any, they have been retained.* His 'peace,' repeated with emphasis[3], is no mere salutation, but recalls the words spoken immediately after the promise of the Paraclete: *a peace that is mine I give you; not as the world gives give I you.* What He gave before the Passion on that night of conflicting emotions He gives once again in the first joy of the Resurrection. But to peace He adds now another gift which is the direct consequence of His triumph over death. The Eleven have before them a new destiny, and for its fulfilment they need a new life. The Lord Himself had received from the Father a commission which He had executed so far as it was to be fulfilled by His personal service on earth. But the commission itself, as the perfect suggests, remained in force, and in virtue of it He now sends the Eleven and the whole Church to carry on His

Jo. xx. 19 ff.

Jo. xiv. 27.

[1] Ἀπέσταλκεν, "the regular word for commissioning" (Hort, *Apocalypse*, p. 6).

[2] For πέμπω cod. D has ἀποστέλλω.

[3] *V.* 21 εἶπεν οὖν αὐτοῖς ὁ Ἰησοῦς πάλιν Εἰρήνη ὑμῖν (cf. *v.* 19).

Part II. iii. ministry in the world. Of such a mission they were in themselves as incapable as an inanimate body is incapable of performing the functions of a living man. Hence the words were followed immediately by an act which symbolized the giving of life. The oldest

Gen. ii. 7. story of the creation of man tells us how *the Lord God formed man of the dust of the ground, and breathed into his nostrils* (LXX. ἐνεφύσησεν εἰς τὸ πρόσωπον αὐτοῦ) *the breath of life, and man became a living soul*[1]. Even so the new humanity, represented by the little company in the upper room, was now inspired by the risen Christ with the breath of the higher life, and His insufflation was the visible sign of this inward grace. Sacramental words accompanied the sign: *take Holy Spirit*[2]. Here are two things to be noted: (1) it is not the person of the Paraclete-Spirit, but the inspiration of His life which is communicated; and (2) the use of λάβετε rather than δέχεσθε[3] implies that the gift is not an *opus operatum*, but a vital force which must be met by personal effort and not passively received.

[1] Gen. ii. 7. The Coptic versions follow the LXX. in Jo. xx. 22 adding 'in their face' (Horner II. p. 571); cf. the Liturgy of S. Mark (Brightman I. D. 116. 3): ἐμφυσήσας εἰς τὰ πρόσωπα αὐτῶν. Compare Ezek. xxxvii. 5 LXX. ἰδοὺ ἐγὼ φέρω εἰς ὑμᾶς πνεῦμα ζωῆς...καὶ δώσω πνεῦμά μου εἰς ὑμᾶς καὶ ζήσεσθε.

[2] Πνεῦμα ἅγιον, not τὸ πνεῦμα τὸ ἅγιον.

[3] Westcott: "The choice of word seems to mark the personal action of man in the reception. He is not wholly passive." So at the institution of the Eucharist the Lord says λάβετε, not δέχεσθε (Mc. xiv. 32).

The Easter gift of the Spirit stands in the most intimate relation with the mission of the Catholic Church, as the great words that follow shew. The business of the Church is the remitting and retaining of the sins of men, a spiritual office which calls for spiritual vitality no less than for the authority of a Divine mission. If *I send you* provides the authority, *take Holy Spirit* gives the vital force which is no less necessary.

The question has often been asked in what relation the gift of Easter Day stands to the gift of Whitsunday. Bishop Westcott, following Godet, replies that "the one answers to the power of the Resurrection and the other to the power of the Ascension," i.e. the one brought the grace of quickening, the other that of endowment. But besides this, if we may judge from the words that follow, the Easter gift was specially connected with the future work of the Body of Christ. Its realization was therefore to be expected not in any immediate quickening or endowing of the Eleven and their company, of which in fact there are but few traces in the history of the forty days between the Resurrection and the Ascension, but rather in that which manifested itself after the Pentecost, as their great task opened gradually before them. For the moment, therefore, the gift was potential rather than actual[1];

[1] This is perhaps what Theodore of Mopsuestia meant by his somewhat crude remark that in Jo. xx. 23 λάβετε is equivalent to λήμψεσθε (Migne *P. G.* LXVI. 783 f.: "id quod dictum est *Accipite* pro *Accipietis* dicit)."

Part II. iii. it became an actuality when the Church began to remit and retain sins; with the need of quickening the quickening which had been assured was experienced. But when it came, at Pentecost or afterwards, it came in virtue of the Resurrection of the Lord and His sacramental insufflation. It had been in the possession of the Church from the moment that the Risen Lord breathed into her the Breath of Life, although before the Pentecost she was scarcely conscious of her new powers, and even after the Pentecost realized them only by degrees[1].

[1] The same law holds good *mutatis mutandis* in reference to the gifts bestowed on infants in Baptism and on children in Confirmation. It operates also in the case of the newly ordained; the youngest priest has received in the *Accipe Spiritum sanctum* the assurance of all the spiritual power that is needed for the discharge of his ministry, but it belongs to the experience of the pastoral life to call the χάρισμα which is him (2 Tim. i. 6) into exercise.

IV.

THE TEACHING OF THE PAULINE EPISTLES (i).

Τὸ εὐαγγέλιον ἡμῶν οὐκ ἐγενήθη εἰς ὑμᾶς ἐν λόγῳ μόνον· 1 Thess. i.
ἀλλὰ καὶ ἐν δυνάμει καὶ ἐν πνεύματι ἁγίῳ καὶ πληροφορίᾳ 5 f.
πολλῇ...καὶ ὑμεῖς μιμηταὶ ἡμῶν ἐγενήθητε καὶ τοῦ κυρίου,
δεξάμενοι τὸν λόγον ἐν θλίψει πολλῇ μετὰ χαρᾶς πνεύματος
ἁγίου.

Ὁ ἀθετῶν οὐκ ἄνθρωπον ἀθετεῖ ἀλλὰ τὸν θεὸν τὸν διδόντα 1 Thess.
τὸ πνεῦμα αὐτοῦ τὸ ἅγιον εἰς ὑμᾶς. iv. 8.

Τὸ πνεῦμα μὴ σβέννυτε, προφητείας μὴ ἐξουθενεῖτε. 1 Thess. v. 19 f.

Αὐτὸς δὲ ὁ θεὸς τῆς εἰρήνης ἁγιάσαι ὑμᾶς ὁλοτελεῖς, καὶ 1 Thess. v.
ὁλόκληρον ὑμῶν τὸ πνεῦμα καὶ ἡ ψυχὴ καὶ τὸ σῶμα ἀμέμπ- 23.
τως...τηρηθείη.

Ἐρωτῶμεν δὲ ὑμᾶς...εἰς τὸ μὴ ταχέως σαλευθῆναι ὑμᾶς 2 Thess. ii.
ἀπὸ τοῦ νοὸς μηδὲ θροεῖσθαι μήτε διὰ πνεύματος μήτε διὰ 1 f.
λόγου μήτε δι' ἐπιστολῆς ὡς δι' ἡμῶν.

Εἵλατο ὑμᾶς ὁ θεὸς ἀπ' ἀρχῆς εἰς σωτηρίαν ἐν ἁγιασμῷ 2 Thess. ii.
πνεύματος καὶ πίστει ἀληθείας. 13.

Ὁ λόγος μου καὶ τὸ κήρυγμά μου οὐκ ἐν πιθοῖς σοφίας 1 Cor. ii. 4.
λόγοις, ἀλλ' ἐν ἀποδείξει πνεύματος καὶ δυνάμεως.

Ἡμῖν γὰρ ἀπεκάλυψεν ὁ θεὸς διὰ τοῦ πνεύματος, τὸ γὰρ 1 Cor. ii.
πνεῦμα πάντα ἐραυνᾷ, καὶ τὰ βάθη τοῦ θεοῦ. τίς γὰρ οἶδεν 10—16.
ἀνθρώπων τὰ τοῦ ἀνθρώπου εἰ μὴ τὸ πνεῦμα τοῦ ἀνθρώπου
τὸ ἐν αὐτῷ; οὕτως καὶ τὰ τοῦ θεοῦ οὐδεὶς ἔγνωκεν εἰ μὴ
τὸ πνεῦμα τοῦ θεοῦ. ἡμεῖς δὲ οὐ τὸ πνεῦμα τοῦ κόσμου
ἐλάβομεν ἀλλὰ τὸ πνεῦμα τὸ ἐκ τοῦ θεοῦ, ἵνα εἰδῶμεν τὰ
ὑπὸ τοῦ θεοῦ χαρισθέντα ἡμῖν· ἃ καὶ λαλοῦμεν οὐκ ἐν
διδακτοῖς ἀνθρωπίνης σοφίας λόγοις, ἀλλ' ἐν διδακτοῖς πνεύματος, πνευματικοῖς πνευματικὰ συνκρίνοντες. ψυχικὸς δὲ

ἄνθρωπος οὐ δέχεται τὰ τοῦ πνεύματος τοῦ θεοῦ...καὶ οὐ δύναται γνῶναι, ὅτι πνευματικῶς ἀνακρίνεται· ὁ δὲ πνευματικὸς ἀνακρίνει μὲν πάντα, αὐτὸς δὲ ὑπ' οὐδενὸς ἀνακρίνεται. τίς γὰρ ἔγνω νοῦν Κυρίου;...ἡμεῖς δὲ νοῦν Χριστοῦ ἔχομεν.

1 Cor. iii. 16 f. Οὐκ οἴδατε ὅτι ναὸς θεοῦ ἐστέ, καὶ τὸ πνεῦμα τοῦ θεοῦ ἐν ὑμῖν οἰκεῖ; εἴ τις τὸν ναὸν τοῦ θεοῦ φθείρει, φθερεῖ τοῦτον ὁ θεός· ὁ γὰρ ναὸς τοῦ θεοῦ ἅγιός ἐστιν, οἵτινές ἐστε ὑμεῖς.

1 Cor. vi. 11. Ἀλλὰ ἀπελούσασθε, ἀλλὰ ἡγιάσθητε, ἀλλὰ ἐδικαιώθητε, ἐν τῷ ὀνόματι τοῦ κυρίου ἡμῶν Ἰησοῦ Χριστοῦ καὶ ἐν τῷ πνεύματι τοῦ θεοῦ ἡμῶν.

1 Cor. vi. 17, 19. Ὁ δὲ κολλώμενος τῷ κυρίῳ ἓν πνεῦμά ἐστιν...ἢ οὐκ οἴδατε ὅτι τὸ σῶμα ὑμῶν ναὸς τοῦ ἐν ὑμῖν ἁγίου πνεύματός ἐστιν, οὗ ἔχετε ἀπὸ θεοῦ;

1 Cor. vii. 40. Δοκῶ γὰρ κἀγὼ πνεῦμα θεοῦ ἔχειν.

1 Cor. xii. 1—3. Περὶ δὲ τῶν πνευματικῶν...οὐ θέλω ὑμᾶς ἀγνοεῖν... γνωρίζω ὑμῖν ὅτι οὐδεὶς ἐν πνεύματι θεοῦ λαλῶν λέγει Ἀνάθεμα Ἰησοῦς· καὶ οὐδεὶς δύναται εἰπεῖν Κύριος Ἰησοῦς εἰ μὴ ἐν πνεύματι ἁγίῳ.

1 Cor. xii. 4—11. Διαιρέσεις δὲ χαρισμάτων εἰσίν, τὸ δὲ αὐτὸ πνεῦμα... ἑκάστῳ δὲ δίδοται ἡ φανέρωσις τοῦ πνεύματος πρὸς τὸ συμφέρον. ᾧ μὲν γὰρ διὰ τοῦ πνεύματος δίδοται λόγος σοφίας, ἄλλῳ δὲ λόγος γνώσεως κατὰ τὸ αὐτὸ πνεῦμα, ἑτέρῳ πίστις ἐν τῷ αὐτῷ πνεύματι, ἄλλῳ δὲ χαρίσματα ἰαμάτων ἐν τῷ ἑνὶ πνεύματι κτλ....πάντα δὲ ταῦτα ἐνεργεῖ τὸ ἓν καὶ τὸ αὐτὸ πνεῦμα, διαιροῦν ἰδίᾳ ἑκάστῳ καθὼς βούλεται.

1 Cor. xii. 13. Ἐν ἑνὶ πνεύματι ἡμεῖς πάντες εἰς ἓν σῶμα ἐβαπτίσθημεν ...καὶ πάντες ἓν πνεῦμα ἐποτίσθημεν.

1 Co. xiv. 1. Ζηλοῦτε δὲ τὰ πνευματικά, μᾶλλον δὲ ἵνα προφητεύητε.

1 Cor. xiv. 12. Ζηλωταί ἐστε πνευματων.

1 Cor. xiv. 32. Πνεύματα προφητῶν προφήταις ὑποτάσσεται.

1 Cor. xv. 44 f. Εἰ ἔστιν σῶμα ψυχικόν, ἔστιν καὶ πνευματικόν· οὕτως καὶ γέγραπται Ἐγένετο ὁ πρῶτος ἄνθρωπος Ἀδὰμ εἰς ψυχὴν ζῶσαν· ὁ ἔσχατος Ἀδὰμ εἰς πνεῦμα ζωοποιοῦν.

2 Cor. i. 22. Ὁ δὲ...χρίσας ἡμᾶς θεός, ὁ καὶ σφραγισάμενος ἡμᾶς καὶ δοὺς τὸν αρραβῶνα τοῦ πνεύματος ἐν ταῖς καρδίαις ἡμῶν.

2 Cor. iii. 3. Ἐστὲ ἐπιστολὴ Χριστοῦ διακονηθεῖσα ὑφ' ἡμῶν, ἐνγεγραμμένη οὐ μέλανι ἀλλὰ πνεύματι θεοῦ ζῶντος.

Διακόνους καινῆς διαθήκης, οὐ γράμματος ἀλλὰ πνεύ- Part II. iv.
ματος· τὸ γὰρ γράμμα ἀποκτείνει, τὸ δὲ πνεῦμα ζωοποιεῖ... 2 Cor. iii.
πῶς οὐχὶ μᾶλλον ἡ διακονία τοῦ πνεύματος ἔσται ἐν δόξῃ; 6, 8.

Ὁ δὲ κύριος τὸ πνεῦμά ἐστιν· οὗ δὲ τὸ πνεῦμα Κυρίου 2 Cor. iii.
ἐλευθερία. ἡμεῖς δὲ πάντες...μεταμορφούμεθα ἀπὸ δόξης εἰς 17 f.
δόξαν, καθάπερ ἀπὸ Κυρίου πνεύματος.

Συνιστάνοντες ἑαυτοὺς ὡς θεοῦ διάκονοι...ἐν πνεύματι 2 Cor. vi. 4,
ἁγίῳ. 6.

Εἰ μὲν γὰρ...πνεῦμα ἕτερον λαμβάνετε ὃ οὐκ ἐλάβετε κτλ. 2 Cor. xi. 4.

Οὐ τῷ αὐτῷ πνεύματι περιεπατήσαμεν; 2 Cor. xii. 18.

Ἡ χάρις τοῦ κυρίου Ἰησοῦ Χριστοῦ καὶ ἡ ἀγάπη τοῦ 2 Cor. xiii.
θεοῦ καὶ ἡ κοινωνία τοῦ ἁγίου πνεύματος μετὰ πάντων ὑμῶν. 13.

For our purpose it is convenient to divide the Epistles of St Paul into two large groups, namely those which precede the Roman captivity and those which were written during the captivity or after it. The first group includes the Epistles to the Thessalonians (2), Corinthians (2), Galatians, and Romans; of these the first four will occupy the present chapter.

1. The two earliest letters of St Paul were addressed about the middle year of the first century[1] to one of the newly planted churches of Macedonia, *the church of the Thessalonians in God the Father* 1 Thess. i.
and the Lord Jesus Christ. At the outset of the 1, 2 Thess. i. 1.
first epistle we learn that in Europe as in Asia Minor the preaching of the Gospel was attended by manifestations of the Spirit. *Our gospel,* the 1 Thess. i.
missionaries say, *came not unto you in word only* 5.
but also in power and in Holy Spirit and much assurance; i.e. 'we delivered our message with a

[1] The dates usually assigned range from A.D. 47 to 53.

Part II. iv.

power beyond that of mere eloquence, with an inspiration which proclaimed its Divine origin and a strength of conviction which left no doubt of our sincerity.' Such were the preachers, and the hearers caught the contagion of their faith: *you became*
1 Thess. i. 6. *imitators of us and of the Lord, having received the word in much tribulation with joy of Holy Spirit.* The same Spirit which gave strength and assurance to the preachers wrought in the converts a joyful acceptance of the message which was not
Cf. Acts xiii. 52, xvii. 5 ff. checked by the violent opposition of the Synagogue aided by a truculent mob.

Nor was it only in this first acceptance of the Gospel and the early enthusiasm of their new faith that the Thessalonians manifested the power of the Spirit. In a Greek seaport town such as Thessalonica, it was a daily struggle for converts from heathenism to maintain purity of life. For this struggle the Apostle arms the Thessalonians with the assurance that they had received the Spirit
1 Thess. iv. 7 ff. of God. *God called us not for impurity but in sanctification. Therefore he who sets at naught* this calling *sets at naught not man but God, who gives his Spirit, the Holy* Spirit, to enter *into you*[1]. The Christian calling moves in a sphere of progressive holiness (ἐν ἁγιασμῷ), and the Divine Gift which is poured continually[2] into the hearts of believers

[1] Reading τὸν διδόντα εἰς ὑμᾶς with Codd. ℵ*BD; δόντα is given by ℵ^c.a AKL, and ἡμᾶς for ὑμᾶς by A. Dr Milligan aptly compares Ezek. xxxvii. 14 LXX. δώσω τὸ πνεῦμά μου εἰς ὑμᾶς.

[2] Lightfoot paraphrases: "Who is ever renewing this witness against uncleanness in fresh accessions of the Holy Spirit."

renders any act of impurity on the part of a Christian a contempt of God, whose presence within him by the Holy Spirit is a constant witness for holiness and warning against the sins of the flesh. Part II. iv.

Further, at Thessalonica the Spirit was manifested not only in the faith of the founders of the Church and the lives of its members, but by the gift—to these Gentile converts, the entirely new gift—of prophecy. It appears that prophecy was in danger of being undervalued in this Greek Church, whether because, as afterwards at Corinth, the more showy 'glossolaly' was preferred to it, or because it had been abused by some who made it the occasion of wild and even dangerous utterances[1]. Against this attitude towards a great spiritual gift St Paul takes a firm stand. *The Spirit extinguish not, prophesyings make not of no account; put all things to the proof, hold fast the good, from every evil form*[2] *abstain.* (1 Thess. v. 19 ff.) 'It is not for believers to throw water on the fire which has been kindled by the Spirit in the heart of a fellow Christian or to make light of utterances which claim to be His inspirations. There is a better course: submit everything of this kind to such tests as may be ready to your hand and as the Spirit itself has given you in the scriptures, in the experience of life, in the consensus of believers, and retain[3] all that can endure this process, refraining[3] from every kind of utterance which

[1] See Lightfoot, *Notes*, p. 82; Milligan, p. 75.

[2] Or perhaps "every form of evil." Dr Milligan illustrates πᾶν εἶδος from *Oxyrhynchus Papyri* 237.

[3] κατέχετε...ἀπέχεσθε.

Part II. iv. may tend to evil.' It happens that the second letter
2 Thess. ii. 2. affords an instance of such an utterance. An impression had been created at Thessalonica that the
Coming of the Lord was imminent or even had
begun (ἐνέστηκεν), and the result of this belief had
Cf. 1 Thess. iii. 6. been to create restlessness and neglect of duty.
How it arose the Apostle does not seem to know,
but he suggests that it may have come *by spirit*[1],
i.e. through a prophet who claimed inspiration.
2 Thess. ii. 3. Even in that case, the idea was to be rejected as
1 Thess. v. 22. deceptive; it belonged to the 'bad class' of prophetic
utterances which would not endure the test of examination, as St Paul proceeds to shew.

To return to the first Epistle; the Apostle con-
1 Thess. v. 23. tinues: *And the God of peace himself sanctify you
in your whole nature* (ὁλοτελεῖς), *and may your spirit
and* your *soul and* your *body be preserved entire*
(ὁλόκληρον)[2], *without blame, at the coming of our
Lord Jesus Christ.* Here, though the Divine Spirit
is not named, His action is involved in the prayer
for sanctification, since it is by His Holy Spirit that
God produces and perfects holiness in the creature.
Whatever may be the judgement which is to be
passed on the utterances of the Christian prophets,

[1] 2 Th. ii. 2 διὰ πνεύματος.

[2] Ὁλοτελεῖς, 'in your completeness'; ὁλόκληρον, 'with every part represented.' Lightfoot points out that the latter word is "applied especially to sacrifices," comparing Rom. xii. 1, where the bodies of Christians are represented as a *θυσία ζῶσα*. The Spirit sanctifies the Christian's sacrifice (i.e. his body and soul and spirit) that it may be found at the Parousia complete in all its parts.

there can be no question as to the value and need of personal sanctity, and this sanctifying work of the Spirit must cover the whole ground of the personal life, the body, the emotions and affections, and finally that side of the individual being which faces God and the spiritual world, the human spirit which in some sense corresponds to the Spirit of God and is the especial seat of His activity. The whole man is to be kept against the Master's return, that it may be ready for His future service, and this can only be if the whole is under the sanctifying power of the Divine Spirit. An entire consecration can alone preserve human nature in the fulness of its powers for the life where God is all in all. Part II. iv.

This ethical side of the Spirit's work in believers comes into sight again in the second Epistle. *God chose you from the beginning*[1] *unto salvation in sanctification of* (*the*) *Spirit and belief of* (*the*) *truth.* The Divine selection of the Thessalonian Church worked itself out in a progressive holiness imparted by the Divine Spirit, and on the side of the converts themselves, by their acceptance of the truth, i.e. of the Gospel of Christ. Thus the work of the Spirit is brought into relation with the purpose of the Father, whose choice it carries into effect[2]; and the whole process is seen to issue in 'salvation,' i.e. that restoration of the composite nature of man to health 2 Thess. ii. 13.

[1] Or, reading ἀπαρχήν with BFG, 'as firstfruits,' i.e. among the earliest converts in Macedonia and Achaia.

[2] Cf. 1 Pet. i. 2.

Part II. iv. and fulness of life which it was the end of the Incarnation to effect.

2. All these references to the Holy Spirit are consistent with the early date of the Epistles to the Thessalonians, for they do not carry us beyond the experience of primitive Christianity. When we proceed to the next two letters, we find that the Apostle has begun, in view of the growing perplexities of his work, to think out his faith in many directions, and not least in reference to the work of the Spirit of Christ.

In the Epistles to Corinth the general outlook is not very dissimilar to that in the Epistles to Thessalonica. Again the Apostle is dealing chiefly with Greek converts living in a commercial city; the same dangers to a great extent threatened the two communities, and the same general counsels were needed. At Corinth, however, influences were at work which were not felt in the Macedonian seaport: a disposition to form rival factions within the Christian body; an anti-Pauline, probably Judaistic, spirit; an intellectualism which stumbled at fundamental Christian truth; a levity which refused to take the great realities of life seriously, and trifled with the most solemn of Christian ordinances and with the spiritual gifts. In dealing with this new situation St Paul is led to present the ministry of the Spirit in new lights which lead us some steps further towards a fuller Pneumatology.

As in his first Epistle to the Thessalonians, St Paul starts by referring to the manifestation of the Spirit in the experience of his own early ministry at Corinth. At Corinth as at Thessalonica his preaching had been effective in a high degree, and its strength had lain in the power of the Spirit. The Apostle altogether disclaims the *rôle* of the Greek rhetor or sophist. *My discourse and my preaching were not in persuasive words of wisdom, but in demonstration of* the *Spirit and power.* The Corinthians had heard from him none of those artifices of speech to which they were accustomed in the lectures of the vagrant philosopher: instead of philosophical proofs (ἀποδείξεις) he had offered a convincing appeal to the consciences of men. It was the moral strength of that appeal that had prevailed rather than its intellectual force, as the Greeks of that age judged intellectual force; and the result was what he had in fact contemplated, that the conversion of the Corinthian Gentiles was not to be ascribed to the preacher, but to the Spirit of God.

Part II. iv.

1 Cor. ii. 4 (cf. 1 Thess. i. 5).

Yet a Christian philosophy, a Divine wisdom there was, and this was known to the preachers of the Cross. *For to us God revealed* the things which He prepared for those who love Him *through the Spirit, for the Spirit searches all things, even the depths of God. For who among men knows* (οἶδεν) *the things of a man but the spirit of the man which is in him? So also the things of God none has discerned* (ἔγνωκεν)[1] *but the Spirit of God.* 'The

1 Cor. ii. 10 ff.

[1] "While οἶδα is simple and absolute, γινώσκω is relative" (Lightfoot, *ad loc.*).

Part II. iv. Spirit is the revealer of the wisdom of God[1], because the Spirit explores the mind of God, even those depths of the Divine knowledge and will which are inscrutable to man[2]. As in man there is a self-conscious life which is conversant with the secrets of his heart, so it is with the nature after which human nature is modelled; the Divine Spirit is cognizant of[3] the secrets of God. And this Spirit has been
1 Cor. ii. 12 f. given to us. *We received not the spirit of the world*, which finds its expression in the wisdom of this present order[4], *but the Spirit which is from* (ἐκ) *God*, issuing from Him whose Spirit it is, *that we might know*, by possessing them (εἰδῶμεν), *the gifts bestowed upon us by God*. This practical knowledge of God, derived from His Spirit which is in us, is our philosophy, and supplies the matter of our higher teaching; *of which* gifts *also we speak, not in* words *taught of human wisdom, but in* words *taught of the Spirit, matching*[5] *spiritual things with spiritual*; keeping the things of the Spirit of God free from intermixture with the non-spiritual ideas and terms of a worldly philosophy, and blending them with truths of the same order, we express them in words which lend themselves to spiritual

[1] Cf. Eph. i. 17 πνεῦμα σοφίας καὶ ἀποκαλύψεως ἐν ἐπιγνώσει αὐτοῦ.

[2] Cf. Rom. xi. 33 ὦ βάθος πλούτου καὶ σοφίας καὶ γνώσεως θεοῦ· ὡς ἀνεξεραύνητα τὰ κρίματα αὐτοῦ.

[3] Ἔγνωκεν takes the place of οἶδεν here in the best texts (אABD): a hint perhaps that the analogy is incomplete.

[4] Cf. *v.* 6 σοφίαν οὐ τοῦ αἰῶνος τούτου.

[5] Cf. 2 Cor. x. 12 συνκρίνοντες ἑαυτοὺς ἑαυτοῖς οὐ συνιοῦσιν.

thoughts. But there are those for whom spiritual thoughts and the words that express them have no meaning. *The psychic man*[1] *does not receive* (δέχεται) *the things of the Spirit of God, for they are folly*[2] *to him, and he cannot take cognizance* (γνῶναι) *of them, because they are scrutinized* (ἀνακρίνεται[3]) *by spiritual methods. But the spiritual man, while he scrutinizes everything, is himself scrutinized by none*; there is in him that which defies scrutiny and remains a mystery to the unspiritual. Men from this point of view consist of two classes; those in whom the lower rational life (ψυχή) predominates, and those who are guided by the higher. The man who belongs to the former class has no conception of spiritual realities; he is incapable of apprehending them or even examining their claims, since they can be investigated only by spiritual faculties which he never possessed, or which through long disuse and atrophy can no longer fulfil their functions. On the other hand the man in whom the spiritual nature is developed can pass in review all the facts of life and form a judgement upon them which is essentially sound and true, although his own position is an enigma to the rest of men who have no capacity for understanding it. *We* Christians *have Christ's mind*[4],

Part II. iv.

1 Cor. ii. 14 f.

1 Cor. ii. 16.

[1] Cf. Jude 19 ψυχικοί, πνεῦμα μὴ ἔχοντες.

[2] Cf. 1 Cor. i. 23 ἔθνεσιν δὲ μωρίαν. Possibly the word was often on the lips of the heathen at Corinth when they commented on the teaching of St Paul.

[3] For ἀνακρίνειν in the technical sense of 'a preliminary examination before a judge,' see Lc. xxiii. 14, Acts iv. 9.

[4] In Isa. xl. 13, of which St Paul is thinking, νοῦς translates

because we have His Spirit, and the mind of Christ in believers places them in a position of superiority
1 Cor. i. 21. to the world which *through* its *wisdom* knew not God. None can comprehend or explore the mind of the Lord, but believers in some measure possess it through the indwelling of the Spirit of Christ.'

Four passages[1] follow which may be grouped together, since they describe the ethical results of this indwelling of the Spirit. In the first and last of these those in whom the Spirit dwells are repre-
1 Cor. iii. 16 f. sented as living sanctuaries (ναοί) of God. *Know you not that you are a temple of God and that the Spirit of God dwells in you? If any one destroys the temple of God, God shall destroy that man; for the temple of God is holy; and such are you.* And
1 Cor. vi. 19 f. again, with a directly personal reference: *Know ye not that your body is a temple of the Holy Spirit that is in you, which you have from God, and that you are not your own, for you were bought for a price? So then glorify God in your body.* As in the Greek temples at Corinth, the temple of Aphrodite on the Acropolis, the temple of Poseidon on the Isthmus, the innermost shrine was occupied by the image that represented the deity; as at Jerusalem the Holy of Holies, though it contained no image of God, was for Israel the Divine dwelling-

רוּחַ. Νοῦς Χριστοῦ however is more appropriate to the subject in hand than πνεῦμα Χριστοῦ would have been. 'Christ's mind' is shared by Christians: they maintain the same general attitude towards the problems of life; their philosophy is His, and not the wisdom of the world.

[1] 1 Cor. iii. 16 f., vi. 19 f., vi. 11, vi. 17.

place on earth; so the Christian congregation in every place where the Church had been planted, and even the body of the individual believer, had become a holy place, a sanctuary of the Divine Spirit which dwells in the Ecclesia collectively and in its members as individuals. Both collectively and individually believers are in virtue of their baptism consecrated shrines of the presence of God, and in both capacities it is laid upon them to guard the sanctity of the Divine abode. The heathen deities did not require from their worshippers any jealous watch against the intrusion of immorality; on the contrary, as the Corinthians knew, the great temple on the Acro-corinthus was a vast home of licensed vice[1]. But the Spirit which dwells in the Church is essentially holy, and the sanctuary of the Holy Spirit must be holy not only by a sacramental consecration but through the maintenance of the strictest ethical purity. As the vengeance of the deity was expected to fall on any who desecrated his shrine, so would the Living God surely visit with His judgements the Church or the baptized soul that defiled the sanctuary of the Spirit. The general lesson is clear: 'You are God's consecrated shrine, through the Spirit's indwelling, and you are therefore relatively holy; beware lest your relation to the Holy Spirit be your ruin. The body has been redeemed, the body has been sanctified; let it fulfil its proper end, that of bringing glory to the God whose temple it is.'

[1] Cf. Strabo viii. 378 τὸ τῆς Ἀφροδίτης ἱερὸν οὕτω πλούσιον ὑπῆρξεν ὥστε πλείους ἢ χιλίας ἱεροδούλους ἐπέκτητο ἑταίρας.

Part II. iv.

The other two references to the Spirit in 1 Cor. vi. reveal the greatness of the change which faith and baptism made in the moral condition of many of the early converts from heathenism. After enumerating ten of the worst vices practised in the most immoral city of Greece St Paul proceeds: *And some*
1 Cor. vi. 11.
of you were such (ταῦτά τινες ἦτε); *but you washed yourselves, but you were sanctified, but you were justified in the name of the Lord Jesus Christ and in the Spirit of our God.* 'You washed away your former defilements[1] in the baptismal bath, you consecrated yourselves to the service of God, you were accepted by God as righteous in His sight, on the basis of faith in Jesus Christ and the recognition of His sovereignty over your lives, and in the power of the Divine Spirit which you received from the Christians' God.' Negatively, they had broken with their past life; positively, they had entered on the life of the consecrated and accepted servants of God; and this great moral revolution was effected by the Holy Spirit sent by Jesus Christ from the Father.

In the last of this group of passages the Apostle finds in the believer's baptismal incorporation into Christ a sufficient dissuasive from the common Greek sin of fornication. According to Gen. ii. 24 a man and his wife are *one flesh*, and this principle

[1] With this ἀπελούσασθε compare Acts xxii. 16 *βάπτισαι* καὶ ἀπόλουσαι τὰς ἁμαρτίας σου, Tit. iii. 6 ἔσωσεν ἡμᾶς διὰ λουτροῦ παλινγενεσίας, 2 Pet. i. 9 λήθην λαβὼν τοῦ καθαρισμοῦ τῶν πάλαι αὐτοῦ ἁμαρτιῶν.

holds good where there is sexual union without the marriage-bond. The body of a Christian belongs to Christ, and is a member of His Body; and he who takes that which is Christ's and unites it with the flesh of a harlot is guilty of an intolerable act of desecration. But the Apostle has a further motive for purity. The union betwixt Christ and His Church is such as may well satisfy the deepest cravings of human nature, and it certainly forbids any union which degrades nature or which ministers to the lusts of the flesh. *He that is joined to the Lord is one spirit*, i.e. by partaking of Christ's Spirit he is spiritually one with Christ, and Christ with him. To believe this true was to be armed against the temptations of the most corrupt society, for it created a strong central force in human life which formed a counter-attraction to the power of evil.

1 Cor. vi. 17.

But the greater number of the references which this Epistle makes to the work of the Holy Spirit are concerned with spiritual gifts which were not directly ethical or common to all Christians: the *charismata* which served to promote the enrichment of the Christian life rather than the ends of personal holiness. To these we must now turn.

Once the Apostle speaks, but incidentally and with great reserve, of his own inspiration. After giving his judgement[1] on a questionable point he claims consideration for it on the ground that he believed himself to share the gift of inspiration with teachers such as Cephas and Apollos:

1 Cor. vii. 40.

[1] 1 Cor. vii. 40 κατὰ τὴν ἐμὴν γνώμην.

Part II. iv. *for*[1] *I think that I also have God's Spirit,* i.e. 'in common with others who are called to be the guides of believers, I am conscious of a Divine assistance[2] in judgements which relate to moral and spiritual questions, over and above that general enlightenment which guides all believers in the fulfilment of their individual duty.' But he recognizes also other special gifts which belonged not only to teachers but to many who held no official position in the Church, and of these he speaks at length in chapters xii.—xiv.

A new section of the Epistle begins at xii. 1, *On the spiritual* gifts[3]. Before entering upon these St Paul lays down a canon which is to be borne in mind when such manifestations of the
1 Cor. xii. 3. Spirit are discussed. *No one, speaking in God's Spirit, says, 'Jesus is anathema'; and no one can say 'Jesus is Lord,' except in Holy Spirit.* The Jewish adversary who anathematized Jesus in the synagogue or before the heathen, had no part in the Spirit of God; the humblest Christian who uttered with conviction the shortest confession of his faith did so in the power of the Divine Spirit, though he might not possess the *charismata.* This premised, the
1 Cor. xii. 4 ff. Apostle proceeds: *There are differences in gifts, but the same Spirit; and there are differences in*

[1] γάρ, not δέ, is the reading of B and some other good uncials, and gives the better sense.

[2] Rutherford: "for God's Spirit is not denied, I dare say, even to me." There is a gentle irony in κἀγώ.

[3] περὶ τῶν πνευματικῶν. Cf. vii. 1, viii. 1; and for τὰ πνευματικά see xiv. 1.

ministries, but the same Lord; and there are differences in workings, and the same God who works all things in all. As there is one Lord whom all Christians serve, and yet there are many forms of service; as we all have one God, and yet there are many operations of the Divine grace; so is there one Spirit, and yet a diversity of His gifts. *To each the manifestation* (φανέρωσις) *of the Spirit is given with a view to the profit* of the Body of Christ. *For to one through the Spirit is given a word of wisdom, and to another a word of knowledge according to the same Spirit; to another faith, in the same Spirit, and to another gifts of healings, in the one Spirit, and to another workings of miraculous powers; to another prophecy, to another discernings of spirits, to another kinds of tongues, and to another interpretation of tongues. But all these the one self-same Spirit works, dividing severally to each according as it wills.* Nine manifestations of the Spirit are enumerated here, and it is easy to discover in the list a certain order. The first two are endowments of the Christian teacher which are rarely found in the same individual; one is distinguished by his insight into Divine mysteries (σοφία), another by the intellectual breadth or acuteness which creates a scientific theology (γνῶσις). The next three belong to the thaumaturgic side of early Christianity, the faith which could move mountains (xiii. 2), the therapeutic powers over disease (χαρίσματα ἰαμάτων) which some believers exhibited and are said still to exhibit, the working of physical signs and wonders (ἐνεργή-

1 Cor. xii. 8—11.

Part II. iv. μα*τα δυνάμεων*). Lastly, we have two pairs of spiritual gifts which were perhaps the most widely exercised: prophecy, with its cognate power of distinguishing the true prophet from the false (προφητεία, διακρίσεις πνευμάτων), and 'glossolaly,' with its necessary accompaniment, ability to interpret 'tongues' for the benefit of the Church (γένη γλωσσῶν, ἑρμηνεία γλωσσῶν).

The Apostle then works back from these manifestations of the Spirit to the original act by which all Christians were incorporated into the Body of Christ, his purpose being to shew that great diversity is consistent with a true unity. In the human body, which is one, the members are many, and they are differentiated by their functions. The Body of Christ, into which we were all admitted by the one Baptism of the Spirit, in like manner consists of many members who, notwithstanding their corporate unity, are distinguished by the diversity of their powers and services. These gifts and functions, proceeding from one Spirit and exercised in one Body, are not only different in purpose but of varying importance, and the Apostle arranges them in the orderly sequence of a descending scale[1].

1 Cor. xii. 28. *God appointed some in the Church, first apostles, secondly prophets, thirdly teachers, then miraculous powers, then gifts of healings, then the helps*[2] which

[1] 1 Cor. xii. 28 πρῶτον...δεύτερον...τρίτον...ἔπειτα...ἔπειτα.

[2] Ἀντιλήμψεις. Cf. Acts xx. 35 δεῖ ἀντιλαμβάνεσθαι τῶν ἀσθενούντων.

support the weak and the *powers of guidance*[1] which pilot the course of the Church; and lastly, *the* various *kinds of tongues* which make themselves heard in the assemblies of the Saints. All cannot be apostles or all prophets, nor can all speak with tongues; for this would destroy the completeness, the balance, and even the efficiency of the Body of Christ; the lower gifts and functions are not less necessary to the life and work of the whole organism than the higher, and all are in their degree manifestations of the presence of the Divine Spirit of which all believers are partakers through the first draught[2] of the water of life. Part II. iv.

At this point there comes the great episode of St Paul's praise of love. It is important to note its connexion both with what has preceded and with
what is to follow. *Be zealous*, the Apostle writes, 1 Cor. xii. 30.
for the greater gifts, for those which stand higher in the scale rather than for the lower and less noble, however showy and popular the latter may be: e.g.
for prophecy rather than for tongues. '*And further* 1 Cor. xii. 31.
I point out a way of life *which surpasses*[3] even the
best *charismata*, a way apart from which no gifts of 1 Cor. xiii. 3.
tongues or prophecy or knowledge or faith can avail anything, a way which will endure when all these
have had their day and been forgotten, which is 1 Cor. xiii. 13.

[1] Κυβερνήσεις. Cf. Acts xxvii. 11, Apoc. xviii. 17.

[2] 1 Cor. xii. 13 πάντες ἓν πνεῦμα ἐποτίσθημεν.

[3] Ζηλοῦτε in xiv. 1 takes up ζ. in xii. 31. Μᾶλλον δὲ ἵνα προφητεύητε shews what was in the Apostle's mind when he spoke of τὰ χαρίσματα τὰ μείζονα.

Part II. iv. greatest even of the three great abiding elements of the spiritual life.' So having placed the permanent gifts of the Spirit in their true relation to the *charismata*, he returns to the attitude of the Church towards the latter, which was the point that pressed for immediate consideration. While love is to be the great object of pursuit, inferior gifts might be lawfully desired, especially the best of them. *Pursue love, yet be zealous for the spiritual gifts, but more* than all *that you may prophesy.* Then follows an instructive comparison of prophecy with the gift of tongues, and rules are laid down for the guidance of the Corinthian Church in the use of both these manifestations of the Spirit. At Corinth as at

Cf. 1 Thess. v. 20. Thessalonica the Christian prophet scarcely had his due; he was eclipsed by the more attractive glossolalete, and the Apostle labours to reverse the order which the two held in the estimation of the Church. However high the mysteries which the speaker in unknown tongues might utter, he could profit none but himself, unless an interpreter

1 Cor. xiv. 2 ff., 24 f. happened to be at hand; whereas the prophet could 'build up' the Church by exhorting and consoling its members, and even winning unbelievers who entered its assemblies. Nevertheless, the Apostle does not either forbid glossolaly, or suffer prophecy to run riot uncontrolled. Both were gifts of the Spirit, and each had its place in the manifestation of spiritual life which was necessary and profitable under the conditions of the Apostolic age. But both must be exercised under proper restraints.

The glossolalete may not speak in the congregation unless an interpreter is at hand, nor may he use his gift in the ministry of public prayers or Eucharist. Not more than two or three glossolaletes or prophets may claim a hearing at the same assembly, and a prophet who is speaking must be ready to give way to another who believes himself to have received a revelation. By such rules St Paul endeavours to check the disorders threatened by an unbridled licence in the public use of the *charismata*. Further, he lays down the important principle that *prophets' spirits are under prophets' control*[1], i.e. in Christian prophecy the reason and will are not overpowered by spiritual influences, but the prophet is left master of his own powers, and is therefore responsible for their use. If he abuses his gift, or if he is a mere pretender or is under influences which are not those of the Spirit of God, there is another gift, the 'discerning of spirits,' by which he can be called to account[5]; and this also, it seems, was to be exercised, doubtless under proper safeguards, by the prophets whose turn it was to listen. A free criticism of prophetic utterances by men who were qualified by the possession of the critical spirit is not only permitted but encouraged[2]. No infallibility is claimed for the prophet; the human element which

Part II. iv.

1 Cor. xiv. 13—19, 28.

1 Cor. xii. 10, xiv. 29.

[1] Πνεύματα προφητῶν προφήταις ὑποτάσσεται: the axiomatic form suggests that this canon was already familiar to the Pauline Churches.

[2] 1 Cor. xiv. 29 οἱ ἄλλοι διακρινέτωσαν: cf. xii. 10 διακρίσεις πνευμάτων.

Part II. iv. is ever mingled with the Divine, the possibility not only of imposture or self-deception, but of imperfections in the delivery of a Divine message through personal vanity or want of balance, is plainly contemplated by the Apostle, notwithstanding his conviction that prophecy itself was a manifestation of the Holy Spirit, and that the prophet ranked next after the Apostle in the order of the charismatic ministry.

From these temporary problems, St Paul passes to the great doctrine of the Resurrection. Here also there is a reference, though indirect and in passing, to the work of the Spirit of Christ. The
1 Cor. xv. 44 ff. human body *is sown a psychic body, it is raised a spiritual body. If there is a psychic body, there is also a spiritual. So also it is written, The first man, Adam, became* (ἐγένετο εἰς) *a living soul* (ψυχὴν ζῶσαν)*; the last Adam became a life-giving spirit* (πνεῦμα ζωοποιοῦν). *But not first the spiritual, but the psychic*, and *then the spiritual.* The student of the Epistle will recall the contrast between the 'psychic' and the spiritual in ch. ii. There, however, two types of men are compared, here two conditions of the human body; our present bodies are psychic, our bodies when raised from the dead will be spiritual. But our present bodies are not psychic in regard to their material; from that point of view
2 Cor. iii. 3. they are carnal—σαρκικά or rather σάρκινα. They are 'psychic,' only in so far as they are adapted to the purposes of that lower rational life which St Paul
1 Thess. v. 23. calls the *psyche*; the passions, affections and emo-

tions of the soul are revealed and work themselves out into act through the body as it now exists. Similarly, the risen body for which we look will be the expression and instrument of the higher spiritual nature which is in us, when that has been developed and matured by the Spirit of God. The Spirit dwells in our mortal bodies, but does not make them 'spiritual'; to the end they will yield themselves readily to the desires of the flesh, and thus express the *psyche* rather than the *pneuma*. This will be reversed by the Resurrection. It is reasonable, St Paul argues, to expect that as there is a body adapted to the present visible order, so there is, in God's purpose, a body akin to the spiritual and invisible order. The first man, as we read in Genesis, *came to be a living soul*, i.e. he was invested with an Gen. ii. 7.
animal nature, which originally was inbreathed by God, and had affinities with the Supreme Life. But the last Adam, the man in whom at length humanity reached its goal, has passed by the Resurrection into a spiritual existence which has the power to communicate the higher life to the new humanity which He represents. The risen and ascended Christ is not 'psychic' but 'pneumatic'; He is the Heavenly 1 Cor. xv. 48 f.
Man, and those who are heavenly[1] ought to wear[2] the image of the Heavenly in every part of a renewed manhood. Here the Holy Spirit is not directly named; yet if it be asked how the humanity of the

[1] ὁ ἐπουράνιος, οἱ ἐπουράνιοι (cf. Heb. iii. 1 κλήσεως ἐπουρανίου μέτοχοι).

[2] φορέσωμεν ℵACD: φορέσομεν B.

Part II. iv.

Lord exercises this life-giving power, the answer must be, 'By imparting the Spirit of life by which it has itself been raised and glorified.' As St Paul has elsewhere written, *We wait for a Saviour, the Lord Jesus Christ, who shall transfigure the body of our humiliation so that it shall be conformed to the body of his glory according to the working by which he can even subject all things to himself.* (Phil. iii. 20 f.)

3. The second Epistle to the Corinthians is essentially practical, and while it has passages which are rich in teaching, there is no systematic treatment of the great questions of faith or practice such as are found in the first Epistle. Yet the work of the Spirit in the Christian body comes into view repeatedly, and here and there new lights are cast upon it.

(2 Cor. i. 17.) In ch. i. 17 St Paul has occasion to combat a charge of levity to which a change of plans had exposed him. His ministry, he contends, like the Gospel which he preached, was characterized by definiteness, certainty, fixity of purpose and aim. (2 Cor. i. 21.) The position of believers in Christ is 'guaranteed[1]' by *God, who anointed us* in Baptism with the unction of His Christ[2], *who also sealed us* with His own royal seal, and lastly *put in our hearts the first instalment of the Spirit* (τὸν ἀρραβῶνα τοῦ πνεύματος)[3].

[1] Ὁ δὲ *βεβαιῶν ἡμᾶς...θεός*. On *βεβαίωσις* as a legal term see Deissmann, *Bible Studies*, p. 104 f.

[2] *χρίσας* is suggested by *εἰς Χριστόν* which immediately precedes. Cf. 1 Jo. ii. 20, 27.

[3] "*Ἀρραβών* is properly a deposit paid as a security for the rest of the purchase money; and then, by a natural transference,

Though the Spirit is named only in connexion with the *arrhabo*, all the metaphors used in this passage describe its workings under different aspects. The gift of the Spirit is at once the unction, the sealing, and the first recompense of faith. As the Spirit anointed Jesus, so it anoints the members of the Christ; as the Son was sealed by the Father, so the adopted sons receive through the Spirit the impress of His character; and the measure of light and power which they already possess in the Spirit is an anticipation of the fulness of spiritual gifts which will be theirs after the resurrection. It may be noted that the last of these metaphors is peculiarly appropriate in a letter addressed to a great mercantile city, where it would be at once understood. Part II. iv.

Quite another figure is used in ch. iii. 3. Here the Spirit is the ink with which the Christ writes, when He impresses His mind on the hearts of men in characters which all can read. *Ye are being manifested as an epistle of Christ*[1], *ministered by us, inscribed not with ink*[2], *but with the Spirit of the living God; not on stone tables*[3], *but on tables* which are *hearts of flesh*[4]. In the conversion of the 2 Cor. iii. 3.

the first instalment of a treasure given as a pledge for the delivery of the remainder" (Westcott on Eph. i. 14).

[1] I.e., 'Your life shews with increasing distinctness the autograph of Christ, the characteristic marks of His hand, which can be detected by every one who knows you.'

[2] Cf. 2 Jo. 12, 3 Jo. 13.

[3] Exod. xxxi. 18 LXX. πλάκας λιθίνας γεγραμμένας τῷ δακτύλῳ τοῦ θεοῦ (cf. Lc. xi. 20), xxxiv. 1 ff.

[4] Reading καρδίαις with codd. ℵBACD.

Part II. iv. Gentiles the part performed by the Apostles was ministerial only; the first believers were their converts in the sense in which St Paul's Epistle to the Romans was written by Tertius[1]. It was Christ Himself who was the Author of the great change which had passed over them, and He had wrought it by the Spirit of the Living God, the power which 'alone can order the unruly wills and affections of sinful men.' Not more truly had the Law been written with the Finger of God on the two tables of stone than the New Law had been inscribed by the Spirit on the hearts of those who believed the preaching of the Gospel in the heathen cities of Asia Minor and Greece.

Yet another aspect of the Spirit's work is seen
2 Cor. iii. 6—11. as the chapter proceeds. The reference which has been made to the Tables of the Law suggests a comparison between the Law and the Gospel or, as they are here called, the Old Covenant and the New. [God] *made us sufficient to be ministers*[2] *of a new covenant*[3], *not of letter but of spirit*[4], *for the letter kills but the spirit gives life.* The Old Covenant offered a written code of duty, the New Covenant dispenses spiritual life; the code kills hope and love, the Spirit quickens what is ready to die. If the Old Covenant had its splendours, *how*

[1] Rom. xvi. 22 ἐγὼ Τέρτιος ὁ γράψας τὴν ἐπιστολήν.

[2] Cf. *v.* 3 ἡ διακονηθεῖσα ὑφ' ἡμῶν.

[3] Contrast τῆς παλαιᾶς διαθήκης (*v.* 4), and cf. Heb. viii. 13 τὸ δὲ παλαιούμενον...ἐγγὺς ἀφανισμοῦ.

[4] Cf. Rom. vii. 6 δουλεύειν ἐν καινότητι πνεύματος καὶ οὐ παλαιότητι γράμματος.

shall not the ministry of the Spirit be more in glory? Part II. iv.
*for if the ministry of condemnation is glory, how
much more does the ministry of righteousness surpass
in glory!...For if that which passes away was with
glory, much more is that which abides in glory.* The
religion of the Spirit, the religion which brings
righteousness, the religion which alone possesses
finality, must needs exceed in glory the religion of
the Law, which brought condemnation and from its
very nature was transitory and propaedeutic. That 2 Cor. iii.
the Law was not permanent or final had been sym- 13—18.
bolized by the fading away of the radiance on the
face of Moses, which he sought to screen from the
eyes of the Israelites by throwing a veil over it[1].
This veil remains on the hearts of his followers,
for Israel cannot yet see that the Old Covenant has
served its end and found its fulfilment in the religion
of the Spirit. But whenever the day shall come for
Israel to turn to the Lord Christ, the veil will be
taken off, even as Moses uncovered his face when
he went back into the Divine Presence. With Exod.
believers, whether Jews or Greeks (ἡμεῖς πάντες), xxxiv. 34 f.
this time has already come; they enter the Presence
with unveiled face, and reflecting as on the burnished
brass of a mirror the glory of the ascended Lord, they
are by degrees transfigured into His image as from
a Lord who is spirit. The last words have caused
much difficulty, and, as a matter of grammar, may
doubtless be variously rendered. But in view of

[1] Cf. Exod. xxxiv. 33 ff. The interpretation πρὸς τὸ μὴ ἀτενίσαι εἰς τὸ τέλος τοῦ καταργουμένου is St Paul's.

Part II. iv.

1 Cor. xv. 45—49 the explanation which has just been given seems to be probable. The transforming process by which Christians are made to wear the image of the Heavenly comes direct from the glorified Lord, whose humanity is now *quickening spirit*, instinct with the powers of the Spirit of life.

2 Cor. vi. 4 ff.

Some incidental references to the work of the Spirit which occur in the course of the Epistle may be briefly noticed here. In ch. vi. the Apostle marshals the evidences of a ministry which is truly of God, and midway among these he places its relation to the Holy Spirit: *in everything commending ourselves as God's ministers...in purity, in knowledge, in longsuffering, in kindness, in Holy Spirit, in unfeigned love, in word of truth, in power of God.* It is surprising at first sight that the Holy Spirit should be placed thus in the midst of its gifts: a modern writer would surely have named it either first or last according as he thought of purity, knowledge and the rest as emanating from the Spirit or culminating in it. But St Paul is as far as possible from the conventionalities of the professed theologian; he writes, especially in this Epistle, as the words offer themselves, with the freedom of the informal letter which pays little regard to the logical requirements of the sentence. Moreover it is not the person of the Spirit but the gift that is intended, and the gift with special reference to the holiness which it brings (ἐν πνεύματι ἁγίῳ); so that 'Holy Spirit' here is nearly equivalent to the spirit of holiness which ought to be the central feature of the ministerial character, the spirit which is common to all true ministers of God, distinguishing them from *false apostles*. *Walked we not*—Titus and I—(St Paul appeals) *in the same spirit? in the same steps?* It was *a different* (ἕτερον) *spirit* which animated pretenders to apostleship (ψευδαπόστολοι), whatever their claims to sanctity might be, and which they imparted to those who followed them; even as the Jesus whom they preached was another (ἄλλον) than the Person preached by St Paul.

Part II. iv.

2 Cor. xii. 18.

2 Cor. xi. 4, 13 f.

The Epistle ends with a benediction which is fuller than St Paul's usual form, and trinitarian in character. His two letters to the Thessalonians and the first of his letters to the Corinthians are concluded by a simple commendation to *the grace of our Lord Jesus Christ*, and these words are found at the end of his later letters to the Churches—Galatians, Romans (xvi. 20), Ephesians, Colossians. But at the end of 2 Corinthians the parting prayer is extended in two directions. On the one hand it includes *the love of God*[1], which is the ultimate source of all Divine blessings; and on the other *the fellowship* of the Holy Spirit, by which the Father's love and the grace of the Son are brought down into the hearts of men. This fellowship or joint participation (κοινωνία) is that which the Holy Spirit effectuates by uniting the human spirit to God in Christ and in Christ and in God to other human spirits which are partakers of the same Spirit. Such

2 Cor. xiii. 13.

[1] Cf. 2 Cor. xiii. 11 ὁ θεὸς τῆς ἀγάπης.

Part II. iv. a conclusion is especially appropriate. In an epistle which is full of the jarring notes of discord, there is fitness in closing words which speak of the blessing of a fellowship which rests on the grace of Christ and the love of God. Only with some reserve can words written with such a purpose be used for the purpose of establishing a doctrine. Nothing could have been further from the thought of St Paul than to formulate dogma. Yet the manner in which this Apostolic benediction brings together the Father, the Son, and the Spirit in Their relation to the Church suggests beyond a doubt that beneath the religious life of the Apostolic age there lay a profound though as yet unformulated faith in the tripersonality of God.

V.

THE TEACHING OF THE PAULINE EPISTLES (ii).

Ἐξ ἔργων νόμου τὸ πνεῦμα ἐλάβετε ἢ ἐξ ἀκοῆς πίστεως; Gal.iii. 2 ff.
...ἐναρξάμενοι πνεύματι νῦν σαρκὶ ἐπιτελεῖσθε;...ὁ οὖν
ἐπιχορηγῶν τὸ πνεῦμα καὶ ἐνεργῶν δυνάμεις ἐν ὑμῖν, ἐξ
ἔργων νόμου ἢ ἐξ ἀκοῆς πίστεως;

Ἵνα τὴν ἐπαγγελίαν τοῦ πνεύματος λάβωμεν διὰ τῆς Gal. iii. 14.
πίστεως.

Ὅτι δέ ἐστε υἱοί, ἐξαπέστειλεν ὁ θεὸς τὸ πνεῦμα τοῦ υἱοῦ Gal. iv. 6.
αὐτοῦ εἰς τὰς καρδίας ἡμῶν, κρᾶζον Ἀββά ὁ πατήρ.

Ὁ κατὰ σάρκα γεννηθεὶς ἐδίωκε τὸν κατὰ πνεῦμα. Gal. iv. 28.

Ἡμεῖς γὰρ πνεύματι ἐκ πίστεως ἐλπίδα δικαιοσύνης Gal. v. 5.
ἀπεκδεχόμεθα.

Πνεύματι περιπατεῖτε καὶ ἐπιθυμίαν σαρκὸς οὐ μὴ τελέ- Gal. v. 16
σητε· ἡ γὰρ σὰρξ ἐπιθυμεῖ κατὰ τοῦ πνεύματος, τὸ δὲ πνεῦμα —18.
κατὰ τῆς σαρκός· ταῦτα γὰρ ἀλλήλοις ἀντίκειται, ἵνα μὴ ἃ
ἐὰν θέλητε ταῦτα ποιῆτε. εἰ δὲ πνεύματι ἄγεσθε, οὐκ ἐστὲ
ὑπὸ νόμον.

Φανερὰ δέ ἐστιν τὰ ἔργα τῆς σαρκός...ὁ δὲ καρπὸς τοῦ Gal. v.
πνεύματός ἐστιν ἀγάπη, χαρά, εἰρήνη, μακροθυμία, χρηστότης, 19 ff.
ἀγαθωσύνη, πίστις, πραΰτης, ἐγκράτεια.

Εἰ ζῶμεν πνεύματι, πνεύματι καὶ στοιχῶμεν. Gal. v. 25.

Ὑμεῖς οἱ πνευματικοὶ καταρτίζετε τὸν τοιοῦτον [= τὸν Gal. vi. 1.
προλημφθέντα ἔν τινι παραπτώματι] ἐν πνεύματι πραΰτητος.

Ὁ δὲ σπείρων εἰς τὸ πνεῦμα ἐκ τοῦ πνεύματος θερίσει Gal. vi. 8.
ζωὴν αἰώνιον.

Τοῦ ὁρισθέντος υἱοῦ θεοῦ ἐν δυνάμει κατὰ πνεῦμα ἁγιω- Rom. i. 4.
σύνης ἐξ ἀναστάσεως νεκρῶν.

Rom. v. 5. Ἡ ἀγάπη τοῦ θεοῦ ἐκκέχυται ἐν ταῖς καρδίαις ἡμῶν διὰ πνεύματος ἁγίου τοῦ δοθέντος ἡμῖν.

Rom. viii. 2. Ὁ γὰρ νόμος τοῦ πνεύματος τῆς ζωῆς ἐν Χριστῷ Ἰησοῦ ἠλευθέρωσέν με ἀπὸ τοῦ νόμου τῆς ἁμαρτίας καὶ τοῦ θανάτου.

Rom. viii. 4 ff. Ἵνα τὸ δικαίωμα τοῦ νόμου πληρωθῇ ἐν ἡμῖν τοῖς μὴ κατὰ σάρκα περιπατοῦσιν ἀλλὰ κατὰ πνεῦμα. οἱ γὰρ κατὰ σάρκα ὄντες τὰ τῆς σαρκὸς φρονοῦσιν, οἱ δὲ κατὰ τὸ πνεῦμα τὰ τοῦ πνεύματος. τὸ γὰρ φρόνημα τῆς σαρκὸς θάνατος, τὸ δὲ φρόνημα τοῦ πνεύματος ζωὴ καὶ εἰρήνη...ὑμεῖς δὲ οὐκ ἐστὲ ἐν σαρκὶ ἀλλὰ ἐν πνεύματι εἴπερ πνεῦμα θεοῦ οἰκεῖ ἐν ὑμῖν. εἰ δέ τις πνεῦμα Χριστοῦ οὐκ ἔχει, οὗτος οὐκ ἔστιν αὐτοῦ. εἰ δὲ Χριστὸς ἐν ὑμῖν, τὸ μὲν σῶμα νεκρὸν διὰ ἁμαρτίαν, τὸ δὲ πνεῦμα ζωὴ διὰ δικαιοσύνην. εἰ δὲ τὸ πνεῦμα τοῦ ἐγείραντος τὸν Ἰησοῦν ἐκ νεκρῶν οἰκεῖ ἐν ὑμῖν, ὁ ἐγείρας ἐκ νεκρῶν Χριστὸν Ἰησοῦν ζωοποιήσει καὶ τὰ θνητὰ σώματα ὑμῶν διὰ τοῦ ἐνοικοῦντος αὐτοῦ πνεύματος ἐν ὑμῖν.

Rom. viii. 13—16. Εἰ δὲ πνεύματι τὰς πράξεις τοῦ σώματος θανατοῦτε ζήσεσθε. ὅσοι γὰρ πνεύματι θεοῦ ἄγονται, οὗτοι υἱοὶ θεοῦ εἰσίν. οὐ γὰρ ἐλάβετε πνεῦμα δουλείας πάλιν εἰς φόβον, ἀλλὰ ἐλάβετε πνεῦμα υἱοθεσίας, ἐν ᾧ κράζομεν Ἀββά ὁ πατήρ. αὐτὸ τὸ πνεῦμα συνμαρτυρεῖ τῷ πνεύματι ἡμῶν ὅτι ἐσμὲν τέκνα θεοῦ.

Rom. viii. 23. Τὴν ἀπαρχὴν τοῦ πνεύματος ἔχοντες.

Rom. viii. 26 f. Τὸ πνεῦμα συναντιλαμβάνεται τῇ ἀσθενείᾳ ἡμῶν...αὐτὸ τὸ πνεῦμα ὑπερεντυγχάνει στεναγμοῖς ἀλαλήτοις· ὁ δὲ ἐραυνῶν τὰς καρδίας οἶδεν τί τὸ φρόνημα τοῦ πνεύματος, ὅτι κατὰ θεὸν ἐντυγχάνει ὑπὲρ ἁγίων.

Rom. xii. 11. Τῷ πνεύματι ζέοντες.

Rom. xiv. 17. Οὐ γάρ ἐστιν ἡ βασιλεία τοῦ θεοῦ βρῶσις καὶ πόσις, ἀλλὰ δικαιοσύνη καὶ εἰρήνη καὶ χαρὰ ἐν πνεύματι ἁγίῳ.

Rom. xv. 13. Ὁ δὲ θεὸς τῆς ἐλπίδος πληρώσαι ὑμᾶς πάσης χαρᾶς καὶ εἰρήνης ἐν τῷ πιστεύειν, εἰς τὸ περισσεύειν ὑμᾶς ἐν τῇ ἐλπίδι ἐν δυνάμει πνεύματος ἁγίου.

Rom. xv. 16. Ἵνα γένηται ἡ προσφορὰ τῶν ἐθνῶν εὐπρόσδεκτος, ἡγιασμένη ἐν πνεύματι ἁγίῳ.

Rom. xv. 18 f. Κατειργάσατο Χριστὸς δι᾽ ἐμοῦ εἰς ὑπακοὴν ἐθνῶν, λόγῳ

καὶ ἔργῳ, ἐν δυνάμει σημείων καὶ τεράτων, ἐν δυνάμει πνεύ- Part II. v.
ματος ἁγίου.

Παρακαλῶ δὲ ὑμᾶς...*διὰ τοῦ κυρίου ἡμῶν* Ἰησοῦ Χριστοῦ Rom. xv.
καὶ διὰ τῆς ἀγάπης τοῦ πνεύματος. 30.

THE Epistle to the Galatian Churches and the Epistle to the Romans are addressed to widely different communities in circumstances partly similar. The first went to central Asia Minor, the second to Italy; the first appealed to provincials, the second to a cosmopolitan Church at the heart of the Empire. On the other hand both Epistles arose out of the same great questions of faith and life which were raised by the conflict of Pauline Christianity with the Judaizing movement in the Churches. But while in Galatia this controversy was at its height and assumed the form of a personal struggle between the Apostle and the Judaizers, at Rome it was as yet inchoate, or perhaps had scarcely begun, and personal considerations did not enter. Moreover, the wider outlook of the Church of the metropolis afforded an opportunity for a more systematic exposition of the Gospel of St Paul than the Galatians were prepared to receive. For these reasons we shall find in these two Epistles, together with striking coincidences, a marked difference of general treatment. We begin with Galatians, which will naturally precede Romans, not only on chronological grounds, but as presenting St Paul's teaching in a less mature or at least a less fully reasoned form.

Part II. v.

Gal. iii. 2 ff.

1. In Galatians the work of the Spirit first comes into view in ch. iii., where the Apostle uses the fact that the Spirit had been given through his ministry as an argument in favour of the Gospel that he preached. *This only would I learn from you: From works of law received ye the Spirit, or from hearing of faith? Are you so void of understanding? Having begun with spirit are you now being perfected by flesh?...He therefore who supplies to you the Spirit and works miracles* (δυνάμεις) *among you*, is it *from works of law or from hearing of faith* that he proceeds? The appeal is a twofold one; it points in the first place to the original bestowal of the Spirit at the baptism of the Galatians (ἐλάβετε τὸ πνεῦμα), and secondly to the continued supply of the Spirit and of the miraculous gifts of the Spirit vouchsafed through the hands of those who carried on St Paul's work among them. Had the Judaizing teachers anything of this kind to shew? Could they point to any spiritual results which followed their ministration of legal ordinances? And would men who knew from their own experience what spiritual powers meant be content to enter on the down-grade road of external rites, to descend from the spiritual to the material, and after such an initiation into their new life (ἐναρξάμενοι πνεύματι) seek to consummate it by a carnal ordinance (σαρκὶ ἐπιτελεῖσθε)? Was it not pure folly to reverse the true order of progress—to go from spirit to flesh, not from flesh to spirit? Was it possible to do this in the face of present

facts? The Spirit was still given before their eyes; signs of Divine power were daily witnessed. But in no instance as the result of legal teaching or of compliance with it (*ἐξ ἔργων νόμου*); only as following the message of the Gospel apprehended by faith on the part of the hearers (*ἐξ ἀκοῆς πίστεως*).

Such an *argumentum ad hominem* might well have given pause to the keenest partizan on the side of the legalists. But the Apostle presses his advantage further. How were the facts to which reference had been made to be interpreted? Why was the Spirit given only through the preaching of St Paul and of those who followed in his steps? Why had the Judaizers uniformly failed to shew any similar effects of their mission? It was because the one party in this controversy had followed and the others had refused God's way of righteousness. Abraham believed God and was justified by his faith. In Abraham all the nations of the world were to be blessed. How? By sharing his faith and thus sharing his righteousness. It is not the Law which will bring righteousness to the Gentile world, but faith in the promise of God. The promise of God to mankind appeals to the trust, the loyalty, the self-surrender of the human heart; where these are given, the promise fulfils itself. It fulfils itself in the gift of the Spirit, which is the immediate consequence of believing in Jesus Christ and being incorporated into His Body, the Church. Thus it is through faith that the Spirit is received, and not through legal rites.

Gal. iii. 7—9.

Gal. iii. 14.

Part II. v.

Gal. iii. 26 ff.

Gentiles who believed were therefore the true *sons of Abraham*, since they inherited Abraham's faith. But they were more; they were *sons of God.* In Baptism they had put on Christ, i.e. they had been invested with Christ's character and sonship. Two recent Divine missions had made this

Gal. iv. 4—6.

possible. *God sent forth*[1] *his Son made of woman, made under law, that he might redeem those under law, that we might receive the adoption. And because you are sons, God sent forth*[1] *the Spirit of his Son into your hearts, crying, Abba, Father.* The purpose of the Son's mission was to give the rights of sonship; the purpose of the Spirit's mission, to give the power of using them. As the former was realized in human history at the moment of the Incarnation, so the latter connects itself historically with the moment of the Pentecostal coming. But in view of his readers' experience, St Paul prefers to think of the mission of the Spirit as having taken effect when He entered each individual life[2] at Baptism or the Laying on of Hands. Further, the Apostle is led by his line of thought to speak of the Spirit as the Spirit of the Son. The Spirit of the Only-Begotten Son is sent into the hearts of the adopted sons, because it is the very Spirit of sonship. It does not make them sons, for they are such by their union with the Incarnate Son, but it makes them conscious of

[1] For this use of ἐξαποστέλλειν cf. Lc. xxiv. 49.

[2] Gal. *l.c.* εἰς τὰς καρδίας ὑμῶν. Cf. Rom. v. 5, viii. 27, 2 Cor. iii. 2 f., Eph. i. 18, iii. 17, 1 Pet. iii. 4.

their sonship and capable of fulfilling their responsibilities. It enters the heart, the centre of the moral and intellectual nature of every baptized member of Christ and child of God, and its voice is heard within, acclaiming God as the Father of the personal life, *crying, Abba Father*[1]! The words which are uttered belong to the human subject and not to the Divine Spirit, and when they appear again in Rom. viii. 15, this is made evident by a verbal change in the phrase with which they are introduced; in the later Epistle it stands *in which we cry*[2]. But *crying* in Galatians has its own truth to teach; the Spirit of God inspires the cry which the human spirit utters. The bilingual form of the cry is worthy of notice, whether we regard it as a reminiscence of words actually used by our Lord in Gethsemane, or suppose the Marcan Ἀββά ὁ πατήρ to reflect the liturgical use of the early Church of Jerusalem. In the former case it will suggest that the adopted children of God reveal their sonship in the same spirit of filial submission which marked the Only Son; in either case, it points to the meeting of Jew and Gentile, men of Aramaic and men of Greek speaking lands, in the Divine Family of the Church[3]. Both Jewish and Gentile Christians possess in Christ the right to call God Father, and the Spirit voices

Mc. xiv. 36; cf. Heb. v. 7.

[1] Gal. iv. 6 κρᾶζον Ἀββά ὁ πατήρ.

[2] Rom. viii. 15 ἐν ᾧ κράζομεν Ἀ. ὁ π.

[3] See the writer's notes on Mc. xiv. 36 and Apoc. i. 7. Bp Chase (*Texts and Studies* I. 3, p. 23 f.) thinks that there is a reference to the Lord's Prayer, which in the shorter form (Lc. xi. 2 ff.) begins Πάτερ, ἁγιασθήτω κτλ.

Part II. v. this common claim in the hearts of all, and thus gives effect to the Son's redemptive work. That all believers have the right to say 'Our Father' comes from the Incarnate Son; that, having the right, they have also the strong desire to use the privilege of sons, comes from the indwelling in their hearts of the Spirit of the Son. Without the mission of the Spirit the mission of the Son would have been fruitless; without the mission of the Son the Spirit could not have been sent. In order of time the mission of the Son preceded the mission of the Spirit, since adoption, the fruit of redemption, must precede the awakening of the filial spirit. But the two are alike necessary, and the Divine Love which gave the Son and the adoption of sons has included in the gift the Spirit of the Son which is its proper complement.

A group of passages follows in which the contrast between Spirit and Flesh, already suggested in ch. iii., is worked out in detail. It appears in
Gal. iv. 29. ch. iv. in connexion with an allegorical treatment of the story of Ishmael and Isaac. The two sons of faithful Abraham are taken to represent the contending parties in the Churches of Galatia; the Judaizers are the children of the slave girl Hagar, while those who looked to be justified by faith are children of the free woman and true wife, Sarah. *We, brethren* (the Apostle proceeds), *after the manner of Isaac are children of promise; but as then the son born after the flesh persecuted the son born after the Spirit, even so it is now.* As Ishmael,

who came into the world in the way of natural generation (κατὰ σάρκα), derided Sarah's son who was the child of promise and born out of the course of nature, so the more spiritual members of the Galatian congregations must expect to encounter the hard speeches of the legalists. There is a play here upon words; 'after the flesh,' 'after the Spirit' bear a sense in reference to Ishmael and Isaac which must be modified when they are applied to the Judaizers and the Pauline Christians of Galatia. In the latter case 'after the flesh' means 'in the way of a carnal, external ordinance,' and 'after the Spirit,' in the way of spiritual regeneration. Much the same meaning must be attached to πνεύματι in ch. v. 5: *we* (ἡμεῖς)[1] *by spirit from faith wait for hope of righteousness*—a strangely compressed sentence which appears to mean: 'our hope of final acceptance, which rests upon the basis of faith, is spiritually generated and maintained; it belongs to the higher life of man in which the Spirit of God itself operates upon the human spirit and inspires it with the hope which is founded on faith.' A little further down, at *v.* 16, 'by spirit' (πνεύματι) occurs again, and from this point the contrast between spirit and flesh is carried forward far into ch. vi. The whole passage is of great interest, and portions of it must be examined here at some length.

Gen. xxi. 9. Cf. Rom. iv. 19 ff.; Heb. xi. 11 f.

Gal. v. 5.

Gal. v. 16.

But I say, Walk by spirit and you shall not fulfil fleshly lust (ἐπιθυμίαν σαρκός). *For the flesh*

Gal. v. 16 ff.

[1] Emphatic: '*We*, who seek justification not from the Law but from faith,' as contrasted with οἵτινες ἐν νόμῳ δικαιοῦσθε.

Part II. v. *lusts against the spirit, and the spirit against the flesh; for these are opposed to one another, that whatsoever things you would, these you may not do. But if you are led by spirit, you are not under Law.*

The antagonism between Flesh and Spirit is now seen to be far more radical than has hitherto appeared. Not only does the flesh stand for the external and natural, and the spirit for the internal and Godward; but the former is the sphere of sinful lusts, while the latter is the champion of the better life, leading men to battle with their lusts. The two are thus diametrically opposed, and men have to choose between them; for they cannot do simply what they please, but must take part in the contest under the leadership of one or of the other. When
Gal. v. 16, 25. the Spirit leads a man, he *walks by spirit* (πνεύματι περιπατεῖν, στοιχεῖν): there is movement and
Gal. vi. 16 (κανόνι στοιχεῖν). progress in his life as step after step he follows the straight line of the Spirit's rule, each moment bringing him nearer to the goal. In so far as this is so he is *not under law*; the external command or prohibition is gradually superseded by the growing agreement of his ideals and conduct with the purpose of the highest law, until its control over him ceases altogether because its end has been attained.

Gal. v. 16 ff. But what is to be understood by *the flesh* and *the spirit*? The Apostle does not define either, but he gives a detailed account of the effects they severally produce. The flesh proceeds by way of
Cf. James i. 15. uncontrolled desire (ἐπιθυμία σαρκός) to overt acts of sin. Such acts in great variety met the eye in

every Greek city; it was impossible to overlook or mistake them. *Manifest are the works of the flesh, such as are fornication, impurity, lasciviousness, idol-worship, witchcraft, enmities, strifes, rivalries, fits of passion, factions, divisions, selfwilled partizanships, envious tempers, drinking bouts, revels, and the like to these.* For these things no place would be found in the Kingdom of God. But there was another order which was already at work in human society and was bearing goodly and lasting fruit. *The fruit of the Spirit is love, joy, peace, long-suffering, graciousness, goodness, faithfulness, meekness, self-restraint; against such things there is no law:* law as a prohibitory or condemning power has no existence (οὐκ ἔστιν) where they are found. 'Fruit' is doubly a contrast to 'works.' Fruit-bearing is a natural and not a mechanical process, revealing the presence of an inner life; and the use of the singular (καρπός, not καρποί) points to the unity of the character which the Spirit creates. But its unity is manifold, and the nine products enumerated correspond to three sides of the manifold Christian experience; some find their sphere in that inner life which is privy to God and the individual consciousness[1], some in the life of fellowship with men[2], and some again in the personal character which interprets itself in the words and deeds[3] or even in the face[4] and the manner of the man. The

Part II. v.

Gal. v. 19f.

Gal. v. 21 ff.

[1] Ἀγάπη, χαρά, εἰρήνη.

[2] Μακροθυμία, χρηστότης, ἀγαθωσύνη.

[3] Πίστις, πραΰτης, ἐγκράτεια.

[4] See Acts vi. 15.

Part II. v. Spirit—here the Holy Spirit in His operations, rather than the spiritual life which He creates in believers—bears fruit in every region of human life. All in life that is worthy of the name of fruit—all that fulfils the end of life by bringing glory to God—is of the Spirit. By the Spirit the True Vine abides in the branches and the branches abide in the Vine, apart from which they can do nothing, in union with which they bear 'much fruit[1].' By the Spirit[2] we live, i.e. receive and maintain our spiritual life, our very existence in the higher possibilities of our nature; by the Spirit we may also take step after step along the way of life (εἰ ζῶμεν πνεύματι, πνεύματι καὶ στοιχῶμεν). Thus in *v.* 26 the Apostle returns to the practical rule with which he set out in *v.* 16.

Gal. vi. 1. A particular instance follows of the influence of the Spirit upon daily life. *Even if* (ἐὰν καί) *a man be surprised in some trespass, you, the spiritual* members of the Church, *restore one that is such in a spirit of meekness.* True spirituality shews itself in yielding the fruit of the Spirit, for which opportunities are given in intercourse with other members of the Body of Christ. It is by the regular discharge in the Spirit of Christ of the duties that arise from

[1] Jo. xv. 4 f. The metaphor is found already in Hosea xiv. 8; for its use in the N.T. see Mc. iv. 20, 28, Jo. xv. 1—10, Rom. vi. 22, Phil. i. 11, iv. 17, Col. i. 6, 10, Heb. xii. 11, Jas. iii. 18.

[2] πνεύματι. Lightfoot prefers 'to the Spirit,' comparing Rom. vi. 2, xiv. 6, 2 Cor. v. 15. But this involves the use of the dative in two senses within the same short sentence, for he translates the second πνεύματι 'by the Spirit.'

the relations of the present life that Christians are trained for their future life with God. *Whatsoever a man has sown, that shall he also reap; for he that sows to his own* (ἑαυτοῦ) *flesh shall of the flesh reap corruption, whereas he that sows to the Spirit shall of the Spirit reap eternal life.* To sow to a man's own flesh is to live for the gratification of his lower nature; to sow to the Spirit[1] is to follow the higher intuitions which come from the Holy Spirit in the heart. From the former course of action there results the decay of all that is best in human nature, and at length the utter corruption of the dead soul; from the latter, the quickening and ripening of a character which, when it has been matured, will be the lasting possession of those who have cultivated it during the present life. Life in the Spirit is eternal life sown and growing to maturity; eternal life is life in the Spirit matured and harvested in the Kingdom of God.

Part II. v.

Gal. vi. 7 f.

2. "The Epistle to the Galatians stands in relation to the Roman letter as the rough model to the finished statue[2]." But on the whole the doctrine of the Spirit comes to the front in Romans less often

[1] ἑαυτοῦ is not repeated, for the Spirit is not the man's own, or if his own spirit is intended, it is regarded as taught and filled by the Spirit of God.

[2] See Lightfoot, *Galatians*[5], p. 49. He adds, "Or rather, if I may press the metaphor without misapprehension, it is the first study of a single figure, which is worked into a group in the latter writing." This extension of the figure may help to explain the somewhat different proportions which the subjects of Galatians assume in Romans.

Part II. v. than in Galatians; there are casual references to it throughout the Epistle, but nothing like a systematic treatment of the subject is attempted except in ch. viii. That chapter, however, carries the teaching of the Galatian Epistle some way further, and places St Paul's conception of the work of the Spirit in a new and highly interesting light, by bringing out its connexion with his soteriology.

Rom. i. 3 f. The antithesis *according to flesh, according to spirit*, appears at the very beginning of the Epistle to the Romans, but in reference to the Incarnation and Resurrection of Christ, *who was made of the seed of David according to* the *flesh; who was declared*[1] *Son of God in power according to* the *spirit of holiness by* (ἐξ) *resurrection from the dead.* Jesus Christ became son of David by a generation which though, as the Church now knows, it was mediated by the Holy Spirit, in every other respect followed the course of nature (κατὰ σάρκα)[2]. But notwithstanding His truly human birth, He was Son of God, and His Divine sonship was vindicated by an event which did not belong to the natural order of things but was due to supernatural and spiritual forces (κατὰ πνεῦμα), even to that *spirit of holiness*[3] which characterized His whole life, and triumphed over death[4].

[1] ὁρισθέντος, defined, marked out, not made (γενομένου, Gal. iv. 4). Cf. Acts x. 42 ὁ ὡρισμένος...κριτής, xvii. 31 μέλλει κρίνειν...ἐν ἀνδρὶ ᾧ ὥρισεν, πίστιν παρασχὼν πᾶσιν ἀναστήσας αὐτόν.

[2] Cf. Rom. ix. 5 ἐξ ὧν ὁ χριστὸς τὸ κατὰ σάρκα.

[3] I.e. the spirit whose note was holiness.

[4] Cf. Rom. viii. 11 τὸ πνεῦμα τοῦ ἐγείραντος τὸν Ἰησοῦν.

In ch. i. 11 there is a passing reference to the spiritual gifts imparted by the ministry of the Apostle. But it is in ch. v. that the ethical work of the Spirit first comes into view as a consequence of our Lord's work of redemption and justification. The passage occurs at the end of the great argument which establishes justification on the basis of faith. Jesus Christ *was raised because of our justification. Therefore being justified on the ground of faith let us have peace with God through our Lord Jesus Christ...and let us rejoice in hope of the glory of God...Let us also rejoice in our tribulations, knowing that tribulation works endurance, and endurance probation, and probation hope, and hope does not put to shame.* Of this we are confident, *because the love of God has been poured out in our hearts through Holy Spirit that was given to us.* 'Since the day (the Apostle would say) when the Spirit was given to each of us[1], there has been perpetually in our hearts the sense of God's love to us in His Son, poured out upon them by the Spirit which was then received.' Here the Spirit is regarded as the source of Christian experience in so far as it realizes the Divine Love of redemption. It is due to the Spirit that the love of God is to believers not a mere doctrine, but a fact of their inner life, continually present to their consciousness, and inspiring a certain hope of future blessedness.

Rom. i. 11.

Rom. iv. 25; v. 1, 3—5.

[1] δοθέντος, not διδομένου. On the other hand the experience which ensues upon the first gift is continuous (ἐκκέχυται, not ἐξεχύθη).

Part II. v.

Rom. vii. 5 ff. The seventh chapter strikes the keynote of 'spirit' *versus* 'flesh' which dominated the closing chapters of Galatians. *When we were in the flesh the passions of our sins, which were through the Law, were active in our members. But as things now are* (νυνὶ δέ), *we are discharged from the Law*, our old relations with the Law are broken off...*so that we may serve in newness of spirit and not in oldness of written ordinance.* 'Not that the Law is itself the cause of sin or death, or a mere written form; on the contrary, it is spiritual in its purpose and
Rom. vii. 14 ff. requirements. It is I, the human *ego*, that am fleshly (σάρκινος) and therefore the slave of sin. In me, at least in my flesh, in my lower nature, good does not dwell; if my higher self, my rational nature (ὁ νοῦς), consents to the Divine Law—*video meliora proboque*—my lower self is from time to time taken captive by the law of Sin, a ruling power which resides in the body and uses its members as its
Rom. vii. 25. instruments. Thus in my one personality (αὐτὸς ἐγώ) I am divided between two masters, my mind serving the law of God, my flesh the law of Sin. So miserable (ταλαίπωρος ἐγὼ ἄνθρωπος) is my condition apart from Christ.'

But all is changed when Christ enters the field of human life and is received by faith. The law of Sin and Death is now vanquished by a new and
Rom. viii. 1 ff. stronger principle, *the law of the Spirit of life in Christ.* What is the history of this new force in human life? It begins with the mission of the Son of God, who took *the likeness of flesh of sin*, i.e.

flesh such as ours in every respect except its sin, and in this flesh, this visible bodily nature, exposed to all the temptations which beset such a nature, condemned sin and put it to death by dying to it, and by this victory of a true humanity over sin opened the way for the attainment by men in the flesh of the righteousness which the Law demands (τὸ δικαίωμα τοῦ νόμου), but has hitherto demanded in vain. For the victory of Christ has not only a negative, but a positive result; on the one hand it has destroyed the power of the principle of Sin, on the other it has brought to us through the Resurrection the power of the Spirit of Christ. This new power dominates those who yield themselves to it and *walk not according to flesh but according to spirit.* (Rom. viii. 4 ff.) To them the higher nature of man, which even in the heathen is on the side of righteousness, no longer resists the impulses of the flesh unaided and suffers hopeless defeat, but is reinforced by the Spirit, which leads it to victory. Thus we are brought back to the struggle between flesh and spirit. But though the conflict is the same which is described in Galatians, the treatment is entirely fresh and goes more deeply into the heart of the matter. *For those who are according to flesh set their minds upon the things of the flesh, but those* who are *according to spirit, upon the things of the Spirit. For the mind set upon the flesh is death, but the mind set upon the Spirit is life and peace; because the mind set upon the flesh is hostility towards God, for it is not in a state of subjection to the law of God (for*

Part II. v. *neither can it be*), *but those who are in flesh cannot please God.*

The argument is not easy to grasp, but it seems to be as follows. 'I spoke of the attainment of righteousness by those who walk after spirit and not after flesh. For there are two opposite conditions of mind, that in which men's thoughts and affections are centred on the life of sense, and that in which they find their satisfaction in things that are spiritual and eternal. And these two states cannot lead to the same end, for the one is a state of spiritual death and the other is life and peace, the life of the Spirit and the peace of God, which comes from union with Christ. The mind which is dominated by the flesh cannot please God or fulfil the law of righteousness, for it habitually resists the Divine Will and is, openly or secretly, consciously or unconsciously, the enemy of God[1].'

Rom. viii. 8 ff. *But you*[2] (the Apostle continues) *are not in flesh but in spirit, if the Spirit of God really* (εἴπερ) *dwells in you. But if any has not Christ's Spirit, that man is not his. If, however, Christ is in you, the body indeed is dead because of sin, but the spirit is life because of righteousness. But if the Spirit of him who raised Jesus from the dead dwells in you, he who raised Christ Jesus from the dead shall quicken even your mortal bodies because of his Spirit that dwells in you.*

[1] Cf. Jas. iv. 4.

[2] Emphatic: '*You* who walk after the Spirit, in whom the Spirit dwells.'

In other words: 'You, Roman believers, are not in the condition of those whose affections are set upon the flesh; you are "in spirit[1]," in a state of spiritual activity, if the Spirit of God does in very truth dwell in you, as indeed He does if you are members of Christ; for the man who has not Christ's Spirit, which is the Spirit of God, is not Christ's. Christ is in all His members by His Spirit. But if Christ is in you, the life of righteousness has begun in your human spirit, quickened by the Spirit of God. For the time, indeed, the new life does not shew itself in the body, which is still dead[2] because it is the seat of sin. But the body, too, must eventually yield to the law of the spirit of life; as Jesus Himself was raised according to the spirit of holiness, so will the Spirit of God which dwells in you bring about the same result.' If we accept the Alexandrian reading (διὰ τοῦ ἐνοικοῦντος πνεύματος[3]) the Spirit is the Agent—if the 'Western' reading (διὰ τὸ ἐνοικοῦν πνεῦμα[4]), He is the Cause, of the resurrection of the body. In either case the effect is due to the indwelling of the Spirit, and not to a power working *ab extra*; there is no resurrection after the likeness of Christ's Resurrection except for those who already are alive in spirit through the

[1] κατὰ σάρκα, κατὰ πνεῦμα, are now exchanged for ἐν σαρκί, ἐν πνεύματι. It is not conduct which is now in view so much as the sphere in which a man's inner life is lived.

[2] νεκρόν, not simply θνητόν: dead potentially and relatively. From another point of view the bodies of believers are a 'living sacrifice' (Rom. xii. 1).

[3] So codd. ℵAC.

[4] So codd. BD.

Part II. v. immanent presence of the Spirit of God and of Christ.

Even in this most systematic of his Epistles St Paul repeatedly pauses to point the moral of his argument. So he does here. The indwelling of the Spirit lays the believer under an obligation which must be discharged by living as the Spirit directs.
Rom. viii. 12 f. *So then, brethren, we are debtors not to the flesh, to live according to flesh* [but to the Spirit, to live after the Spirit], *for if you live according to flesh, you are on the point* (μέλλετε) *to die, but if by the Spirit you put to death* (θανατοῦτε) *the deeds of the body, you shall live.* 'The flesh has no claim upon you, for it works death; the Spirit, which kills the flesh, brings you life. And consider what the life of the Spirit
Rom. viii. 14. means. *As many as are led by God's Spirit, these are God's sons* (υἱοί). *For you received not a spirit of slavery*, leading you *again to fear, but you received a spirit of adoption, in which we cry*[1], *'Abba, Father'; the Spirit bears witness jointly with our own spirit that we are God's children* (τέκνα). As the slave is marked by the slavish spirit, so the filial spirit is the sure sign of sonship. But the Spirit received at baptism is a filial Spirit; it inspires the daily *Pater noster* of the Church; in those who are led by it, it is a joint-witness with their own consciousness that they possess the nature as well as the rights of

[1] Not κρᾶζον, as in Gal. iv. 6 (see p. 205), nor κράζετε, as the context might seem to require (οὐ γὰρ ἐλάβετε...ἀλλ' ἐλάβετε... ἐν ᾧ κτλ.), but κράζομεν, as a statement which is true of all Christians.

sons[1]. There is no return in their case to the state of fear[2] in which they lived under the Law, for they know God to be their Father, and themselves His accepted sons. More than this, they know themselves to be His heirs. *But if* we are *children*, we are *also heirs, heirs of God and joint-heirs with Christ, if in truth we suffer jointly with him, that we may also be jointly glorified*[3]. Rom. viii. 17. As the only begotten Son is *the Heir*[4], the adopted and regenerated children are also heirs, but on the condition that they share the sufferings of the Son. Present suffering, if borne in fellowship with Christ, is so far from casting a doubt upon the reality of our sonship that it lies on the direct road to its realization in *the glory of the children of God.* Rom. viii. 22. All nature suffers in this imperfect state, and its sufferings extend even to those who are under the law of the Spirit of life. *We ourselves also, though we have the firstfruits of the Spirit—we ourselves also groan within ourselves, waiting for adoption, namely the emancipation of our body.* Rom. viii. 23. For adoption has been as yet received only in part; the Spirit in us is but the firstfruits of the great harvest of spiritual life; Cf. Gal. vi. 8. our emancipation is incomplete, for the body is still subject to death and the instrument of sin. 'First-

[1] They are τέκνα θεοῦ and not only υἱοί by a process of υἱοθεσία. Cf. Jo. i. 12 f. τέκνα θεοῦ...ἐκ θεοῦ ἐγεννήθησαν, 1 Jo. iii. 1 ποτάπην ἀγάπην δέδωκεν ἡμῖν ὁ πατὴρ ἵνα τέκνα θεοῦ κληθῶμεν· καὶ ἐσμέν.

[2] οὐ...πάλιν εἰς φόβον.

[3] Cf. 2 Tim. ii. 11.

[4] Cf. Mc. xii. 7 (so also Mt., Lc.), and see Heb. i. 2, vi. 17.

Part II. v.

fruits' (ἀπαρχή) applied to the Spirit in believers recalls St Paul's use of 'first instalment' (ἀρραβών) in 2 Cor. i. 22, v. 5. The present metaphor is drawn from the ceremonial of the Passover, the other from the mercantile life of the Greek towns; while the latter was specially appropriate in a letter to Corinth, the former would appeal to the large Jewish element in the Church at Rome. Both yield the same general sense. The spiritual life already imparted to the Church is inchoate, and cannot be perfected until the body has been set free from the law of sin and death. When at length the body has been emancipated and made 'spiritual,' the adoption will be complete. The firstfruits will be merged in the harvest, the first instalment in the full inheritance of the sons of God.

Rom. viii. 26 ff.

Yet one further contribution is made by this great chapter to St Paul's doctrine of the Spirit. He has spoken of the groans of suffering Nature being shared by the half-emancipated children of God. Meanwhile, however, we are not left without effective help in our struggle with sin and death. *In like manner also the Spirit supports our weakness; for what we should pray* so as to pray *as we ought we know not, but the Spirit itself entreats for us with groans which are not to be expressed in words. But he who searches the hearts* of men *knows what is the mind*[1] *of the Spirit, because* it is *in accordance with* the will of *God*[2] *that he entreats for saints.* The

[1] τὸ φρόνημα, the contents of the mind, its purpose and intent.

[2] κατὰ θεόν: cf. 2 Cor. vii. 10.

very Spirit of God within us bears His part[1] in our present difficulties. As He cries in us and we in Him *Abba, Father*, so He shares the groans of our imperfect nature, converting them into prayers without and beyond words. There are times when we cannot pray in words, or pray as we ought; but our inarticulate longings for a better life are the Spirit's intercessions on our behalf, audible to God who searches all hearts, and intelligible and acceptable to Him since they are the voice of His Spirit, and it is according to His will that the Spirit should intercede for the members of His Son. Part II. v.

There is perhaps nothing in the whole range of New Testament Pneumatology which carries us so far into the heart of the Spirit's work. He is seen here in His most intimate relations with the human consciousness, distinct from it, yet associated with its imperfectly formed longings after righteousness, acting as an intercessor on its behalf in the sight of God, as the glorified Christ does[2]; not however in heaven, but in the hearts of believers. The mystery of prayer stands here revealed, as far as it can be in this life; we see that it is the Holy Spirit who not only inspires the filial spirit which is the necessary condition of prayer, but is the author of the 'hearty desires' which are its essence.

[1] For συναντιλαμβάνεσθαι cf. Lc. x. 40 (περιεσπᾶτο...συναντιλάβηται).

[2] Cf. *v.* 34. As the Spirit ὑπερεντυγχάνει, so also the Ascended Christ ἐντυγχάνει ὑπὲρ ἡμῶν. Or, as St John expresses the same truth, the Son is also our παράκλητος, but πρὸς τὸν πατέρα (1 Jo. ii. 1).

Here the systematic teaching of Romans ends; but the second half of the Epistle yields several incidental notices of the place which the Holy Spirit fills in the Christian life. If the members of Christ's body are *fervent in spirit*[1], it is because the fire of the Spirit has raised their natural lukewarmness to the boiling heat of a great enthusiasm. If they are distinguished by a joyous spirit which triumphs over circumstances however adverse, it is because *the Kingdom of God* which the Christ came to establish upon earth *is righteousness and peace, and joy in Holy Spirit*[2]; if they *abound in hope*, it is *in the power of Holy Spirit*; if the Apostle would appeal to the sympathy of men, most of whom were personally unknown to him, he beseeches them *by the love of the Spirit*, that brotherly love which the one Spirit implants in all Christian hearts. In the mission work of the Church there was no less need and there had been no less evidence of the Spirit's presence. To the Spirit, in fact, was due the conversion of the Gentiles; St Paul had received a special gift of Divine grace in virtue of which he was the *ministering priest of Jesus Christ for the Gentiles, doing the sacrificial work of the Gospel of God* by offering up the Gentile Churches[3]. But he

Rom. xii. 11.

Rom. xiv. 17.

Rom. xv. 13.

Rom. xv. 30.

Rom. xv. 16.

[1] τῷ πνεύματι ζέοντες. Cf. Acts xviii. 25 and contrast Apoc. iii. 16 χλιαρὸς εἶ, καὶ οὔτε ζεστὸς οὔτε ψυχρός.

[2] Cf. Acts xiii. 52, Gal. v. 22, 1 Thess. i. 6. Our Lord Himself, on the one occasion when He is said to have been stirred by an emotion of joy, ἠγαλλιάσατο τῷ πνεύματι τῷ ἁγίῳ (Lc. x. 21; see p. 60).

[3] It is impossible to miss the import of the series of sacrificial

knows that his offering could not have been acceptable unless it had been *sanctified in Holy Spirit*, the Spirit of God falling upon the hearts of the new disciples like fire from heaven upon a sacrifice and consecrating them to the service of the Living God. All that the great Apostle had done at the time when this Epistle was written—and it came at the end of his missionary journeys, when he had practically finished his evangelistic work in Asia Minor and Greece—had been wrought by Christ through his hands *in the power of* the *Spirit*[1]. The greatest of Christian missionaries realized that his power lay not in himself but in the Spirit of Christ, who used him as the instrument of His grace.

Part II. v.

Rom. xv. 18 f.

words (λειτουργός, ἱερουργεῖν, προσφορά, εὐπρόσδεκτος). Cf. Rom. xii. 1, 1 Pet. ii. 5.

[1] κατειργάσατο Χριστὸς δι' ἐμοῦ...ἐν δυνάμει πνεύματος (+ ἁγίου ACD, + θεοῦ ℵL). The relation of Christian work to Christ, the Spirit, and the human agent is here clearly seen.

VI.

THE TEACHING OF THE PAULINE EPISTLES (iii).

Phil. i. 19. Τοῦτό μοι ἀποβήσεται εἰς σωτηρίαν, διὰ τῆς ὑμῶν δεήσεως καὶ ἐπιχορηγίας τοῦ πνεύματος Ἰησοῦ Χριστοῦ.

Phil. i. 27. Ἀκούω ὅτι στήκετε ἐν ἑνὶ πνεύματι, μιᾷ ψυχῇ συναθλοῦντες τῇ πίστει τοῦ εὐαγγελίου.

Phil. ii. 1. Εἴ τις κοινωνία πνεύματος...πληρώσατέ μου τὴν χαρὰν ἵνα τὸ αὐτὸ φρονῆτε.

Phil. iii. 3. Ἡμεῖς γάρ ἐσμεν ἡ περιτομή, οἱ πνεύματι θεοῦ λατρεύοντες ...καὶ οὐκ ἐν σαρκὶ πεποιθότες.

Col. i. 8. Ὁ καὶ δηλώσας ἡμῖν τὴν ὑμῶν ἀγάπην ἐν πνεύματι.

Eph. i. 13. Ἐν ᾧ καὶ πιστεύσαντες ἐσφραγίσθητε τῷ πνεύματι τῆς ἐπαγγελίας τῷ ἁγίῳ, ὅ ἐστιν ἀρραβὼν τῆς κληρονομίας ἡμῶν, εἰς ἀπολύτρωσιν τῆς περιποιήσεως.

Eph. i. 17 f. Ἵνα ὁ θεὸς...δῴη ὑμῖν πνεῦμα σοφίας καὶ ἀποκαλύψεως ἐν ἐπιγνώσει αὐτοῦ, πεφωτισμένους τοὺς ὀφθαλμοὺς τῆς καρδίας ὑμῶν κτλ.

Eph. ii. 18 ff. Δι' αὐτοῦ ἔχομεν τὴν προσαγωγὴν οἱ ἀμφότεροι ἐν ἑνὶ πνεύματι πρὸς τὸν πατέρα...ἐν ᾧ καὶ ὑμεῖς συνοικοδομεῖσθε εἰς κατοικητήριον τοῦ θεοῦ ἐν πνεύματι.

Eph. iii. 5. Ἀπεκαλύφθη [τὸ μυστήριον τοῦ χριστοῦ] τοῖς ἁγίοις ἀποστόλοις αὐτοῦ καὶ προφήταις ἐν πνεύματι.

Eph. iii. 16 f. Ἵνα δῷ ὑμῖν κατὰ τὸ πλοῦτος τῆς δόξης αὐτοῦ δυνάμει κραταιωθῆναι διὰ τοῦ πνεύματος αὐτοῦ εἰς τὸν ἔσω ἄνθρωπον, κατοικῆσαι τὸν χριστὸν διὰ τῆς πίστεως ἐν ταῖς καρδίαις ὑμῶν ἐν ἀγάπῃ.

Eph. iv. 3 f. Σπουδάζοντες τηρεῖν τὴν ἑνότητα τοῦ πνεύματος ἐν τῷ συνδέσμῳ τῆς εἰρήνης. ἓν σῶμα καὶ ἓν πνεῦμα...εἷς κύριος, μία πίστις, ἓν βάπτισμα, εἷς θεὸς καὶ πατὴρ πάντων.

Ἀνανεοῦσθαι δὲ τῷ πνεύματι τοῦ νοὸς ὑμῶν, καὶ ἐνδύ- Part II. vi.
σασθαι τὸν καινὸν ἄνθρωπον. Eph. iv. 23.
Μὴ λυπεῖτε τὸ πνεῦμα τὸ ἅγιον τοῦ θεοῦ, ἐν ᾧ ἐσφραγίσ- Eph. iv. 30.
θητε εἰς ἡμέραν ἀπολυτρώσεως.
Μὴ μεθύσκεσθε οἴνῳ, ἐν ᾧ ἐστὶν ἀσωτία, ἀλλὰ πληροῦσθε Eph. v.
ἐν πνεύματι, λαλοῦντες ἑαυτοῖς ψαλμοῖς καὶ ὕμνοις καὶ ᾠδαῖς 18 f.
πνευματικαῖς.
Καὶ τὴν μάχαιραν τοῦ πνεύματος [δέξασθε], ὅ ἐστιν ῥῆμα Eph. vi.
θεοῦ, διὰ πάσης προσευχῆς καὶ δεήσεως προσευχόμενοι ἐν 17 f.
παντὶ καιρῷ ἐν πνεύματι.

Ὃς ἐφανερώθη ἐν σαρκί, ἐδικαιώθη ἐν πνεύματι. 1 Tim. iii. 16.
Τὸ δὲ πνεῦμα ῥητῶς λέγει ὅτι κτλ. 1 Tim. iv. 1.
Ἀναμιμνήσκω σε ἀναζωπυρεῖν τὸ χάρισμα τοῦ θεοῦ, ὅ
ἐστιν ἐν σοὶ διὰ τῆς ἐπιθέσεως τῶν χειρῶν μου· οὐ γὰρ 2 Tim. i.
ἔδωκεν ἡμῖν ὁ θεὸς πνεῦμα δειλίας, ἀλλὰ δυνάμεως καὶ 6 f.
ἀγάπης καὶ σωφρονισμοῦ.
Τὴν καλὴν παραθήκην φύλαξον διὰ πνεύματος ἁγίου τοῦ 2 Tim. i.
ἐνοικοῦντος ἐν ἡμῖν. 14.
Ἔσωσεν ἡμᾶς διὰ λουτροῦ παλινγενεσίας καὶ ἀνακαινώ- Tit. iii. 5.
σεως πνεύματος ἁγίου, οὗ ἐξέχεεν ἐφ' ἡμᾶς πλουσίως διὰ
Ἰησοῦ Χριστοῦ τοῦ σωτῆρος ἡμῶν.

Συνεπιμαρτυροῦντος τοῦ θεοῦ σημείοις τε καὶ τέρασιν καὶ Heb. ii. 4.
ποικίλαις δυνάμεσιν καὶ πνεύματος ἁγίου μερισμοῖς κατὰ τὴν
αὐτοῦ θέλησιν.
Καθὼς λέγει τὸ πνεῦμα τὸ ἅγιον. Heb. iii. 7
Ἀδύνατον γὰρ τοὺς ἅπαξ φωτισθέντας γευσαμένους τε (cf. ix. 8,
τῆς δωρεᾶς τῆς ἐπουρανίου καὶ μετόχους γενηθέντας πνεύ- x. 15).
ματος ἁγίου καὶ καλὸν γευσαμένους θεοῦ ῥῆμα κτλ. Heb. vi. 4.
Ὃς διὰ πνεύματος αἰωνίου ἑαυτὸν προσήνεγκεν ἄμωμον Heb. ix.
τῷ θεῷ. 14.
Ὁ τὸν υἱὸν τοῦ θεοῦ καταπατήσας, καὶ τὸ αἷμα τῆς Heb. x. 29.
διαθήκης κοινὸν ἡγησάμενος ἐν ᾧ ἡγιάσθη, καὶ τὸ πνεῦμα τῆς
χάριτος ἐνυβρίσας.

Part II. vi.

It is characteristic of St Paul that he does not return, except incidentally or for a practical purpose, to a subject which he has treated at any length in a particular Epistle or group of Epistles. Thus the doctrine of Justification by Faith, which is laboured in the Epistles to the Galatians and Romans, reappears but twice[1] in the later letters. In like manner the doctrine of the Spirit, also treated in those Epistles, does not again come on for discussion. But the work of the Holy Spirit enters so largely into the life of the Church, and held so great a place in the thought of the first age, that no Apostolic letter to the Churches could ignore it altogether; and references to it will be found in all the Epistles attributed to St Paul with the exception of the short private letter to Philemon.

1. The long imprisonment at Rome was to St Paul in some respects a season of leisure and even of liberty. He was free to think, to write, to teach, and to preach[2]; and the enforced confinement to hired lodgings offered opportunities for these employments, especially for the two former, which could rarely have been found during the years of travel and active work that preceded his arrest. It would be surprising if no letters to the Churches had been written in this interval, and those which have reached us, the Epistles to the Philippians and Colossians, and the encyclical to the Churches of Asia which is

[1] See Phil. iii. 6 ff., Tit. iii. 5 ff.

[2] The Acts end with the significant words *κηρύσσων...καὶ διδάσκων...μετὰ πάσης παρρησίας ἀκωλύτως.*

known as the Epistle to the Ephesians[1], bear the stamp of St Paul's mind and heart too plainly to be attributed to a mere imitator of the great Apostle. Part II. vi.

For our present purpose we will take these three Epistles in the order already given. It is probably the chronological order[2], and it will have the advantage of keeping to the last the most important references to our subject in this group of letters.

(*a*) At Rome St Paul's vigorous personality had roused the zeal of other preachers of the Gospel, some of whom preached a Gospel which was not his, and preached it in a spirit of partizanship, and even with the malicious hope of adding bitterness to the prisoner's lot. Yet he rejoiced in this state of things; the name of Christ was proclaimed even by those whose purpose was to hurt His Apostle; and the very pain which their malice caused would help on the Apostle's own highest interests. *For* Phil. i. 19.
I know (he writes to the Philippians) *that this shall turn to me for salvation*[3] *through your supplication and supply of the Spirit of Jesus Christ.* The prayers of the Philippian Church and the supply of the Spirit to St Paul in his lodgings at Rome are so closely correlated that in the Greek one article

[1] In support of the Pauline authorship of Ephesians see Hort, *Prolegomena to Ephesians and Philippians*, p. 45 ff.; and on the other side von Soden, *History of early Christian literature* (E. tr.), p. 294 ff., or Jülicher, *Introduction to the N.T.*, p. 138 ff.

[2] Hort, *Prolegomena*, p. 101 f. In favour of placing Philippians last see von Soden, *op. cit.* p. 47.

[3] Cf. Lc. xxi. 13 ἀποβήσεται ὑμῖν εἰς μαρτυρίαν.

Part II. vi. suffices for the two (διὰ τῆς ὑμῶν δεήσεως καὶ ἐπιχορηγίας). Writing to the Galatians four or five years before, St Paul had spoken of the Spirit as 'supplied' through the ministry of the Church[1]. Now he traces his own supply of the Spirit to the prayer of the Church. He was confident that, as his converts prayed, a fresh abundance of the Spirit which was in Jesus Christ and had been sent by Him[2] would be poured into his heart, making for his final salvation whether the present captivity should result in life or in death.

Phil. i. 27—ii. 2. In the next passage St Paul's thoughts are turned to the Philippians themselves. They also had need of the Spirit of Jesus Christ, but for other reasons. Against the persecutor they had shewn a firm front; they had learned not only to believe on Christ, but to suffer for Him. Yet there was evidently among them, though in a less developed form than among the Corinthians, the spirit of dissension and division. They needed not only to resist the enemy, but to resist him with a united
Phil. i. 27. front; to *stand firm in one spirit, with one soul striving in concert for the faith of the Gospel.* The Apostle presently returns to this point, which he
Phil. ii. 1f. knows to be vital. *If then there is any exhortation* (παράκλησις) *in Christ, if any consolation of love,*

[1] Cf. Gal. iv. 5 ὁ ἐπιχορηγῶν ὑμῖν τὸ πνεῦμα. This seems to decide in favour of taking τοῦ πνεύματος in Phil. as the genitive of the object. The Spirit is supplied, not the supplier.

[2] πνεῦμα Ἰησοῦ, Acts xvi. 7; πνεῦμα Χριστοῦ, Rom. viii. 9, 1 Pet. i. 11.

if any fellowship of spirit, if any feelings of tenderness and mercy, complete my joy that you be of the same mind, having the same love, being of one soul, setting your minds on the one thing. I.e. 'if you can be moved by an appeal based on your Christian faith or by the persuasiveness of the love it inspires or by that common life in the Spirit which you share with your brethren or by the stirrings within you of God's own character of tender mercy, by all these I entreat you to let nothing disturb your harmony or divide you from one another; thus you will fill my cup with joy[1].' Here the Apostle returns to a phrase which he had used in an earlier Epistle; the 'fellowship of the Holy Spirit' has met us already in 2 Corinthians, where it is associated in the parting benediction with the 'grace of our Lord Jesus Christ' and the 'love of God.' There the personal Spirit of God is directly in view; here perhaps rather the spiritual life which is His work in believers. But 'fellowship of spirit' is more than oneness of spirit; it is that joint participation in the Spirit's gifts and powers which was in the Apostolic Church the acknowledged bond of unity and communion between the baptized. Part II. vi.

One more reference to the Spirit occurs in this Epistle. In ch. iii. 2 ff. the Apostle warns the Philippians in no measured language against his old adversaries, the Judaizing party, who were seeking to undermine his work at Rome and were perhaps Phil. iii. 2 ff.

[1] The Apostle had already causes for rejoicing in his bonds (i. 18); this would make his cup full.

Part II. vi.

not wholly unknown at Philippi[1]. *Beware of the 'dogs[2],' beware of the 'evil workers,' beware of the 'Mutilation.' For we[3] are the 'Circumcision,' who serve by God's Spirit, and glory in Christ Jesus, and have not put our trust in the flesh.* Circumcision, considered as a mere rite, is simple mutilation; the true circumcision is that of the heart, in the spirit and not in the letter[4]. Spiritual Christians, therefore, are 'the Circumcision,' for it is in them that the rite finds its fulfilment. Such are Israelites indeed, who with circumcised hearts render the spiritual service which only the Divine Spirit can inspire. The thought is in general the same as in Jo. iv. 23 f., Rom. i. 9[5], where the human spirit is in view; but in Philippians, if we accept the reading which has the best support[6], the Spirit of God is specifically mentioned as the power by which the human spirit is enabled to worship in spirit and in truth.

[1] It is unexpected to find a reference to the Judaizers in an Epistle addressed to a city where there was not even a synagogue. But St Paul's steps seem to have been dogged everywhere by the Pharisaic party, and the fame of the Philippian Church may well have brought them to Philippi by 59 or 60.

[2] Lightfoot: "St Paul retorts upon the Judaizers the term of reproach by which they stigmatized the Gentiles as impure." Ἐργάται perhaps hints at their insistence on mere works, κατατομή at their perversion of circumcision, which, as they taught it, was a mere cutting of the flesh, without spiritual significance.

[3] ἡμεῖς, emphatic: 'we, and not they, as they claim.'

[4] Cf. Rom. ii. 29.

[5] The words in Rom. i. 9 come very near in other respects to Phil. iv. 3 (ὁ θεὸς...ᾧ λατρεύω ἐν τῷ πνεύματί μου).

[6] θεοῦ ℵ*ABCD^c: θεῷ ℵ^{ca}D* is 'Western.'

(*b*) In the Epistle to the Colossians the Apostle's thoughts are carried by a new controversy into another field, and he mentions the Spirit only once. St Paul begins the letter as usual with a sympathetic reference to the proofs of sincerity which the Colossians had given: he had heard of their faith in Christ Jesus and the love which they had towards all their brethren in Christ (i. 4). Such love as Epaphras who knew them well had described could only be *in spirit* (i. 8); it had its origin in hearts quickened and warmed by the indwelling of the Spirit of Christ. Of love as an evidence of the Spirit's presence we have already heard much in earlier Epistles[1].

Col. i. 4–8.

(*c*) The Epistle to the Ephesians has been suspected because of its frequent coincidences with Colossians. In one important respect, however, it offers a striking contrast to Colossians; it abounds in references to the Holy Spirit. Nor are these references by any means mere recollections of earlier thoughts: some are such, no doubt, but in others a distinct note of progress may be heard, as if the writer were feeling his way to new points of view upon a road which he had but in part explored.

The first mention of the Spirit (i. 13 f.) has many points of resemblance to 2 Cor. i. 22. *In whom—the Beloved* (*vv.* 3, 6)—*having also believed* and not only heard the Gospel (*v.* 13), *you* Gentiles *were sealed with the Spirit of promise, the Holy Spirit, which is an earnest of our inheritance, unto*

Eph. i. 13 ff.

[1] Cf. 1 Cor. xii. 31, xiii. 1 ff.; Gal. v. 22, Rom. xv. 30.

Part II. vi. *the redemption of the possession, to the praise of his glory.* Hearing was in the case of the Asian Christians followed by faith in Christ, and faith by the seal of the promised Spirit, which was the consecrating power in the life of believers and the first instalment (ἀρραβών) of their future inheritance, that final emancipation from sin and death of the new Israel, the Possession of God, which will issue in the recognition by all His creatures of the moral glory of God manifested in the completed history of Redemption. In this passage the metaphors of the seal and the earnest are reminiscences of the similar passage in 2 Corinthians, and the '*Spirit of Promise*' recalls the *promise of the Spirit* in Galatians; but the setting is new, and it carries us into regions of thought which are now for the first time connected with the work of the Spirit. We learn what it is that the Spirit as an earnest guarantees, namely, our inheritance in the life to come, and the place it fulfils in the purpose of God, working out the final deliverance of His purchased people from the law of sin and death, and calling forth the last great *Te Deum laudamus* of angels and men.

Gal. iii. 14.

Cf. Rom. viii. 17.

Cf. Rom. viii. 22.

With this passage it is natural to associate Eph. iv. 30, *Grieve not the Spirit, the Holy* Spirit, *of God, in which*[1] *you were sealed unto* the *day of emancipation.* Here two of the keywords of ch. i. 13 occur again. Believers in their baptism received the *seal* of the Spirit with a view to their complete *emancipation* at a future day. As in 1 Thess. iv. 8

Eph. iv. 30.

[1] ἐν ᾧ, the element in which the sealing took place.

the Apostle finds an argument against the indulgence of sin in an emphatic reference to the holiness of the Divine Gift: 'the Spirit which sealed you is the Holy Spirit, for it is the Spirit of God[1], whose nature recoils from all contact with evil.' The thought of a 'day of emancipation[2]' adds another motive, placing the present struggle against sin in the light of the day of Christ, which held so large a place in early Christian thought. Lastly, the exhortation not to 'grieve the Spirit' represents the Spirit as personal, identifying it with the Heart of God, as in Isaiah lxiii. 10[3]. To have received the seal of the Spirit is not only a cause for thankfulness, but a source of increased responsibility. The first instalment of spiritual life which it brings is not an absolute guarantee of final deliverance; it makes for that end, but may be frustrated by the conduct of the person who has received it. 'You were sealed with the Spirit,' the Apostle pleads; 'then do not break the seal[4].'

To return to the first chapter; in *v.* 17 the Apostle again refers to the Spirit, but with another purpose. 'You are often named in my prayers; I give thanks to God for your faith, but I desire for you yet larger gifts. I pray that God *may give you* Eph. i. 17.

[1] τὸ πνεῦμα τὸ ἅγιον τοῦ θεοῦ is intentionally reduplicative; the Holy Spirit is the Spirit of God, but the Apostle wishes to press both points.

[2] The ἡμέρα ἀπολυτρώσεως is doubtless the ἡμέρα τοῦ κυρίου or the Parousia; cf. 2 Cor. v. 5, Phil. i. 6, 10; cf. Rom. viii. 19, 23.

[3] LXX. παρώξυναν τὸ πνεῦμα αὐτοῦ (עִצְּבוּ 'pained').

[4] Theophylact: μὴ λύσῃς τὴν σφραγῖδα.

Part II. vi. *a spirit of wisdom and revelation* (ἀποκαλύψεως) *in knowledge of him, you having the eyes of your heart enlightened to the end that you may know what is the hope of his calling, what the wealth of the glory of his inheritance...and what the surpassing greatness of his power*...The Spirit was given to the Church at the Pentecost, and to each individual at baptism, and the gift is continuous unless it is checked by a course of sin. It is not then for this that St Paul prays, but for a particular endowment of the Spirit, 'a spirit,' i.e. a spiritual influence, productive of a certain type of character or mind. As we read elsewhere in his Epistles of a *spirit of meekness* (1 Cor. iv. 21), a *spirit of faith* (2 Cor. iv. 13), a *spirit of adoption* (Rom. viii. 15), so the Apostle speaks here of a *spirit of wisdom and revelation*[1]—the wisdom that apprehends God's will, the revelation that makes Divine mysteries intelligible, by lifting the veil from the heart, so that the glory of the Christian calling with its hope for the future and its promise of strength for the present is disclosed to enlightened eyes. It is not the charismatic *word of wisdom* (1 Cor. xii. 8), or the power of apocalyptic utterance (1 Cor. xiv. 6) which is here in view, but the inward illumination which is the normal outcome of faith and love. St Paul desires this experience for all his converts. Not all are prophets or seers[2]; not all see visions or write apocalypses, but all may

[1] Cf. Col. i. 9 ἵνα πληρωθῆτε τὴν ἐπίγνωσιν τοῦ θελήματος αὐτοῦ ἐν πάσῃ σοφίᾳ καὶ συνέσει πνευματικῇ.

[2] Cf. 1 Cor. xii. 19 f

Part II. vi.

have their eyes open to see the true meaning of their life in Christ[1].

Eph. ii. 14 ff.

In ch. ii. 14 the Apostle strikes another note which is heard at intervals through the next two chapters. The union of Jew and Gentile in the Body of Christ has created a new humanity; a reconciliation has taken place between the two factors which hitherto have been kept apart, in virtue of the reconciliation of both to God by the Cross of Christ. *For through him we both have access in one Spirit to the Father.* Here the work of the Spirit is seen in its relation to the work of the Son and the love of the Father. 'Access to God' is the first great result of the Atonement, and it comes to men through the mediation of the Son. 'Access' is another word taken over from the Epistle to the Romans (v. 2). There however the Apostle thinks chiefly of the terms of admission to the favour of God, here he contemplates admission to His Presence[2]; we are on the track of the ideas afterwards worked out in the Epistle to the Hebrews. But St Paul, while he emphasizes the redemptive work of the Son, does not lose sight of its necessary sequel, the guiding, inspiring work of the Spirit; if the Son has opened a new and living way into the Father's

[1] For this ἀποκάλυψις see Mt. xi. 25 f., ἀπεκάλυψας αὐτὰ (the mystery of the Kingdom of Heaven, cf. Mc. iv. 11) νηπίοις...οὐδὲ τὸν πατέρα τις ἐπιγινώσκει εἰ μὴ ὁ υἱὸς καὶ ᾧ ἐὰν βούληται ὁ υἱὸς ἀποκαλύψαι. The Father reveals through the Son, the Son by the Spirit.

[2] In this sense it occurs again in Eph. iii. 12.

Part II. vi. Presence, it is the Spirit in whom we cry Abba, Father; in whom our hearts draw nigh. And it is the oneness of the Spirit of access which makes all who draw near to God through Jesus Christ to be one in Him. Jew and Gentile now approach God in one *Pater noster*, in one Eucharist; they are one Body, nay one man[1], since they have one Spirit. A common spiritual life animates and coordinates the two great sections of the Christian Society.

Eph. iv. 1 ff. This conception is worked out in detail at the beginning of the fourth chapter. Here the distinction between Jew and Gentile disappears altogether. The Apostle enumerates seven unities which ought to triumph over all the elements of discord that tend to keep believers apart: there is *one body and one Spirit...one hope...one Lord, one faith, one baptism, one God and Father of all.* But it is the *unity of the Spirit* on which especial stress is laid, for if this is wanting, the others lose their power to preserve union. An earnest effort therefore must be made (σπουδάζοντες) to keep this unity in the bond (συνδέσμῳ) of peace[2], i.e. to maintain in the Body of Christ the charity which binds its members into a perfect whole; whatever disturbs the peace of the Church impairs the unity of the Spirit which inhabits the Body. As the commentators point out[3],

[1] εἰς ἕνα καινὸν ἄνθρωπον. Cf. Gal. iii. 28 οὐκ ἔνι Ἰουδαῖος οὔτε Ἕλλην...πάντες γὰρ ὑμεῖς εἷς ἐστὲ ἐν Χριστῷ Ἰησοῦ.

[2] Col. iii. 14 τὴν ἀγάπην, ὅ ἐστιν σύνδεσμος τῆς τελειότητος.

[3] See the commentaries of Dean Armitage Robinson and Bp Westcott *ad loc.*

it is not easy to distinguish here between the two senses of 'spirit'; the 'one spirit' may be either the community of thought and feeling, of interest and life, which marks the living organism, or the Divine Spirit through which this community is gained. But if the first meaning is present in the words, it passes insensibly into the second; the 'One Spirit' of *v.* 4 cannot be divorced from the 'One Lord' and the 'One God and Father' of *v.* 5. Viewed in connexion with the 'one Body,' it is the spirit of the Church; but it also stands in relation to Christ and to God, and is the very Spirit of Both.

Eph. iv. 7—16.

From the unity of the Spirit St Paul passes at once to the manifold gifts of grace which create a diversity of ministries without breaking the harmony of the Body (iv. 7—16). The passage has affinities with 1 Cor. xii. 4—28, Rom. xii. 4 ff., but it has also characteristics which are its own. The gifts are connected with the Ascension of the Christ; the ascended Lord gave them to the world, and their purpose is to perfect the Church in Him. The Spirit is not mentioned here by name, but no reader of St Paul can doubt that His work is throughout in the background of the Apostle's thought[1].

Of the special gifts possessed by St Paul himself and by other apostles and prophets mention has been made at an earlier point in the Epistle (iii. 3, 5), where the Apostle speaks of *the stewardship of that grace of God which was given* him for the

Eph. iii. 3, 5.

[1] In τῆς ἐπιχορηγίας (*v.* 16) it almost comes into sight; cf. Gal. iii. 5, Phil. i. 19.

Part II. vi. benefit of the Gentile churches. *The mystery was made known to me in the way of revelation* (κατὰ ἀποκάλυψιν)...*the mystery of the Christ, which in other generations was not made known to the sons of men as it has now been revealed* (ἀπεκαλύφθη) *to his holy apostles and prophets in spirit.* St Paul knew himself to have been fitted for his 'stewardship' by an insight into God's great purpose of a catholic mission which was not possessed by the prophets of the older covenant, but at the time when he wrote (νῦν) was shared by all the leading teachers, the Apostles and Prophets[1], of the Christian Church. To a less extent and in a lower region of thought this gift was bestowed on not a few of the non-official members of the Church; it was one of the commoner *charismata* in the Church at Corinth, and doubtless also in Asia Minor, at the time when this encyclical was sent to the Asian Churches. Another form of 'revelation,' which was possessed by St Paul himself, consisted in ecstatic raptures that seemed to carry the man who was under their influence into Paradise or to disclose to him the person of the glorified Christ. But to these manifestations there is no reference in Ephesians; the high level of thought maintained throughout this Epistle does not lend itself to a reference to the lower charismatic gifts[2].

1 Cor. xii. 26.

1 Cor. xii. 1, 7.

The Spirit's work upon the individual life of the

[1] Cf. 1 Cor. xii. 28, Eph. iv. 11.

[2] Contrast the list in Eph. iv. 11 with the much fuller one given in 1 Cor. xii. 28.

ordinary believer receives illustration later in the same chapter (iii. 16) where for the second time the Apostle prays for the Churches addressed. *I bend my knees to the Father...that he may give to you according to the wealth of his glory to be strengthened with power through his Spirit* poured *into the inner man, that the Christ may dwell through faith in your hearts in love, you being rooted and grounded*[1], *that you may have full strength to apprehend with all the saints what is the breadth and length and height and depth and to know the knowledge-surpassing love of the Christ, that you may be filled unto all the fulness of God.* Though the Spirit is named only at the opening of this great prayer, it is necessary to have the whole before the eye while we attempt to grasp the place which He occupies in the process described. Beginning at the end of the prayer and working back we see that the goal of the Christian life is 'the fulness of God'; that this is reached by the road of a knowledge which surpasses all the intelligence of men, intuitively realizing the love of Christ and apprehending the vastness of the Divine idea of Redemption; that this knowledge comes from the faith by which Christ dwells in the heart, and the love in which the root and foundation of the higher life is laid. For no step in this progress is human nature sufficient; behind it all there lies the strengthening[2] of the

Part II. vi.

Eph. iii. 16 f.

[1] So Westcott in his posthumous Commentary on Ephesians; the text of WH. gives *in love, rooted and grounded.*

[2] With this κραταιωθῆναι διὰ τοῦ πνεύματος cf. Lc. i. 80

Part II. vi.

will, the understanding, the whole spiritual nature or 'inner man' by the Spirit of God. Thus the present prayer goes further and deeper than the prayer of i. 16 ff. Spiritual strength is the primary and most fundamental need of human nature on its way to God, more fundamental than wisdom and revelation, which are the adornments rather than the essentials of the Christian life.

Eph. iv. 23 ff.

The inner life is again in view in ch. iv. 23 ff. St Paul's converts had been taught (ἐδιδάχθητε), before their baptism or at an early stage in their baptismal life, *to put off*, *in relation to* their *former manner of life*, *the old man...and to be renewed in the spirit of* their *mind and put on the new man which was created after God in righteousness and holiness of the truth.* A new self must take the place of their former self; a self renewed continually in the region of the spiritual life, and like unfallen man, created after the image of God, in the righteousness and holiness which spring from and are in harmony with the truth. The *spirit of the mind*, where the great change is wrought, is not the Divine Spirit, but it is the sphere of the Holy Spirit's operations, and its renewal and re-creation are due to them. In a later epistle we shall find this connexion explicitly stated[1]; here it is implicit only, but scarcely obscure.

ἐκραταιώθη πνεύματι, ii. 40 ἐκραταιοῦτο πληρούμενον σοφίᾳ. The present passage is remarkable for bringing together all the words which signify strength or force (δυνάμει...κραταιωθῆναι...ἵνα ἐξισχύσητε).

[1] See Tit. iii. 5 διὰ...ἀνακαινώσεως πνεύματος ἁγίου.

Part II. vi.

Two other passages in the Epistle to the Ephesians place the work of the Spirit in relation with the experience of the Christian life. The exhilarating, uplifting, power of the Spirit is contrasted by St Paul with the effect of overmuch wine upon the intemperate. *Be not drunken with wine, in which there is excess, but be filled in spirit, speaking one to another in psalms and hymns and spiritual songs, singing and making music with your heart to the Lord.* (Eph. v. 18 f. (cf. Col. iii. 16).) It is of course not the use of wine[1] that is deprecated, but its abuse—a use *in which there is excess.* Such carousals were too familiar in the Greek cities of Asia Minor[2], and they were the negation of all spiritual influences[3]. But if Christians were called to abstain from this shallow mirth, they received immediate compensation; their spirits were filled with the wine of God, their hearts rose under the power of the new Spirit of Christ; and for the drinking songs of heathendom, they had the psalms of the Old Testament and Christian psalms based upon them[4], the hymns and odes which the Church under the impulses of the Spirit was already beginning to compose[5]. St Paul, however, would not

[1] See 1 Tim. iii. 8, v. 23 (μὴ οἴνῳ πολλῷ προσέχοντας...οἴνῳ ὀλίγῳ χρῶ).

[2] 1 Peter iv. 3 ἀρκετὸς γὰρ ὁ παρεληλυθὼς χρόνος τὸ βούλημα τῶν ἐθνῶν κατειργάσθαι, πεπορευμένους ἐν οἰνοφλυγίαις.

[3] Gal. v. 19 ff. τὰ ἔργα τῆς σαρκὸς...μέθαι, κῶμοι καὶ τὰ ὅμοια τούτοις.

[4] Jas. v. 13 εὐθυμεῖ τις; ψαλλέτω: cf. 1 Cor. xiv. 15, 26.

[5] Traces of such hymns are probably to be found in Eph. v. 14, 1 Tim. iii. 16.

Part II. vi. limit thanksgiving to moments of exhilaration; in the Spirit all life could be a giving of thanks (*v.* 20).

Yet life in Christ has another aspect; it is a warfare with the powers of evil. And in this also the Spirit bears its part, supplying the soldiers of God with their chief weapon of attack and the Eph. vi. 17 f. power to use it. *Take...the sword of the Spirit, which is God's word* (ῥῆμα)[1], *with all manner of prayer and supplication praying at every season in spirit.* Any utterance of God, whether it comes through a prophet or is addressed directly to the heart, is a sword of the Spirit, through whom it reaches us, to be used for a home-thrust at the powers of evil. But it must be wielded *by way of* (διά) *prayer and supplication*, i.e. prayer rising to the fervency of earnest entreaty. Such prayer, in all its forms, is necessary not at some seasons only but at all. Since the enemy is always with us, the sword must be always in the hands of the Christian soldier, and the prayer which gives it effect in his heart. Both are due to the Holy Spirit; for as it is by the Spirit that God speaks in and to men, so it is by the Spirit that the spirits of men hold communion with God.

2. If the Epistles of the Captivity differ in purpose and tone from St Paul's earlier letters, the Pastoral Epistles are still further removed from them, and it is not difficult to make out a case for the widely accepted view that 1, 2 Timothy and Titus cannot in their present form be attributed to

[1] Cf. Heb. iv. 12.

the author of 1 Thessalonians, 1 and 2 Corinthians, Galatians, and Romans. But the advocates of the non-Pauline origin of the Pastorals are apt to overlook an important element in the controversy. It is forgotten that a writer of St Paul's versatility and genius must have known how to adapt himself to changed circumstances and a new theme. Certainly the purpose of the Pastorals sufficiently accounts for the absence of theological discussion; if we meet with little or no reference to justification by faith or to the inner life of believers, the purpose of these letters explains this circumstance. Yet even in the Pastoral Epistles Pauline theology is not unrepresented, and in particular they contain several characteristic allusions to St Paul's doctrine of the Spirit.

1 Tim. iii. 16.

In 1 Tim. iii. 16 the contrast of flesh and spirit appears in a famous Christological passage. *Great is the Mystery of religion* (τῆς εὐσεβείας), *who was manifested in flesh, was justified in spirit.* The central truth of the Christian Religion is a mystery, a Divine secret, long hidden but now revealed to faith; and this central mystery is the Person[1] who, preexistent and invisible, has been manifested[2] to men in human form, and whose claim to be the Righteous one was made good in the sphere of the spirit, by the force and elevation of His life and death, by the miracle of His resurrection and

[1] τὸ...μυστήριον, ὅς....

[2] With ἐφανερώθη used in reference to the Incarnation compare 1 Jo. i. 2, iii. 5, 8.

 ascension[1]. 'Spirit' is here, as in Rom. i. 4, the human spirit of our Lord, in union with the Divine, and filled with the Holy Spirit which anointed Him for His Messianic work.

Several passages in the Pastoral Epistles speak of the work of the Holy Spirit in the prophetic utterances of the Apostolic Church. Thus in 1 Tim. iv. 1, *The Spirit expressly* (ῥητῶς) *says that in the latter times some shall apostatize from the faith, giving heed to deceiving spirits and teachings of demons*, there can be little doubt that a Christian prophecy is cited, whether we have here the very words of an utterance which had impressed itself on the mind of the Church and become a tradition, or only the substance of words such as might often be heard in the churches from members of the prophetic order. Further on in the same chapter (*v.* 14) Timothy is reminded of the part which the prophetic Spirit had borne in his own ordination: *neglect not the gift that is in thee, which was given thee through prophecy with laying on of the hands of the presbytery*. The words 'through prophecy' (διὰ προφητείας) are best explained by the reference in ch. i. 18 to *the prophecies that led the way to* Timothy, i.e. that marked him out for the future companion of St Paul and led to his ordination to that work. It is true that in the Acts no mention is made either of the presence of prophets at Derbe or Lystra at the time when Timothy went forth with St Paul, or of any formal ordination by the

1 Tim. iv. 1.

1 Tim. iv. 14.

[1] Cf. Rom. i. 4, viii. 11.

presbytery acting in concert with St Paul in the laying on of hands. But the scene described in the Epistles to Timothy accords with the account of a primitive ordination given in Acts xiii. At Derbe as at Antioch the first step may have been taken at the suggestion of a prophet or prophets, who speaking in the Spirit pointed out Timothy as the future colleague of Paul and Silas[1]. Paul on his part accepted Timothy[2]: the elders of the local Church joined with the Apostle in the solemn imposition of hands, and the heavenly spark was imparted which needed only from time to time to be fanned into a flame[3].

2 Tim. i. 7.

The nature of this ordination gift is defined in 2 Tim. i. 7. After speaking of the *charisma* which was in Timothy through the laying on of his hands the Apostle proceeds: *for God gave us not a spirit of cowardice, but a spirit of power and love and discipline* (σωφρονισμοῦ). The last word is of doubtful interpretation; if it is to be taken intransitively, it will mean *a sound mind* (A.V.) or rather 'sobriety of mind,' 'self control[4].' But in the few other instances where σωφρονισμός occurs in literature, it bears the transitive sense 'chastening,' 'discipline[5],' and this is supported by the use of the

[1] 1 Tim. i. 18, iv. 18.

[2] Acts xvi. 3 τοῦτον ἠθέλησεν ὁ Παῦλος σὺν αὐτῷ ἐξελθεῖν.

[3] 2 Tim. i. 6 ἀναμιμνήσκω σοι ἀναζωπυρεῖν τὸ χάρισμα. On the whole passage see Hort, *Ecclesia*, p. 181 f.

[4] So Bp Ellicott *ad loc.*; cf. Vulg. *sobrietatis*.

[5] Plutarch, *Cato maior* 5 ἐπὶ σωφρονισμῷ τῶν ἄλλων, Joseph.

Part II. vi.

cognate verb in Tit. ii. 4[1]. The ministerial spirit, St Paul would say, is not that of the weakling who refrains from speaking the truth because it is distasteful and will provoke resentment, but that of the strong man who can exercise discipline without abandoning love[2]. For discipline there was doubtless frequent occasion in the churches newly gathered from heathenism; and there was no part of the apostle's or the evangelist's work which needed more urgently a special endowment of the Spirit of Christ. Another difficult duty which fell to the lot of the first preachers of the Gospel was to *guard the good deposit* of Christian truth (2 Tim. i. 14; cf. 1 Tim. vi. 20) against the attacks open or insidious of the false teachers who abounded in the Apostolic age. This also must be done, St Paul is careful to say, *through the Holy Spirit which dwells in us*. *In us* may mean 'in all believers[3],' but in this context it is more probably 'in you and me, who have been *put in trust with the Gospel*[4] and specially endowed with the Spirit for the fulfilling of our charge.'

Tit. iii. 4.

However this may be, there is at least one clear reference in the Pastoral Epistles to the work which the Spirit accomplishes in all the members of Christ. In Tit. iii. 4 ff., a passage full of Pauline ideas, we

Antt. xvii. 9. 2 ἐπὶ σωφρονισμῷ καὶ ἀποτροπῇ (similarly *B. J.* ii. 13). At Athens a trainer of *Ephebi* was known as σωφρονιστής.

[1] ἵνα σωφρονίζουσι τὰς νέας.

[2] Cf. Apoc. iii. 19 ἐγὼ ὅσους ἐὰν φιλῶ ἐλέγχω καὶ παιδεύω.

[3] Cf. Rom. viii. 11.

[4] Cf. Gal. ii. 7, 1 Thess. ii. 4, 1 Tim. i. 11, Tit. i. 3.

read: *When the goodness and the philanthropy of our Saviour God appeared*, it was *not on the ground of works* (οὐκ ἐξ ἔργων) *that were in righteousness, which we* (ἡμεῖς) *did, but according to his mercy* that *he saved us, through a washing of second birth and renewal of Holy Spirit*[1], *which he poured out upon us richly through Jesus Christ our Saviour; that, justified by his* (ἐκείνου, God's) *grace, we might become heirs according to hope*, the hope *of an eternal life*. 'God, of His generous bounty (χρηστότης) and His special love for our race (φιλανθρωπία), saved us by a pure act of mercy, without an equivalent of righteous actions on our part. He saved us through a sacramental washing[2] which He was pleased to make the sign and means of a second birth[3] and a renewed life[4], wrought in us by the gift of the Holy Spirit which was abundantly bestowed upon the Church through Christ.' No context in the New Testament exhibits more clearly the place

[1] The construction is ambiguous. Πνεύματος ἁγίου is the genitive of the agent and qualifies ἀνακαινώσεως, but it remains uncertain whether ἀνακαινώσεως depends on διά or on λουτροῦ, i.e. whether regeneration and renewal are regarded as two separate acts or processes, or are both sacramentally included in the baptismal washing. The latter is the interpretation adopted by the Vulgate (*per lavacrum regenerationis et renovationis*), the former is supported by codd. D*EFG which repeat διά before ἀνακαινώσεως. On the whole perhaps it is simpler to treat both genitives as marking the contents of spiritual baptism; it involves not only a new birth but a new life.

[2] Cf. Eph. v. 26 καθαρίσας τῷ λουτρῷ τοῦ ὕδατος ἐν ῥήματι.

[3] Cf. Jo. iii. 5 ff., and for the word, Mt. xix. 28.

[4] Cf. Rom. xii. 2, Col. iii. 10.

Part II. vi. of the Spirit in the economy of human salvation; its relation to the justifying grace of God, the redeeming work of our Lord, the sacramental life of the baptized, the eternal life of the saved. No words could more fitly conclude an examination of St Paul's teaching upon the subject of this book. It is here summed up in a single sentence and correlated with the other main features in Pauline theology.

3. There remains an Epistle which it is convenient to consider here, although its attribution to St Paul was doubted in ancient times and has been abandoned by modern scholarship. If Hebrews has no claim to rank as a Pauline Epistle, yet it has affinities to the Pauline writings which justify us in treating it as an appendix to them.

In the judgement of Origen the Epistle to the Hebrews is not inferior in point of thought to the Apostolic writings; "the thoughts are St Paul's," if the wording and composition are those of a disciple rather than of the master[1]." A closer examination of the Epistle has shewn that though there is "a sense in which Origen is right," the writer of Hebrews "approaches each topic from a different side from that which would have been St Paul's[2]." It may be added that there are topics that meet us everywhere in the genuine writings of St Paul upon which this writer barely touches. In

[1] Eus. *H. E.* vi. 25 τὰ νοήματα οὐ δεύτερα τῶν ἀποστολικῶν γραμμάτων...τὰ μὲν νοήματα τοῦ ἀποστόλου ἐστίν, κτλ.

[2] Westcott, *Hebrews*, p. lxxviii.

Hebrews there is no theology of the Spirit[1]. The historical fact of the outpouring of the Spirit on the Church is mentioned more than once, but there is no reference to Christian prophecy, no working out of the relation which the Spirit bears to the Christian life; and it is chiefly as the inspirer of the Old Testament Scriptures that the Spirit is mentioned by this writer. When it is remembered that Hebrews is but little shorter than Romans or 1 Corinthians, its comparative silence in regard to the work of the Holy Spirit is remarkable, even if we make due allowance for the absorbing interest of its great subject, the Person and High Priesthood of the Son. Part II. vi.

The Spirit is first named in ch. ii. 4, where its workings are regarded as an evidence of the truth of the Gospel. *God added his witness*, witnessing *with the first preachers* of the word *by signs and wonders and various works of power and by distributions*[2] (μερισμοῖς) *of Holy Spirit according to his will.* The writer perhaps has in mind the tongues of fire distributing themselves among the company at the Pentecost; possibly also he recalls St Paul's words as to the Spirit dividing its gifts *to each one severally as he will.* But the conception is not quite the same as St Paul's; in Hebrews it is God who divides the gifts of the Spirit. Heb. ii. 4. 1 Cor. xii. 11.

[1] Westcott (p. 331) finds a reason for this in the design of the Epistle: "the action of the Holy Spirit falls into the background ...from the characteristic view which is given of the priestly work of Christ."

[2] Cf. Acts ii. 3, 1 Cor. xii. 4, 11, Apoc. i. 4.

Part II. vi.

Heb. vi. 4 ff.

There is a second reference to the distribution of the Spirit among the baptized in ch. vi. 4. For *those who were once for all enlightened*[1] *and tasted the heavenly gift and became partakers of Holy Spirit and tasted*[2] *God's good word* (ῥῆμα) *and powers of a future age, and fell away, it is impossible again to renew them unto repentance.* To the convert of the first age Baptism brought a whole circle of new experiences which are here described in an ascending order. There came to him the breaking of a new light upon the mind: a conviction of the reality and glory of the gift which had come from heaven in the person of Jesus Christ, a consciousness of possessing a share in the life and power of the Spirit of Christ, and as the Spirit wrought upon him, a growing sense of the beauty of the Divine word and of the nearness and strength of the invisible order. The whole constituted a body of evidence derived from personal knowledge which could not be rejected without a deliberate sinning against conscience; and such a sin the writer despaired of being able to reduce to repentance by any words that he could find.

Heb. x. 29.

Similarly in Heb. x. 29 the apostate is said to have *outraged the Spirit of grace* (τὸ πνεῦμα τῆς χάριτος ἐνυβρίσας). Apostacy is an act of ὕβρις, an insult to the Holy Presence which is the seal and

[1] Cf. Heb. x. 32. In Eph. i. 18 (πεφωτισμένους τοὺς ὀφθαλμοὺς τῆς καρδίας) the reference is somewhat different.

[2] For γεύεσθαι in this sense see 1 Pet. ii. 3 (Ps. xxxiii. = xxxiv. 9).

manifestation of the Divine favour bestowed upon believers in Christ. The title *Spirit of grace* is unique in the New Testament, but it is used by the prophet Zechariah in a promise[1] which looks forward to Messianic times. This promise has been realized in the experience of the Church; the grace of the Spirit has been poured out upon her. But the Divine gift is forfeited by any member of the Church who by returning to Judaism or heathenism does violence to the august Guest who is the pledge of its bestowal. The teaching is similar to that of Eph. iv. 30, but the case in view is a more extreme one, and the language proportionately stronger.

In another group of passages the Holy Spirit is represented as speaking through the writers of the Old Testament; thus a Psalm is quoted with the formula *as says the Holy Spirit* (iii. 7), and a prophecy with *the Holy Spirit also bears witness to us* (x. 15); an interpretation of a Levitical ordinance, again, is said to give the meaning which the Holy Spirit intended to be attached to it (ix. 8)[2]. The Holy Spirit is here, as in the Old Testament, God Himself in operation; God putting a word into the hearts of the legislators, psalmists, and prophets of Israel. He spoke in them, not as He has spoken

[1] Zech. xii. 10 LXX. ἐκχεῶ ἐπὶ τὸν οἶκον Δαυεὶδ...πνεῦμα χάριτος καὶ οἰκτιρμοῦ (רוּחַ חֵן וְתַחֲנוּנִים).

[2] See Westcott on Heb. iii. 7: "it is characteristic of the Epistle that the words of Holy Scripture are referred to the Divine author and not to the human instrument"; and compare his note "On the use of the O.T. in this Epistle," especially pp. 474 f., 493 f.

Part II. vi. to us in one who was a Son, but as it was possible
Heb. i. 1 f. to speak through servants, in the fragments of a broken and partial revelation, in many modes corresponding to the many stages of the national life. Yet it was the voice of the Spirit of God which they heard, and that voice is heard by believers still as they read Moses and the Law and the Prophets.

Heb. ix. 14. In one remarkable passage the Christ is said to have *through an eternal spirit* (διὰ πνεύματος αἰωνίου) *offered himself an unblemished* sacrifice *to God. Eternal spirit* is anarthrous in the Greek, and it is perhaps overbold to render 'the Eternal Spirit,' as both our English versions do. On the other hand to think here of our Lord's human spirit as "the seat of His Divine Personality[1]" seems too much like an attempt to read the formal theology of a later age into a document of the first century. It is safer not to connect the term definitely either with the Holy Spirit, or with our Lord's human spirit or His Divinity, but to take the words in a more general and non-technical sense. The spirit which impelled our Lord to offer His great sacrifice was not the spirit of the world, narrow, time-bound, but a larger, longer outlook upon the whole of life; the spirit that views all things *sub specie aeternitatis*, that takes its standpoint in the invisible and eternal, and not in this short existence. Through that spirit He was strong to undergo the death of the Cross. As the Priest of the good things to come, He was upheld by a sense of the great issues of life and in

[1] See Westcott, *Hebrews*, p. 262.

view of them could offer up Himself to God. This interpretation of the words does not of course exclude the thought of the Spirit of God acting upon the human spirit of the Redeemer. Such an 'eternal spirit' was in fact due to the interpenetration of His human spirit by the Divine, which enabled His whole manhood to respond to the call of the higher world. In our measure the same spirit is possible for us, *while we look not at things seen but at things not seen; for the things seen are for a season, but the things not seen are eternal.* But in the life of our Lord the 'eternal spirit' was always paramount; while no earthly relation was neglected and no work that the Father had given Him to do here remained undone, the eternal things that are not seen were always in full view. No other power could have upheld Him on His way to the Cross or gained for Him the victory which He won upon it.

Part II. vi.

2 Cor. iv. 18.

VII.

THE TEACHING OF OTHER NEW TESTAMENT WRITINGS.

James iv. Ἢ δοκεῖτε ὅτι κενῶς ἡ γραφὴ λέγει Πρὸς φθόνον ἐπιποθεῖ
5 f. τὸ πνεῦμα ὃ κατῴκισεν ἐν ἡμῖν; μείζονα δὲ δίδωσιν χάριν·
διὸ λέγει Ὁ θεὸς ὑπερηφάνοις ἀντιτάσσεται, ταπεινοῖς δὲ
δίδωσιν χάριν.

1 Pet. i. 1, Ἐκλεκτοῖς παρεπιδήμοις διασπορᾶς......κατὰ πρόγνωσιν
2. θεοῦ πατρός, ἐν ἁγιασμῷ πνεύματος, εἰς ὑπακοὴν καὶ ῥαν-
τισμὸν αἵματος Ἰησοῦ Χριστοῦ.

1 Pet. i. Περὶ ἧς σωτηρίας ἐξεζήτησαν καὶ ἐξηραύνησαν προφῆται
11 f. οἱ περὶ τῆς εἰς ὑμᾶς χάριτος προφητεύσαντες, ἐραυνῶντες
εἰς τίνα ἢ ποῖον καιρὸν ἐδήλου τὸ ἐν αὐτοῖς πνεῦμα Χριστοῦ
προμαρτυρόμενον τὰ εἰς Χριστὸν παθήματα καὶ τὰς μετὰ
ταῦτα δόξας· οἷς ἀπεκαλύφθη ὅτι οὐχ ἑαυτοῖς ὑμῖν δὲ διη-
κόνουν αὐτά, ἃ νῦν ἀνηγγέλη ὑμῖν διὰ τῶν εὐαγγελισαμένων
ὑμᾶς πνεύματι ἁγίῳ ἀποσταλέντι ἀπ᾽ οὐρανοῦ.

1 Pet. iii. 4. Ὁ κρυπτὸς τῆς καρδίας ἄνθρωπος ἐν τῷ ἀφθάρτῳ τοῦ
ἡσυχίου καὶ πραέως πνεύματος.

1 Pet. iii. Θανατωθεὶς μὲν σαρκὶ ζωοποιηθεὶς δὲ πνεύματι.
18.

1 Pet. iv. Τὸ τῆς δόξης καὶ τὸ τοῦ θεοῦ πνεῦμα ἐφ᾽ ὑμᾶς ἀνα-
14. παύεται.

2 Pet. i. 21. Οὐ γὰρ θελήματι ἀνθρώπου ἠνέχθη προφητεία ποτέ,
ἀλλὰ ὑπὸ πνεύματος ἁγίου φερόμενοι ἐλάλησαν ἀπὸ θεοῦ
ἄνθρωποι.

Jude 19 ff. Οὗτοί εἰσιν οἱ ἀποδιορίζοντες, ψυχικοί, πνεῦμα μὴ
ἔχοντες. ὑμεῖς δέ, ἀγαπητοί, ἐποικοδομοῦντες ἑαυτοὺς τῇ
ἁγιωτάτῃ ὑμῶν πίστει, ἐν πνεύματι ἁγίῳ προσευχόμενοι,

ἑαυτοὺς ἐν ἀγάπῃ θεοῦ τηρήσατε προσδεχόμενοι τὸ ἔλεος τοῦ κυρίου ἡμῶν Ἰησοῦ Χριστοῦ εἰς ζωὴν αἰώνιον.

Ὁ τηρῶν τὰς ἐντολὰς αὐτοῦ ἐν αὐτῷ μένει, καὶ αὐτὸς ἐν 1 Jo. iii. 24.
αὐτῷ· καὶ ἐν τούτῳ γινώσκομεν ὅτι μένει ἐν ἡμῖν, ἐκ τοῦ
πνεύματος οὗ ἡμῖν ἔδωκεν.

Μὴ παντὶ πνεύματι πιστεύετε, ἀλλὰ δοκιμάζετε τὰ 1 Jo. iv.
πνεύματα εἰ ἐκ τοῦ θεοῦ ἐστίν· ὅτι πολλοὶ ψευδοπροφῆται 1—6.
ἐξεληλύθασιν εἰς τὸν κόσμον. ἐν τούτῳ γινώσκετε τὸ πνεῦμα τοῦ θεοῦ· πᾶν πνεῦμα ὃ ὁμολογεῖ Ἰησοῦν Χριστὸν ἐν σαρκὶ ἐληλυθότα ἐκ τοῦ θεοῦ ἐστίν, καὶ πᾶν πνεῦμα ὃ μὴ ὁμολογεῖ τὸν Ἰησοῦν ἐκ τοῦ θεοῦ οὐκ ἔστιν· καὶ τοῦτό ἐστιν τὸ τοῦ ἀντιχρίστου...ἐκ τούτου γινώσκομεν τὸ πνεῦμα τῆς ἀληθείας καὶ τὸ πνεῦμα τῆς πλάνης.

Ἐν τούτῳ γινώσκομεν ὅτι ἐν αὐτῷ μένομεν καὶ αὐτὸς ἐν 1 Jo. iv. 13.
ἡμῖν, ὅτι ἐκ τοῦ πνεύματος αὐτοῦ δέδωκεν ἡμῖν.

Οὗτός ἐστιν ὁ ἐλθὼν δι' ὕδατος καὶ αἵματος, Ἰησοῦς 1 Jo. v. 6 f.
Χριστός· οὐκ ἐν τῷ ὕδατι μόνον ἀλλ' ἐν τῷ ὕδατι καὶ ἐν τῷ αἵματι. καὶ τὸ πνεῦμά ἐστιν τὸ μαρτυροῦν, ὅτι τὸ πνεῦμά ἐστιν ἡ ἀλήθεια. ὅτι τρεῖς εἰσὶν οἱ μαρτυροῦντες, τὸ πνεῦμα καὶ τὸ ὕδωρ καὶ τὸ αἷμα, καὶ οἱ τρεῖς εἰς τὸ ἕν εἰσιν.

Χάρις ὑμῖν καὶ εἰρήνη ἀπὸ ὁ ὢν καὶ ὁ ἦν καὶ ὁ ἐρχό- Apoc. i. 4:
μενος, καὶ ἀπὸ τῶν ἑπτὰ πνευμάτων ἃ ἐνώπιον τοῦ θρόνου cf. iii. 1, iv.
αὐτοῦ, καὶ ἀπὸ Ἰησοῦ Χριστοῦ. 5, v. 6.

Ἐγενόμην ἐν πνεύματι ἐν τῇ κυριακῇ ἡμέρᾳ. Apoc. i. 10: cf. iv. 2.

Ὁ ἔχων οὖς ἀκουσάτω τί τὸ πνεῦμα λέγει ταῖς ἐκκλη- Apoc. ii. 7:
σίαις. cf. ii. 11, 17, 29; iii. 6, 13, 22.

Ναί, λέγει τὸ πνεῦμα. Apoc. xiv. 13.

Ἀπήνεγκέν με εἰς ἔρημον ἐν πνεύματι. Apoc. xvii. 3: cf. xxi. 10.

Ἡ γὰρ μαρτυρία Ἰησοῦ ἐστὶν τὸ πνεῦμα τῆς προφη- Apoc. xix.
τείας. 10.

Ὁ θεὸς τῶν πνευμάτων τῶν προφητῶν ἀπέστειλεν τὸν Apoc. xxii.
ἄγγελον αὐτοῦ δεῖξαι τοῖς δούλοις αὐτοῦ ἃ δεῖ γενέσθαι ἐν
τάχει. 6.

Καὶ τὸ πνεῦμα καὶ ἡ νύμφη λέγουσιν Ἔρχου. Apoc. xxii. 17.

Part II. vii.

THE group of letters known as the Catholic Epistles may be regarded as representing the correspondence of the non-Pauline teachers of the Apostolic age. It will be interesting to see how far these letters agree with the Pauline letters in regard to the doctrine of the Holy Spirit; what aspects of the Spirit's work they emphasize; what new lines they mark out in this field of Christian thought and life. It will be convenient to begin with the Epistles of St James, St Peter and St Jude; the Johannine letters will naturally be considered with the Apocalypse of St John.

1. (*a*) The Epistle of St James, which is singularly reticent on Christian topics, contains one reference to the Holy Spirit. It occurs in a passage as to the meaning of which interpreters differ widely. The writer is warning his readers against worldli-

Jas. iv. 4 f. ness. *Whosoever is minded to be a friend of the world constitutes himself an enemy of God. Or suppose you that it is to no purpose that the scripture says,* Πρὸς φθόνον ἐπιποθεῖ τὸ πνεῦμα ὃ κατῴκισεν ἐν ἡμῖν? For the moment the words must be left untranslated, but we shall assume that they are a citation from some inspired writing; the phrase '*the scripture says*' is too well recognized a form of citation to permit us to punctuate as the Revised Version does[1]. If nothing in the Old Testament

[1] "Or think ye that the Scripture speaketh in vain? Doth the Spirit," etc. For (ἡ) γραφὴ λέγει as a *formula citandi* see Jo. xix. 37, Rom. iv. 5, ix. 17, x. 11, xi. 2, Gal. iv. 30, 1 Tim. v. 18; cf. λέγει (sc. ἡ γραφή, or ὁ θεός) in this context (*v.* 6).

comes near enough to the words which follow[1], they must be attributed, it would seem, to some lost Jewish or Christian writing. The latter is suggested by the last four words, if they are to be regarded as part of the scriptural quotation.

To begin with these last words. Whether we read the verb as transitive (κατῴκισεν[2]) or intransitive (κατῴκησεν), 'the Spirit which He made to dwell,' or, 'the Spirit which dwelt,' there is a clear reference to the Spirit of Christ, and the term is in full agreement with the language of St Paul[3], which is seen in this respect to be common to the Pauline and non-Pauline Churches. But what is πρὸς φθόνον ἐπιποθεῖ? The verb is fairly common in the Greek of both the Old and the New Testaments, in the sense of longing or yearning for some object of desire, usually a personal object. The adverbial phrase (πρὸς φθόνον[4]) qualifies this longing; the Spirit of Christ in us longs after us, but jealously, with a love which resents any counteracting force such as the friendship of the world. His attitude towards such an antagonist is not merely ζῆλος but

[1] The nearest approach is made in Gen. vi. 3, if לֹא יָדוֹן means 'shall not strive,' or such a passage as Exod. xx. 5, where ζῆλος is attributed to God.

[2] So codd. ℵAB.

[3] St Paul uses ἐνοικεῖν (Rom. viii. 11, 2 Tim. i. 14) or οἰκεῖν ἐν (Rom. viii. 9, 11, 1 Cor. iii. 16) in reference to the Spirit, and κατοικεῖν of Christ dwelling in the heart by the Spirit (Eph. iii. 17).

[4] Dr J. B. Mayor compares the classical phrases πρὸς ὀργήν, πρὸς βίαν, πρὸς ἡδονήν, etc.

Part II. vii.

φθόνος; His claim upon the allegiance of the human heart is that of one who can brook no rival; there is a righteous jealousy, as there is a righteous wrath, which is worthy of God and indeed is a necessary consequence of the greatness of His love. Any false conception of the Divine Character which might be suggested to the mind is at once dismissed by a second quotation. *But he gives greater grace;*
Prov. iii. 34 (LXX.). *wherefore it says, 'God sets himself against* the *overbearing, but to* the *humble he gives grace.'* 'It is only those who resist God that God resists; men of humble hearts have no cause to fear the jealousy of the Divine Inhabitant, but will find themselves growing in His favour and in the gifts of the Spirit by which that favour is manifested.'

Thus the general sense of the passage seems to be: 'The friends of God cannot also be friends of the world. As the sacred writing says, the Spirit which God has planted within Christians yearns for the whole-hearted devotion of the hearts in which it dwells, with a jealous love which will not tolerate an intruder. But this Divine jealousy is consistent with an ever-growing generosity towards those who surrender themselves to the control of the Holy Spirit that is within them. It is the greatness of God's love towards us which resists the sin that sets itself up against Him, and excludes the friendship of the world from hearts in which His Spirit dwells.'

(*b*) The First Epistle of St Peter has affinities both of thought and diction with St Paul's Epistles, especially with Romans and Ephesians. This is admitted by so cautious a critic as Dr Hort[1], and it is hard to see how it can be denied even by those who are not prepared to allow that there is any literary connexion between these writings. But St Peter's Epistle is no mere imitation, and sheds new light on topics handled by St Paul even when it seems to adopt Pauline phraseology.

Part II. vii.

The Epistle opens with a salutation to *elect sojourners of the Dispersion...according to God the Father's foreknowledge, in sanctification of* the *Spirit, unto obedience and sprinkling of Jesus Christ's blood.* 'In sanctification of the Spirit' (ἐν ἁγιασμῷ πνεύματος) is a Pauline phrase which meets us in the first group of St Paul's Epistles (2 Thess. ii. 13), and in a passage not unlike this: *God chose you from the beginning unto salvation, in sanctification of* the *Spirit and belief of the truth.* But in the present context (1) the reference to the Holy Spirit is placed beyond doubt by the mention of God the Father and of Jesus Christ; and (2) the Holy Spirit's work of sanctifying the elect is brought into more direct connexion with the redeeming work of Christ. God's foreknowledge, as viewed by St Peter, works itself out in the hallowing of the human spirit by the Divine, which leads a man to obey the summons of

1 Pet. i. 1.

[1] On 1 Peter, p. 4: "the Epistle is certainly full of Pauline language and ideas." He adds, however, "But it also differs from St Paul's writings both positively and negatively." Dr Bigg (*St Peter and St Jude*, p. 20) characterizes the resemblances as "quite superficial."

Part II. vii.

the Gospel and to be sprinkled with the Blood of Christ, i.e., to undergo the moral purification[1] which comes from faith in the sacrifice of the Cross when it goes along with loyal obedience to the Lord who bought us with His blood.

1 Pet. i. 11 ff.

A little further on (i. 11) we come to a notable passage on the Christological aspect of ancient prophecy. *Concerning which salvation prophets carefully sought and searched, who prophesied of the grace* in store *for you, searching to what manner of season the Spirit of Christ*[2] *which was in them was pointing when it witnessed beforehand of the sufferings* destined *for Christ and the glories that* came *after these; to whom it was revealed that not to themselves but to you they ministered them; which things were in these days* (νῦν) *reported to you by those who brought you the gospel by a Holy Spirit sent from heaven.* 'The Messianic salvation was, as a matter of fact, foretold by certain of the Old Testament prophets; further, the Spirit of Christ, that Spirit which Jesus Christ Himself received and bestows, and which was already in them as the Spirit of prophecy, testified of the sufferings which were to befall Christ and the glories of His subsequent triumph, leaving only for their own consideration the question of the time, actual or approximate, when these prophecies were to be fulfilled. They

[1] Cf. Heb. x. 21. Dr Hort explains ῥαντισμός differently, referring to Exod. xxiv. 3—8.

[2] Dr Hort translates "the Spirit of Messiah," holding that the anarthrous Χριστός may bear this sense.

knew, however, that their ministry was for the benefit of a future generation rather than of their own; they foresaw the present age with its proclamation of the Gospel brought to you in Gentile lands, and confirmed by a special mission from heaven. What the Spirit long ago foretold in the prophets, a new outpouring of the Holy Spirit has now, through the preachers of the Gospel, announced to the world as fulfilled in the Death, the Resurrection, and the exaltation of the historical person, Jesus Christ.'

Part II. vii.

This context is the *locus classicus* for the New Testament doctrine of Messianic Prophecy[1]. It comes appropriately from the pen of the Apostle who on the day of Pentecost first expounded the Old Testament in the light of the Gospel of Christ.

There is an indirect reference to the Spirit's work of building up the Christian character, when in ch. iii. 4 St Peter speaks of *the hidden man of the heart in the incorruptibility* (τῷ ἀφθάρτῳ) *of the quiet and gentle spirit which is in God's sight* a *costly* ornament. The Apostle had just deprecated the expenditure, common among Gentile women, of time and money upon a personal adornment which was purely external (ὁ ἔξωθεν...κόσμος); against this he sets the adornment of the inner life with the spiritual jewels which no wealth can purchase, and which God only knows how to estimate at their true value. 'Spirit' is here as in Gal. vi. 1

1 Pet. iii. 4.

[1] A good summary of its teaching on this point may be seen in Edghill's *Evidential value of Prophecy*, p. 546 ff.

Part II. vii.

(ἐν πνεύματι πραΰτητος) the tone of the personal life shewing itself in daily conduct. But this is not the result of natural temperament; it is imparted by the Spirit of Christ[1].

1 Pet. iii. 18.

In ch. iii. 18 (*Even Christ died once for all for sins,...put to death on the side of the flesh but made alive on that of* (*the*) *spirit, in which also he took his journey and preached to the spirits in ward*) the 'spirit' seems clearly to be the human spirit of the Lord, as in the relative clause that follows 'the spirits' are the human spirits to which He preached after He had left the body. The 'quickening' to which St Peter refers is the new vital power of which His spirit was conscious when delivered from the burden of the flesh, and the direct reference to the Holy Spirit as the Giver of life which is suggested by the Authorized Version[2] cannot be maintained. Yet here again the quickening of the Lord's human spirit cannot be dissociated from the action of the Divine Spirit which in death as in life was present with it.

1 Pet. iv. 12 ff.

The 'sufferings destined for Christ[3]' were already being extended to His Body, the Church[4]. This, St Peter says, was cause for rejoicing. *If you are reproached in the name of Christ, you are happy* indeed, *because* in that case *the Spirit of glory and the* Spirit *of God rests upon you* (ἐφ' ὑμᾶς ἀναπαύεται)[5];

[1] Cf. Mt. xi. 29 πραΰς εἰμι τῇ καρδίᾳ.

[2] A.V. "quickened by the Spirit; by which also," etc.

[3] 1 Pet. i. 11.

[4] 1 Pet. iv. 13 κοινωνεῖτε τοῖς του̂ Χριστου̂ παθήμασιν.

[5] Cf. Isa. xi. 2 LXX. ἀναπαύσεται ἐπ' αὐτὸν πνεῦμα του̂ θεου̂.

i.e. 'what was said in the Prophets of the Messiah will be true of you also.' St Peter is thinking of Isaiah's great prophecy of Messiah (xi. 2). But he amplifies Isaiah's description of the Spirit; the Spirit as revealed to Christians is the Spirit of glory as well as the Spirit of God. The 'glory' which characterizes the Spirit of Christ makes a strong contrast to the reproach which was heaped on Christians for Christ's sake. There may be a reference to the *glory of the Lord* that filled the tabernacle of the Exodus under the cloud that lay upon it[1]. Even the cloud was lit up as by an inward fire at night. So the Spirit of glory filled the Apostolic Church; even the cloud shone in the night of heathendom with the fire of love which revealed itself in the patience of the saints. Nor was the light a momentary flash which went out in darkness; it rested on the Church so long as she bore the reproach of Christ. Part II. vii.

(*c*) The Second Epistle of St Peter has but one reference to the Holy Spirit, and it is perhaps characteristic of the writer's point of view that this has to do not with the life of the Church, but with the inspiration of the Old Testament prophets.

After describing the Transfiguration, of which St Peter was a witness, the Petrine writer proceeds: *And we have the prophetic word* thus made *more sure; to which* word *you do well to take heed as to a lamp shining in a dark room, until day has dawned and* the *daystar arisen in your hearts; recognizing this first, that no prophecy of Scripture is of private* 2 Pet. i. 19 ff.

[1] Cf. Exod. xl. 34 (28) ff.

Part II. vii.

interpretation; for it was not *by man's will* that any *prophecy was ever brought, but as they were borne along by Holy Spirit men spake from God.*

The general sense of this difficult passage seems to be as follows: The written word of prophecy has been confirmed by the vision of our Lord's glory seen by the three ἐπόπται on the Mount of Transfiguration, and Christians may well trust themselves to its guidance in this dark world till a light has dawned which will render the lamp of an external revelation unnecessary. Meanwhile, however, there is need to be careful in regard to the use to which prophecy is turned. It is not a puzzle which each man may solve as best he can; it has a definite purpose or message which is to be seized and followed. No prophecy in Scripture may be interpreted as each individual pleases; it did not proceed from human volition, but though it was spoken by man prophecy came from God through the breath of the Divine Spirit by which the prophets were carried on their course[1]. The nearest parallel in the New Testament to this view of prophetic inspiration is in 2 Tim. iii. 16 (πᾶσα γραφὴ θεόπνευστος), but that passage does not suggest, as this does, the supersession of the prophet's intellect and will by the action of a superior force. The Petrine writer's teaching on inspiration is more

[1] Compare the addition in cod. D to Acts xv. 29 φερόμενοι ἐν τῷ ἁγίῳ πνεύματι, and for other examples of this use of φέρεσθαι see Job xiii. 25 χόρτῳ φερομένῳ ὑπὸ πνεύματος; Acts ii. 2, where however φέρεσθαι is used of the wind itself. The epithet πνευματοφόρος (אִישׁ רוּחַ) in Hos. ix. 7, Zeph. iii. 4, transfers this conception to the *afflatus* of the prophet; cf. πνευματοφορεῖσθαι, Jer. ii. 24.

in accord with Philo's[1] or with that of the Christian fathers of the second century[2] than with the doctrine of the Apostolic age, and in using it as evidence account must be taken of the possibility that this Epistle may not be a genuine product of the days of St Peter and St Paul[3].

(*d*) The Epistle of Jude also has but one distinct reference to the work of the Holy Spirit. Jude, following or followed by 2 Peter (iii. 3), cites a prophecy which he attributes to the Apostles (*v.* 17 ff.): *They said to you, In the last time there shall be mockers, walking after their own lusts of impieties;* and he proceeds, *These are they who make nice distinctions*[4], *psychic persons such as have no spirit. But ye, beloved, building yourselves on your holiest faith, praying in Holy Spirit, keep yourselves in God's love, awaiting the mercy of our Lord Jesus Christ* which leads *unto eternal life.* On the one hand the writer places before us a type of Christians Jude 19 f.

[1] See p. 5 f.

[2] See, e.g., the passages collected by Bp Westcott in an appendix to the *Canon of the N.T.* Montanism, in claiming inspiration, carried this view to an extreme length which the Church reprobated: cf. Gore in *Lux Mundi*, p. 343.

[3] On the genuineness and date of 2 Peter see Bp Chase in Hastings' *D. B.*, III. p. 817 ff.; Dr J. B. Mayor in *Jude and 2 Peter*, p. cxxvii; Dr Bigg's introduction.

[4] See Mayor's note on ἀποδιορίζοντες. Possibly the distinctions were such as those between πνευματικοί and ψυχικοί, the words being used not as by St Paul in 1 Cor. ii. 14 f., but in a spirit of uncharitable self-exaltation. Those who thus assumed to themselves the style of 'pneumatic' Christians were in truth 'psychic,' and destitute of the Spirit of Christ.

who, while professing to be on a higher plane than their brethren, are in truth under the guidance of their lower rational nature, destitute of spiritual aspirations and intuitions, with no element in their personality that is in fellowship with the Spirit of God. Against these he sets those who hold a faith that demands the strictest sanctity, and build themselves upon it through the spirit of prayer, which is the voice of the Divine Spirit in man[1], and the vigilant self-discipline which preserves the consciousness of the Divine love[2]. The difference between these two classes of believers is not nominal, but vital, and will reveal itself in the day of Christ, for which the truly spiritual wait. In this context the trinitarian form of *v.* 20 (ἐν πνεύματι ἁγίῳ...ἐν ἀγάπῃ θεοῦ...τὸ ἔλεος τοῦ κυρίου ἡμῶν Ἰησοῦ Χριστοῦ) is too manifest to be overlooked. The fellowship of the Spirit, the love of the Father, the mercy of the Son, form, as in other passages in the Epistles, a closely related group[3], the mention of any one of which leads naturally to the mention of the other two. The Spirit in believers leads them to the Father, and the love of the Father issues through the mercy of the Son in the fulness of an enduring life.

[1] Cf. Rom. viii. 26 f., Eph. vi. 18.

[2] Cf. Rom. v. 5.

[3] See 2 Cor. xiii. 14, Eph. iv. 4 ff., 1 Pet. i. 1 f., etc. The order of the Persons differs, and almost every possible arrangement is found: the Son, the Father, the Spirit; the Spirit, the Son, the Father; the Father, the Spirit, the Son; the Spirit, the Father, the Son; the Father, the Son, the Spirit.

Part II. vii.

2. Two Johannine writings remain to be considered, and both are fruitful in contributions to the doctrine of the Holy Spirit.

1 Jo. iii. 24.

(*a*) The first Epistle of St John[1] mentions the Spirit first in ch. iii. 24: *He who keeps his* (God's) *commandments abides in him, and he* (God) *in him; and in this we know that he abides in us, from the Spirit which he gave us* (ἔδωκεν). This is repeated with slight changes in ch. iv. 13: *in this we know that we abide in him and he in us, because he has given* (δέδωκεν) *us of his Spirit.* The abiding fellowship of God with any man[2] and of the man with God becomes a matter of personal knowledge through his possession of the Spirit of God. If we keep God's commandments, the Spirit which we received when we believed and were baptized into Christ remains with us as a permanent gift: its continual presence in our hearts is placed beyond a doubt both by our consciousness of its workings within us, and by the witness of our lives. But the indwelling of the Spirit of God in men is the indwelling of God Himself; for it is by His Spirit that God dwells and works in us. That in one passage God is said to give the Spirit (τὸ πνεῦμα), but in the other a portion or measure of the Spirit (ἐκ τοῦ πνεύματος), is not material; the Spirit was

[1] The Second and Third Epistles of St John—short letters addressed to private friends—contain no direct reference to the Holy Spirit.

[2] See Additional Note on Divine fellowship in Westcott's Commentary on the Epp. of St John (p. 274 ff.).

Part II. vii. given in its fulness, but is received by each man according to his capacity for spiritual gifts.

1 Jo. iv. 1 ff. The greater the significance of the gifts of the Spirit, the more urgent the need of distinguishing between the Spirit of God and spirits which are not of God. And so, immediately after his first mention of the Spirit which God gave us, the writer proceeds: *Believe not every spirit, but test*[1] *the spirits* to see *if they are from God; for many false prophets have gone out into the world.* The prophets and teachers of the Church are not the only missionaries who are abroad; there are false prophets inspired by spirits which are not from God. There is a propaganda of evil as well as of good. Therefore the spiritual forces (τὰ πνεύματα) which are at work in the world must be tried by some test which will reveal their true character, before they can be trusted as manifestations of the Spirit of God. Such a test

1 Jo. iv. 3 ff. can be found. *In this you recognize the Spirit of God. Every spirit which confesses Jesus Christ* as *come in the flesh is from God, and every spirit which confesses not Jesus is not from God; and this is the spirit of the Antichrist, of which you have heard that it is coming, and now it is in the world already... We are from God; he that knows God hears us; he who is not from God hears us not. From this we know the Spirit of the truth and the spirit of error*[2]. The Spirit that issues from God (τὸ ἐκ τοῦ θεοῦ) is 'the

[1] Cf. 1 Thess. v. 21.

[2] Cf. *Test. xii. Patriarch.* Jud. 20 (ed. Charles, p. 95 f.): δύο πνεύματα σχολάζουσι τῷ ἀνθρώπῳ, τὸ τῆς ἀληθείας καὶ τὸ τῆς πλάνης.

Spirit of the truth,' and it cannot but confess the truth. But the central truth is the Person of the Incarnate Lord, Jesus Christ come in the flesh. Here then is to be found the crucial test of spiritual influences; they are of God in so far as they acknowledge Jesus: if they acknowledge Him not[1], they are not of God, they are the workings of the spirit of Antichrist, the power which opposes the Christ of God by substituting for Him some rival force in the region of conscience and thought. St John supplies a crucial test for his own age, when Ebionite and Docetic interpretations of the Person of Jesus were already abroad. It is not, it will be observed, a test of personal character that he offers such as our Lord Himself gives in Mt. vii. 15ff., but one which relates to teaching only. Whatever the personal merits of a teacher may be, he is no true prophet, not taught by the Spirit of Christ, if he propagates error on the vital point of the Lord's Person and His place in human life. The Spirit of Christ is known by the witness which He bears to Christ[2]. A secondary test, but one more easy of application and generally not less sure in its results, is to be found in readiness to accept the testimony of the authorized teachers of the truth. No man who was taught by the Spirit of Christ could reject the witness of His duly accredited messengers.

[1] ὃ μὴ ὁμολογεῖ τὸν Ἰησοῦν. On the reading of the Latin versions (*qui solvit Iesum*) see Additional Note in Westcott, p. 163 ff.

[2] Cf. Jo. xv. 26, xvi. 14; 1 Cor. xii. 3.

Part II. vii.

This is obviously a very important passage for the guidance of the Church in her attitude towards religious teachers. Whether they 'follow with us' or not may be immaterial; whether they hold fast the vital teaching of the Apostolic Church in reference to the Incarnation of our Lord is the criterion by which they must be judged. According as they do this or not their claim to be spiritual men is to be admitted or refused.

And as the true prophet is distinguished by his acknowledgement of the Person of Jesus Christ and his acceptance of the accredited teachers of the Church, so the true Christian is known by his faith in Jesus and love to the children of God (v. 1).

1 Jo. v. 1 ff. *Every one who believes that Jesus is the Christ has been begotten of God*[1], *and every one who loves the begetter loves him who has been begotten of him.* And the life which flows from a Divine birth is a victory, partly accomplished already, partly still in progress[2]: *all that has been begotten of God conquers the world.* Its faith is its victory, for faith realizes in the experience of each believer that conquest of the world which was once for all gained in the life and death of the Lord; *This is the victory that overcame the world* (ἡ νικήσασα), *our faith.* But faith rests on witness, and witness to Jesus is not wanting.

1 Jo. v. 6. *This is he who came by way of water and blood, Jesus Christ; not in the Water only but in the Water and in the Blood.* The Lord's Messianic

[1] Cf. 1 Jo. ii. 29, iii. 9, iv. 9.

[2] Cf. 1 Jo. ii. 13 f., iv. 14 (νενικήκατε); v. 4 (νικᾷ).

course led Him through two baptisms, a baptism of water and a baptism of blood; and each was a witness that He answered to the character of the Christ, and satisfies the needs of men, both as their Teacher and their Sacrifice. But there is a third Witness which confirms and consummates the evidence of the life and death of the Lord. *And the Spirit is that which bears witness* (τὸ μαρτυροῦν), *for the Spirit is the truth.* The gift of the Spirit to the Church is the crowning, abiding, living proof that Jesus is the Christ. The Ministry, the Passion, ought to have sufficed to convince the world. But these belong to history, and the world asks for evidence which is present and tangible. It has received such evidence in the Spirit, which lives and manifestly works in the Body of Christ. It is fitting that the Spirit should be the supreme witness to the Christ, for the Spirit is the very Truth of God, knowing and speaking only the truth. Thus three witnesses agree together to declare Jesus to be the Christ; His baptism with water and the Spirit, with the wondrous Ministry which flowed from it; His baptism with blood, and the conquest over sin and death which was its issue; and chiefest of all, the living Spirit which according to His promise came upon the Church, and still abides with her, the Truth of God's innermost Being testifying day by day in the life of Christendom to the Truth incarnate in Jesus Christ our Lord. He who believes upon the Son of God has this supreme witness in himself; it belongs to the experience of his inner life. The

1 Jo. v. 7.

Part II. vii.

unbeliever lacks this inward testimony of the Spirit, but the external evidence is sufficient to convict him of charging God with untruth. For God Himself speaks to the conscience in the life and death of Jesus and through the continual miracle of the spiritual life which flows from them and is daily seen in the Christian Church.

(*b*) The Apocalypse of St John is in form a letter to the Churches of Asia[1], and as such it opens with a salutation after the manner of the Epistles of St Paul. *John to the seven churches which are in the* Province *Asia: Grace to you and peace from him who is and who was and who is coming, and from the seven spirits which* are *before his throne, and from Jesus Christ.* The grace and peace which in all the Pauline letters to the Churches are invoked as flowing from God the Father and the Lord Jesus Christ[2] are here traced to a threefold source, the Eternal Father, the Incarnate Son, and, placed between Them, the seven spirits before the Father's Throne. Are the 'seven spirits'[3] to be understood as equivalent to the Holy Spirit, the Apocalyptic writer having written ἀπὸ τῶν ἑπτὰ πνευμάτων for ἀπὸ τοῦ ἁγίου πνεύματος for some reason connected with the peculiar purpose and style of his book? Or are the seven spirits to be understood as refer-

Apoc. i. 4 f.

[1] Cf. Apoc. i. 4, xxii. 21.

[2] Compare the opening words of Romans, 1, 2 Corinthians, Galatians, Ephesians, Philippians, Colossians, 1, 2 Thessalonians.

[3] τὰ ἑπτὰ πνεύματα τοῦ θεοῦ occurs again in Apoc. iii. 1, iv. 5, v. 6; in interpreting i. 4 these later passages must be borne in mind.

ring to created or imaginary spirits and not to the Spirit of God? There is support, both ancient and modern, for the view that they are the seven angels of the Presence mentioned in Tobit, and it is slightly in favour of this interpretation that angelic heptads occur elsewhere in this Apocalypse[1]. But the position of these seven spirits between the Eternal Father and the glorified Christ is unsuitable even for the highest of created spirits in a salutation which is in fact a benediction[2]; the adjuration in 1 Tim. v. 21[3] is not a true parallel, for the order is different; and the well-known passage in Justin which seems to class the Spirit of prophecy with the holy angels[4] must not be used to determine the practice of a writer in the New Testament who belonged to the Apostolic age. Furthermore, though the description of the seven spirits as *fiery torches blazing before the throne* (iv. 5) is not inappropriate to angels of the Presence, and the glorified Christ

[1] Tobit xii. 15 εἷς ἐκ τῶν ἑπτὰ ἁγίων ἀγγέλων οἳ προσαναφέρουσιν τὰς προσευχὰς τῶν ἁγίων καὶ εἰσπορεύονται ἐνώπιον τῆς δόξης τοῦ ἁγίου. Cf. Enoch xx. 7. The Apocalypse mentions groups of seven angels in ch. viii. 2 ff. and xv. 1 ff.

[2] See Hort, *Apocalypse* i.—iii. p. 11: "Nothing suggests seven angels or anything of that sort. Evidently the seven spirits are spoken of as in the strictest sense Divine."

[3] διαμαρτύρομαι ἐνώπιον τοῦ θεοῦ καὶ Χριστοῦ Ἰησοῦ καὶ τῶν ἐκλεκτῶν ἀγγέλων does not correlate the elect angels with God and Christ except as belonging to the spiritual order which is invisibly present.

[4] *Apol.* I. 6 ἐκεῖνόν τε καὶ τὸν παρ' αὐτοῦ υἱὸν ἐλθόντα...καὶ τὸν τῶν ἄλλων ἑπομένων καὶ ἐξομοιουμένων ἀγαθῶν ἀγγέλων στρατόν, πνεῦμά τε τὸ προφητικὸν σεβόμεθα καὶ προσκυνοῦμεν.

Part II. vii.

might be represented as using these highest of created intelligences to carry His messages to the world (v. 6), it is not easy to understand why they are described as the *eyes of the Lamb*. The personal relation to the Lord which is implied in this metaphor, and the permanent place in the presence of God assigned to them in their character of blazing lights, are appropriate to the Divine Spirit and wholly unsuitable to created spirits. On the whole, then, it is best to regard the seven spirits of God as answering to the operations or aspects of the One Spirit of God. We have already noticed more than once the use of the plural in connexion with the work of the Holy Spirit, which, one in essence, is manifold in its workings and manifestations[1]. But why is the number seven chosen? As we learn from ch. v. 6 the writer of the Apocalypse has in view the *seven eyes* of Zech. iii. 9, but this reference does not explain the first appearance of the number in ch. i. 4; rather it was the number that suggested the reference to Zechariah. The spirits are seven because the churches are seven. Why seven churches are addressed, neither more nor less, we need not here enquire; but their number being seven, the spirits also are seven; i.e. the Spirit is regarded in its relations to each of them. The Spirit is one (τὸ πνεῦμα)[2], yet in reference to the seven churches

[1] See e.g. 1 Cor. xiv. 12, 32; 1 Jo. iv. 1. The διαιρέσεις χαρισμάτων of 1 Cor. xii. 4, and the πνεύματος ἁγίου μερισμοί of Heb. ii. 4, look the same way.

[2] Cf. ii. 7, etc.

there are seven spirits, for there is one manifestation, one aspect of the Spirit's manifold life for each, according to the needs of each. Part II. vii.

Putting together the four passages where mention is made by the Apocalyptist of the *septiformis Spiritus*, they are seen to yield some important teaching, part of which is new. The Spirit appears in its relation to the ascended Christ as the eyes of the Lamb, the organ by which He exercises His oversight of the world. It is ever before the throne of God, the Light of heaven; and yet it is carrying forward a mission which implies its presence in every region of the earth[1]. Towards the Churches it has a special office, which it fulfils to each Christian community by inspiring it with the special endowments required by special circumstances. The Head of the Church alone possesses the fulness of the Spirit (iii. 1 ὁ ἔχων τὰ ἑπτὰ πνεύματα); but He possesses it in order that He may supply each brotherhood with its own peculiar 'spirit'—its own spiritual character, and its own measure of grace.

A somewhat different conception is conveyed in the refrain (ii. 7, 11, 17, 29, iii. 6, 13, 22), which comes near the end of each of the separate messages to the churches: *He that has an ear, let him hear what the Spirit says to the churches.* Since each message begins with a formula which attributes it to the glorified Christ, the voice of the Spirit is here Apoc. ii. 7, etc.

[1] ἀπεσταλμένοι (*v. l.* ἀπεσταλμένα) εἰς πᾶσαν τὴν γῆν. Cf. Mt. xxviii. 20.

Part II. vii.

identified with the voice of the Christ. The Spirit is the *vicaria vis*[1] of the ascended Christ, but it is not an impersonal force, and not a mere deputy. Its message to the churches is identical with Christ's message, and yet it is its own; *the Spirit speaks* though *not from itself*[2]. It speaks in its essential unity: the seven are one when the churches are addressed in general[3].

Apoc. i. 3, etc.

The Apocalypse concerns itself chiefly with one particular mode by which the Spirit communicated His mind to the Apostolic Church. The Spirit of this book is 'the Spirit of prophecy[4].' Apostles and Prophets are the only ministries recognized in it, and the prophetic order is prominent throughout (i. 3, x. 7, xi. 18, xvi. 6, xviii. 20, 24, xix. 10, xxii. 6, 9). The prophets were members of the congregations who were distinguished by their 'spirits[5],' i.e. by possessing spiritual powers developed in an unusual degree by contact with the Spirit of God in His character as the prophetic Spirit. The process which the prophets underwent is described from the writer's own experience. *I found myself in the Spirit*, he twice relates[6], i.e., in a state of mental

Apoc. i. 10, iv. 2.

[1] Tertullian, *praescr.* 13.

[2] Apoc. xiv. 13, xxii. 17; cf. Jo. xvi. 13.

[3] Each message, notwithstanding its special adaptation to one particular community, is ultimately addressed to all the Asian brotherhoods (τὸ πνεῦμα λέγει ταῖς ἐκκλησίαις).

[4] τὸ πνεῦμα τῆς προφητείας (xix. 10).

[5] Apoc. xxii. 6 θεὸς τῶν πνευμάτων τῶν προφητῶν. Cf. 1 Cor. xii. 10, xiv. 12, 32, 1 Jo. iv. 1.

[6] ἐγενόμην ἐν πνεύματι. Cf. Acts xxii. 17 ἐγένετο...γενέσθαι με ἐν ἐκστάσει.

exaltation, in which "the ordinary faculties of the flesh are suspended, and inward senses opened[1]." In this condition his local surroundings were suddenly changed, or he became conscious of sights and sounds which to other men were invisible and inaudible. Thus in his first vision St John sees and hears the glorified Lord; in the second, he looks through the open door of Heaven and beholds the glory of God; later in the book he is transported[2] at one time into a wilderness (xvii. 3), at another to a high mountain (xxi. 10), and on both occasions his eyes are opened to new wonders.

But the 'ecstasy' was not the only manifestation of the prophetic Spirit, and perhaps not the ordinary one. The Spirit in the prophets of the later Apostolic Church was evidently the source of the higher Christian teaching in the congregations to which they ministered. There is no trace in the Apocalypse of any such abuse of prophetic powers as is implied in St Paul's account of the assemblies at Corinth. Forty years had passed since 1 Corinthians was written; and prophecy, in the Asian Churches at least, had entered on another stage, in which it fulfilled its purpose by serving the highest ends. The order of Prophets knew itself now to be charged with the great duty of bearing witness to Jesus, the very function of the Spirit itself; for, as St John adds, *the witness of Jesus is the Spirit of* Apoc. xix. 10.

[1] Hort, *Apocalypse*, p. 15.

[2] Cf. Ezek. xxxvii. 1, Bel 36 (LXX.); Gospel acc. to the Hebrews, fragm. ap. Origen *in Joann.*, t. ii. 6; 2 Cor. xii. 2.

Part II. vii.

prophecy[1], i.e. the two are in practice identical. To be a true prophet is to witness to Jesus, and to witness to Jesus is to have the prophetic Spirit; testimony is the *raison d'être* of prophecy.

But the Spirit of the Apocalypse, while it "spoke by the prophets," spoke also in the Church and in each believer, answering the voice of Christ in the prophets. The voice of Christ is heard saying, *Behold I come quickly; the Spirit and the Bride say, Come.* That the hope of the Parousia was still alive at the end of the first century was doubtless due in large measure to the impassioned anticipations of prophets like St John. The Spirit which inspired the prophets responded in the Church, the Bride of Christ. Every believer in the depths of his own heart was ready with the same cry, *Come, Lord Jesus*; and this also was of the Spirit, which *intercedes for the saints according to* the will of *God*[2]. Nor does the Apocalyptist forget the initial work of the Spirit upon those who though not yet of the Church are feeling after God: *he that is athirst, let him come; he that will, let him take the water of life freely.* It is the last echo in the New Testament of the Lord's great offer of grace: *if any man thirst, let him come unto me and drink*[3].

Apoc. xxii. 17, 20.

Our detailed examination of the writings of the New Testament is now ended; but the witness of the

[1] Cf. Jo. xv. 26.
[2] Rom. viii. 26.
[3] Jo. vii. 37.

book as a whole remains to be considered. Hitherto we have dealt with the characteristic presentation of the doctrine of the Holy Spirit in each writing or group of writings; in the case of St Paul it has even been possible to observe the growth of his thought upon the subject during the dozen years or more over which his letters extend. It is, however, not only permissible but necessary also to review the testimony of the New Testament without regard to the attitude of the individual writers. Apart from its canonical authority, the New Testament undoubtedly represents the belief of the Apostolic age, and from the sum of its teaching we gain the best conception that can now be formed of the doctrinal position which was reached by the first generation of believers under the guidance of the Spirit of Jesus Christ.

PART III.

SUMMARY OF THE NEW TESTAMENT DOCTRINE OF THE HOLY SPIRIT.

I. The Spirit of God.

II. The Spirit of Jesus Christ.

III. The Spirit in the Church.

IV. The Spirit and the Ministry.

V. The Spirit and the written word.

VI. The Spirit and the personal life.

VII. The Spirit and the life to come.

λεγέσθω τοίνυν ὑφ᾽ ἡμῶν περὶ ἁγίου πνεύματος μόνα τὰ γεγραμμένα. εἰ δέ τι μὴ γέγραπται, μὴ πολυπραγμονῶμεν. αὐτὸ τὸ πνεῦμα τὸ ἅγιον ἐλάλησε τὰς γραφάς· αὐτὸ καὶ περὶ ἑαυτοῦ εἴρηκεν ὅσα ἐβούλετο ἢ ὅσα ἐχωροῦμεν. λεγέσθω οὖν ἃ εἴρηκεν· ὅσα γὰρ οὐκ εἴρηκεν ἡμεῖς οὐ τολμῶμεν.

Cyril of Jerusalem.

I.

THE SPIRIT OF GOD.

1. 'SPIRIT' in the New Testament covers a wide range of ideas. Once or twice it is used for the wind[1]; once or twice for the animal life of which the breath is the most obvious sign[2]. More commonly it stands for the spiritual side of man's being, his conscious self[3], the will[4], the deeper emotions[5], the seat of the intellectual powers[6], the sphere in which worship and fellowship with God and Christ are enacted[7], the higher rational life as contrasted not only with the life of the body but with the soul (ψυχή)[8]; that in human nature which proclaims men to be the offspring of God, the Father of spirits[9], and which at death passes into His hands[10]. Part III. i.

The word also connotes the spiritual influences which dominate the lives of men, whether for good

[1] Jo. iii. 8, Heb. i. 7.

[2] Jas. ii. 26, Apoc. xi. 11, xiii. 15; cf. 2 Th. ii. 8.

[3] 1 Cor. ii. 11.

[4] Mc. xiv. 38, Acts xix. 21.

[5] Lc. i. 47, Jo. xi. 33, xiii. 21.

[6] Mc. ii. 8, Eph. iv. 23.

[7] Rom. i. 9, Gal. vi. 18, Phil. iv. 23.

[8] 1 Th. v. 23.

[9] Heb. xii. 9.

[10] Lc. xxiii. 46, Acts vii. 59.

Part III. i.

2 Cor. iv. 13. Rom. i. 4. Rom. viii. 15. Eph. i. 17. 1 Cor. iv. 21, Gal. vi. 1. Rom. viii. 2. 2 Tim. i. 7. Rom. xi. 8. 1 Jo. iv. 6. 1 Tim. iv. 1. 1 Cor. ii. 12. Eph. ii. 2. Eph. vi. 12.

or for evil. Thus the New Testament recognizes a *spirit of holiness*, a *spirit of faith*, a *spirit of adoption*, a *spirit of wisdom and revelation*, a *spirit of meekness*, a *spirit of life*, a *spirit of power*; and on the other hand, a *spirit of cowardice*, a *spirit of slavery*, a *spirit of slumber*, a *spirit of error*. In the thought of the Apostolic age the spiritual forces of evil take shape in the form of personal or quasi-personal existences; thus we hear not only of a *spirit of error* (πνεῦμα πλάνης), but of *deceiving spirits* (πνεύματα πλάνα); the Epistles speak of *the spirit of the world, the spirit that now works in the children of disobedience, the world-rulers of this darkness. the spiritualities* (τὰ πνευματικά) *of wickedness in the heavenlies*. In the Synoptic Gospels, the Acts, and the Apocalypse, these perverted spiritual powers appear constantly as impure (ἀκάθαρτα)[1] or bad (πονηρά)[2] spirits, or as 'demons' (δαιμόνια, δαίμονες[3]), and they are associated with the infliction of physical diseases[4] from which the sufferers were set free by the superior spiritual power which dwelt in the Christ and, by His gift, in the Apostles. There was a disposition to see the handiwork of these evil spirits in the immoralities of heathendom, and to regard its images of the gods as representing their activities[5]; in one passage the mantic art of a

[1] E.g. Mc. i. 23, 26.

[2] Acts xix. 12 ff.

[3] The latter only in Mt. viii. 31.

[4] Cf. Mc. ix. 17, 25 ἄλαλον καὶ κωφὸν πνεῦμα. Lc. xiii. 11 πνεῦμα ἀσθενείας.

[5] 1 Cor. x. 20; cf. Apoc. xvi. 14.

ventriloquist is ascribed to *a python-spirit*[1]. As the pagan world presented itself to early Christian thought, its atmosphere was seen to be full of evil forces, of spiritual incorporeal natures which, though beaten back by the Gospel, perpetually assailed the Church and sought to regain their hold upon her members. Against these were arrayed on the side of goodness and truth an innumerable host of pure spirits, 'liturgic' powers, whose mission it was to minister[2] to the tempted members of Christ's Body as in the days of His flesh they had ministered to the Lord Himself[3]. And about the Church was an ever-growing concourse of human spirits, spirits of righteous men made perfect, spectators of the course which the imperfect have yet to run[4].

Part III. i.

Acts xvi. 16.

2. But the ultimate antagonist of evil and source of goodness in the world is the Divine Spirit itself. For as there is a *spirit of man which is in him*, so there is a Spirit of God, a Divine Selfconsciousness and Selfknowledge which searches the very depths of the Infinite Nature that no creature can explore, and at the same time issues forth from God (τὸ ἐκ τοῦ θεοῦ), and is operative in the world. For this supreme spiritual Power the New Testament has several names, each of which has its own significance. It is *the Spirit of God* (τὸ πνεῦμα τοῦ θεοῦ, πνεῦμα

1 Cor. ii. 10 f.

1 Cor. ii. 14, vii. 40.

[1] ἔχουσα πνεῦμα πύθωνα, μαντευομένη, i.e. she was believed to possess a spirit of divination. Cf. Plutarch, *defect. orac.* 9 τοὺς ἐγγαστριμύθους...νῦν...πύθωνας προσαγορευομένους.

[2] Heb. i. 7, 14, xii. 22. [3] Mc. i. 13.

[4] Heb. xii. 1, 23.

Part III. i.

Acts v. 9, viii. 39, 2 Cor. iii. 17. Lc. x. 21, Acts i. 8, Rom. xiv. 17.

θεοῦ) or *of the Lord* (πνεῦμα Κυρίου), *the Holy Spirit* (τὸ πνεῦμα τὸ ἅγιον, τὸ ἅγιον πνεῦμα, or πνεῦμα ἅγιον), or simply *the Spirit* or *Spirit*, *par excellence* (τὸ πνεῦμα, πνεῦμα)[1]. All these designations had been used by the LXX., but in different proportions; in the Old Testament *the Spirit of the Lord* (Jahveh) is the prevalent form, and *the Spirit of God* (Elohim) next in frequency, while *the Holy Spirit* is rare[2]. In the New Testament, on the other hand, *the Holy Spirit* predominates, occurring 88 times, and *the Spirit of God* or *of the Lord* is found but seldom in comparison, about 25 times in all. 'The Spirit,' without any defining genitive or adjective, is rarely found in the Old Testament[3]; in the New Testament it is used to denote the Divine Spirit in 46 passages, not taking into account the numerous instances in which 'Spirit' without the article seems to stand for the working of the Spirit of God upon the spirit of man.

3. These figures are not without importance, for they reveal a change in the point of view from which the Divine Spirit is regarded by writers who lived after the Incarnation. (1) The New Testament gives prominence to the ethical side of the Spirit's nature and work which is expressed by the name 'Holy Spirit.' This is emphasized by the omission of the pronoun which accompanies the name when

[1] E.g. Mc. i. 12.

[2] It occurs only in Ps. li. 11, Isa. lxiii. 10 f.; cf. Dan. iv. 5 (Th.), v. 12 (LXX.), vi. 3 (LXX.), Sus. 45 (Th.), Sap. i. 5, ix. 17.

[3] I.e. in Num. xi. 26, xxvii. 18, and in Ezekiel (viii. 3 etc.).

it is used in the Old Testament. In Psalm li. 11 and Isaiah lxiii. 10 the Hebrew has *the spirit of thy* (*his*) *holiness*, and the LXX. faithfully reproduces the pronoun in both passages[1]. In the New Testament, on the contrary, it is but very occasionally that we read of *the Holy Spirit of God*[2]. The 'Holy Spirit' is sufficiently definite—the Spirit that is essentially, characteristically, uniquely holy; which being holy breathes the atmosphere of holiness into any spiritual nature that it enters and inhabits. (2) The prevalence in the New Testament of the yet simpler designation 'the Spirit' or even 'Spirit,' without the article, which in St Paul[3] and St John is almost the normal expression for the Divine Spirit when regarded as operative in the Church or in the individual human life, is significant of the new place which the Holy Spirit had come to fill in the experience of life. The presence and working of the Spirit of God are no longer conceived of as rare and isolated phenomena, but as entering into all Christian thought and work, an element in life so universal, so constantly meeting the observer, that the briefest of names was sufficient to indicate it.

Part III. i.

Eph. iv. 30, 1 Th. iv. 8.

[1] τὸ πνεῦμά σου τὸ ἅγιον, τὸ πνεῦμα τὸ ἅγιον αὐτοῦ. In Isa. lxiii. 11, however, the LXX. drops αὐτοῦ, but the suffix is given by the present Hebrew text.

[2] Later Jewish use employs רוּחַ קֻדְשָׁא as equivalent to רוּחַ אֱלֹהִים; see Dalman, *Words of Jesus*, p. 202 f. For the transition see Dan. v. 11 θ′ πνεῦμα θεοῦ (+ ἅγιον AQ), ο′ πνεῦμα ἅγιον, vi. 3 θ′ πνεῦμα περισσόν, ο′ πνεῦμα ἅγιον (יַתִּירָא).

[3] τὸ πνεῦμα or πνεῦμα occurs in St Paul nearly 50 times, and in St John (Ev., Epp., Apoc.) nearly 30 times.

Part III. i. When the Spirit was named every Christian reader would think at once of the Holy Spirit, unless the immediate context decided otherwise. 'Spirit' without the article is often ambiguous[1], but the ambiguity is one which could not have been altogether avoided, because it lies deeper than words—in the intimate relation and interaction of the human and the Divine within the spiritual life.

4. The Holy Spirit in the New Testament and more especially in the Epistles is regarded chiefly in relation to the Church and the Christian life, and the question of the Spirit's relation to God is never formally raised, and receives only a partial answer. It is clear indeed that in the New Testament as in the Old the Holy Spirit belongs to the sphere of the Divine and the uncreated. The Spirit of God which searches the depths and knows the heart of God is Divine, as the spirit of man is human. The Arian representation of the Spirit as a 'creature' and even 'the creature of a creature[2]' finds no support in Biblical theology, and is inconsistent with the whole conception of the Spirit's mission and work as it is unfolded by the writers of the New Testament. If the Holy Spirit does not receive the name of God, if there is no statement in regard to the godhead of the Spirit which corresponds to St John's *θεὸς ἦν ὁ λόγος* or to St Paul's *ἐν μορφῇ θεοῦ ὑπάρχων*, the fact is implied in passages which attribute to the Spirit the Divine prerogatives: in the remarkable

[1] See Additional Note O, 'Spirit' and 'the Spirit' (p. 397 f.).

[2] *κτίσμα, κτίσμα κτίσματος*. Cf. Epiph. *haer.* lxxvi. 3.

saying of our Lord about the unpardonable sin; in St Peter's representation of an attempt to deceive the Holy Spirit as 'lying unto God'; in St Paul's description of the Church and even of the body of the baptized Christian as a sanctuary of God, seeing that the Spirit of God dwells in them. But the divinity of the Spirit does not rest on isolated sayings; it is involved in the view which is given of the Spirit's work considered as a whole. The spiritual Power which is immanent in God and by His gift in men; which regenerates, renews, sanctifies, teaches, guides, supports, strengthens all believers, and convicts the unbelieving world, cannot but be Divine. In the New Testament as in the Old the Spirit of God is God at work in the world, with this difference only that the field of His spiritual operations is vastly widened, and the manifestations of Divine power and wisdom connected with the Spirit are proportionately more impressive and more permanent.

Part III. i.

Acts v. 3 f.

1 Cor. iii. 16, vi. 19.

5. Thus the Spirit of God is beyond doubt differentiated from all created life. Is it also differentiated from God Himself? *God is spirit*; is the Spirit of God God, in such a sense that the conceptions are absolutely interchangeable? To this question the New Testament seems to give a negative answer. For the Spirit proceeds from God, is sent by God, is God's gift to the Church and to the individual believer. Here a distinction is clearly drawn between the Giver and the Gift, and a like distinction is seen in the relative functions ascribed to the Spirit and to

Jo. iv. 24.

Part III. i.

Rom. viii. 27.

God; as for example where the Spirit is said to intercede for the saints according to the will of God, while the Searcher of hearts understands what the Spirit desires, seeing that the intercession is made by His own appointment. This is but one instance of many in which the Spirit of God is distinguished from God in regard to the offices which it fulfils. The differentiation is more complete in passages where God is called the Father, and the Father and the Son are coordinated or contrasted with the Spirit; as in the Johannine promises of the Paraclete, and the words in which, according to the first Gospel, our Lord instituted Christian Baptism. The distinction which in such passages is clearly drawn between the Father, the Son, and the Spirit, when it is taken together with the personal attributes which are assigned to each, points to some profound mystery in the Being of God which makes it possible to say, as the Church says, 'The Spirit of God is God, yet not the Father nor the Son.' And if so, we seem to be forced to admit a threefold personality in God, and a personal life of the Holy Spirit which is its own. But the New Testament does not pursue this line of thought; the ideas of personality and of tripersonality are foreign to its intensely practical purpose, and in its nearest approaches to a metaphysical theology it stops short at such a revelation of God—Father, Son, and Spirit—as answers to the needs and corresponds with the facts of the spiritual life in man.

6. But though the Holy Spirit is not definitely

hypostatized in the New Testament, as a person in the unity of a tripersonal Essence, personal qualities are freely attributed to it as an agent in the field of human experience. Even the Old Testament represents the Spirit as speaking by the prophets, and as grieved by the sin or indifference of men[1]. In the Acts and Epistles this is carried much further[2]; the Spirit is said to be tempted and resisted; it can send men forth to a new work, or forbid them to enter on it; it can bear witness, it can intercede, it can endow men with its gifts, distributing to each severally as it wills. Is this mere personification, due to the habit of regarding the Spirit as the energy of the Living God[3]? can we attach any further significance to it in view of the still larger class of passages where the Spirit is treated as the breath that fills, the unction that anoints, the fire that lights and heats, the water that is poured out, the gift in which all believers partake? Or are these impersonal representations to be explained as belonging only to the temporal manifestation of an Eternal Spirit, which in its gifts and working is as breath or unction, fire or water, but in its essence is a centre of conscious personal life? That the

[1] 2 Sam. xxiii. 2, Isa. lxiii. 10.

[2] Acts v. 9, vii. 51, xiii. 4, xvi. 6, xx. 23; Rom. viii. 26, 1 Cor. xii. 7—11.

[3] I. V. Wood, *The Spirit of God in Biblical Literature*, p. 227: "Certainly it was personal, for God is personal." But the question is whether the N. T. represents the Spirit *qua* Spirit as personal, i.e., as a selfconscious subject. On St Paul's attitude towards this question see Stevens, *Theology of the N. T.*, p. 443 ff.

Part III. i.

latter is the true interpretation of the facts seems to follow from the great context in the fourth Gospel where the Spirit is represented as *another Paraclete*. It may be possible to exaggerate the force of the masculine παράκλητος and the corresponding masculine pronoun (ἐκεῖνος)[1], just as it is possible to make too much of the neuter gender of πνεῦμα or of the feminine gender of *rûaḥ*. But it cannot be doubted that throughout the whole discourse the *rôle* of a personal advocate is ascribed to the Spirit. He takes the place of the absent Christ. He is sent by Christ from the Father, and when He has come He will guide believers as Christ had guided them hitherto, will teach as Christ taught, will take of that which is Christ's and declare it to them, will convict the world which the ministry of the Christ failed to convict. That this advocate will be invisible and purely spiritual does not make against His personality; it is in that which is most spiritual in ourselves that we find evidence of our own personal life. That He fulfils the whole of our Lord's personal functions towards the Church, that He belongs to the category of Paraclete—Teacher, Director, Protector, Counsellor—this invests Him with all the essential attributes of that which we understand by personality.

Jo. xiv., xvi.

[1] Yet the choice of ὁ παράκλητος, where τὸ παράκλητον (πνεῦμα) might have been written, is significant; and even more so is the steady use of ἐκεῖνος, e.g. in Jo. xvi. 13 f., where τὸ πνεῦμα would naturally suggest a transition to ἐκεῖνο. ὁ λόγος...ἐκεῖνος (Jo. xii. 48) is scarcely a true parallel.

7. As seen in the New Testament the Spirit of God is the very life and energy of God, issuing from the fountain-head of Deity; the selfconsciousness of God, 'exploring the depths' of the Divine heart and mind; the 'Spirit of the' absolute 'truth,' nay, 'the truth' Itself; the 'finger of God,' by which His work is done in the spiritual world. The life, the consciousness, the truth, the power of God is God; God living, thinking, teaching, working. But God thus manifested is in the thought of the New Testament clearly differentiated from God in His own infinitude, the fountain of the Divine life, the Father, and from God the Word and Son of the Father. The Spirit is neither the Father nor the Son, although He is God. And though in His workings and gifts He is regarded as a power and a gift rather than a person, and described under figures borrowed from external and inanimate nature, yet in His own Divine life it is impossible to doubt that He possesses that which answers in some higher and to us incomprehensible way to personality in man. Even in His relation to the Church and to the world He bears a personal name and fulfils the *rôle* of a personal office. But beyond these lines of thought the Apostolic age did not penetrate. It was occupied with the appreciation of the Spirit's work rather than with the doctrine of His Person or of His relation to the Father and the Son. The Christology of the first century is more advanced than its Pneumatology; partly because, while the questions which arose in the Apostolic Church compelled its leaders to

1 Cor. ii. 10.

Jo. xiv. 17. 1 Jo. v. 6. Lc. xi. 20.

Part III. i. examine the nature of the Son, no controversy had as yet arisen in reference to the Holy Spirit; partly and perhaps chiefly because the Spirit had come to
Jo. xvi. 14. glorify Jesus, and not to direct attention to His own relation to God.

II.

THE SPIRIT OF JESUS CHRIST.

THE New Testament, as it speaks of the Spirit of God, speaks also of the Spirit of Jesus[1], of Christ[2], and of Jesus Christ[3]. The Spirit of the Father[4] is also the Spirit of His Son[5]. These designations clearly indicate a relation between our Lord and the Holy Spirit which is not shared by the members of the Church. The Spirit is not correlated in like manner with any other name. Part III. ii.

What is the teaching of the Apostolic age as to this unique relation of Jesus Christ to the Spirit of God?

1. Two of the Gospels trace it back to His Conception. *That which was begotten in* Mary was *of Holy Spirit*; the Holy Spirit came upon her, the Power of the Most High overshadowed her in such wise that that which was born of her was entitled to be called *holy, son of God.* The incipient humanity of our Lord was 'of the Spirit' on the one hand, as it was of Mary on the other; its substance was hers, Mt. i. 20, Lc. i. 35.

[1] Acts xvi. 7.
[2] Rom. viii. 9, 1 Pet. i. 11.
[3] Phil. i. 19.
[4] Mt. x. 20.
[5] Gal. iv. 6.

but the vitalizing power which brought it into life was His. As in the mystery of natural generation the human father impresses on his child the lineaments of his own character, so by the action on Mary which superseded paternity the Holy Spirit imparted to her son, not the human nature (which was wholly of the Virgin Mother), but the sinless image and likeness of God. The facts are related only by the writers of the first and third Gospels, but they are in the background of St Paul's doctrine of the "Last Adam" or the "Second Man[1]." The Second Man is of heaven; His life was from above, its whole course was a victory over sin, and it issues in the quickening of the race. The Apostle, as his subject requires, hastens on to the magnificent end; the Gospels shew us the beginning. The whole began with a creative act on the part of the Holy Spirit of God. Jesus was in relation with the Divine Spirit from the first moment of His human existence. The Spirit of God was from that moment the Spirit of Jesus, the vivifying sanctifying power by which He entered on His life as the Son of Man and lived it to the end.

2. As the years went by, a fresh relation with the Spirit began. The Spirit of Jesus became the Spirit of the Christ. All the Gospels describe the consecration of Jesus to the Messianic office: how

[1] 1 Cor. xv. 47 ὁ δεύτερος ἄνθρωπος ἐξ οὐρανοῦ. It is not meant that St Paul was aware of the circumstances connected with the Conception. On the Conception as the basis of the new humanity see Gore, *Dissertations*, p. 63 ff.

God anointed Him with the Spirit for the Christ-life. The Christ-life began, as the human life itself began, with a special act of the Holy Spirit. As in the Conception the Spirit descended on Mary, so at the Baptism it descended on her Son, anointing Him to be the Prophet, the Priest, the King. As the Spirit of the Conception gave sweetness and strength to His childhood, youth, and early manhood, so the Spirit of the Baptism gave power to the mature years of the Ministry, to the crisis of the supreme Sacrifice and to the risen life, and gives power to the larger activities of the Lord's present life in Heaven. The Spirit of the Christ is the secret source of the Christ's ceaseless energies: *in the power of the Spirit* explains all—miracles[1], teaching, victory over temptation and death, and that vast authority which He now wields in heaven and on earth.

Part III. ii.

Lc. iv. 14.

3. But as the Baptist already knew, the Christ was not only baptized with the Spirit, but was the true Baptizer; receiving the Spirit without measure in order that He might impart it in measure to His brethren. *He upon whom thou shalt see the Spirit*

Jo. i. 33.

[1] Bishop Weston (*The One Christ*, p. 236 ff.) argues that the activity which effected the miracles was that of the Eternal Son acting through the Spirit under the conditions of manhood, the purpose of the Conception and the Baptism being to give the manhood such spiritual power as would enable it to answer to the calls of the incarnate life. According to this view the miracles are witnesses to (1) the activity of the Divine Son, who "always acts for the Father through the Spirit"; (2) the strengthening and developing of the human faculties by the Spirit to "make them able and fit to assimilate and communicate the Divine power."

Part III. ii. *descending and abiding upon him, the same is he that baptizes in Holy Spirit.* The Spirit of Christ is not only the Spirit that anointed the Christ, but the Spirit with which the Christ anoints. The Epistles of the New Testament, which are silent about the fact of the Lord's Baptism[1], as they are about most of the other facts of the Gospel history, speak freely of the anointing received by all Christians from the Holy One, i.e. the ascended Christ[2]. Perhaps it was because of the witness which it bore to the continuation of the Messianic anointing in the Body of Christ that the Church accepted the name of 'Christian' applied to her by the heathen, although out of reverence for the Lord she did not usually or at first speak of her members as 'Christs[3].'

Even in the Synoptic Gospels the Christ is sometimes represented as preparing His disciples for an era of fuller spiritual life. In the fourth Gospel this extension of the Spirit's work forms the subject of a series of instructions which extends from the third chapter to the last but one. These discourses are in substance the Lord's own comment upon the relation which as the Christ He bears to the Spirit, and which the Spirit bears to Him and His.

[1] Except the allusions in 1 Tim. iii. 16, 1 Jo. v. 6.

[2] 2 Cor. i. 21, 1 Jo. ii. 20, 27.

[3] Those who had received a χρίσμα might well have been called χριστοί. But the New Testament seems to avoid the plural of χριστός, though it is used by the LXX. (1 Chron. xvi. 22, Ps. civ. (cv.) 15), and is sometimes applied to Christians by later writers.

According to the fourth Gospel the Spirit is the principle of spiritual life by which men are born into the Kingdom of God. This new life of the Spirit it belongs to Jesus, in virtue of His own anointing as the Christ, to impart and to maintain. In Him 'the whole fountain of the Holy Spirit[1]' is stored for the use of mankind, and from it He gives the living water to all who ask of Him or come to Him for it. This was said to those who were not even disciples, such as the Samaritan woman, and the mixed crowd in the Temple-courts. A fuller teaching was reserved for the inner circle of His Apostles. On the night before the Passion, in circumstances of peculiar solemnity, the Lord spoke at last of the Spirit's coming as imminent, and revealed the relations in which the Christ-gift stands both to the Father and to Himself. The Father is still the ultimate Source and Giver; He whose love gave the Son gives, in the last resort, the Spirit also[1]. Nevertheless, since the Son is the way and the truth and the life for men, and no man can come to the Father but by Him, the Son will send the Spirit from the Father; i.e. the Spirit will come to men not immediately from the Father, but mediately through the Son. Not only is the Spirit given at the request of Jesus (ἐγὼ ἐρωτήσω) and in His name (ἐν τῷ ὀνόματί μου), but by His act (ἐγὼ πέμψω); He will mediate in the mission of the

Part III. ii.

Jo. iii. 3, 5.

Jo. iv. 14, vii. 37.

Jo. xiv. 16, 26, xv. 26.

[1] *Ev. sec. Hebr.* "descendit fons omnis sancti spiritus et requieuit super eum"; cf. Jo. iii. 34 οὐ γὰρ ἐκ μέτρου δίδωσιν τὸ πνεῦμα [sc. ὁ θεὸς τῷ χριστῷ].

Part III. ii. other Paraclete, and thus will baptize with the Holy Spirit, as He Himself was baptized by the Father[1]. The Paraclete Spirit is the Spirit of Christ not only as received by Christ from the Father, but as bestowed by Christ upon the Church and all her members.

4. But this is not all. The Spirit sent by
Jo. xiv. 16. the Christ is His second Self, ἄλλος παράκλητος, 'another,' distinct from the Paraclete who is taken away, a second of the same and not of a different order[2]. That the second Paraclete is not identical with the first is sufficiently clear from the words *I will send him.* The Spirit is not the Christ, but the Chrism; not the Son, but the Spirit of the Son. Yet the correspondence is so close, the equivalence so complete, that the Lord again and again in this discourse identifies Himself with the Spirit: *I will*
Jo. xiv. 18, xvi. 22, 25. *not leave you bereaved, I come to you...again I shall see you...there comes an hour when I shall no more speak to you in proverbs but shall plainly declare to you concerning the Father.* These words may have an ulterior reference to the Parousia, but it can scarcely be doubted that they point primarily to the coming of the Spirit of Christ in His name. And the measure of identification which they imply is justified by the experience of the Apostolic Church.

[1] ἔχρισεν αὐτὸν ὁ θεός (Acts x. 38).

[2] See Lightfoot on Gal. i. 6 f.: "ἄλλος adds, while ἕτερος distinguishes." On the question whether this distinction holds good in St John see Abbott, *Johannine Grammar*, 2676 f. It is impossible to conceive of ἕτερον παράκλητον standing in this context.

The Spirit in its working was found to be in effect the equivalent of Jesus Christ. Thus St Paul writes, *If any has not Christ's Spirit, that man is not his (Christ's); but if Christ is in you, the body indeed is dead...but the spirit is life...*, where the possession of the Spirit of Christ is clearly regarded as tantamount to an indwelling of Christ Himself[1]. The same line of thought seems to be followed in the words, *The Lord is the Spirit, but where the Spirit of the Lord is, there is liberty.* But *we all... are being transformed...as by the Lord the Spirit*, where 'the Spirit of the Lord' and 'the Lord the Spirit' (i.e. Christ in the power of His glorified life) are viewed as being in practice the same. Men who lived within a short space of time after the Ministry, the Ascension, and the Pentecost realized that where the Spirit was Christ was, and what the Spirit wrought was wrought in fact by Christ. Even in the words spoken by His Spirit through the prophets they recognized the voice of Christ. Though the Spirit of Christ, through whom the glorified Lord comes to His Church[2] and sees as with eyes of flame and works and speaks, is neither the human spirit of Christ, nor the pre-existent Logos who was made flesh, yet it is so absolutely one in will and thought with the Divine-Human Christ that Christ is still in the Spirit present and at work on earth, dwelling in men and revealing Himself to them after a manner more expedient for them than if He were still visibly

Part III. ii.

Rom. viii. 9 f.

2 Cor. iii. 17.

[1] Cf. Eph. iii. 16 f.

[2] Apoc. ii. 1, 7 etc.

Part III. ii. in their midst. Whether this equivalence is due to the perfect interpenetration of the Lord's glorified humanity by the Spirit, or to His oneness with the Spirit in the mystery of the Divine Life, neither St John nor any of the New Testament writers has taught us; the question did not lie within their scope, and possibly does not lie within the grasp of the human mind. The Spirit alone searches the depths of God, and where the Spirit is silent as to their contents it is hazardous and indeed vain to speculate.

5. The Spirit of Jesus, the Spirit of Christ, is
Gal. iv. 6. also described as the Spirit of the Son of God. *God sent forth the Spirit of his Son into your hearts.* The Son is here the Incarnate Son, not the pre-existent Word, and no direct inference can be drawn as to the relation of the Spirit to the Logos. The Spirit of the Son is the perfect spirit of sonship which was manifested in the human life of Jesus Christ. It was this Spirit which made it His meat and drink to do His Father's will, which maintained in Him unbroken fellowship with God, which inspired the supreme cry
Mc. xiv. 36. of filial submission *Abba, Father; not what I will, but what thou.* That which was in Him the Spirit of sonship becomes in His members the Spirit of adoption. Sons such as He is they cannot be, for He is the Only-begotten; adopted sons they can be and are[1], and the Spirit of the Only-begotten has been sent to give them the filial character which was in Him.

[1] 1 Jo. iii. 1.

6. The Spirit is expressly and repeatedly associated with the glorified life of our Lord in Heaven. The Apocalyptic *seven spirits of God*, while they blaze like torches before the Eternal Throne, are at the same time the eyes of the Lamb which are sent forth by Him into all the earth. This figure connects the sevenfold energies of the Spirit with the person of the Ascended Christ. The Spirit *was not* in the world in the fuller sense until Jesus was glorified: *having been by the right hand of God lifted up and having received from the Father the promise of the Holy Spirit, he poured forth* the Pentecostal effusion; *if I depart*, He Himself had said, *I will send him* (the other Paraclete) *unto you.* That in the last days of the Messianic age the Spirit should be poured out not on the prophetic order only but on all the people of Jahveh had been clearly foretold; it was the great promise of the Father, conveyed through Isaiah and Jeremiah, Joel and Zechariah, and on the eve of its fulfilment revived by the Lord Himself. But the gift was kept in the hands of God until it could be claimed by a sinless and victorious humanity: until the Paraclete with the Father obtained from the Father the mission of the second Paraclete who was to abide with men to the end of time. Thus the outpouring of the Spirit was the direct result of the glorification of the Son, and a witness to that great event. Of the Ascension there were few witnesses, and they saw only the form of the Son of Man disappearing in a cloud. Stephen in an ecstasy saw the same form standing at the right hand of God.

Part III. ii.

Apoc. iv. 5, v. 6.

Jo. vii. 39.

Acts ii. 33.

Jo. xvi. 7.

Part III. ii.

Col. iii. 3.

But to the Church in general the exaltation is matter of faith and not of sight: *your life is hid with Christ in God.* Yet in the coming of the Spirit and the life of the Spirit we have a continual witness of the fact; the experience of the Christian life is a daily witness to believers that Jesus Christ is in the presence of God, *ever living to intercede for* men. *The Spirit which* God has *made to dwell in us* is the Spirit of the glorified Lord.

Heb. vii. 25.
Jas. iv. 5.

7. The question will be asked whether the New Testament recognizes an eternal relation between the Only-begotten Son and the Holy Spirit, such as the ancient Church had in view when she spoke of the Spirit as our Lord's 'very own,' or in the West confessed that He 'proceeds from the Son' and not from the Father only[1]. And the answer must be that there is no explicit teaching upon this point in the Apostolic writings. Even the statement that the Holy Spirit proceeds from the Father does not explicitly teach the doctrine of an Eternal Procession as it is conveyed in the modified terms of the Creed[2], while for the Eternal Procession from the Son no direct support from the New Testament has ever been claimed. Nevertheless it is a fair inference from the teaching of the New Testament that the Spirit of God belongs eternally to the Divine Essence, and that the Only-begotten Son who as

[1] Cyril Alex. *anathem.* 9 ἴδιον αὐτοῦ, *Symb. Nicaenum* (in the Ordinary of the Roman Mass): "qui ex patre filioque procedit."

[2] Jo. xv. 26 ὃ παρὰ τοῦ πατρὸς ἐκπορεύεται. The Creed runs: τὸ ἐκ τοῦ πατρὸς ἐκπορευόμενον. Cf. Hort, *Two Dissertations*, p. 86.

the Word was in the beginning with God stands in a timeless relation to the Divine Spirit. If the Spirit of the Father was the Spirit of the Incarnate Son, dominating the whole human life of the Word made flesh, who can doubt that it was also in the most intimate relation with that pre-existent Life which was with the Father before the world was? All this lies in the background of New Testament thought, ready to be drawn into fuller light by the consciousness of the Church as she pondered on her inheritance of Apostolic truth.

III.

THE SPIRIT IN THE CHURCH.

Part III. iii.

—

1. OUR Lord's teaching upon the Holy Spirit touches but rarely and lightly on His own unique endowment with the Spirit. There is no reference in His words to the Holy Conception and scarcely any to the Baptism. On the other hand He spoke freely and sometimes at considerable length of the distribution of His Spirit to the Church. In His earlier references to the Spirit the gift is offered to individuals. *The Father who is of heaven will give Holy Spirit to those who ask him; unless one has been born of water and Spirit, he cannot enter into the kingdom of God; if any thirsts, let him come unto me and drink.* But as the end approached and the Pentecostal effusion drew near, Jesus spoke of the Spirit as to be given to His disciples collectively[1]. The discourse of John xiv.—xvi. was perhaps addressed to the Eleven only, and it might have seemed to them at the time that the promise of the Paraclete was limited to their own body; a similar impression might have been created by the Lord's parting

Lc. xi. 13, Jo. iii. 5, iv. 14, vii. 37 ff.

[1] Jo. xiv.—xvi. (δώσει ὑμῖν, πέμψω ὑμῖν, ὑμᾶς διδάξει, ὁδηγήσει ὑμᾶς, ἀναγγελεῖ ὑμῖν).

words in Acts i. 5, 8. If so, the error was corrected by the course of events. When after the Resurrection the Spirit was given with a sacramental breathing, accompanied by the words which have long been used at ordinations in the West, other believers were present with the Apostles[1], probably all who were then in Jerusalem. Thus the assembly which received the Easter gift of the Spirit was representative of the whole Church, and not of the Apostles only and their successors in the ministry of the Church. The party in the upper room which awaited the coming of the Spirit numbered one hundred and twenty[2], and though the word is not used in the Acts before ch. v. 11, this assembly was in fact the assembled Ecclesia. All were still together when the Spirit came[3], and if each was separately visited[4], the illapse was simultaneous and collective; the Church as a whole received the Paraclete. Such an effusion of the Spirit was vouchsafed only once again, when the firstfruits of the Gentile Church were baptized with the Holy Spirit as the firstfruits of the Jewish Church had been on the day of Pentecost[5]. In all other cases the Spirit came to new converts when they were added to the body of

[1] Lc. xxiv. 33 interprets St John's *οἱ μαθηταί* as *οἱ ἕνδεκα καὶ οἱ σὺν αὐτοῖς*. They were closely packed in the upper room, though it was large: *εὗρον ἠθροισμένους*.

[2] Acts i. 15.

[3] Acts ii. 1 *ἦσαν πάντες ὁμοῦ ἐπὶ τὸ αὐτό*. The reference appears to be to the assembly of i. 15.

[4] ii. 3 *ἐκάθισεν ἐφ' ἕνα ἕκαστον αὐτῶν*.

[5] Acts x. 41 ff., xi. 15 ff., xv. 7 f.

Part III. iii.

the Church by baptism and its complementary rite, the laying on of hands on the baptized[1]. The Spirit was the corporate possession of the Body of Christ, and it became the property of the individual convert when he was made a member of the Ecclesia. No man could be Christ's who had not Christ's Spirit, and ordinarily no man could have Christ's Spirit but by being "added" to the brotherhood of Christ's disciples. When St Peter says that God gave the Holy Spirit "to them that obey Him," the notes of obedience which were in his mind were doubtless the same that he required on the Day of Pentecost, namely repentance, faith, and baptism. The Apostle of the Uncircumcision did not differ herein from the Apostle of the Circumcision, as his conversation with the disciples of the Baptist at Ephesus plainly shews. No gift of the Spirit could be expected, he taught them, until they had been baptized into Christ and made members of His Church[2].

Acts v. 32.

Acts xix. 39.

2. It was given to St Paul beyond the other Apostles to develop the conception of the Christian Ecclesia, and together with it the doctrine of the Spirit's relation to the Church. This is done chiefly in two of his Epistles, 1 Corinthians and Ephesians. In 1 Corinthians it is his aim to check "the excess of individuality" and "the diminished sense of corporate responsibilities[3]" which were due to the temperament

[1] Acts viii. 15 f., xix. 5 f.

[2] In Heb. vi. 1 f. the foundation stones of the Christian life are given in the order μετάνοια, πίστις, βαπτισμοί, ἐπίθεσις χειρῶν.

[3] Hort, *Ecclesia*, p. 129.

of Greek thought and life. He meets these tendencies by setting forth the relation of the Spirit to the Ecclesia. The local congregation of baptized believers is a sanctuary (ναός), in which God dwells by His Spirit; it is a Body of Christ, into which all its members have been admitted by being baptized in one Spirit. Such a community as the Corinthian Church might well create upon the mind of an observer the impression of diversity and not of unity; its social differences, its class distinctions, its variety of spiritual gifts would suggest the presence of incompatible or hostile elements which made corporate life impossible. But no diversities could shake the fundamental unity which comes from the indwelling Spirit; and the multiplicity of the members and the manifoldness of their functions and gifts can no more prevent a Christian Church from being one than the unity of the human body is destroyed by the complexity of its structure.

Part III. iii.

1 Cor. iii. 16.

1 Cor. xii. 13.

The Epistle to the Ephesians carries this argument into a larger field. Here it is not the disparity of gifts or temperaments in a local society that threatens unity, but the strife between Jew and Gentile which affected all Christian societies in the first century. Again the danger of disunion is met by unfolding the work of the Spirit in the Ecclesia. *Through him* (Christ) *we both have our access in one Spirit unto the Father...in whom* (Christ) *each several building*[1]

Eph. ii. 18 ff.

[1] I.e. "each local community" (Hort, *Ecclesia*, p. 164, and so apparently Westcott, *Comm. on Eph.*, ad loc.). Dean Armitage Robinson, while reading πᾶσα οἰκοδομή, supports the rendering of the A. V. (*Ephesians*, pp. 70 f., 164 f.).

Part III. iii.

grows into a holy temple in the Lord...in whom you also are builded together for a habitation of God in the Spirit. Here as in 1 Corinthians (iii. 16) each separate congregation is regarded as a local sanctuary, and the various churches are so many spiritual buildings springing up everywhere throughout the provinces of the Empire, and designed as so many dwelling-places of the Living God. But as the Epistle proceeds, the Apostle sees before him the vision of an Ecclesia which is not limited to a single city or a single province but includes all the baptized in all the provinces of the Roman world. Perhaps this greater Ecclesia was suggested, as Dr Hort inclines to think[1], by the sense of the vastness of the Roman Empire which grew upon the Apostle during his residence in Rome. However this may be, it is only in this Epistle and in the kindred Epistle to the Colossians, written about the same time[2], that we hear of a Church of all believers, an *universitas fratrum Christianorum.* As Dr Hort acutely remarks, this universal Church is not regarded by St Paul as the sum of all the local churches, but as the sum of all the baptized; "the members which make up the One Ecclesia are not communities but individual men[3]." As the Holy Spirit, dwelling in the heart of each member of the local community, binds all together in a corporate unity; so, by dwelling in all the faithful everywhere, it creates

[1] *Ecclesia*, p. 143 f.

[2] Eph. i. 22 f., iii. 10, 21, v. 23 ff., Col. i. 18, 24.

[3] *Op. cit.*, p. 168.

the worldwide unity of a Catholic Church. There is *one Body and one Spirit*, even as there is *one Lord, one faith, one baptism, one God and Father of all.* The unity of the Church in a particular city or province, the unity of the whole congregation of Christ's flock, alike come from the one Spirit which gives to both their corporate life.

Part III. iii.

Eph. iv. 4 ff.

3. The Holy Spirit, then, is the bond of unity in the Christian Society, whether the unit is the congregation or the universal Church. But the Church, local or catholic, is not regarded in the New Testament as a mere aggregate of atoms or an inanimate organization composed, like an instrument, of many separate parts. The individuals who compose the Church are the members of a living body; it is the common life of the body which makes them one, and this life is inspired by the Spirit of Christ. The Church is the body of Christ; the glorified Lord is its head; Christ is incomplete without His Church as the Church is incomplete without Christ[1]. From the exalted Head the life of the Spirit flows down into all the members; there is vitality and there is growth in every part which is in real union with the Lord, and in the body as a whole[2]: *from whom all the body, constructed and drawn together by every ligament of the supply, according to the working in the measure of each single part, causes the growth of the body.* The Spirit is not named here, yet the word 'supply' (τῆς ἐπιχορηγίας) points not obscurely to its gifts. The "supply of the Spirit of Jesus

Eph. iv. 16.

[1] Eph. i. 22 f. [2] Eph. iv. 16.

Part III. iii.

Christ[1]" is represented as descending from Christ into the Church through certain channels of communication, among which it is not overbold to reckon the usual means of grace, and as operating in Christ's members individually to the advantage of the whole body, which thus *grows*, as the Epistle to the Colossians adds, *the growth of God*—with a more than human, a Divine increase.

Col. ii. 19.

4. And as this Divine life and growth of the Body of Christ is of the Spirit, so it is by the Spirit in her that the Church fulfils her proper work. Life and growth imply work, and a work proper to a particular organization. What does the New Testament represent as the special work of the Body of Christ under its present conditions? The answer is, in a word, To witness to the invisible Christ. According to the Acts the very last words spoken by our Lord before He withdrew into the unseen assigned this work to the Church, and connected her discharge of it with the coming of the Paraclete: *ye shall receive power when the Holy Spirit has come upon you, and ye shall be my witnesses...unto the end of the earth.* The Spirit is the primary witness of the Christ: *the Paraclete...the Spirit of the truth...he shall bear witness of me: the Spirit is that which bears witness, because the Spirit is the truth.* But the witness of this Spirit is borne in and through the Body of Christ.

Acts i. 8, Jo. xv. 26, 1 Jo. v. 6.

The first generation bore witness of what they had seen and heard in the days of Christ's flesh: *ye also*

Jo. xv. 27; cf. Lc. xxiv. 19, Acts i. 8.

[1] Cf. Gal. iii. 5, Phil. i. 19.

bear witness, because ye are with me from the beginning. Their testimony, i.e. the witness of the Apostolic Church, remains in the four Gospels. But even in the Apostolic age it was realized that what met the eye and the ear in the Lord's brief Ministry was but a small part of that which He is and came to do and teach. In reviewing His own teaching, even that which had been given to the innermost circle of the disciples, the Lord could say, *These things I have spoken unto you in proverbs: the hour comes when I shall no more speak unto you in proverbs but shall tell you plainly* (παρρησίᾳ) *of the Father.* That hour came when the Spirit came. The Spirit not only recalled our Lord's words, but revealed heights and depths in Him hitherto unsounded, declaring that which is His, and thereby (since whatsoever the Father has is His) declaring also that which is the Father's. It was in some sense a new Christ that the Church came to know after the Pentecost: *even though we have known Christ after the flesh, yet now we know him* thus *no more*[1], i.e. we know Him after the Spirit, by a process different from that of bodily intercourse, and by which He is placed in a new light. Of this deeper and fuller revelation of Jesus Christ the Apostolic Church taught by the Spirit of Christ also bore witness, and in the Fourth Gospel and the Epistles of St Paul and St Peter and St John we have a record of this interpretation of our Lord's

Part III. iii.

Jo. xvi. 25.

2 Cor. v. 16.

[1] Dr Rutherford paraphrases: "if indeed there was a time when we knew Christ in the world's way, we do not so know Him now."

Part III. iii.

teaching and person which corresponds with the glorification of Him by the Spirit that had been foretold. Nor is there any reason to limit the Spirit's witness in the Church to the lifetime of those who were *eyewitnesses and ministers of the word.* The life of the Church is continuous, and the Paraclete came to abide with her for ever. The interpretation of Christ has, as a matter of fact, been carried forward by the Catholic Church in the formulation of Creeds, and the evolution of Christian thought and of the manifold types of Christian life. This is not the place to enter on that great subject, but we may note the light which it receives from the New Testament doctrine of the Spirit. Our Lord's words about the Paraclete justify us in attributing to His presence in the Church the progressive witness of Christendom to Christ during the centuries which have passed since the end of the Apostolic age.

5. The continued witness of the Spirit in the Church implies a continual teaching of the Church by the Spirit. This also has a place in the Lord's
Jo. xiv. 26, xvi. 13. great promise of the Paraclete: *He shall teach you all things*[1]...*He shall lead the way for you* to enter *into all the truth.* When St John wrote his first Epistle the experience of half a century had proved
1 Jo. ii. 20, 27. the truth of these words: *You have an anointing from the Holy One; all of you know*[2]. *As for you, the anointing which you received from him abides in*

[1] In this He carried on Christ's work, taking His place; cf. Mt. xxiii. 8 εἷς γάρ ἐστιν διδάσκαλος, where ὁ χριστός is a true gloss.

[2] Or, reading πάντα, "*you know all things.*"

you, and you have no need that any teach you...his anointing teaches you concerning all things, and it is true. This appeal is not addressed to Apostles or Prophets, but to the members of the Church in general. It recognizes that the promise of Christ was not for the Eleven only or for their successors, but for the whole Christian society.

Yet in what sense was it true that the congregations of the province of Asia to which St John wrote knew all things, or even that they all knew the truth and needed not to be taught? It is clear that complete knowledge of the contents of their faith could not have been theirs in actual possession. But it was potentially and implicitly conveyed to them in the gift of the Spirit, and would be progressively realized in their experience if they for their part were loyal to their Teacher. What happens in the case of individuals happens on a great scale in the history of the Church. The Divine Teacher is always with her, and the teaching in itself is complete, although its assimilation by human thought and in human life is progressive, and at times, even for long periods of time, may seem to recede. In the abiding presence of the Paraclete the Body of Christ possesses the fulness of the truth, even in an age when it is least able to understand or to interpret His teaching. But advance in spiritual knowledge depends upon the Church herself; it is as she follows her Guide and learns His lessons of truth that she attains to fuller measures of Divine illumination. Thus the promise of Divine teaching is not a promise that the

Part III. iii.

judgements of the Church shall be infallible or irreformable; on the contrary, it holds out the hope of a progress in knowledge proportionate to the faithful use of light already given.

6. The perfecting of the Body of Christ is the final purpose of the coming of the Paraclete. Churches and the members of churches are being *builded together* in the fabric of the Universal Church, that they may become *a habitation of God in the Spirit*. The process is to continue *until we arrive, all of us, at the unity of the faith and knowledge of the Son of God*: until we attain *to a perfect man, to the measure of the stature of the fulness of the Christ*. When this end has been reached the work of the Paraclete will have been accomplished, and the long history of the Church's immature years will find its consummation in perfect unity, perfect knowledge, and the perfect life. Much that now seems to be final in creed and in life, much that is and ought to be final under present conditions, will then be lost in the full light of day. *When that which is perfect is come, then that which is in part shall be done away.* What is limited, defective, belonging to human imperfection, shall disappear; what is of the Spirit shall remain, the imperishable possession of the perfected Church.

Eph. ii. 22, iv. 13.

1 Cor. xiii. 10.

IV.

THE SPIRIT AND THE MINISTRY.

1. THE Church of Christ is, as St Peter teaches, a *spiritual house* built of living stones and designed to be not a Sanctuary only but a Priesthood: *a holy priestly function*[1], *to offer up spiritual sacrifices acceptable to God through Jesus Christ.* Its members constitute *a royal priesthood, a holy nation, a people* destined *for a* Divine *possession*; a new Israel succeeding to the high privileges of the ancient people of God[2]. St John has the same conception, and amplifies it after his manner. *He* (Jesus Christ) *made us a kingdom, priests to his God and Father*; *they* (the saints and martyrs) *shall be priests of God and of Christ.* Some glimpse of the priestly character of the Church is caught also by St Paul and in Hebrews: *present your bodies a living sacrifice, holy, acceptable to God, your reasonable service*: *let us offer up a sacrifice of praise to God continually.* In these passages the New Testament teaches the priesthood of the Church without

Part III. iv.

1 Pet. ii. 5, 9.

Apoc. i. 6, v. 10, xx. 6.

Rom. xii. 1.

Heb. xiii. 15.

[1] On ἱεράτευμα here see Dr Hort's commentary *ad loc.*

[2] Cf. Exod. xix. 5 f.

Part III. iv.

recognizing any distinction in this matter between her official and non-official members. All who in baptism and the laying on of hands have received the Spirit of Christ have been thereby consecrated to the Christian priesthood[1].

2. On the other hand the New Testament speaks with equal clearness of the existence within the Church of special ministries which are not common to the whole Christian society, but possess a priestly character and are in some measure analogous to the special priesthood that distinguished the tribe of Levi from the other tribes of the priestly nation of Israel. Though no emphasis is laid on the fact, it comes into view incidentally more than once in the
Acts xiii. 2. Acts and Epistles. The ministry of the prophets and teachers in the Church of Antioch is represented as a *λειτουργία* rendered to the Lord[2], a word which with its cognates is repeatedly used in the LXX. in reference to the official ministrations of the
Rom. xv. 15 ff. Priests and Levites. In a famous context St Paul describes his labours among the Gentiles as sacerdotal, borrowing term after term[3] from the Greek vocabulary of Levitical worship. It may be said that such a passage is metaphorical, and therefore must not be pressed, but it is neither more nor less metaphorical than the passages which speak of the

[1] This is not a 'priesthood of the laity,' as it is sometimes called, but a priesthood of the Church, without distinction of orders.

[2] λειτουργούντων δὲ αὐτῶν τῷ κυρίῳ.

[3] λειτουργός, ἱερουργεῖν, προσφορά.

priesthood and sacrifices which are common to all Christians. In both cases the priesthood and the sacrifices are spiritual, and in both they present nevertheless a real analogy to the hierarchy and the sacrificial offerings of the Old Testament. This analogy is so close that it is made by St Paul the basis of an argument for the support of the preachers of the Gospel; those who preach the Gospel have as much right to *live of the Gospel* as the ministers of the Jewish altar had to *share with the altar*. Thus in a true sense the Christian ministry succeeded to the Levitical priesthood[1], although the whole Levitical system has become obsolete and the only sacrifices which remain are spiritual and personal.

All Christian service, and in particular the special form of service which falls to the share of the Christian ministry, is rendered *by the Spirit of God*. The ministry of the New Covenant is a *ministry of the Spirit* as contrasted with the mechanical performance of the prescribed functions which constituted the bulk of the Levitical worship. And being such, it demands the special assistance of the Holy Spirit. As the whole Church is consecrated for its spiritual priesthood by the gift of the Spirit, so the ministry of the Church, which is

Phil. iii. 3.

2 Cor. iii. 6 ff.

[1] The Christian ministry is sacerdotal in so far as it discharges the functions of a sacerdotal body, the Church. But, as Lightfoot rightly urges (*Philippians*, p. 182 ff.), its *sacerdotium* is not exclusive or personal; "as individuals all Christians are priests alike."

Part III. iv. directly concerned with spiritual things, needs in a high degree the anointing of the Spirit of Christ. We turn to the New Testament to see what provision is made for the supply of this need.

3. The New Testament mentions ministries of many kinds, some which exhausted themselves in the apostolic or sub-apostolic age; others, which took root in the Churches and grew into permanent orders of men. The distinction cannot always be very clearly made out; in the lists which are given in 1 Cor. xii. and Eph. iv. apostles, prophets and evangelists evidently belong to the former class, but it is less certain to which we ought to refer pastors and teachers, helps and governments. Probably in many instances the charismatic gifts were possessed by persons who at the same time held office in the local Christian societies as 'presbyters' or 'bishops.' But however this may have been, the New Testament associates both types of ministerial life with special gifts of the Holy Spirit.

In the case of the charismatic ministries this needs no demonstration. Apostles and prophets possessed powers which marked them out as under the direct teaching of the Holy Spirit; they were gifts of the ascended Christ, who works by the Spirit[1]; the mystery of Christ[2] was revealed to them in the Spirit; they *brought the gospel* to the world *by a Holy Spirit sent from heaven.* The Christian

1 Pet. i. 12.

[1] Eph. iv. 8, 11 (ἀναβὰς...ἔδωκεν δόματα...καὶ αὐτὸς ἔδωκεν τοὺς μὲν ἀποστόλους κτλ.).

[2] Eph. iii. 4 f.

Part III. iv.

Prophets were the mouthpiece of the Spirit[1], insomuch that when they spoke under His influence the Spirit is said to have spoken. Their words were coloured, it is true, by individual character or by circumstances, and they were responsible for the manner in which they exercised the prophetic gift; in matter of fact it was not always used wisely or well[2]. But so far as they were effective instruments for the building up of the Church or the conversion of unbelievers[3], this was due to the Spirit of prophecy—a gift entrusted to the prophetic order and not common to the whole body of believers[4]. Of the reality of this gift and of its generally beneficial results the New Testament writers entertain no doubt[5].

In comparison with these directly spiritual ministries the local office-bearers of the several Churches occupied an inferior place: *thirdly teachers, then...helps, governments*. They were appointed, it appears, by the Apostle or his deputy[6], who selected grave and trustworthy persons, capable of serving their brethren and presiding over the local congregation, but not necessarily possessing any special gift of the Spirit such as the power of prophesying or speaking with tongues. The elder or overseer did not

1 Cor. xii. 28; cf. Eph. iv. 11.

[1] Cf. Acts xiii. 2, xvi. 6 f., xx. 23, xxi. 11, 2 Th. ii. 2, 1 Tim. iv. 1, Apoc. ii. 7, etc.; xxii. 17.

[2] 1 Cor. xiv. 29 ff.

[3] 1 Cor. xiv. 3, 24 f.

[4] 1 Cor. xii. 29.

[5] 1 Cor. xii. 10, xiv. 1 ff., 1 Th. v. 20, 1 Jo. iv. 2, Apoc. xix. 10.

[6] Acts xiv. 23, Tit. i. 5.

Part III. iv.

always possess even the gift of teaching; it was desirable that he should be apt to teach[1], but this was not indispensable. Systematic teaching in the first age was probably left almost entirely in the hands of the Apostle, the Prophet, and the Evangelist; the college of elders was rather concerned with the business and the discipline of the society which it ruled[2]. Yet even under these conditions St Paul held that the presbyters or bishops of the local communities derived their authority from

Acts xx. 28.

the Holy Spirit: *take heed to yourselves, and to all the flock in which the Holy Spirit* (τὸ πνεῦμα τὸ ἅγιον) *appointed you overseers* (ἐπισκόπους). The words may refer to the solemn ceremony of ordination described in the Epistles to Timothy[3], and the prophesyings by which it seems to have been preceded. The prophets, speaking in the Spirit, appear to have taken an important part in the choice of fit persons for certain ministries[4], and the appointment of overseers may have been controlled by their judgement; in that case it would be attributed to the Holy Spirit itself[5]. But besides this it cannot be doubted that a special *charisma*

[1] 1 Tim. iii. 2, v. 17.

[2] The elder was a προϊστάμενος (Rom. xii. 8, 1 Thess. v. 12, 1 Tim. v. 17) or ἡγούμενος (Heb. xiii. 17, 24) rather than a teacher. Even in ποιμήν the leading idea is discipline rather than instruction.

[3] 1 Tim. iv. 14, 2 Tim. i. 6 f. On 1 Tim. v. 22 see Hort, *Ecclesia*, p. 214 f.

[4] Acts xiii. 1 f., 1 Tim. i. 18.

[5] Cf. 2 Tim. 1. 6.

accompanied the laying on of hands by which the presbyters were set apart for their ministry—not necessarily the gift of prophecy, but one which was more needful for their office, a *spirit of power and love and discipline*, such as fitted them for the difficult duties of ruling and guiding the primitive Churches in the midst of the heathen society from which they had but recently escaped. 2 Tim. i. 7.

4. But the reason for the association of the Christian Ministry with the Holy Spirit lies deeper than this. If we allow ourselves to think of the early Church merely as a human society, a *collegium* among the many *collegia* or guilds of the Empire—an aspect which it doubtless wore in the eyes of its pagan contemporaries—its rulers may well seem to have needed no more than a good natural capacity for business and for leadership. But the Christian society as it is seen in the New Testament has another character which belongs only to itself. It is *the house of God*, the *congregation of the living God, pillar and basement of the truth*. Such a view of the Church naturally affects our estimate of the ministry of the Church. The officers of a spiritual body are charged with spiritual work, and need spiritual power to do it. To remit and retain sins is the mission of the Church, and the Lord, who knew the extreme difficulty of this most exacting of tasks, endowed her for it with a special gift of 'Holy Spirit[1].' But the Church's duty in this respect is chiefly fulfilled, at least since the end of 1 Tim. iii. 15.

[1] Jo. xx. 23.

the Apostolic age, by the three orders of the regular ministry, and the Easter gift of the Spirit goes with this exercise of responsibility. On these grounds the Western Church was justified when it ordered the use of *Accipe Spiritum sanctum* at all ordinations to the diaconate[1], the presbyterate, and the episcopate; and the Anglican Church when it followed the Latin Church so far as to retain the words at the Ordering of Priests and the Consecration of Bishops, adding on both occasions the solemn invocation of the Holy Spirit in the hymn *Veni Creator Spiritus.*

5. The few and simple rites of primitive Christianity are represented in the New Testament as spiritual acts, effectual signs of the life of the Spirit of Christ, and therefore instinct with the powers of the world to come. When the Lord spoke to Nicodemus of a birth from above[2] by which men were born of water and spirit, He struck a keynote which Christian experience took up and worked into a doctrine of baptismal grace. The event shewed that in Christian Baptism the outward visible sign was indeed accompanied by an inward spiritual power. Men who as heathens had been defiled by the worst vices of Greek life, in baptism washed themselves clean, were sanctified and justified[3] in the name of the Lord Jesus and in the Spirit of our God. The Bridegroom of the Church sanctified

[1] *Accipe Spiritum Sanctum* was said in the Sarum rite to the Deacon, though the following words, *quorum remiseris peccata*, etc., were reserved for the Priest.

[2] Jo. iii. 5.

[3] 1 Cor. vi. 11.

and cleansed His Bride with the washing[1] of the baptismal water accompanied by a form of solemn words. God of His mercy saved men by the washing of a second birth and a renewal[2] of their nature wrought by the Holy Spirit. Baptism saved them, not the external use of water, but that reawaking of the conscience to the call of God[3] which the Resurrection of the Lord had brought through the gift of the Spirit in the sacramental act. The completion of the ceremony of baptism by the laying on of hands shed a yet clearer light upon the working of the Holy Spirit through the ministries of the Church. Even Simon of Samaria could see that *through laying on of the apostles' hands the Holy Spirit was given*, for external effects followed this act in the first age[4]. Lastly, the Eucharist, if not expressly associated in the New Testament with the Holy Spirit, is represented as a series of spiritual acts which are inconceivable apart from the Spirit's presence and operation. A cup of mingled wine and water, blessed by the ministers of the Church, becomes to those who drink of it a participation in the Blood of Christ[5]. A cake of bread, similarly blessed and broken, becomes to those who eat of it a participation in the Body of Christ. This identification of the Cup and the Bread with the sacrificed humanity of the Lord is so complete, so truly a fact in the spiritual world,

Part III. iv.

Acts viii. 18.

[1] Eph. v. 26. [2] Tit. iii. 6.
[3] 1 Pet. iii. 21. [4] Acts xix. 6.
[5] 1 Cor. x. 16 f.

Part III. iv.

that to eat and drink unworthily is to incur the guilt of profaning the Lord's Body and to attract such Divine chastisements as sickness and death[1]. But these accounts of the spiritual significance of the Eucharist seem to involve the intervention of the Spirit of God, who alone can make material substances or human acts spiritually efficacious. In the words of a great Church writer of the second century, a diligent student of the New Testament, the Eucharist 'consists of two things, an earthly and a heavenly[2].' If so, the heavenly thing in it must be due to the Divine Spirit; and it was doubtless the recognition of this truth that led the early composers of liturgies to invoke the Holy Spirit on the elements as well as on the communicants. The *Epiclesis* is an acknowledgement of the Spirit's work in the highest act of Christian worship.

The teaching of the New Testament on the relation of the Holy Spirit to the ministry of the Church is admirably summarized in the *Ecclesiastical Polity*[3]. "We have (writes Richard Hooker) for the least and meanest duties performed by virtue of ministerial power that to dignify, grace, and authorize them which no other offices on earth can challenge. Whether we preach, pray, baptize, communicate, condemn, give absolution, or whatsoever, as dis-

[1] 1 Cor. xi. 27, 29.

[2] Irenaeus iv. 18 οὐκέτι κοινὸς ἄρτος ἐστὶν ἀλλ' εὐχαριστία ἐκ δύο πραγμάτων συνεστηκυῖα, ἐπιγείου τε καὶ οὐρανίου.

[3] v. lxxvii. 8.

posers of God's mysteries, our words, judgements, acts, and deeds are not our own but the Holy Ghost's." The words are cast in a mould shaped by the exigencies of an age far removed from Apostolic times, but the main thought which breathes in them is one which underlies all that the New Testament teaches about the Christian ministry. It is a ministry of the Spirit, and whatever spiritual power it exerts is from the Spirit who, dwelling in the Body of Christ, makes His presence felt in the acts and words of those who fulfil its work[1].

[1] It was a fine saying of Bp George Ridding (*Life*, p. 241): "God's magnet is a man of God electrified by the Spirit of God." This is true in the highest degree of the priest whose heart is in his work. But "the effect of Christ's ordinance" is not taken away by the wickedness or insincerity of the minister; as the Anglican article (xxvi) rightly insists, the Sacraments are "effectual because of Christ's institution and promise." The Spirit of Christ works in such cases through the acts of evil men, since they are done in Christ's name and by His authority.

V.

THE SPIRIT AND THE WRITTEN WORD.

Part III. v.

1. 'SPIRIT' suggests 'inspiration,' and it would not have been surprising if the idea of inspiration and the word itself had been common in the New Testament, which speaks so constantly of the Spirit. But the word does not occur, and the idea occurs but seldom. In John iii. 8 there is a play upon the two senses of πνεῦμα, wind or breath and spirit, which might have been maintained and widely used; but it is dropped at once and is rarely found again either in the Gospels or in the Epistles. There is a reference to it in the act of breathing which accompanied the Easter gift of the Spirit, and in the wind that filled the house where the Church was assembled at the Pentecost. But when a metaphor is wanted, it is usually borrowed not from wind but from water; partly because the latter figure had been employed by the prophets of the Old Testament, partly from the association of the Spirit with the baptismal rite. The New Testament speaks of an effusion (ἔκχυσις) of the Spirit rather than of an inspiration (ἔνπνευσις) of men or their works by it; the latter word, although

used by the LXX.[1], is not once found in the Apostolic writings. When the Spirit is regarded as a power which works in the human mind or heart, it is not said to 'inspire,' but to 'fill' men as with new wine; or to 'dwell in' them as in a sanctuary. Such phrases as 'the inspiration of good thoughts,' and 'the cleansing of the thoughts through the inspiration of the Holy Spirit,' familiar as they are to us through the English Prayerbook and the Latin sacramentaries which lie behind the collects of the Prayerbook, are unknown to the New Testament. On two occasions, however, it appears to speak of the inspiration of the prophets and their writings in the sense which the term bears in popular theology. Of one of these passages little need be said here; in 2 Peter i. 21, where the Prophets are said to have spoken as they were borne along (φερόμενοι, Vulg. *inspirati*) by the Holy Spirit, the idea conveyed is not so much inspiration as rapture; the Wind of God carries men before it so that they go where they are driven. But in 2 Tim. iii. 16 the *divinitus inspirata* of the Latin versions is justified by the Greek (θεόπνευστος). On the other hand the rendering of our Authorized version "all scripture is given by inspiration of God," a phrase which is largely responsible for the use of the word *inspiration* among English-speaking Christians, is too dogmatic in form: "every scripture inspired of God," as the Revised version translates, is doubtless right, and the difference is material. The writer does not assert the inspiration of all

[1] In Ps. xvii. (xviii.) 16.

Part III. v. scripture, but that every scripture which is inspired is also profitable. His purpose is to teach not the inspiration of the Old Testament scriptures but their use. In what sense they are inspired, and whether their inspiration is such as to protect them from error, we are not taught, but only for what ends they were given. It is interesting to note that the first two of those ends correspond with two of the functions fulfilled by the Paraclete; He came in person, as He had come through the Hebrew prophets, to teach and to convince (*πρὸς διδασκαλίαν, πρὸς ἐλεγμόν*)[1]. The field of the Spirit's work under the Old Testament was limited, but it bore fruit which is in part at least identical with that which we are taught to connect with the mission of the Spirit of Christ.

2. Though it is only in 2 Timothy that inspiration is directly ascribed to the Old Testament scriptures, there can be no doubt that belief in this inspiration was shared by all the leaders of the Apostolic Church, who quote the Old Testament as a final authority or as the word of God. The same attitude seems to be attributed to our Lord in more than one of His arguments with the Jews[2], and in the direct teaching of the Sermon on the Mount[3]. It is not indeed easy to determine how far the use of the *argumentum ad hominem* should be held to account for the former class of passages; and what is said in the Sermon

[1] Cf. Jo. xiv. 26, xvi. 8.

[2] E.g. Mc. xii. 35 ff., Jo. x. 34 ff.

[3] Mt. v. 17.

as to the permanence of the Law must certainly be interpreted in the light of other sayings in the same context which modify or set aside things that were *said to them of old time.* However, it is certain that our Lord did not protest against the prevalent belief in the inspiration of the Old Testament[1] as He did against other Pharisaic doctrines, but rather on the whole lent His sanction to some form of it. The Old Testament is the court of appeal before which He summons the false traditions of the Scribes[2]; the touchstone by which He tries the suggestions of the Tempter[3]; the treasury of devotion upon which He draws even in the hour of death[4]. *It is written* is His final justification of courses of action, the ground on which He bases principles[5]. *All the things that have been written about* Himself *in the Law of Moses and the Prophets and the Psalms must needs be fulfilled.* Utterances of this kind shew that our Lord did not disallow the popular estimate of the Old Testament, but on the contrary to some extent endorsed it, handing it on to His Church as one of the elementary *credenda* of Christianity. And such it continued to be. There was some danger, it appears, of Christian prophecy being despised, but none of its superseding the

Part III. v.

Mt. v. 21 ff.

Mc. ix. 12 f., xi. 17, xiv. 21, Lc. xx. 17.

Lc. xxiv. 44.

[1] Jo. v. 39 is directed not against a belief in the inspiration of the Law and the Prophets, but against a superstitious trust in the letter. See Westcott *ad loc.*

[2] Mc. vii. 8 ff.

[3] Mt. iv. 4, 6, 7, 10.

[4] Mc. xv. 34, Lc. xxiii. 46.

[5] Mc. ix. 12 f., xi. 17, xiv. 21, Lc. xx. 17.

Part III. v. prophecy of the Old Covenant. The older prophecy was regarded as written for the instruction and consolation of the Christian Church[1]; the Hebrew prophets were moved by the Spirit of Christ which was in them[2], and thus were able to predict the sufferings and the glory destined for the Christ. The ancient Catholic Church rightly voiced the mind of the Apostolic age when she taught her children to confess their faith in "the Holy Spirit ...who spake by the prophets[3]." The omission of any reference to the work of the Paraclete in the present creed of Christendom may be regretted, but it makes the mention of the Old Testament prophets the more significant. No words in the Catholic Creed are more certainly primitive than these.

3. When the Apostolic writers refer to 'inspired Scripture' or to 'the sacred writings,' they mean the books of the Hebrew Canon. There is an apparent exception in 2 Peter iii. 16, where the

2 Pet. iii. 16. Petrine author writes: *Our beloved brother Paul according to the wisdom given to him wrote to you ...in all his epistles...in which there are some things hard to understand, which the untaught and unstable torture, as they do the rest of the scriptures* (τὰς

[1] Rom. xv. 4.

[2] 1 Pet. i. 11.

[3] τὸ λαλῆσαν ἐν τοῖς προφήταις was preceded in the Creed of Jerusalem by τὸ παράκλητον, but the latter does not appear in the Constantinopolitan Creed; see Hort, *Two Dissertations*, p. 142 f. Τὸ παράκλητον was perhaps removed to make room for τὸ ἐκ τοῦ πατρός κτλ. (*ibid.* p. 78).

λοιπὰς γραφάς), *unto their own destruction.* Even assuming that *the rest of the scriptures* are the scriptures of the Old Testament[1], it is evident that this writer places the Epistles of St Paul as a body of writings on a level with the Canon. But there is no other trace in Christian literature of such a view before the end of the first quarter of the second century, and its appearance in 2 Peter excites a suspicion of the genuineness of this Epistle which is strengthened by other considerations. The case against the Epistle is indeed so strong that notwithstanding its inclusion in the New Testament by the judgement of the fourth and fifth centuries it cannot be with any confidence assigned to the Apostolic age[2].

Putting 2 Peter on one side, what claim to inspiration is made in the New Testament on behalf of the Apostolic writings?

There is no indication that any of the writers of the New Testament was conscious of contributing to a second canon of inspired scriptures. No ulterior purpose of creating a Christian literature or of ministering to the spiritual needs of posterity appears on the surface of the books[3]. It is a

[1] So Spitta and Zahn. But see J. B. Mayor, *St Jude and St Peter*, p. 168; Bp Chase, in Hastings' *D. B.* III., p. 810.

[2] Bp Chase (*op. cit.*) suggests as a provisional date "a few years before or a few years after the middle of the 2nd century"; Dr Mayor (p. cxxvii) says, "I think 125 A.D. is about the earliest possible date."

[3] On this see Deissmann, *New Light on the N. T.*, pp. 54 ff. (esp. pp. 62—4).

Part III. v.

somewhat different question how far, while writing letters and books which were designed to meet the immediate wants of individuals or churches, they were conscious of being assisted by the Holy Spirit. The prophets of the Old Testament knew themselves to be the subjects of a Divine afflatus. In the New Testament only one book—the Apocalypse—is directly prophetic, and there the claim to inspiration is made as distinctly as in the prophecies of Ezekiel and Zechariah[1]. The Epistles of St Paul are not formal prophecies, but they contain the substance of Divine revelations[2]: the writer has experienced ecstatic visions and has heard unspeakable words: some of his teachings are based upon a *word of the Lord*, perhaps a personal revelation; now and again he has a mystery, a Divine secret, to communicate[3]. St Paul thinks that he, as well as certain others, has the Spirit of God[4]: he knows that he has the mind of Christ; he is an Apostle of Jesus Christ and speaks with the authority of his office. His letters are to be read in the Churches and obeyed; the prophet or spiritual person who seeks recognition must first acknowledge that the things which Paul writes to the Church are the commandment of the Lord[5]. Yet he is conscious that some of the counsels he gives do not fall under that category, and when he would establish a

1 Th. iv. 15.

[1] Cf. Sanday, *Inspiration*, p. 375 f.

[2] 1 Cor. ii. 10, Gal. i. 12, 16, Eph. iii. 3 ff., 2 Cor. xii. 1 ff.

[3] 1 Cor. xv. 51.

[4] 1 Cor. vii. 40.

[5] 1 Cor. xiv. 37 f.

doctrine he does not support it by authority but by argument. Certainly he does not claim that all he writes is protected from error, or that all is equally or uniformly inspired.

The historical books of the New Testament from the nature of their contents shew fewer signs of spiritual influence exerted upon their writers. They deal not with revelations but with facts, which could be collected and verified by the ordinary processes of memory or research. If inspiration was needed by the writers of the Synoptic Gospels and the Acts, it was needed to guide them in selecting their materials wisely with a view to the edification of the Church; and of such guidance they may well have been unconscious. The promise that the Paraclete would recall to memory the words of Christ found its fulfilment in the Apostolic preaching and in the oral tradition of the first age rather than in the written Gospels which are based upon them. St Luke writes as if he had depended entirely upon his own researches; and if St Luke and the writer of the first Gospel had St Mark before them, as is now commonly supposed, they certainly treated the second Gospel with a freedom which suggests that they did not recognize it as inspired scripture. But while this is freely admitted, it must not be forgotten that the Gospels and the Acts are, even more than the 'Former Prophets' of the Old Testament, didactic histories, and in purpose didactic rather than historical; books, therefore, in which the voice of the Spirit may be heard, teaching by their words the whole Church to the end of time. In this sense a prophetic character and a prophetic inspiration may be claimed for writings such as St Mark's Gospel and the Acts; if spiritual profit marks the presence of inspiration[1], it is to be found everywhere in the New Testament, and not least in the histories which tell us all that we know of the life of our Lord and of the beginnings of the Church. As for the Gospel of St John, it is perhaps an interpretation of the life and teaching of Jesus rather than a formal history; but it is an interpretation which exhibits the Lord's person and work in the light of the Spirit, and thus it possesses a claim to inspiration of a high order, although the claim is not made by the writer, and he may have been unconscious of his gift.

4. Of the nature and effects of Inspiration the writers of the New Testament say but little. In quoting the prophecies of the Old Testament they use the customary formulas of citation. The words were spoken *through the prophet*, or more precisely *by the Lord through the prophet*. (Mt. i. 22, ii. 15.) In the Psalms *David spoke in the Holy Spirit*, or *God spoke by the Holy Spirit* through *the mouth of David*. (Mc. xii. 36, Acts iv. 25.) The inspiration of the Prophet is transferred to his writings, and the writing is sometimes personified. *The Scripture*, we read, *foreseeing that God would justify the Gentiles through faith, preached the Gospel beforehand unto Abraham*, (Gal. iii. 8 (Gen. xii. 1 ff.).) where the meaning clearly is that the Holy Spirit foresaw the issue

[1] πᾶσα γραφὴ θεόπνευστος καὶ ὠφέλιμος.

when He spoke to Abraham as the Scripture relates; *the Scripture shut up all things under sin*, i.e. God did this through the Scripture. *The Scripture says*, or *What says the Scripture?* is St Paul's familiar form of appeal to the Old Testament. In all such modes of speech the written word is regarded as a standing witness to the mind and will of God, who speaks through it in virtue of the inspiration of the writers. Much the same inference may be drawn from the constant occurrence in the New Testament of the formula *It is written*[1]. All this seems to shew that the Apostolic age turned to the Old Testament as a written record of God's dealings with Israel, when it wished to obtain indications of the principle upon which He governs His people. It evidently realized that every part of this record had its warnings, its consolations, or its teachings for the new Israel, and that this abiding voice of the Spirit was not to be neglected even by a generation which was conscious of having received a far larger outpouring of life and light; that on the contrary, the coming of the Paraclete had reinterpreted the ancient Scriptures and made them valuable allies of the Church in her work of evangelizing the world.

Part III. v.

Gal. iii. 22.

Rom. iv. 3, ix. 17, x. 11, xi. 2, Gal. iv. 30, 1 Tim. v. 18.

5. As the Apostolic age appealed to the Old Testament, so the next age or the next but one, while maintaining the primitive estimate of the Hebrew Canon, naturally looked with growing reverence to the writings of the Apostles and Apostolic men, and

[1] The Synoptists, the Acts, and St Paul use γέγραπται; St John for the most part has γεγραμμένον ἐστίν.

Part III. v. began to see in them a new collection of inspired Scriptures. For this the New Testament, as we have seen, is not directly responsible. Nevertheless there was solid ground for the attitude of the Church towards these writings. The anointing which teaches all things and is true, the Spirit which came to guide believers into all the truth, could not have failed to guide and teach in an especial degree those leaders of the Church to whom it was given to shape the first beginnings of Christian life and thought. The Spirit which moved a David or an Isaiah could not have failed to move a Paul or a John. Their writings and others such as theirs are permanent records of the highest teaching which the Paraclete gave to the first generation. Men who lived at so critical an era, under such direct and constant guidance, were, we cannot doubt, as fully inspired as the prophets and teachers of the older Israel. A long experience has confirmed the judgement of the second and third centuries which ascribed to the New Testament the same inspiration that its writers attribute to the Old.

But if the Apostolic writers were inspired men, we may safely apply to their writings what St Paul has said of the ancient scriptures. They, too, *were written for our learning, that we through patience and comfort of* these Apostolic *scriptures might have hope*. They are *profitable for teaching, for conviction, for correction, for instruction which is in righteousness, that the man of God may be complete,*

Rom. xv. 4.

2 Tim. iii. 16 ff.

furnished completely unto every good work. It is in the practical use of the Old and New Testaments that their inspiration appears. Inspiration is not defined in Scripture, and the Church has shewn a wise self-restraint in refusing to enter upon this ground. But no Christian who makes the prophetic and Apostolic writings the guide of his religious thinking and daily living will doubt that there is a true sense in which these books stand alone as a Divine library. Full as they are of the personal characteristics and infirmities of their human authors, they are also full, according to their several measures, of the wisdom and power of the Spirit of God and of Christ. The human element in the written word coexists with the Divine after a manner inscrutable to our comprehension. It is so in the mystery of the Christian life; it is so, to take the highest instance, in the mystery of the Word made flesh. We believe, we experience the truth of the union, and it is enough.

VI.

THE SPIRIT AND THE PERSONAL LIFE.

Part III. vi.

WITH one or two possible exceptions the Old Testament makes no reference to the ethical action of the Spirit of God upon the individual man[1]; the Hebrew writers view the Spirit in relation to Israel, the Messiah, and the prophetic order. Nor do the Synoptic Gospels carry us much further[2], for the baptism of the personal life by the Spirit of Christ did not begin till the Ministry was ended;
Jo. vii. 39. the *Spirit was not yet*. Even Acts scarcely enters upon this field; by its scope the book is nearly limited to the effects of the Spirit's coming upon the Church and the world. It is St Paul to whom the honour belongs of having called attention to the change which the Pentecost made in the possibilities of the individual human life; the Pauline Epistles which exhibit the relation of the Spirit to the Body of Christ are not less full of its workings in the members of the Body. St Paul was followed herein

[1] Even in Ps. li. it is doubtful whether the writer speaks of his own experience, or in the name of Israel.

[2] Lc. xi. 13 is scarcely an exception: see p. 120.

by other teachers of the Apostolic age, and especially by St John, who late in the first century, in the light of a long experience, recalled and reinterpreted sayings in which the Lord had foreshadowed the work of the Spirit in the hearts of men. Part III. vi.

1. (*a*) In the earliest of St Paul's Epistles an insight is given into his psychology which supplies a starting-point for the doctrine of the Spirit's relation to human nature. Man in his completeness consists of body, soul, and spirit. It is doubtless true that no actual trichotomy is contemplated here[1], but there is at least a mental distinction made between three elements in our nature which are regarded as necessary to its perfection. Of the 'soul' in connexion with our present subject the Apostle says little, except that he applies the epithet 'psychic' to men who are not under the control of the Spirit of God, and to the body in its present condition, 'psychic' being in both instances contrasted with 'pneumatic' or spiritual. Of the human spirit, on the other hand, frequent mention is made in the Epistles; it is evidently the sphere in which the ethical work of the Holy Spirit is carried forward[2]. Elsewhere that work is connected with the 'inward man[3],' i.e. the true self; or with the 'spirit of the mind[4],' i.e. the spiritual nature on the side of the intellectual powers; or again with the 'conscience[5],' 1 Th. v. 23. 1 Cor. ii. 14, xv. 44 ff.

[1] See Milligan on 1 Thess. v. 23.

[2] Rom. viii. 16, Gal. vi. 18, Phil. iv. 23, 2 Tim. iv. 22, Philem. 25.

[3] Eph. iii. 16.

[4] Eph. iv. 23.

[5] Rom. ix. 1, Gal. iv. 6, Rom. viii. 27.

Part III. vi. i.e. the self-conscious life which is the note of personality, or with the heart, which is its seat.

(*b*) The Holy Spirit does not create the 'spirit' in man; it is potentially present in every man, even if rudimentary and undeveloped. Every human being has affinities with the spiritual and eternal. In each
1 Cor. ii. 11. individual of the race *the spirit of the man which is in him* answers to the Spirit of God, in so far as the finite can correspond with the infinite; though there are men who are psychic and not spiritual, who may even be said not to 'have spirit[1],' human nature is incomplete without it, and vainly seeks satisfaction in sensual or even in intellectual enjoyment[2]. But though the Spirit of God finds in man a spiritual nature on which it can work, the human spirit is in so imperfect or depraved a condition that a complete renovation, even a re-creation, is
2 Cor. v. 17. necessary. *If any is in Christ*, there has been in his case *a new creation; the old things passed away; behold, they have become new.* St Paul describes in his letters the process of renovation as he had himself witnessed it in the lives of thousands of Gentile converts.

(*c*) If a moment is named at which the change began or an act in which it was potentially included, that moment and that act are identified with the admission of the convert into the Church by baptism[3]

[1] Jude 19. [2] Eph. iv. 17 ff.

[3] In Acts xix. 2 the first gift of the Spirit is connected with the first act of Christian faith (πιστεύσαντες). But the first overt act of faith in the Apostolic age was baptism; cf. e.g. Gal. iii. 25 ff.

into the death and Resurrection of the Lord Jesus. Part III. vi.
In the act of Baptism the 'old man,' i.e. the former self, was crucified together with the Lord, that a new self, a risen Christ, might take its place within him. It was his *palingenesia*, his second birth, Tit. iii. 5.
his renovation by the Spirit of Christ[1], giving the promise of a new life. The baptized man might by his subsequent conduct grieve the Holy Spirit[2], outrage Him[3], and even extinguish the Divine fire in his heart[4]; but from that moment he could never again be in the position of one to whom the Spirit had not come; he had been *made partaker of Holy* Heb. vi. 4 ff.
Spirit, and had tasted the good word of God and the powers of the coming age. From that moment, with that great sacramental act, the life of the Spirit[5] began.

(*d*) The life of the Spirit, as it proceeds, encounters a hostile force which St Paul calls the Flesh, and the history of the Christian life is the history of a lifelong war: *the flesh lusts against the Spirit* Gal. v. 7.
and the Spirit against the flesh, for these powers *are opposed to one another.* The flesh in this antithesis is neither human nature as such, nor the corporeal and external as contrasted with the spiritual and invisible, nor even the seat of the passions which make for sin, but human nature regarded as fallen and sinful, corrupt and morally decaying; the precise

[1] Tit. iii. 6. [2] Eph. iv. 30.
[3] Heb. x. 29. [4] 1 Th. v. 19.
[5] On this life see Gore, *Lux Mundi*[1], p. 316 ff.; Denney in Hastings, *D. C. G.*, p. 738 b.

Part III. vi.

opposite in man of the principle of life which is communicated by the Spirit of God. In view of this antinomy men fall into two categories, those who are 'in flesh,' and those who are 'in Spirit'; or, having regard to the practical working of the two conditions, those who live or walk 'after flesh,' and those who live or walk 'after Spirit.' Neither class pursues its course without resistance from the opposite force, but St Paul takes cognizance only of the struggle which the Spirit makes in baptized men against the principle of spiritual death. As the Spirit gains upon the flesh, there grows up within a man the 'mind of the Spirit,' an attitude of thought and will which changes the direction of the inner life, inclining it to the Divine and the eternal. There follows a corresponding change of the standards and habits of outward conduct; those who live by the Spirit are bound to live after its rule. From this high ground St Paul is able to attack with absolute confidence the sensuality, the flippant levity, the gross vices of heathendom which still threatened the Gentile churches; such things were impossible for men who had put away the old man and were being renewed in the power of the Holy Spirit, which had now become the very 'spirit of their minds[1].' To live by the Spirit, to walk by the Spirit, this was the one safeguard against relapsing into the lusts of the flesh[2].

Rom. viii. 5, 8 f.

(*e*) But the Spirit is not merely in St Paul's view an aggressive force leading the human spirit against

[1] Eph. iv. 17 ff.

[2] Gal. v. 16 ff.

the flesh, or a defensive power shielding it from attack. Stoicism, as interpreted by Seneca and Epictetus[1], was able to go some way in this direction. St Paul opens another door of hope; his indwelling Spirit is also a constructive power which builds up a new life within, cooperating with the spirit of man in the work of restoring human life to the image of God. The Holy Spirit "sanctifieth me and all the elect people of God." Perhaps the familiar words have led English Christians to think of the Holy Spirit too exclusively as the Sanctifier, a character which in the New Testament is not uniformly ascribed to the Third Person in God[2]. Yet whenever the Apostolic writers speak of the members of the Church as 'saints' or 'sanctified,' the Spirit's work is implicitly in view. No one term, indeed, so fully covers the effects upon human nature of the presence in it of the Holy Spirit of God as the word 'sanctification.' It expresses at once the hallowing or consecration to the service of God which is the first result of the coming of the Spirit, and the actual equipment for service of each of the faculties of men. In the former sense the change is merely one of relation and non-moral; thus even the body receives consecration from the Divine indwelling[3],

[1] See *St Paul and Seneca* (Lightfoot, *Philippians*; cf. pp. 278, 311 ff.). Seneca knew of a *sacer spiritus* (ib. p. 294).

[2] The chief passages are Rom. xv. 16, 1 Cor. vi. 11, 2 Thess. ii. 13, 1 Pet. i. 2. In other places, perhaps more numerous, sanctification is connected with our relation to Jesus Christ; see 1 Cor. i. 1, 30; Eph. v. 26, Heb. ii. 11, x. 10, 29, xiii. 12.

[3] 1 Cor. vi. 19.

Part III. vi.

and a heathen who has married a Christian woman is sanctified by the union[1]. But the progressive sanctification which follows the act of Baptism is of another kind; and though St Paul does not often use the term, the steps of this great spiritual process are described by him at length.

(*f*) The Holy Spirit enables the members of Christ to realize their consecration by creating in them a sense of their filial relation to God, and opening and maintaining communication between God and the individual life. The Spirit in the human heart is 'the spirit of the adoption' which corresponds with the spirit of sonship in the Christ, and cries in us as in Him *Abba, Father*. It is through the Christ that we have our access to the Father[2], but we have it in the Spirit. If we worship the Father in spirit and in truth, we do so by the Spirit of God[3]. If we pray, it is the Spirit who supports our weaknesses, and inspires those unuttered and unutterable longings after the Divine which God recognizes as the voice of His Spirit and in accordance with His will[4].

Rom. viii. 14 ff., Gal. iv. 6.

Having thus reopened fellowship between God and the human spirit, the Holy Spirit builds up the ruins of our spiritual nature, restoring the Divine life in man. The love of God is poured into the heart, awakening a response of love on man's part to God[5]; hope, peace, and joy follow in the region

[1] 1 Cor. vii. 14.
[2] Eph. ii. 18.
[3] Phil. iii. 3.
[4] Rom. viii. 26 f.
[5] Rom. v. 5.

of the spirit[1]. Another powerful instrument of sanctification is the knowledge of Divine truth as it is learnt in the experience of the Christian life; and this also is in the hands of the Holy Spirit, who is the teacher of all Christians, and without whose instruction the things of God have no reality or convincing power[2]. In order to utter with sincerity and conviction the shortest of Christian creeds a man must have been taught by the Spirit of Christ[3]. Truth thus imparted to the mind is a power in life which makes for righteousness and holiness of truth, and is not a mere part of its intellectual furniture[4]. Words of God thus put by the Spirit into the hands of men are swords by which home-thrusts may be dealt at His enemy and ours[5]. Part III. vi.

(*g*) If the apostle is asked to specify the results of this work of sanctification, his answer is ready; the *fruit of the Spirit*[6] is the Christian character in its manifoldness, and in its unity. He names nine great products of life in the Spirit. When this list is scrutinized it is found to include the most characteristic features of practical Christianity, as it was exhibited in the first age. The list begins with those which indicate the attitude of the inner self to God, for the Spirit first creates right relations between the soul and God, and from these it proceeds Gal. v. 22.

[1] Rom. xiv. 17, xv. 13, Gal. v. 5, 1 Th. i. 6.
[2] 1 Cor. ii. 10 ff., Eph. i. 17 ff., 1 Jo. ii. 20, 27.
[3] 1 Cor. xii. 3.
[4] Eph. iv. 23.
[5] Eph. vi. 17.
[6] Gal. v. 22.

Part III. vi. to remodel personal and social life. As St Paul saw the religion of the Spirit, it not only filled men with love, joy, and peace, but it surrounded them with an atmosphere of forbearance, kindness, goodness, honesty of purpose, ability to endure affront, and self-control. That such a character should have been realized even in part within a generation after the coming of the Spirit, in the midst of heathen surroundings, and in the lives of men who had recently escaped from heathenism, went far to establish the Divine authority of the Gospel—further indeed than the greatest of physical miracles. God, it was evident, had set His seal on men who manifested such signs of a supernatural life, some of which could be seen by all observers. To use
2 Cor. iii. 3. another Pauline metaphor, they were an open *letter of Christ*, which all the world could read, written with the Spirit of the living God.

(*h*) For the life of the Spirit of Christ in the individual believer is the very life of Christ in him, reproducing the character of Christ by 'forming
1 Cor. vi. 17. Christ[1]' within his heart. *He that is joined to the Lord is one spirit;* there is a spiritual unity between Christ and himself, of which the human spirit is the sphere, and the Spirit of Christ the author. The indwelling of the Spirit is the indwelling of Christ; and Christ, dwelling in the heart by the Spirit, be-
Gal. ii. 20. comes the life of our lives. *I live, and yet no longer*
Rom. viii. 10. *I, but Christ liveth in me. If Christ is in you...the spirit is life because of righteousness.* It is thus that

[1] Gal. iv. 19.

the inner life of men is strengthened and enriched, until at last it is *filled unto all the fulness of God.* Part III. vi. Eph. iii. 19.

2. Our other great New Testament authority on the life of the Holy Spirit in the individual is St John. His interpretation of the teaching of Christ may be coloured more or less deeply by the experience of the sixty years or more which had intervened between the coming of the Spirit and the date of the fourth Gospel. But the theology of St John is at least not a mere replica of the Pauline theology, in regard either to the Son or to the Holy Spirit. While there are points of resemblance between them which imply a common basis of belief, minor differences both of presentation and of detail suggest that the writers lived at different stages in the growth of the Christian consciousness, and differed in their outlook upon the field of Christian thought[1].

(*a*) Like St Paul, St John recognizes that the work of the Spirit in the personal life begins with a spiritual birth which is connected with the water of Baptism. But the conception is worked out independently. It is true that we have in St John as in St Paul the antithesis of flesh and Spirit: *that which has been born of the flesh is flesh, and that which has been born of the Spirit is spirit*; but the flesh is here the symbol not of moral corruption, but of the external and animal side of human nature. The lower animal life can only propagate itself by natural birth; the higher life must be derived from Jo. iii. 6; cf. i. 13.

[1] On this point see Sanday, *Criticism of the Fourth Gospel*, pp. 208 ff., 226 ff.

Part III. vi.

the Spirit by a birth from above. The fundamental thought connected with the Spirit's action in the first half of the fourth Gospel is not, as with St Paul, burial with Christ, or cleansing from sin, but rather the origination, the satisfaction, the preservation of life. It is the Spirit which regenerates: which as living water, issuing from the Christ[1], allays the thirst of men and becomes in them a perennial fountain of life which overflows for the quickening or the refreshment of all that it can reach. So the Lord foreshadowed, or the Evangelist interpreting His words by the event expressed, the effect of the Pentecostal outpouring of the Spirit: the new life which sprang up in the hearts of believers, its freshness, its brightness and joy, its unfailing supply, the law of self-extension which it invariably follows. The Acts are full of the workings of this law; each believer in the first days became a centre of spiritual life. St Paul's whole life was shaped by his recognition of the fact, but it is to St John that we owe the sayings of our Lord which explain it. The energies of the indwelling Spirit of Christ can no more be limited to the individual life than a perennial fountain can be held in by narrow barriers. Spiritual life communicates itself from person to person as torch is lit from torch.

Jo. iii. 5, iv. 14, vii. 37 f.

(*b*) It is, however, only in a secondary sense that either the individual believer or the Church com-

[1] St Paul approaches this point of view in his allegory of the spiritual Rock (1 Cor. x. 4), but does not stop to draw out the teaching.

municates the Spirit. The water of life, through its vital energy, springs up within the personal life and overflows in acts and words which minister spiritual life to other men; a whole household, a whole region may owe its conversion to God to the personal influence which is itself due to the power of the indwelling Spirit of Christ. But in the last resort it is from Christ and not from the individual members of Christ that the water of life proceeds; both the original gift and the perennial supply are from Him who baptizes with the Holy Spirit. Thus the personal life of all believers depends upon the incarnate Lord. Each human being that receives the Holy Spirit receives it by the gift of Christ. The mystery of the Incarnation, the Sacrifice, the Resurrection and Ascension, the glorification of the Word made flesh, lies behind every manifestation of the Spirit in the words and actions of men. The anointing which teaches the most ignorant as man cannot teach is from the Holy One who Himself was anointed by the Father. The life which springs up in the depths of the most degraded personality, and makes the desert to rejoice and blossom as the rose, issues out of the throne of God and of the Lamb. The Spirit of Christ is on earth and in the hearts of men because Christ is at the Father's right hand in heaven[1].

[1] Jo. i. 33, iv. 10, vii. 37, xiv. 16, 26, xv. 26, xvi. 7, xx. 22, Acts ii. 33, 1 Jo. ii. 20, Apoc. xxii. 1.

VII.

THE SPIRIT AND THE LIFE TO COME.

Part III. vii.

1. It is unnecessary to enter here upon the large and thorny field of New Testament Eschatology. For our purpose it is enough to know that the Apostolic writings recognize everywhere that there is a state beyond death in which the spiritual life is continued under new and more favourable conditions. In the Synoptic teaching of our Lord to 'enter into' or 'inherit' this life (ἡ ζωή, ζωὴ αἰώνιος) is set forth as the highest aim of man[1]. In the Johannine discourses 'eternal life' is a constantly recurring phrase[2], and although the believer is said to 'have' this life by having Christ Himself, and thus to have already made the great transition from death to life[3], it belongs in its fulness to another stage of existence which begins with what is called the 'resurrection of life' (ἀνάστασις ζωῆς)[4]. The Epistles of the New Testament distinguish yet more clearly between the

[1] Mc. ix. 43, 45; x. 17, 30.

[2] Jo. iii. 36, vi. 54, x. 28; cf. 1 Jo. v. 11 f.

[3] Jo. v. 24; cf. 1 Jo. iii. 14.

[4] Jo. v. 29, vi. 40, 54, 57 f.: cf. Jo. iv. 14, xii. 25.

initial spiritual life of the present state and its perfection in the future. *The end* is *eternal life; he who sows to the Spirit shall of the Spirit reap eternal life.* There is a 'life to come' (ζωὴ ἡ μέλλουσα) of which godliness has promise; it is hidden now but will be manifested at the Parousia; it is *the crown of life which the Lord promised to them that love him.* Even the state of the dead members of Christ holds something far better than their present life in Him[1]. But it is the fuller life to be disclosed at the coming of the Lord which is the heritage[2] of Christians, their land of promise, their birthright as the sons of God[3]. This is *the glory which is to be revealed*, the *eternal weight of glory* which must be placed in the scale against present loss; the *wealth of glory* belonging to God's *inheritance in the saints*; the *unfading crown of glory* which is to be placed upon their heads.

Part III. vii.

Rom. vi. 22, Gal. vi. 8, 1 Tim. iv. 8, Col. iii. 3, Jas. i. 12.

Rom. viii. 18, 2 Cor. iv. 17.

Eph. i. 18. 1 Pet. v. 14.

What place does the New Testament assign to the Holy Spirit in this mature and perfected life? Is the work of the Spirit preparatory only, ceasing with death or the Parousia, or is it permanent, extending to the world to come?

2. All that has been said makes for the real continuity of the spiritual life in the future order. Physical death has no power over the life of the Spirit;

[1] Phil. i. 21 ff.

[2] On κληρονομεῖν, κληρονομία, κληρονόμος in the N.T. see Westcott, *Hebrews*, p. 167 ff.; cf. Dalman, *Words of the Lord Jesus*, E. tr., p. 125.

[3] Rom. viii. 17, Gal. iv. 7.

Part III. vii. the Lord's return will manifest the sons of God, but it
cannot change their relation to Him. But if *neither*
Rom. viii. 38 f. *death nor life...nor things present nor things to come*
...can separate us from the love of God which is in
Christ Jesus our Lord, it is inconceivable that they
can separate us from the Spirit of God and of Christ,
Rom. v. 5. by which *the love of God has been shed abroad in our*
hearts, and which is the very bond of our union with
God through Christ. Nor are we left to a mere
inference. The present indwelling of the Spirit is
the firstfruits of the harvest, the first instalment of
the inheritance. But the harvest is homogeneous
with the firstfruits, and the inheritance with the
instalment. Both metaphors clearly teach that the
life of the world to come will be, as our present life
in Christ is, a life in the Spirit, although immeasurably larger, fuller, and more abiding. The gift of
the Spirit which is ours now is 'in part'; the great
promise of the Father awaits its complete fulfilment
in a future state.

3. It is possible to examine more closely the
contents of this hope so far as it affects the future of
the body. In the present state, while the spirit is
Rom. viii. 10. *life because of righteousness*, the body is *dead because*
of sin. It fails to respond to the already emancipated spirit, and indeed chains and drags it down.
Rom. vii. 24. *Quis liberabit?* is the constant cry of the spirit as it
groans under *the body of this death*. The Gospel
recognized the burdens of life and did not profess to
set men free from them. It discouraged the pagan
practice of suicide, counselling brave endurance of

suffering, and dwelling on its disciplinary purpose. Nor did it offer a prospect of release from the body in a future life. Not the destruction of the body but its liberation was the hope which it held forth to the world. Human nature is to be perfected not by the abandonment of one of its factors, but by the emancipation of the whole man; humanity is to be preserved in its entirety for the coming Christ[1]. And the emancipation of the body is attributed to the same Spirit which has regenerated the spiritual nature of men. *If the Spirit of him that raised up Jesus from the dead dwells in you, he that raised up Christ Jesus from the dead shall quicken also your mortal bodies through his Spirit that dwells in you.* But a quickening of the body by the Spirit of the risen Christ cannot be a mere resuscitation of the flesh. There can be no return to the unspiritual conditions of mortality: *flesh and blood cannot inherit the Kingdom of God.* The Spirit which quickens will change; the body shall be raised not 'psychic' but 'pneumatic,' an organ of the highest life, a sacrament of the Spirit's presence, an instrument to carry out His inspirations.

Part III. vii.

Rom. viii. 11.

1 Cor. xv. 50.

4. Thus the resurrection of the body is so far from being the last work of the indwelling Spirit that it will be the starting point of a new activity of spiritual life. It was in order to bring human nature to this point that the Spirit regenerated and renewed it, bearing with the limitations and the sins which beset the process of its recovery; and it is not to

[1] Rom. vii. 24, viii. 10 f., 23, 1 Thess. v. 23.

Part III. vii. be believed that when the end has been reached and the emancipated spirit and body are capable of answering fully to His touch, He will forsake the work of His own hand. The New Testament does not indeed enter in detail into the life of the world to come; it is sufficiently occupied with the work of claiming for God the life that now is. But such indications as it gives confirm us in the belief that the Spirit's presence in human nature is not to be
1 Cor. xiii. 10. withdrawn *when that which is perfect has come.*
Jo. iv. 14. The water of life *springs up into eternal life*, not that it may cease when the life has come, but that it may find in the great future its ultimate issue and its fullest scope. The Paraclete was sent that He
Jo. xiv. 16. might abide with the Church *for ever* (εἰς τὸν αἰῶνα)[1], not to the end of this dispensation only, but *to all the generations of the age of the ages*, as St Paul paraphrases[2]. The movements of the Spirit of which the first century was conscious are recognized
Heb. vi. 5. as *powers of a coming age*, of which the full experience belongs to the future though in the present they are 'tasted' by believers. These are but hints, yet they all point one way, connecting the present life of the Spirit in men with the next order which lies beyond the return of the Lord.

5. One book breaks the usual silence of the New Testament about the life to come. The

[1] Cf. Mc. iii. 29 (Mt. xii. 31), Jo. vi. 51, 58, viii. 51 f., x. 28, xi. 26, 2 Jo. 2. Εἰς τοὺς αἰῶνας, which is used regularly in the Apoc., does not occur in the Gospel and Epistles of St John.

[2] Eph. iii. 21 εἰς πάσας τὰς γενεὰς τοῦ αἰῶνος τῶν αἰώνων.

Apocalypse places its reader side by side with the seer before the open door of heaven, and permits him to see *things which must come to pass hereafter.* Two of its great outlooks into the future refer to the Spirit under St John's usual symbol, as the Water of Life. In the vision of ch. vii. we read: *They shall hunger no more, neither thirst any more, neither shall the sun strike upon them, nor any heat; for the Lamb which is in the midst of the throne shall be their shepherd, and shall guide them unto fountains of waters of life.* The double plural (πηγὰς ὑδάτων) suggests the indefinite multiplication of the reservoirs of spiritual life which are opened to refresh and finally to satisfy the thirst after God and righteousness. The glorified Christ is represented as Himself guiding the saints, as if He had taken into His own hands again the work which had been committed to the Paraclete-Spirit[1]. Yet though the mission of the Paraclete as the Vicar of Jesus Christ has come to an end, He is seen to be still the giver of spiritual life; if the Lamb now leads in person, He leads to ever fresh supplies of the Spirit, fountains of waters of life, means of grace hitherto unknown or inaccessible, but open to those who are *accounted worthy to attain to that world.* The same view of the Spirit's place in the life to come is given, with slight differences, in the vision of the New Jerusalem. *He shewed me a river of water of life, bright as crystal,*

Part III. vii.

Apoc. iv. 1.

Apoc. vii. 16 f.

Apoc. xxii. 1 f.

[1] ὁδηγήσει, said here of the Lamb, is used of the Spirit of Christ in Jo. xvi. 13.

Part III. vii.

proceeding out of the throne of God and of the Lamb...on this side of the river and on that was the tree of life bearing twelve manner of fruits, yielding its fruit every month, and the leaves of the tree were for the healing of the nations. It may be said that this is a picture of the Christian Society in the world, the Catholic Church in which the Spirit already dwells; for have we not already *come unto Mount Zion, and unto the city of the living God, the heavenly Jerusalem*? are not the River of Life and the Tree of Life already in our midst? Yet St John's vision is certainly not exhausted by present experience. It is the ideal City which he sees, and though the Church strives to realize the vision, she fails age after age, for in its fulness it belongs to the perfect life. Meanwhile the vision witnesses to the continuity of the life of perfectness with the life of grace, and to the permanence of the great facts of the spiritual order. Nothing can be clearer than that the River of the Water of Life is one of these permanent features; whatever fulfilments it may find in the present mission of the Spirit, we are encouraged by the vision to believe that it will continue to fulfil itself in ages to come. Without its broad stream of crystal water flowing through its central street, and its great avenue of ever green, ever fruitbearing trees on either side of the river, the New Jerusalem would lack its most characteristic glory. The Church without the Spirit would cease to be the true City of God.

Heb. xii. 22.

The River of Life is seen by St John proceeding out of the throne of God and of the Lamb. So he traces to its ultimate source both the present temporal mission of the Holy Spirit and His future work upon the spirits of the just made perfect. The whole flood of life which will, world without end, make glad the City of God, issues forth from the glorified humanity of the Incarnate Son. The throne on which He reigns with the Eternal Father is the exhaustless fountain-head from which the Spirit will be for ever poured into the hearts of the redeemed.

Here our view of New Testament teaching upon the Being and work of the Holy Spirit must end. The result of the whole enquiry has been to place before the mind not a doctrine but an experience. The Spirit has revealed itself to us in the history and life of the first age: in the ministry of the Forerunner and of the Lord, in the work of the primitive Church, in the witness of Apostolic teachers, especially of St Paul and St John. We have seen the Divine Energy, of which the Old Testament spoke as the Spirit of God, manifesting itself in new relations, and by new processes of spiritual life. It has been revealed as the Spirit of Christ, and the Spirit of the Body of Christ; it has made for itself a sanctuary in the heart of man, consecrating his whole being to the service of God, in whose image it has created him anew. The whole amazing picture is drawn for us by men who speak of what they knew and had seen in the life of the age which immediately followed the great day of Pentecost. If at any time they go beyond their personal knowledge, it is only to give expression to hopes which were justified by events which had occurred in their own day.

No age of the Church can depart fundamentally from this experience. The same Spirit inspires the whole Body to the end of time. But each age receives its own manifestation of the Spirit's presence. Loyalty to the Apostles' teaching and fellowship does not exclude readiness to follow the guidance of the Spirit of truth when it leads into paths which the first generation were not called to tread. The New Testament marks out the great lines of Christian truth which can never be changed; but it leaves to successive generations the task and the joy of pursuing them into new regions of thought and life, as the Divine Guide points the way.

APPENDIX

OF

ADDITIONAL NOTES

O REX GLORIAE, DOMINE UIRTUTUM, QUI TRIUMPHATOR SUPER OMNES CAELOS ASCENDISTI: NE DERELINQUAS NOS ORPHANOS, SED MITTE PROMISSUM PATRIS IN NOS SPIRITUM UERITATIS.

ALLELUIA.

APPENDIX

Additional Note A. THE DOVE AS A SYMBOL OF THE HOLY SPIRIT.

" " B. THE BAPTISM IN THE EARLY HERETICAL SYSTEMS.

" " C. THE δαιμόνια OF THE GOSPELS.

" " D. THE 'OTHER PARACLETE.'

" " E. THE RELATION OF THE ASCENSION TO THE PENTECOSTAL EFFUSION OF THE SPIRIT.

" " F. THE RELATION OF THE PENTECOSTAL EFFUSION TO EARLIER COMINGS OF THE SPIRIT.

" " G. THE GIFT OF PROPHECY.

" " H. THE GIFT OF TONGUES.

" " I. THE LAYING ON OF HANDS.

" " J. UNCTION.

" " K. RAPTURE AND ECSTASY.

" " L. THE INSPIRATION OF SACRED BOOKS.

" " M. REGENERATION.

" " N. SANCTIFICATION.

" " O. FLESH AND SPIRIT.

" " P. 'SPIRIT' AND 'THE SPIRIT.'

" " Q. THE HOLY SPIRIT IN JEWISH APOCALYPTIC WRITINGS.

" " R. THE HOLY SPIRIT IN SOME EARLY CHRISTIAN UNCANONICAL GOSPELS, ACTS, AND APOCALYPSES.

" " S. READINGS OF COD. BEZAE WHICH BEAR UPON THE SUBJECT OF THIS BOOK.

A.

THE DOVE AS A SYMBOL OF THE HOLY SPIRIT.

All the Gospels relate that the descent of the Spirit on the newly baptized Christ was symbolized by the appearance of a bodily form (Lc. iii. 22) which resembled a dove (Mc. i. 10, Mt. iii. 16, Lc. *l.c.*, Jo. i. 32). Whether the dove was real or spectacular, it was clearly symbolical of the Spirit which henceforth rested on the humanity of the Lord.

What was the exact meaning of the symbol? Why was the dove chosen rather than some other symbol of the Spirit, such as water, fire, or wind?

In the O.T. the dove meets us in the story of the Flood (Gen. viii. 8 ff.), and in connexion with sacrificial rites (Gen. xv. 9, Lev. i. 14, &c.; cf. Lc. ii. 24, Mc. xi. 15). Its flight is the type of swiftness and beauty (Ps. lv. 6, lxviii. 13); its gentleness and grace supplied the Eastern lover with an image for the person or the eyes of his beloved (Cant. i. 15, ii. 14, iv. 1, v. 2, 12, vi. 9). In other passages it seems to be used as a symbol of Israel, inoffensive and defenceless among the nations of the earth (Ps. lxxiv. 19, Hos. vii. 11, xi. 11). More than one ancient writer remarks upon the sacredness of the dove in Syria (Lucian, *dea Syra* 54 *περιστερὴ χρῆμα ἱρότατον καὶ οὐδὲ ψαύειν αὐτῶν δικαιεῦσι*: Tibullus i. 7 alba Palestino sancta

Add. Note A. columba Syro), but whether this feeling prevailed in Israel there is not sufficient evidence to shew.

Our Lord (Mt. x. 16) speaks of the dove as the embodiment of the harmlessness which was characteristic of His own human life (Heb. vii. 26; cf. Clem. Al. *paed.* i. 14), and ought to characterize His disciples.

Mr F. C. Conybeare (*Expositor* IX. ix. p. 454) has pointed out that Philo regards the dove as the symbol of the Divine Wisdom; the *τρυγών* is *φιλέρημος, τὴν μόνωσιν ἀγαπῶσα*, the *περιστερά* is *ἥμερος, διαίτῃ τῇ μετὰ θνητῶν ἀσμενίζουσα*, and Wisdom has both qualities. It is more than precarious to suppose that Philo influenced the Christian tradition of the Baptism. But it is possible that the association of the dove with Wisdom or the Holy Spirit was familiar to his generation, and if so, the choice of the symbol may be in some measure due to that circumstance.

But behind this or any other symbolism there probably lay the reference in Gen. i. 2 to the birdlike hovering of the Spirit of God over the waters of the chaos. At the Baptism the New Creation took its rise out of the waters of the Jordan; the Spirit of God again moved upon the face of the waters, bringing forth an ordered life. The form of the descending bird represented this great mystery; that the bird was a dove may be explained by the associations already mentioned.

For the use of the dove in early Christian art see Cabrol, *Dictionnaire d'archéologie chrétienne* fasc. XIII., col. 346 ff., where many illustrations are given.

B.

THE BAPTISM OF CHRIST IN THE EARLY HERETICAL SYSTEMS.

The following passages will serve to illustrate the views of the chief early heretical teachers on the subject of the Baptism.

CERINTHUS according to Irenaeus (i. 26. 1) taught "post baptismum descendisse in eum [Iesum] ab ea principalitate quae est super omnia Christum figura columbae, et tunc annuntiasse incognitum Patrem et uirtutes perfecisse; in fine autem reuolasse iterum Christum de Iesu et Iesum passum esse et resurrexisse; Christum autem impassibilem perseuerasse, exsistentem spiritalem" (cf. Hippolytus, *phil.* vii. 33). Similarly Epiphanius (i. 28. 1): Cerinthus held *μετὰ τὸ ἁδρυνθῆναι τὸν Ἰησοῦν τὸν ἐκ σπέρματος Ἰωσὴφ καὶ Μαρίας γεγεννημένον, κατεληλυθέναι τὸν Χριστὸν εἰς αὐτόν, τουτέστιν τὸ πνεῦμα τὸ ἅγιον ἐν εἴδει περιστερᾶς ἐν τῷ Ἰορδάνῃ.*

The EBIONITES, who like the Cerinthians regarded Jesus as the son of Mary and Joseph by natural generation (Iren.), agreed with them also in attaching the greatest significance to the Baptism. It was the moment when He became the Christ and the Son of God by the Father's choice: cf. Justin, *dial.* 49 *οἱ λέγοντες ἄνθρωπον γεγονέναι αὐτὸν καὶ κατ' ἐκλογὴν κεχρίσθαι καὶ Χριστὸν γεγονέναι.* When Epiphanius (i. 30. 14) adds *βούλονται...Χριστὸν ἐν αὐτῷ* (sc. *τῷ Ἰησοῦ*) *γεγενῆσθαι τὸν ἐν περιστερᾶς εἴδει καταβεβηκότα,* he attributes to the Ebionites a Gnostic view which was probably not known to primitive Ebionism.

The BASILIDIANS shewed their sense of the importance of the Baptism by observing the day as a festival and spending the previous night in a vigil-service: Clem. Al.

Add. Note B.

strom. i. 21 (146) *οἱ δὲ ἀπὸ* Βασιλείδου *καὶ τοῦ βαπτίσματος αὐτοῦ τὴν ἡμέραν ἑορτάζουσι προδιαννκτερεύοντες ἀναγνώσεσι*[1]. Clement adds that they regarded the dove as the 'Minister' or 'Ministering Spirit': *fragm.* 16 *καὶ ἡ περιστερὰ δὲ σῶμα ὤφθη, ἣν οἱ μὲν τὸ ἅγιον πνεῦμά φασιν, οἱ δὲ ἀπὸ* Βασιλείδου *τὸν διάκονον* (cf. *strom.* ii. 8. 449, and see Hort in *D. C. B.* I. p. 276). The effect of the descent of the Aeon on Jesus was to reveal to him the Gospel which he thenceforth preached: Hippol. vii. 26 *κατῆλθεν ἀπὸ τῆς ἑβδομάδος τὸ φῶς...ἐπὶ τὸν* Ἰησοῦν *τὸν υἱὸν τῆς* Μαρίας, *καὶ ἐφωτίσθη συνεξαφθεὶς τῷ φωτὶ τῷ λάμψαντι εἰς αὐτόν.*

The VALENTINIANS were agreed in regarding the Power which descended on Jesus as an Aeon, but differed widely in details. See Iren. i. 7. 2 *εἰσὶ δὲ οἱ λέγοντες... εἰς τοῦτον ἐπὶ τοῦ βαπτίσματος κατελθεῖν ἐκεῖνον τὸν ἀπὸ τοῦ πληρώματος ἐκ πάντων* Σωτῆρα *ἐν εἴδει περιστερᾶς*: iii. 16. 1 sunt qui dicunt Iesum quidem receptaculum Christi fuisse, in quem desuper quasi columbam descendisse Christum. Hippolytus (vi. 35) thus distinguishes the views of the Italic and Anatolic schools: *οἱ μὲν ἀπὸ τῆς* Ἰταλίας...*ψυχικόν φασι τὸ σῶμα τοῦ* Ἰησοῦ *γεγονέναι, καὶ διὰ τοῦτο ἐπὶ τοῦ βαπτίσματος τὸ πνεῦμα ὡς περιστερὰ κατελήλυθε, τουτέστιν ὁ λόγος ὁ τῆς μητρὸς ἄνωθεν τῆς σοφίας...οἱ δ' αὖ ἀπὸ τῆς ἀνατολῆς λέγουσιν... ὅτι πνευματικὸν ἦν τὸ σῶμα τοῦ σωτῆρος· πνεῦμα γὰρ ἅγιον ἦλθεν ἐπὶ τὴν* Μαρίαν, *τουτέστιν ἡ σοφία.* What place the latter school assigned to the baptismal descent does not appear. Clement, however, in the excerpt already cited (*fragm.* 16) says: *οἱ δὲ ἀπὸ* Οὐαλεντίνου (the Anatolic school) *τὸ πνεῦμα τῆς ἐνθυμήσεως τοῦ πατρός τὴν κατέλευσιν πεποιημένον ἐπὶ τὴν τοῦ λόγου σάρκα.*

The significance which the early Catholic Church attached to the Baptism is well shewn by Irenaeus, iii. 18. 3:

[1] See Cabrol, *Dict. d'arch. chrét.*, fasc. XIII., col. 350.

in Christi enim nomine subauditur qui unxit, et ipse qui unctus est, et ipsa unctio in qua unctus est. Et unxit quidem Pater, unctus est uero Filius, in Spiritu qui est unctio.

C.

THE ΔΑΙΜΟΝΙΑ OF THE GOSPELS.

The word *δαιμόνιον* is widely distributed through the N.T., appearing in each of its sections, though most frequent in the Gospels, especially the Synoptists (Mt.[9], Mc.[13], Lc.[20], Jo.[6], Acts[1], Paul[5], Jas.[1], Apoc.[3]). *Δαίμων* occurs once (Mt. viii. 31) with no perceptible difference of meaning.

The *δαιμόνια* are *πνεύματα*, but *πνεῦμα* where so used is commonly qualified by *ἀκάθαρτον* (Mt. x. 1, xii. 43, Mc. i. 23 ff., iii. 11, 30, v. 2, 8, 12, vi. 7, vii. 25, ix. 25, Lc. iv. 36, vi. 18, viii. 29, ix. 42, xi. 24, Acts v. 16, viii. 7, Apoc. xvi. 13, xviii. 2) or *πονηρόν* (Mt. xii. 4, Lc. vii. 21, viii. 2, xi. 26, Acts xix. 12 ff.). *Πνεῦμα δαιμονίου* (*ἀκαθάρτου*) is found in Lc. iv. 33, Apoc. xvi. 14; cf. *πνεῦμα πύθων* in Acts xvi. 16.

In the Acts and Epistles the word bears the sense which it usually has in the O.T.; the *δαιμόνια* are the evil forces which lie behind the immoral worships of the heathen world (1 Cor. x. 20, 21, Apoc. ix. 20; cf. Deut. xxxii. 16 f., Ps. xc. (xci.) 6, xcv. (xcvi.) 5, cv. (cvi.) 37, Isa. lxv. 3, 11, Baruch iv. 7), or they are the powers of evil generally (Jas. ii. 19, 1 Tim. iv. 1). The wisdom of the world on its worst side is said to be *δαιμονιώδης*, of the sort which is akin to the character of the *δαιμόνια* (Jas. iii. 15).

In the Gospels the *δαιμόνια* appear as unclean spirits which enter into men (Lc. viii. 30), who are thereupon said

Add. Note C.

ἔχειν δαιμόνιον (Mt. xi. 18, Lc. vii. 33, Jo. vii. 20, viii. 48 ff., x. 20), or to be 'demonized' (δαιμονίζεσθαι Mt. iv. 24, viii. 16, 28, 33, ix. 33, xii. 22, xv. 22, Mc. i. 32, v. 15 ff., Lc. viii. 36, Jo. x. 21). In some cases more than one demon takes up his abode in the same human victim (ἑπτά 'Mc.' xvi. 9, Lc. viii. 2; πολλοί ἐσμεν, Mc. v. 9). The effects of their indwelling are madness (Jo. x. 20), epilepsy (Mc. ix. 20 ff.), and other diseases—chiefly, as far as can be seen, such as are mental or connected with the nervous system. The person who is under the influence of a demon is not master of himself; the evil spirit speaks through his lips or makes him dumb at pleasure (Mc. i. 34, iii. 11, ix. 25), drives him whither it wills (Lc. viii. 29) and generally uses him as its tool, sometimes imparting for this end a superhuman strength (Mc. v. 3 f.).

Exorcism seems to have been freely used by the Jews of our Lord's time to overcome the power of the demons (Mt. xii. 27, Acts xix. 13). Jesus used no formula or incantation, but relied on the power of His own word; at His bidding or at the bidding of men authorized by Him the demons were constrained to leave their victims, and go elsewhere (Mc. v. 10 ἔξω τῆς χώρας, Lc. viii. 31 εἰς τὴν ἄβυσσον).

It is not clear in what relation these evil spirits stand to the personal or quasi-personal 'Satan.'

In some passages the action of the δαιμόνια is identified with that of Satan; e.g. in Acts x. 38 where our Lord is said to have gone from place to place ἰώμενος πάντας τοὺς καταδυναστευομένους ὑπὸ τοῦ διαβόλου, i.e. τοὺς δαιμονιζομένους; and Mc. iii. 23 f. where His casting out of the demons is treated as synonymous with the casting out of Beelzebul, i.e. Satan, who is ὁ ἄρχων τῶν δαιμονίων. Similarly in Lc. xiii. 11 the woman who had a πνεῦμα ἀσθενείας for eighteen years which prevented her from lifting herself up is said to have been bound by Satan.

The δαιμόνια are thus regarded as Satan's subalterns, doing his work. It would appear that they are to be identified with the 'angels' who are classed with the Devil in Mt. xxv. 41, Apoc. xii. 8 f., and perhaps also with the πνευματικὰ τῆς πονηρίας of Eph. vi. 12, which are at once ἐν τοῖς ἐπουρανίοις (belonging to the unseen world) and yet are κοσμοκράτορες τοῦ σκότους τούτου.

However this may be, it seems that the teaching of the New Testament, both in the Gospels and the Epistles, supports the doctrine that there is a spiritual order of beings or forces which is directly antagonistic to Christ and to His Spirit in the Church. In the days of His flesh our Lord, full of the Holy Spirit, cast these unclean spirits out of the bodies of the possessed, even as He Himself in the Spirit had driven away their Ruler. When after the Ascension He came again in the Spirit the same antagonism appeared, but the battle was fought thenceforth in the inner life of man. The Ruler of this world (Jo. xii. 31 f., xvi. 11), the Ruler of the power of the air (Eph. ii. 2), already potentially condemned and cast out by the victory of the Cross, still retains his precarious hold on the world of heathendom, and wages war upon the Body of Christ (Eph. vi. 12 ἔστιν ἡμῖν ἡ πάλη...πρὸς τὰς ἀρχάς), working through his agents, the countless forces of spiritual evil which only the Parousia will finally disperse. Such a view of the mystery of life may be inconsistent with present modes of thought, but that it was held by the generation to whom we owe the New Testament, and that they represent our Lord as having held it, there is no reason to doubt.

D.

THE 'OTHER PARACLETE.'

Ἄλλον παράκλητον δώσει ὑμῖν seems to imply that when the Fourth Gospel was written the term παράκλητος was already applied in Christian circles to Jesus Christ, and this is confirmed by its direct use in reference to our Lord in 1 Jo. ii. 1. It is even possible that the Lord had so described Himself in conversations with the Twelve, using the Aramaic פרקליטא (= Neo-Hebrew פרקליט, *Aboth* iv. 15; cf. C. Taylor *ad loc.*), and that ἄλλον παράκλητον is a direct reminiscence of His last discourse.

That in 1 Jo. ii. 1 the word is rightly translated *Advocate* is not questioned, and the same meaning is claimed for it in Jo. xiv. 16, 26, xv. 26, xvi. 7 by Bp Lightfoot (*On a fresh revision of the N. T.*, p. 50) and Bp Westcott (*St John*, ed. 1908, II. p. 188 ff.). The form is undoubtedly passive, and *advocatus* is the natural interpretation of a passive verbal formed from παρακαλεῖν. Against this it is urged (e.g. by Jülicher, in *Enc. Bibl.* 3569) that usage seems to have favoured an active sense; in Job xvi. 2 Aquila and Theodotion substitute παράκλητοι for LXX. παρακλήτορες, and in Philo παράκλητος occurs in the sense of 'counsellor' (*De mund. opif.* 6 οὐδενὶ δὲ παρακλήτῳ...μόνῳ δὲ ἑαυτῷ χρησάμενος ὁ θεός), or 'intercessor' (*vit. Mos.* iii. 14, where the Logos is so described); see Hatch, *Essays*, p. 82 f. The Advocate passes naturally into the Intercessor or the Counsellor or the Comforter, as the needs of the case may require.

The question is complicated by the use of παράκλησις in the Acts and Epistles. When in Acts ix. 31 we read of the παράκλησις τοῦ ἁγίου πνεύματος, we are tempted to connect this word, whether in the sense of 'exhortation' or of 'comfort,' with St John's title for the Holy Spirit. But there is no evidence that παράκλητος was used beyond the Johannine circle, or that it suggested the Christian use of παράκλησις, which would naturally arise from the constant need of a name to express one of the commonest of Christian duties. The παράκλησις of the Holy Spirit is that deepest encouragement or appeal which is addressed to the hearts of men by the voice of God.

On the whole it seems best to translate παράκλητος 'Advocate' in the Gospel as well as in the Epistle. The ἄλλος παράκλητος must be such as His predecessor was and is. But the Advocate who pleads our cause in the heart does not merely defend and protect; He intercedes, He counsels, He instructs, He comforts. Thus the name of 'Comforter,' which has held its place in English versions of St John's Gospel from the time of Wyclif, is not wholly misleading, although it might have been better if the English reader had been from the first accustomed to the more comprehensive 'Paraclete.'

E.

THE RELATION OF THE ASCENSION TO THE PENTECOSTAL EFFUSION OF THE SPIRIT.

That the departure of the Incarnate Son to the Father was a necessary condition of the coming of the Spirit from the Father is taught explicitly in Jo. xvi. 7 ἐὰν μὴ ἀπέλθω, ὁ παράκλητος οὐ μὴ ἔλθῃ πρὸς ὑμᾶς. And as a matter of fact, as the Evangelist writing after the event remarks, there was 'no Spirit,' no coming or effusion of the Spirit, until Jesus had been glorified (Jo. vii. 39). The sending of the

Add. Note E.

Spirit was the direct and almost immediate consequence of His glorification, i.e. His return to the Father (Lc. xxiv. 49, Acts ii. 33). There was an interval of "not many days," which was necessary in order that the Church might be prepared by a period of waiting and prayer, and that the Coming might coincide with the Pentecost when Jerusalem would be full of pilgrims from all parts. On Christ's part all was ready from the moment of the Ascension.

The two phrases which St John uses for the Ascension explain the relation in which it stands to the Descent of the Spirit.

1. The Ascension was a departure, to be followed by an arrival (ἀπέλθω...ἔλθῃ). It was the withdrawal of a visible Presence, the *terminus ad quem* of the earthly life and the *terminus a quo* of a Presence purely spiritual. The two modes of Christ's presence could not be conterminous or coexist; the second could not begin till the first had reached its end. The Ascension completed the days of the Son of Man, the life which He lived in the flesh. The Resurrection had begun the great change; from Easter morning He was already ascending (Jo. xx. 17 ἀναβαίνω); the final rapture on the Mount of Olives ended the ascent (ἀναβέβηκα) and ushered in that life in the Spirit in which He could come to His own again, and abide with them for ever.

2. The Ascension was the glorification of the Son of Man (Jo. xii. 16 ἐδοξάσθη Ἰησοῦς, xvii. 5 νῦν δόξασόν με σύ, πάτερ, παρὰ σεαυτῷ): the humanity, perfected by suffering (Heb. ii. 10, v. 9) and victorious over death, entered the Divine Presence to take its place in union with the Person of the Eternal Son at the right hand of the Father. But the glorification of humanity in Christ has for its end the endowment of humanity in the rest of the race. He ascended up that He might fill all things (Eph. iv. 10) As the righteous, victorious Head of the Church He

claimed and received for her the promised gift of the Spirit (Acts ii. 33) by which members of the Christ are to be in due course brought to the glory of their Head. Add Note E.

F.

THE RELATION OF THE PENTECOSTAL EFFUSION TO EARLIER COMINGS OF THE SPIRIT.

The Pentecostal coming of the Spirit is represented in the N.T. as a mission parallel to the mission of the Son, and consequent upon it. Cf. Jo. xiv. 24, 26 *τοῦ πέμψαντός με πατρός...τὸ πνεῦμα τὸ ἅγιον ὃ πέμψει ὁ πατὴρ ἐν τῷ ὀνόματί μου*; Gal. iv. 4, 6 *ἐξαπέστειλεν ὁ θεὸς τὸν υἱὸν αὐτοῦ ...ἐξαπέστειλεν ὁ θεὸς τὸ πνεῦμα τοῦ υἱοῦ αὐτοῦ.* As the Son "came into the world" at the Advent (Jo. xvi. 28), so the Spirit came at the Pentecost; before the Pentecost there was "no Spirit" in this sense.

Yet the O.T. prophets claim that the Spirit was at work in Israel even in the days of the Exodus (Isa. lxiii. 11 ff.), while the broader thought of Alexandrian Judaism held that the Spirit 'filled the world' and was to be found in the lives of all wise and good men. Is this belief consistent with the Christian doctrine of the Pentecostal Coming?

The same difficulty arises in connexion with the Incarnation of the Word. If the Son was not sent into the world until the fulness of the times had been reached, yet He was in the world from the first (Jo. i. 9 *ἦν...ἐρχόμενον*, 10 *ἐν τῷ κόσμῳ ἦν*; compare the doctrine of the Divine Wisdom in Prov. viii. 27–31). Similarly the Spirit of God has ever been in the world from the moment when it

Add. Note F.

moved on the face of the waters, calling forth vitality and a cosmic order. As man emerged from the mere animal into a conscious intellectual life, the Spirit wrought upon him; and the history of Israel in particular is one long manifestation of His presence and working in the Chosen People. Yet there was no indwelling of the Spirit in men, no effusion of His life and power upon the race in general, till He received the special mission which sent Him to carry forward the work of the Incarnate Son. The new order involved in that mission is characterized as having its sphere in believers (Jo. xiv. 17 *ἐν ὑμῖν ἔσται*). The entrance of the Spirit into the Body of the Church, and into the hearts of its members individually, corresponds with the entrance of the Word into the womb of Mary; though not like that an incarnation, it is a permanent inhabitation of humanity (Jo. xiv. 16 *ἵνα ᾖ μεθ' ὑμῶν εἰς τὸν αἰῶνα*).

Thus the Pentecostal effusion of the Spirit in no way conflicts with the doctrine of the Spirit's world-long activity in nature and in man, while on the other hand it is seen to inaugurate a new association of the Spirit with humanity far more intimate and enduring than any which had previously existed.

G.

THE GIFT OF PROPHECY.

This note will deal only with prophecy as a *χάρισμα*, i.e. as one of the gifts bestowed upon the Church by the Spirit of Christ.

1. The gift was not universal (1 Cor. xii. 10 *ἄλλῳ δὲ προφητεία*, 29 *μὴ πάντες προφῆται;*), but it was widely

diffused in the churches, at least in those founded by St Paul (Acts xx. 23 τὸ πνεῦμα τὸ ἅγιον κατὰ πόλιν διαμαρτύρεταί). In the congregation at Corinth it was evidently usual to hear several prophetic utterances at every assembly, and the Apostle even contemplates the possibility of every member of the Church prophesying in turn (1 Cor. xiv. 28 ff.). Probably, however, only a relatively small number of believers were 'established to be prophets,' forming a charismatic order to which a recognized position was given in the Church. Such persons were said ἔχειν προφητείαν (1 Cor. xiii. 2), and known as οἱ προφῆται (Eph. ii. 20, iii. 5, Apoc. xviii. 20, xxii. 6), being thus distinguished from those who occasionally 'prophesied' (Acts xix. 6, 1 Cor. xi. 4 f., xiv. 31).

2. At first there was a disposition in the Gentile churches to undervalue the gift of prophecy, and even to make light of the utterances of the prophets (1 Thess. v. 19 f. τὸ πνεῦμα μὴ σβέννυτε, προφητείας μὴ ἐξουθενεῖτε); probably because the gift of tongues was more novel and attractive. In 1 Corinthians St Paul sets himself to correct this error of judgement, placing the prophetic order next after the Apostolate (xii. 28 δεύτερον προφήτας), and pointing out the value of prophecy as a means of edification and conversion (xiv. 3 ff., 24 ff.). The prophets seem to have been in fact to a great extent the teaching ministry of the primitive Church, and to have acquired before the end of the century an influence which overshadowed that of the bishops and deacons (see the writer's *Apocalypse*, p. xx f.). Their gift was sometimes exercised in the selection of other ministers (Acts xiii. 1 ff., xx. 28, 1 Tim. i. 18, iv. 14); together with the Apostles they might be regarded as the foundation stones of the Church (Eph. ii. 20), sharing with the highest order the task of initiating and consolidating all Christian work. It is easy to understand the great importance of a body of men

under the immediate guidance of the Spirit at a time when the local ministry was drawn from new converts who possessed a very imperfect knowledge of their faith, and had undergone little preparation in the way of moral or spiritual training.

3. Nevertheless, while placing a high value on the order of prophets, St Paul was conscious of its limitations. He realized that the imperfection of the instrument might seriously distort the impression which the Holy Spirit had purposed to convey. In his own experience he had found it to be his duty to neglect a command given to him *through the Spirit* (Acts xxi. 4); contrast his ready obedience when he was convinced that the Spirit itself prohibited progress (Acts xvi. 6 f.). *Spirits of prophets*, he taught, *are subject to prophets* (1 Cor. xiv. 32), i.e. the prophets were responsible for their use of their gift. The utterances of the prophets might be subjected to tests, which could be applied by other members of the congregation who possessed gifts of discrimination (1 Thess. v. 21, 1 Cor. xii. 10, xiv. 29). Prophets must prophesy according to the proportion of their faith (Rom. xii. 6), i.e. their power to use the gift aright varied with the measure of their own spiritual attainments. Christian prophecy was no mantic art, but a spiritual power which needed a spiritual man to turn it to good account.

4. The great purpose of Christian prophecy was to bear witness to Jesus Christ (Apoc. xix. 10). The Spirit of prophecy was the Spirit of witness which belonged to the Church as a whole (Jo. xv. 26, Acts i. 8), but was specially manifested in the mission of the prophetic order. As the Church grew in knowledge and faith, it became increasingly able to bear its witness through the regular ministry and in the lives of its members generally. Prophecies therefore, in the sense of specially inspired utterances, gradually ceased in the Church, the place of the

prophet being taken partly by the teaching bishop or presbyter, partly by the testimony which every well-instructed believer bears by word or act to the name of the Lord Jesus. There is in the history of the Church an increasing advance towards the ideal state when 'all the Lord's people' shall be 'prophets' in this sense. But when that has been reached, prophecy, as St Paul knew it, will be at an end. For prophecy as a special gift of the Spirit was *in part, but when that which is perfect is come, that which is in part shall be done away* (1 Cor. xiii. 8ff.). Even the greatest and best of the *χαρίσματα* implied imperfection, and was therefore temporary; there was *a still more excellent way* in which the Spirit came to abide with men, the way of faith and hope and, above all, of love.

H.

THE GIFT OF TONGUES.

We begin by placing before us the whole of the N.T. evidence. With the exception of a passing reference to the Tongues in the appendix to St Mark, they are mentioned only in Acts and 1 Corinthians.

The passages are as follows:

'Mc.' xvi. 17 *γλώσσαις λαλήσουσιν καιναῖς* (om. *καιναῖς* C*L and some other authorities).

Acts ii. 4 *ἤρξαντο λαλεῖν ἑτέραις γλώσσαις καθὼς τὸ πνεῦμα ἐδίδου ἀποφθέγγεσθαι αὐτοῖς.*

Acts ii. 11 *ἀκούομεν λαλούντων αὐτῶν ταῖς ἡμετέραις γλώσσαις τὰ μεγαλεῖα τοῦ θεοῦ.*

Acts x. 46 *ἤκουον γὰρ αὐτῶν λαλούντων γλώσσαις καὶ μεγαλυνόντων τὸν θεόν.*

Add. Note H.

Acts xix. 6 ἐλάλουν τε γλώσσαις καὶ ἐπροφήτευον.

1 Cor. xii. 10 ἑτέρῳ [sc. διὰ τοῦ πνεύματος δίδοται] γένη γλωσσῶν, ἄλλῳ δὲ ἑρμηνία γλωσσῶν.

1 Cor. xii. 28 [ἔθετο ὁ θεὸς ἐν τῇ ἐκκλησίᾳ] γένη γλωσσῶν.

1 Cor. xii. 30 μὴ πάντες γλώσσαις λαλοῦσιν;

1 Cor. xiii. 1 ἐὰν ταῖς γλώσσαις τῶν ἀνθρώπων λαλῶ καὶ τῶν ἀγγέλων, ἀγάπην δὲ μὴ ἔχω, γέγονα χαλκὸς ἠχῶν ἢ κύμβαλον ἀλαλάζον.

1 Cor. xiv. 2—5 ὁ γὰρ λαλῶν γλώσσῃ οὐκ ἀνθρώποις λαλεῖ ἀλλὰ θεῷ, οὐδεὶς γὰρ ἀκούει, πνεύματι δὲ λαλεῖ μυστήρια ...ὁ λαλῶν γλώσσῃ ἑαυτὸν οἰκοδομεῖ...μείζων δὲ ὁ προφητεύων ἢ ὁ λαλῶν γλώσσαις, ἐκτὸς εἰ μὴ διερμηνεύῃ κτλ.

1 Cor. xiv. 13 διὸ ὁ λαλῶν γλώσσῃ προσευχέσθω ἵνα διερμηνεύῃ. ἐὰν γὰρ προσεύχωμαι γλώσσῃ, τὸ πνεῦμά μου προσεύχεται, ὁ δὲ νοῦς μου ἄκαρπός ἐστιν.

1 Cor. xiv. 18 πάντων ὑμῶν μᾶλλον γλώσσαις λαλῶ· ἀλλὰ ἐν ἐκκλησίᾳ θέλω πέντε λόγους τῷ νοΐ μου λαλῆσαι, ἵνα καὶ ἄλλους κατηχήσω, ἢ μυρίους λόγους ἐν γλώσσῃ.

1 Cor. xiv. 22 f. αἱ γλῶσσαι εἰς σημεῖόν εἰσιν οὐ τοῖς πιστεύουσιν ἀλλὰ τοῖς ἀπίστοις...ἐὰν οὖν συνέλθῃ ἡ ἐκκλησία ὅλη ἐπὶ τὸ αὐτὸ καὶ πάντες λαλῶσιν γλώσσαις, εἰσέλθωσιν δὲ ἰδιῶται ἢ ἄπιστοι, οὐκ ἐροῦσιν ὅτι μαίνεσθε;

1 Cor. xiv. 26 ff. ὅταν συνέρχησθε ἕκαστος...γλῶσσαν ἔχει, ἑρμηνίαν ἔχει...εἴτε γλώσσῃ τις λαλεῖ, κατὰ δύο ἢ τὸ πλεῖστον τρεῖς, καὶ ἀνὰ μέρος, καὶ εἷς διερμηνευέτω· ἐὰν δὲ μὴ ᾖ διερμηνευτής, σιγάτω ἐν ἐκκλησίᾳ, ἑαυτῷ δὲ λαλείτω καὶ τῷ θεῷ.

1 Cor. xiv. 39 τὸ λαλεῖν μὴ κωλύετε γλώσσαις.

The following points may be noted:

(1) The γλῶσσαι are attributed to the action of the Holy Spirit (Acts ii. 4, x. 45, xix. 6, 1 Cor. xii. 8—10); they belonged to τὰ πνευματικά (1 Cor. xiv. 1).

(2) They were ἕτεραι, not the native tongues of the speakers (Acts ii. 4), and καιναί, a fresh experience, one of the series of καινά brought in by the Incarnation.

(3) They were of various kinds, γένη γλωσσῶν (1 Cor. xii. 10, 28) just as there are various languages spoken among men (γένη φωνῶν ἐν κόσμῳ, 1 Cor. xiv. 10).

(4) At Corinth and in St Paul's experience the sounds uttered were not intelligible to a congregation, unless they were interpreted (1 Cor. xiv. 2 ff.); nor did they convey any meaning to the intelligence of the speaker, although they seem to have served as a means of stimulating spiritual activity and enabling him to hold fellowship with God and thus to gain personal edification (1 Cor. xiv. 2, 4, 14).

(5) On the first occasion when the gift was exercised, it appears that the utterances, which were 'strange' to the Apostles and their company, sounded in the ears of the excited crowd as the words of their mother tongues (Acts ii. 6 ff.). It will be observed, however, that the historian of the Acts does not affirm that the speakers spoke in the tongues of the several nationalities that made up the crowd, but only that the hearers so interpreted their utterances ἤκουσεν εἷς ἕκαστος...ἀκούομεν). It is a subjective effect which is described, and not an objective fact.

(6) Tongues, besides being a means of edification to the speaker, were in heathen lands a warning to non-Christians that the Church possessed an unexplained power which might be Divine (1 Cor. xiv. 22). On the other hand an unwise use of the power might lead to a suspicion that those who possessed it were either drunken or mad (Acts ii. 13, 1 Cor. xiv. 23).

(7) The 'interpretation of tongues' was a distinct gift of the Spirit, not necessarily possessed by the glossolalete (1 Cor. xii. 10); the man who spoke with tongues might pray for the power to interpret his own utterances, but it does not appear that he could acquire it by personal effort. From this it seems to follow that, in St Paul's experience at least, the 'tongues' did not answer to any language which was in actual use.

Add. Note H.

(8) Notwithstanding its liability to abuse St Paul did not forbid the exercise of this gift, which he recognized as an operation of the Spirit (1 Cor. xiv. 39). But he restricted its public use (*ib.* 27 f.), placed it last in his list of spiritual powers (1 Cor. xii. 10), and realized its temporary character (1 Cor. xiii. 8).

(9) On the whole it may be gathered that the gift of tongues was a manifestation of the Spirit conditioned by the circumstances of the first age, and experienced chiefly on occasions of strong excitement such as those described in the Acts, or by communities such as the Church at Corinth, which had been recently brought out of heathenism and lived in an environment unfavourable to the normal development of the Christian life. The spiritual element in the primitive *γλωσσολαλία* lay not in the strange utterances themselves, but in the elevation of heart and mind by which men were enabled to 'magnify God,' to 'speak mysteries,' to 'pray in the Spirit' and 'sing in the Spirit,' even at moments when the understanding was unfruitful, and the tongue refused to utter intelligible sounds.

I.

THE LAYING ON OF HANDS.

For the history of this ceremony in general the reader is referred to an article in Hastings' *D. B.* (III. 84 f.). The present note must be limited to its N.T. use in connexion with the imparting of the gifts of the Spirit.

There is a remarkable anticipation of this use in Deut. xxxiv. 9, a passage which refers to Num. xxvii. 18, 23 (see Driver *ad loc.*). By P, Joshua is represented "as a man in whom is (the) spirit" (אִישׁ אֲשֶׁר רוּחַ בּוֹ), on whom Moses is to lay his hands; D inverts the thought; "Joshua was full of the spirit of wisdom, for Moses had laid his hands upon him" (כִּי סָמַךְ מֹשֶׁה אֶת־יָדָיו עָלָיו). The laying on of hands, it seems to be implied, brought an increase of spiritual power to one who already possessed it.

In Acts the ceremony is twice used by Apostles on persons recently baptized, with the result that they 'received Holy Spirit' (Acts viii. 17) or that 'the Holy Spirit came upon them' (Acts xix. 6). Spiritual gifts followed; in the latter case the men *ἐλάλουν γλώσσαις καὶ ἐπροφήτευον*, in the former the sorcerer Simon was so impressed by what he saw that he offered the Apostles money for the magical power which he supposed them to possess.

There is an apparent reference to this post-baptismal ceremony in Heb. vi. 2 *βαπτισμῶν διδαχῆς* (WH., with Bd, *διδαχήν*) *ἐπιθέσεώς τε χειρῶν*. But the vagueness of the plural *βαπτισμῶν* suggests a wider meaning of *ἐπίθεσις χειρῶν* in this place. If *βαπτισμῶν διδαχή* is 'instruction in the rites of lustration' (Heb. ix. 10), i.e. those which culminated in John's baptism and the spiritual baptism ordained by Christ, *ἐπιθέσεως χειρῶν διδαχή* will in like manner cover the various uses of the laying on of hands under the old covenant and in the Church, including no doubt its use after baptism.

The Apostolic age used imposition of hands also in the setting apart of her members to any special ministry. Cf. Acts vi. 6 (the Seven); xiii. 3 (Barnabas and Saul); 1 Tim. iv. 14, 2 Tim. i. 6 (Timothy); 1 Tim. v. 22 (bishops and deacons ordained by Timothy). This *ἐπίθεσις χειρῶν* also was accompanied by a special *χάρισμα* (1 Tim. iv. 16 *τοῦ ἐν σοὶ χαρίσματος ὃ ἐδόθη σοι διὰ προφητείας μετὰ ἐπιθέσεως τῶν χειρῶν τοῦ πρεσβυτερίου*; 2 Tim. i. 6 *τὸ χάρισμα τοῦ θεοῦ ὅ ἐστιν ἐν σοὶ διὰ τῆς ἐπιθέσεως τῶν χειρῶν μου*). The gift is defined as *πνεῦμα δυνάμεως καὶ ἀγάπης καὶ σωφρονισμοῦ*. (For the interpretation of these

Add. Note I. passages see the foregoing pages, especially pp. 244 ff., 322 ff.).

In none of these instances of the laying on of hands is there any trace of a belief in the magical virtue of the act. It is simply the familiar and expressive sign of benediction inherited by the Apostles from the Synagogue and adapted to the service of the Church. As employed by the Spirit-bearing Body of Christ it was attended by the gifts of the Spirit for which prayer had been made in each case. The Church to-day follows the example of the Apostles in the rites of Confirmation and Ordination, expecting that in answer to her prayers the Apostolic sign will be accompanied in each case by such gifts as the needs of our own age and the duties to which men are severally called may seem to demand.

J.

UNCTION.

The N.T. uses the verb *χρίειν* metaphorically with reference to the Christ in Lc. iv. 18 (Isa. lxi. 1), Acts iv. 27, x. 38, Heb. i. 9 (Ps. xlv. 7); and with reference to Christians in 2 Cor. i. 21. The gift of the Holy Spirit is called *χρίσμα* in 1 Jo. ii. 20, 27.

Both the verb and the noun were adopted from the LXX. Χρίειν in the LXX. with few exceptions answers to מָשַׁח, which usually represents the religious use of oil or unguents, especially in the consecration of persons to high offices (cf. *Enc. Bibl.* I. col. 172 f.; Brown-Driver-Briggs, I. p. 602 f.). In Isa. lxi. 1 (quoted in Lc. *l.c.*) the office in view is that of the prophet; in Ps. xlv. 7 and in the majority of the O.T. references, it is that of king. In P there is frequent reference to the anointing of the high priest and the other priests, for which purpose a special *χρίσμα* was prepared (Exod. xxix. 7 *τὸ ἔλαιον τοῦ χρίσματος*, xxx. 25 *ἔλαιον χρίσμα ἅγιον*, xl. 13 = 15 *χρίσμα ἱερατίας*). This rite seems to have been limited at first to the high priest, who is therefore designated *ὁ ἱερεὺς ὁ χριστός* (Lev. iv. 5); but afterwards it was extended to Aaron's sons (see McNeile on Exodus, p. 188).

The *χρίσμα* in virtue of which Jesus is *ὁ χριστός* is explained in Acts x. 38 as *Holy Spirit and power*—words which connect themselves with Lc. iv. 1, 14 and point to the descent of the Spirit at the Baptism.

With reference to believers, the verb and the noun are each used only in a single context. In 2 Cor. i. 21 we read that it is God *ὁ βεβαιῶν ἡμᾶς...εἰς Χριστὸν καὶ χρίσας ἡμᾶς*, where *χρίσας* is evidently suggested by *Χριστόν*, and it is implied that the Apostle and his colleague shared the unction with which Christ was anointed, i.e. the power of the Spirit. In 1 Jo. ii. 20, 27 this is extended to all believers (*ὑμεῖς χρίσμα ἔχετε ἀπὸ τοῦ ἁγίου...ὑμεῖς τὸ χρίσμα ὃ ἐλάβετε ἀπ' αὐτοῦ κτλ.*). *Ἀπὸ τοῦ ἁγίου* and *ἀπ' αὐτοῦ* are ambiguous, but Christ is probably intended, as in Apoc. iii. 7. The train of thought will then be much the same as in Jo. i. 33, as if St John had written: *ὁ κεχρισμένος, αὐτός ἐστιν ὁ χρίων ἐν πνεύματι ἁγίῳ*[1]. The *χρίσμα* came on the whole Church at Pentecost, and upon individual members of Christ at their baptism (*v.* 27 *ἐλάβετε*). But it is not merely a historical fact or a fact realized once in life; the Unction abides (*ἔχετε, μένει*), and continues to inspire as it inspired at the first (*διδάσκει, ἐδίδαξεν*).

It has been customary to deny that the N.T. in these passages alludes to any post-baptismal ceremony of unction. At Carthage in the early years of the third century a

[1] Cf. Clem. Alex. *paed.* ii. 8 § 65 *τοῦτο σκευάζει Χριστὸς ἀνθρώποις γνωρίμοις, εὐωδίας ἄλειμμα, ἐκ τῶν οὐρανίων συντιθεὶς ἀρωμάτων τὸ μύρον.*

Add. Note J.

post-baptismal unction preceded the laying on of hands; cf. Tertullian *de bapt.* 7 egressi de lauacro perungimur benedicta unctione de pristina disciplina...dehinc manus imponitur. But it is precarious to infer from this passage that the custom descended from the Apostolic age. The writer to the Hebrews, it may be argued, would in this case have written in vi. 2 βαπτισμῶν διδαχῆς καὶ χρίσεως ἐπιθέσεώς τε χειρῶν. Nevertheless, since anointing was with the Jews (cf. Ruth iii. 3, Ezek. xvi. 9) as well as with the Greeks and Romans a normal accompaniment of the bath, it is not impossible that the λουτρὸν παλινγενεσίας was followed almost from the first by the use of oil or unguent, which came to be regarded as symbolical of the descent of the anointing Spirit on the Christ and His members. If so, a reference to the custom may be latent in 2 Cor. i. 21 and 1 Jo. ii. 20, 27.

The unction of the sick (Mc. vi. 13, Jas. v. 14) lies beyond the scope of this note, but it may be observed that ἀλείφειν and not χρίειν is used in this connexion. Of the use of unction at ordinations there is no trace in the N.T.

K.

RAPTURE AND ECSTASY.

1. Of Rapture, i.e. a physical removal from one place to another under the impulse of the Spirit, there is but one instance in the N.T. After the baptism of the Eunuch, "the Spirit of the Lord seized (ἥρπασεν) Philip, and the Eunuch saw him no more...but Philip was found at Azotus" (Acts viii. 39). There is no reason to doubt that he made his way from the Gaza road to Azotus (Ashdod) on foot or by some other ordinary means of transit. But he did so

under an impulse which is ascribed to the Holy Spirit, and possibly in a frame of mind in which he lost count of time and of outward surroundings. It may be imagined that it was not till he reached Azotus that he returned to the normal life of self-consciousness; how he came there he could not tell; all that lay between his sudden departure from the Eunuch and his arrival on the coast was a blank, or filled only by memories of a quickened life in the Spirit. Such an interpretation of the facts is merely conjectural, but it does not seem to be psychologically impossible in the circumstances of Philip's ministry.

2. Ecstasy (*ἔκστασις*), properly a surprise which staggers and overwhelms (Mc. v. 42, xvi. 8, Lc. v. 26, Acts iii. 10), is used thrice in the Acts for the mental condition in which men under the influence of the Holy Spirit become conscious only of things that belong to the heavenly order (Acts x. 10 f., xi. 5, xxii. 17). The state is described by St Paul from his own experience in 2 Cor. xii. 2 ff. *οἶδα ἄνθρωπον ἐν Χριστῷ...εἴτε ἐν σώματι οὐκ οἶδα εἴτε ἐκτὸς τοῦ σώματος...ἁρπαγέντα ἕως τρίτου οὐρανοῦ...ἡρπάγη εἰς τὸν παράδεισον καὶ ἤκουσεν ἄρρητα ῥήματα.* Similar experiences are related by St John in the Apocalypse (i. 10, iv. 2, xviii. 3, xxi. 10), with the assurance that on each occasion he was *ἐν πνεύματι*, i.e. in the sphere of spiritual realities, the Spirit of God working upon the human spirit and lifting it above the earthly and transient into the heart of the heavenly and eternal.

Such 'ecstasies' belong to the *rôle* of the apocalyptic prophet, and are not to be looked for among the ordinary operations of the Spirit. Something of the kind, however, seems to have been occasionally granted to the primitive believer who was not a 'prophet' (1 Cor. xiv. 26 *ἕκαστος... ἀποκάλυψιν ἔχει*); the first age thus literally fulfilled the prophecy *οἱ νεανίσκοι ὑμῶν ὁράσεις ὄψονται* (Acts ii. 17; cf. 1 Cor. xii. 1). Nor need we doubt that at times of great

Add. Note K.

spiritual stress or in individual cases such experiences may occur in any age. But they must always be exceptional; the normal workings of the Spirit of God are not ecstatic, but are conducted through the ordinary processes of human thought and feeling, gradually bringing heaven down to earth rather than by any sudden elevation lifting earth up to heaven.

L.

THE INSPIRATION OF SACRED BOOKS.

The *locus classicus* on this subject is 2 Tim. iii. 15 f., where, after mention of *ἱερὰ γράμματα* (evidently those of the O.T. Canon), the writer proceeds, Πᾶσα *γραφὴ θεόπνευστος καὶ ὠφέλιμος*, "every scripture inspired of God is also profitable." Θεόπνευστος is *ἅπ. λεγ.* in N.T. Greek, and does not occur in the LXX.[1], but its meaning is practically certain (see Ellicott *ad loc.*) and is well given by the Vulg. *divinitus inspirata.* The best comment upon *γραφὴ θεόπνευστος* is to be found in 2 Pet. i. 21 *ὑπὸ πνεύματος ἁγίου φερόμενοι ἐλάλησαν ἀπὸ θεοῦ ἄνθρωποι.* Strictly speaking, the inspiration belonged to the prophets and other writers of Scripture in a secondary sense, and only their words and their writings were *ἀπὸ θεοῦ.* Speech and writing gave expression to the personal inspiration of the authors; and so far as they expressed it they might be said to be inspired.

This 'inspiration' of the Old Testament is assumed throughout the Apostolic writings, and by our Lord, as His words are reported in the Gospels. The following passages will suffice to establish this point:

Mt. xxii. 63 Δαυεὶδ *ἐν πνεύματι καλεῖ κτλ.* = Mc. xii. 46

[1] It is not unknown in the later literary Greek, cf. Plutarch, *mor.* 904 F *τοὺς ὀνείρους τοὺς θεοπνεύστους.*

αὐτὸς Δ. εἶπεν ἐν τῷ πνεύματι τῷ ἁγίῳ. Lc. has simply αὐτὸς Δ. λέγει.

Acts i. 26 τὴν γραφὴν ἣν προεῖπεν τὸ πνεῦμα τὸ ἅγιον διὰ στόματος Δαυείδ (similarly iv. 25); xxviii. 25 καλῶς τὸ πνεῦμα τὸ ἅγιον ἐλάλησεν διὰ Ἠσαίου τοῦ προφήτου.

1 Pet. i. 11 ἐδήλου τὸ ἐν αὐτοῖς (sc. τοῖς προφήταις) πνεῦμα Χριστοῦ.

Heb. iii. 7 καθὼς λέγει τὸ πνεῦμα τὸ ἅγιον (in Ps. xcv.); ix. 8 τοῦτο δηλοῦντος τοῦ πνεύματος τοῦ ἁγίου (in Leviticus): x. 15 μαρτυρεῖ ἡμῖν καὶ τὸ πνεῦμα τὸ ἅγιον (in Jer. xxxi. 33).

That the 'former prophets,' i.e. the historical books, and the Hagiographa, are not quoted with a like claim to inspiration, may be accidental; but the Law, the Psalms, and the Prophets were probably felt to be in a special manner inspired by 'the Spirit of Christ.'

Except in the Apocalypse, which is a prophecy, and in 2 Peter, a book of doubtful genuineness, there is no reference in the N.T. to the inspiration of the Apostolic writings; the Church had as yet no ἱερὰ γράμματα. But the traditional belief in the inspiration of the N.T. finds its justification in the promises of Divine assistance made by our Lord to the Apostles and their company, and the special gifts of the Spirit possessed by the Apostolic age. If the first age was specially guided by the Spirit into a knowledge of all essential truth, its writings have rightly been gathered by the Church into a sacred canon. The Apostolic writings are inspired inasmuch as they are the work of inspired men. It is impossible to believe that the first generation of the Christian Church, fresh from the Pentecostal effusion of the Spirit, and richly endowed with spiritual gifts, spoke and wrote of the things of the Spirit with less θεοπνευστία than the lawgivers, historians, prophets and psalmists of Israel, or that their writings are a less precious heritage than the works of men who wrote before the Spirit came.

M.

REGENERATION.

The word is used but twice in the N.T. In Mt. xix. 28, ἐν τῇ παλινγενεσίᾳ ὅταν καθίσῃ ὁ υἱὸς τοῦ ἀνθρώπου ἐπὶ θρόνου δόξης αὐτοῦ (on which see Dalman, *Words of Jesus*, E. tr., p. 177 ff., and W. C. Allen, comm. *ad loc.*), the meaning appears to be 'the order which will follow the Parousia, the new heaven and the new earth of the prophets and apocalyptists.' In Tit. iii. 5 f., ἔσωσεν ἡμᾶς διὰ λουτροῦ παλινγενεσίας καὶ ἀνακαινώσεως πνεύματος ἁγίου, the reference is clearly to the new birth of the Spirit in Baptism.

Παλιγγενεσία was used by Stoic writers for the periodical restorations (ἀποκαταστάσεις) of the world after successive destructions by fire (ἐκπυρώσεις): thus M. Antoninus (xi. 1) speaks of τὴν περιοδικὴν παλιγγενεσίαν τῶν ὅλων; cf. Philo, *de incorr. mundi* 14 οἵ τε τὰς ἐκπυρώσεις καὶ τὰς παλιγγενεσίας εἰσηγούμενοι τοῦ κόσμου. But the term had a wider connotation; thus Philo elsewhere applies it to the recovery of the world from the Flood (*de vit. Moys.* ii. 12) and to life after death (*de leg. ad Cai.* 41; *de cherub.* 32); Josephus (*antt.* xi. 3. 9) speaks of the παλιγγενεσία τῆς πατρίδος which followed the return from Babylon; Cicero (*ad Attic.* vi. 6), of his own παλιγγενεσία. In Tit. *l. c.* the word is taken by St Paul into the service of the Holy Spirit, to represent the initial step in the great spiritual process by which *the old things passed away* or rather *have been made new* (2 Cor. v. 17 τὰ ἀρχαῖα παρῆλθεν, ἰδοὺ γέγονεν καινά) for those who in the baptismal bath have died with Christ and risen again; the birth of the new creation which rises out of the water over which the Spirit of Christ is pleased to brood. It is not impossible that the Apostle, who had met with Stoic philosophers at Athens, and probably also at Rome and in early life at Tarsus, intended to suggest a contrast between the Stoic παλιγγενεσία and the Christian: the one by fire, the other by water; the one physical, the other spiritual; the one subject to periodical relapses and renewals, the other occurring once for all and issuing in an endless life.

N.

SANCTIFICATION.

Ἁγιάζειν is used in the N.T. with reference to (1) the recognition on man's part of the holiness of God or of Christ (Mt. vi. 9, Lc. xi. 2, 1 Pet. iii. 15); (2) our Lord's consecration to His incarnate life by the Father's mission (Jo. x. 36) and by the offering of His own will (Jo. xvii. 19); (3) the consecration of material things to the service of God (Mt. xxiii. 17, 19, 2 Tim. ii. 21); (4) the consecration of the Church and each of its members to a life of progressive holiness (Jo. xvii. 17, Acts xx. 32, xxvi. 18, Rom. xv. 16, 1 Cor. i. 2, vi. 11, Eph. v. 26, 1 Th. v. 25, 1 Tim. iv. 5, Heb. ii. 11, ix. 12, x. 10, 14, 29, xiii. 12, Apoc. xxii. 11). Ἁγιασμός is used only in the last sense (1 Pet. i. 2, Rom. vi. 19, 22, 1 Cor. i. 30, 1 Th. iv. 3 f., 2 Th. ii. 13, Heb. xii. 14).

An examination of the last-named group of passages gives the following results. (*a*) God, the Father of Christ and of Christians, is the ultimate source of the spirit of consecration in man. He sanctifies men by means of the truth, i.e. the revelation of Himself which He has given in His Son, in which as in a congenial atmosphere the consecrated life springs up and thrives (Jo. xvii. 17 *ἁγίασον αὐτοὺς ἐν τῇ ἀληθείᾳ· ὁ λόγος ὁ σὸς ἀλήθειά ἐστιν.* (*b*) The

Add. Note N.

Father sanctifies through the mediation of the Son (1 Cor. i. 2 *ἡγιασμένοις ἐν Χριστῷ Ἰησοῦ*, vi. 11 *ἡγιάσθητε ἐν τῷ ὀνόματι τοῦ κυρίου ἡμῶν Ἰησοῦ Χριστοῦ*). (*c*) The Incarnate and glorified Son is thus mediately our Sanctifier (Eph. v. 26 *ὁ χριστὸς...ἑαυτὸν παρέδωκεν ὑπὲρ αὐτῆς* (sc. *τῆς ἐκκλησίας*) *ἵνα αὐτὴν ἁγιάσῃ*, Heb. ii. 11 *ὅ τε ἁγιάζων καὶ οἱ ἁγιαζόμενοι ἐξ ἑνὸς πάντες*). (*d*) The sanctifying work of Christ is based on His Sacrifice (Heb. x. 29 *τὸ αἷμα...ἐν ᾧ ἡγιάσθη*; xiii. 12 *ἵνα ἁγιάσῃ διὰ τοῦ ἰδίου αἵματος τὸν λαόν*), and it is realized in those who are united to Him by faith and baptism (Acts xxvi. 18 *ἐν τοῖς ἡγιασμένοις πίστει τῇ εἰς ἐμέ*, cf. 1 Cor. vi. 11 *ἡγιάσθητε...ἐν τῷ ὀνόματι τοῦ κυρίου ἡμῶν* Ἰ. Χ.). Thus our Lord becomes to us Sanctification (1 Cor. i. 30 *ὃς ἐγενήθη...ἁγιασμός*) (*e*) But when this sanctification, which is Christ in us, is translated into the experience of the Christian life, it is seen to belong to the sphere of the Spirit's activities (Rom. xv. 16 *ἡγιασμένη ἐν πνεύματι ἁγίῳ*; 1 Cor. vi. 11 *ἡγιάσθητε ...ἐν τῷ πνεύματι τοῦ θεοῦ ἡμῶν*; 2 Th. ii. 25, 1 Pet. i. 2 *ἐν ἁγιασμῷ πνεύματος*). Lastly (*f*), since the Spirit works through the Word and Sacraments, these are regarded as the means of our sanctification (Eph. v. 26 *ἵνα αὐτὴν ἁγιάσῃ, καθαρίσας τῷ λουτρῷ τοῦ ὕδατος ἐν ῥήματι*). Hence the baptized are described as *ἡγιασμένοι* or *ἅγιοι*, or more strictly as *ἁγιαζόμενοι*, consecrated persons who have at least entered on a life of holiness (1 Cor. i. 2, Heb. ii. 11); and in one place this consecration is extended to the near relatives of the baptized (1 Cor. vii. 14).

Thus in the words of the Anglican Catechism it is "the Holy Ghost who sanctifieth me and all the elect people of God." But the N.T. invites us to trace the work of our sanctification to its sources in God. Behind the work of the Spirit in our lives, there are the sacrificial death and the ascended life of Jesus Christ, who is our Sanctification in that He sends the Spirit and the Spirit is His own presence in the Church; and beyond this again we see the ultimate Source of all holiness, the love of the Father which gave the Son, and through the Son has given the Spirit of grace. Add. Note N.

O.

FLESH AND SPIRIT.

The contrast of flesh and spirit is found already in the O.T. (Isa. xxxi. 3 בָּשָׂר וְלֹא רוּחַ, LXX. *σάρκας καὶ οὐκ ἔστιν βοήθεια*, Α.Σ.Θ. *σάρκες καὶ οὐ πνεῦμα*). In the N.T. it first appears in Mc. xv. 38, Mt. xxvi. 21 (*τὸ μὲν πνεῦμα πρόθυμον, ἡ δὲ σὰρξ ἀσθενής*); see also Jo. iii. 51, vi. 63, 1 Pet. iii. 18, iv. 6, Heb. ix. 31 f., xii. 9. But it is St Paul who uses this antithesis most freely, and carries it into new fields of thought. It will be well to classify his uses of it. He employs it:

1. In reference to the incarnate life of our Lord.

Rom. i. 3 *τοῦ γενομένου ἐκ σπέρματος Δαυεὶδ κατὰ σάρκα, τοῦ ὁρισθέντος υἱοῦ θεοῦ ἐν δυνάμει κατὰ πνεῦμα ἁγιωσύνης ἐξ ἀναστάσεως νεκρῶν.* 1 Tim. iii. 16 *ἐφανερώθη ἐν σαρκί, ἐδικαιώθη ἐν πνεύματι.*

2. In reference to human nature in general.

Rom. ii. 28 f. *ἡ ἐν τῷ φανερῷ ἐν σαρκὶ περιτομή... περιτομὴ καρδίας ἐν πνεύματι οὐ γράμματι.* (Here there is a double contrast, *πνεῦμα* being set over against *σάρξ* on the one hand and *γράμμα* on the other; for the latter see 2 Cor. iii. 6.) 2 Cor. vii. 1 *καθαρίσωμεν ἑαυτοὺς ἀπὸ παντὸς μολυσμοῦ σαρκὸς καὶ πνεύματος.* Gal. iii. 3 *ἐναρξάμενοι πνεύματι νῦν σαρκὶ ἐπιτελεῖσθε;* (i.e. 'Is your life in Christ to be an anticlimax, and your last state worse than the first?'). Gal. iv. 24 ὁ κατὰ σάρκα γεννηθεὶς ἐδίωκε τὸν κατὰ πνεῦμα.

3. In reference to the Christian life viewed as a conflict between opposite principles of action.

(*a*) Gal. v. 16—24, vi. 8. The flesh and the Spirit here appear as irreconcilable enemies engaged in a warfare which continues to the end of life. Subjection to the flesh can be avoided only by following through life the leading of the Spirit. The flesh proceeds by way of lust (ἐπιθυμία) to acts of sensuality and every kind of open (φανερὰ) sin; the Spirit yields the fruit of every holy disposition. The end to which each of these forces leads is as opposite as their whole procedure; from the flesh comes corruption, from the Spirit life. This apparent dualism is tempered however by the repeated reminder (v. 18, 25, vi. 7 f.) that it rests with each individual to decide whether the one or the other shall be his master.

(*b*) Rom. viii. 4—13. Here the general conception is the same, but we are permitted to see further into the process by which the hostile principles work. Each acts upon the human mind, affections, and will, and creates a habit of thought and feeling, a fixed attitude of the inner man (φρόνημα) which governs his life. If the man walks after the flesh, his attitude is one of hostility towards God, and he lives in a state of rebellion against His ruling, which ends in spiritual death; if he walks after the Spirit, he is at peace with God, and the end is life. Here nothing is said of the ἔργα, the outward activities of the flesh, which were so 'manifest' in the heathen world; it is the bent and normal position of the inner life on which attention is concentrated. The distinction between the φρόνημα τῆς σαρκός and the φρόνημα τοῦ πνεύματος is even more vital than that which is drawn in Galatians between the ἔργα τῆς σαρκός and the καρπὸς τοῦ πνεύματος.

In these two contexts (Gal. v.—vi., Rom. viii.) it is

evident that the flesh is not simply human nature, or the external, physical side of human nature. The word carries in St Paul's use of it here an ethical sense; the flesh is the lower self as it exists under present conditions, a source of weakness at all times and of temptation often, but never of strength or goodness; see Rom. vii. 18 *οὐκ οἰκεῖ ἐν ἐμοί, τοῦτ' ἔστιν ἐν τῇ σαρκί μου, ἀγαθόν*, viii. 3 *σαρκὸς ἁμαρτίας*. But what is the spirit in antithesis to the flesh thus understood? Apparently not the Holy Spirit regarded as a Divine Person, nor simply the activity of the Spirit in men, but the higher side of human nature when by the power of the Divine Spirit it is set free from the domination of the flesh. See Rom. viii. 9 *ὑμεῖς δὲ οὐκ ἐστὲ ἐν σαρκὶ ἀλλ' ἐν πνεύματι, εἴπερ πνεῦμα θεοῦ οἰκεῖ ἐν ὑμῖν*. The spirit then as well as the flesh in St Paul's antinomy are both human, but the human spirit lies dormant and powerless till it has been awakened and enabled by the Spirit of God.

P.

'SPIRIT' AND 'THE SPIRIT.'

The New Testament uses the anarthrous *πνεῦμα* in the phrases *πνεῦμα Κυρίου*, *πνεῦμα θεοῦ*, and *πνεῦμα ἅγιον*, as well as where the noun stands without a defining genitive or adjective.

(1) *Πνεῦμα Κυρίου* occurs only in Lc. iv. 18 (a quotation from the O.T.), and Acts viii. 39; in Acts v. 9, 2 Cor. iii. 17 we find *τὸ πνεῦμα Κυρίου*.

(2) *Πνεῦμα θεοῦ* (Mt. iii. 16[1], xii. 28, Rom. viii. 9, 14,

[1] Prepositional phrase.

Add. Note P.

1 Cor. vii. 40[1], xii. 3, 2 Cor. iii. 3, Phil. iii.). Τὸ πνεῦμα τοῦ θεοῦ stands in nearly an equal number of passages.

(3) Πνεῦμα ἅγιον is far more frequent in the N.T. than either τὸ πνεῦμα τὸ ἅγιον or τὸ ἅγιον πνεῦμα, the proportion being 54 : 34. By tabulating all the instances of πνεῦμα ἅγιον we get the following results. The anarthrous form is used (*a*) after prepositions (ἐκ, Mt. i. 18, 20; διά, Acts i. 2, iv. 25, 2 Tim. i. 14; ὑπὸ, 2 Pet. i. 21; ἐν, Mt. iii. 11, Lc. iii. 16, Jo. i. 33, Acts i. 5, xi. 16, Rom. ix. 1, xiv. 17, xvi. 16, 1 Cor. xii. 3, 2 Cor. vi. 6, 1 Th. i. 5, Jude 20); (*b*) in the instrumental dative, without preposition (Mc. i. 8, Acts x. 38); (*c*) in the genitive, under government (Lc. i. 15, 41, 67, Acts ii. 4, iv. 8, vi. 5, vii. 55, ix. 17, xi. 24, xiii. 9, 52, Rom. xv. 13, 1 Th. i. 6, Tit. iii. 5, Heb. ii. 4, vi. 4); (*d*) in the accusative after διδόναι or λαμβάνειν (Lc. xi. 13, Jo. xv. 22, Acts viii. 15, 17, 19, xix. 2); (*e*) in the nominative (Lc. i. 35 πνεῦμα ἅγιον ἐπελεύσεται, ii. 25 πνεῦμα ἦν ἅγιον ἐπ' αὐτόν, Acts xix. 2 οὐδ' εἰ πνεῦμα ἅγιόν ἐστιν ἠκούσαμεν).

In (*a*) the anarthrous πνεῦμα ἅγιον may usually be explained by "the strong tendency to drop the article after a preposition[2]," and the case of (*b*) is not very different. But in (*d*) and (*e*), possibly also in (*c*), Middleton's canon seems to hold good; while τὸ πνεῦμα τὸ ἅγιον or τὸ ἅγιον πνεῦμα is the Holy Spirit considered as a Divine Person, πνεῦμα ἅγιον is a gift or manifestation of the Spirit in its relation to the life of man. Bp Ellicott indeed (on Gal. v. 5) proposes to treat πνεῦμα ἅγιον as a proper name, like the anarthrous Κύριος or θεός. But observation shews that the anarthrous form usually occurs just where a proper name would be inappropriate, i.e. in places where the Spirit is regarded in its operations rather than in its essential life, e.g. in phrases such as πνεύματος ἁγίου

[1] Prepositional phrase.

[2] J. H. Moulton, *Prolegg.*, p. 82.

πλησθῆναι, πνεῦμα ἅγιον διδόναι or λαμβάνειν; whereas when any personal action or relation is ascribed to the Spirit the article at once reappears, e.g. when the Spirit is said to speak (Mc. xiii. 11, Acts i. 16, x. 10, xiii. 2) or be spoken against (Mc. iii. 29), resisted (Acts vii. 51) or grieved, or when it is coordinated with the Father and the Son (Mt. xxviii. 19, 2 Cor. viii. 13), or described as fulfilling a personal office (Jo. xiv. 26, xv. 26), or performing personal work (Acts xiii. 4, xvi. 6, xv. 28, xx. 23). If there are cases where τὸ πνεῦμα τὸ ἅγιον is used of a gift of the Spirit (e.g. in Acts x. 44 f., xi. 15), the article will be found to be due to the requirements of the construction, or to refer to the preceding context, or (as Blass suggests, *Gr. of the N.T.*, E. tr., p. 149) "to the well-known fact of the [Pentecostal] outpouring."

To convey these finer shades of meaning to the English reader in a version of the N.T. is impossible without the use of paraphrase. In this book πνεῦμα ἅγιον has been in almost every case translated "Holy Spirit" in order to draw the attention of the reader to the absence of the article in the Greek; what is the exact meaning of the anarthrous title must be gathered from the context in which it occurs.

4. Of πνεῦμα used without adjective or article there are 46 instances in the N.T., of which 29 occur in the Epistles of St Paul. Much that has been said about πνεῦμα ἅγιον applies also to πνεῦμα. Thus, to deal first with the Gospels only, whereas τὸ πνεῦμα in Mt. iv. 1, xii. 31, Mc. i. 22, Lc. ii. 27, iv. 1, 14, Jo. i. 32 f., iii. 6, 8, 34, vii. 39[a] is the Spirit considered as a Divine Agent, πνεῦμα in Jo. iii. 5 is the inward and spiritual grace of Baptism, a particular operation of the Spirit, and in Jo. vii. 39[b] the particular effusion of the Spirit which took place on the day of Pentecost. In the Pauline Epistles it is often a point of great difficulty to determine whether the action of

Add. Note P.

the Spirit of God upon the human spirit or the human spirit under the power of the Spirit of God is intended when πνεῦμα is anarthrous. This problem is repeatedly presented to the reader of St Paul in the use of the prepositional phrases ἐν πνεύματι (or πνεύματι simply), κατὰ πνεῦμα, and where πνεῦμα is followed by a defining noun in the genitive (e.g. πνεῦμα υἱοθεσίας, πραΰτητος, σοφίας, ἀποκαλύψεως, σωφροσύνης, and the like). In all such cases the Divine Spirit is at least in the background of the thought, for the spiritual conditions described are not attainable apart from Divine help; and yet it is the condition which is in view rather than the Spirit by whom it is realized. On the whole it is perhaps safe in almost all cases to give the anarthrous πνεῦμα, at least in the Pauline writings, a double reference, placing in the foreground of the thought the human spirit awakened, guided, and inhabited by the Spirit of Christ, but never losing sight of the Power by which the spiritual element in man is what it is and may become increasingly dominant until mortality is swallowed up of life.

Q.

THE HOLY SPIRIT IN JEWISH APOCALYPTIC WRITINGS.

It may be worth while to collect references to the Holy Spirit in this group of writings, in order to shew how far the O.T. conception of the Spirit held its ground in the popular belief of the Jewish people between the cessation of Prophecy and the end of the first century of our era.

1. TESTAMENTS OF THE XII. PATRIARCHS (written in its original form, according to Dr Charles, B.C. 109–106).

Symeon iv. 4 Ἰωσὴφ δὲ ἦν ἀγαθὸς ἀνήρ, καὶ ἔχων πνεῦμα θεοῦ ἐν αὐτῷ. *Jud.* xx. 1, 5 δύο πνεύματα σχολάζουσι τῷ ἀνθρώπῳ, τὸ τῆς ἀληθείας καὶ τὸ τῆς πλάνης...καὶ τὸ πνεῦμα τῆς ἀληθείας κατηγορεῖ πάντων. *Ib.* xxiv. 2 ἀνοιγήσονται ἐπ' αὐτῷ οἱ οὐρανοί, ἐκχέαι πνεῦμα εὐλογίαν πατρὸς ἁγίου· καὶ αὐτὸς ἐκχεεῖ πνεῦμα χάριτος ἐφ' ἡμᾶς [but this is possibly a Christian interpolation, though it is not bracketed by Charles].

2. THE BOOK OF JUBILEES (according to Charles not later than 96 B.C.). *C.* i. 21, 23, "Create in them a clean heart and a holy spirit..." "I shall create in thee a holy spirit." *C.* xxv. 14, "The spirit of righteousness descended into his (Jacob's) mouth." *C.* xxxi. 12, "The spirit of prophecy came down into his (Isaac's) mouth."

3. PSALMS OF SOLOMON xvii. 42 (written, according to Ryle and James, B.C. 70–40. Ps. xvii. 42 ὁ θεὸς κατειργάσατο αὐτὸν (the Messiah) δυνατὸν ἐν πνεύματι ἁγίῳ. Ps. xviii. 8 ἐν σοφίᾳ πνεύματος καὶ δικαιοσύνης καὶ ἰσχύος.

4. APOCALYPSE OF BARUCH (written, according to Charles, A.D. 70 and after). *C.* vii. 2 f., "Lo, suddenly a strong spirit raised me and bore me aloft...and the Spirit restored me to the place where I had been standing before." *C.* xxi. 4, "Thou...hast made firm the height of the heaven by the Spirit." *C.* xxiii. 5, "Thy Spirit is the creator of life."

5. ASCENSION OF ISAIAH. *C.* i. 7, "The Spirit which speaketh in me" (Isaiah); cf. iii. 19, iv. 21, v. 14, vi. 6, 8, 10. *C.* iii. 26, "The Holy Spirit will withdraw from many." *C.* iv. 21, "The Psalms which the angel of the Spirit inspired"; the same phrase "angel of the (Holy) Spirit" is used, apparently in reference to the Holy Spirit, in vii. 23, ix. 36, 39, x. 4, xi. 35; in iii. 16, xi. 4 the angel of the Spirit seems to be identified with Gabriel. This angel of

Add. Note Q.

the Spirit is to be worshipped by men (ix. 36), yet he in his turn worships God (ix. 40). *C.* xi. 40, "Watch ye in the Holy Spirit, in order that ye may receive your garments and thrones and crowns of glory which are laid up in the seventh heaven."

The *Ascension* is a composite document of which the Jewish source belongs according to Charles to the first century A.D. But he places the editor as late as the third century, and allows that the other two sources (iii. 13^6—iv. 18, vi.—xi. 40) were Christian. Thus the book can be used as a guide to contemporary Jewish thought only in part and with great reserve.

R.

THE HOLY SPIRIT IN SOME EARLY CHRISTIAN UNCANONICAL GOSPELS, ACTS, AND APOCALYPSES.

A. Gospel according to the Hebrews.

1. Quoted above, p. 39.
2. *ἄρτι ἔλαβέ με ἡ μήτηρ μου τὸ ἅγιον πνεῦμα ἐν μιᾷ τῶν τριχῶν μου, καὶ ἀπήνεγκέ με εἰς τὸ ὄρος τὸ μέγα Θαβώρ.*
3. *καὶ γὰρ ἐν προφήταις, μετὰ τὸ χρισθῆναι αὐτοὺς ἐν πνεύματι ἁγίῳ, εὑρίσκετο ἐν αὐτοῖς λόγος ἁμαρτίας.*
4. *ἔφη αὐτοῖς Λάβετε, ψηλαφήσατέ με, καὶ ἴδετε ὅτι οὐκ εἰμὶ δαιμόνιον ἀσώματον. καὶ εὐθὺς αὐτοῦ ἥψαντο καὶ ἐπίστευσαν, κραθέντες τῇ σαρκὶ αὐτοῦ καὶ τῷ πνεύματι.*

Gospel according to the Egyptians.

The Lord is represented as teaching His disciples τὸν αὐτὸν εἶναι πατέρα, τὸν αὐτὸν εἶναι υἱόν, τὸν αὐτὸν εἶναι ἅγιον πνεῦμα. Add. Note R.

GOSPEL OF THE EBIONITES.

Quoted above, p. 39.

PROTEVANGELIUM.

14. τὸ γὰρ ἐν αὐτῇ ὂν ἐκ πνεύματός ἐστιν ἁγίου.

24. οὗτος [Symeon] γὰρ ἦν ὁ χρηματισθεὶς ὑπὸ τοῦ ἁγίου πνεύματος.

GOSPEL OF THOMAS.

10. ἀληθῶς πνεῦμα θεοῦ ἐνοικεῖ ἐν τῷ παιδίῳ τούτῳ.

15. ἀνοίξας τὸ στόμα αὐτοῦ ἐλάλει πνεύματι ἁγίῳ.

GOSPEL OF THE NATIVITY OF MARY.

3. Spiritu sancto replebitur [Maria] adhuc ex utero matris.

8. cum enim [Ioseph] uirgam suam attulisset et in cacumine eius columba de caelo ueniens consedisset, liquido omnibus patuit ei uirginem desponsandam fore.

HISTORY OF JOSEPH THE CARPENTER.

1. induam uos uirtute de alto, ac implebo uos Spiritu sancto.

5. dilexi...illam...consilio Spiritus sancti.

6. concepit de Spiritu sancto.

ARABIC GOSPEL OF THE INFANCY.

54. Our Lord at the Baptism was acknowledged by the Father's voice, "praesente Spiritu sancto in forma columbae candidae."

GOSPEL OF NICODEMUS.

ii. 2. εἶδον ὡσεὶ περιστερὰν καὶ τὸ πνεῦμα τὸ ἅγιον ἐπ' αὐτὸν ἐρχόμενον.

GOSPEL OF PSEUDO-MATTHEW.

3. Spiritus sanctus requiescet in ea.

5. Anna [the mother of the Virgin] repleta Spiritu sancto in conspectu omnium dixit &c.

11. quod enim in utero eius est, de Spiritu sancto est.

Add. Note R.

39. cum autem Iesus introisset scholam, ductus Spiritu accepit librum de manu didascali...et...in Spiritu Dei uiui loquebatur tanquam si de fonte uiuo torrens aquae egrederetur et fons plenus semper permaneret.

B. Acts of Barnabas.

2. χάριν λαβὼν πνεύματος ἁγίου διὰ Παύλου καὶ Βαρνάβα καὶ Σίλα...τῶν καὶ βαπτισάντων με ἐν Εἰκονίῳ.

8. πορεύου ἐν τῇ χάριτι τοῦ χριστοῦ, καὶ ἡμεῖς ἐν τῇ δυνάμει τοῦ πνεύματος.

13. κατανυχθέντες δὲ ὑπὸ τοῦ ἁγίου πνεύματος ἔπεσον εἰς τοὺς πόδας αὐτοῦ.

17. ᾧ καὶ πνεῦμα ἅγιον ἐδόθη ἐπὶ τοῦ βαπτίσματος.

Acts of Philip in Greece.

4. ἐξελέξατο ἡμᾶς ὄντας τὸν ἀριθμὸν δώδεκα, πληρώσας ἡμᾶς πνεύματος ἁγίου.

Acts of Thomas.

41. τί ἡμῖν καὶ σοί, σύμβουλε τοῦ ἁγίου πνεύματος;

49. τοῦ δὲ ὕδατος προσενεχθέντος εἶπεν Ἐλθέτω τὰ ὕδατα ἀπὸ τῶν ὑδάτων τῶν ζώντων...ἡ ἀπὸ ἀναπαύσεως ἀποσταλεῖσα ἡμῖν πηγή...ἐλθὲ καὶ σκήνωσον ἐν τοῖς ὕδασι τούτοις, ἵνα τὸ χάρισμα τοῦ ἁγίου πνεύματος τελείως ἐν αὐτοῖς τελειωθῇ.

Martyrdom of Bartholomew.

4. πνεῦμα ἅγιον ἐπελεύσεται ἐπὶ σέ.

Acts of Thaddaeus.

4. ἐβάπτισεν αὐτοὺς εἰς τὸ ὄνομα τοῦ πατρὸς καὶ υἱοῦ καὶ ἁγίου πνεύματος, χρίσας αυτοὺς τὸ ἅγιον μύρον.

Acts of John.

6. τὸ δὲ ἅγιον πνεῦμα φαιδρότερον αὐτὸν ἐδείκνυ αὐτοῖς.

9. τὸ ἐν αὐτῷ φάρμακον τῷ ἁγίῳ σου πνεύματι

συγκέρασον καὶ ποίησον αὐτὸ πόμα ζωῆς καὶ σωτηρίας.

LEUCIAN ACTS OF JOHN (ed. James).

11. δόξα σοί, πνεῦμα ἅγιον· δόξα σου τῇ δόξῃ.

13. ὁ σταυρὸς οὗτος ὁ τοῦ φωτὸς ποτὲ μὲν λόγος καλεῖται ὑπ' ἐμοῦ δι' ὑμᾶς...ποτὲ υἱός, ποτὲ πατήρ, ποτὲ πνεῦμα.

C. APOCALYPSE OF PAUL (cf. *Visio Pauli*, ed. James).

8, 10, 14. καὶ ἰδοὺ τὸ πνεῦμα [τοῦ θεοῦ] πρὸς αὐτούς (Spiritus [dei] processit in occursum eis).

11. καὶ ἐγενόμην ἐν πνεύματι ἁγίῳ.

14. et Spiritus similiter ait, Ego sum Spiritus uiuificationis adspirans in eam [animam].

16. et Spiritus similiter ait, Ego sum Spiritus qui inhabitabam in eam ex quo facta est; in se autem noui, et non est secuta meam uoluntatem.

45. ἔλαβέν με ἐν ῥιπῇ τοῦ πνεύματος (impetu Spiritus sancti), καὶ εἰσήγαγέν εἰς τὸν παράδεισον...καὶ ἰδοὺ ἐκεῖ δένδρον παμμεγέθη ὡραῖον, ἐν ᾧ ἐπανεπαύσατο τὸ πνεῦμα τὸ ἅγιον (Spiritus autem Dei requiescebat super arborem illam), κτλ.

It will be seen from these extracts that, with the exception of some very early traditions in the Gospel according to the Hebrews, these documents contain nothing that is not substantially present in the N.T., or might have been derived from it by the exercise of the writer's imagination, or by a misconception of its teaching (G. acc. to the Egyptians, Leucian Acts of John).

Add. Note S.

S.

READINGS OF CODEX BEZAE WHICH BEAR UPON THE SUBJECT OF THIS BOOK.

Mt. iii. 16 *εἶδεν πνεῦμα καταβαίνοντα ἐκ τοῦ οὐρανοῦ ὡς περιστερὰν καὶ ἐρχόμενον εἰς* (D^b *ἐπ'*) *αὐτόν.*

„ xxviii. 19 *πορεύεσθε νῦν μαθητεύσατε πάντα τὰ ἔθνη βαπτίσαντες αὐτούς κτλ.*

Mc. i. 7 f. *ἐγὼ μὲν ὑμᾶς βαπτίζω ἐν ὕδατι, ἔρχεται δὲ ὀπίσω μου ὁ ἰσχυρότερός μου οὗ οὐχ ἱκανὸς κτλ...καὶ αὐτὸς ὑμᾶς βαπτίζει ἐν πνεύματι ἁγίῳ.*

„ „ 10 *εἶδεν ἠνοιγμένους τοὺς οὐρανούς.*

„ „ 12 *τὸ πνεῦμα τὸ ἅγιον ἐκβάλλει αὐτόν.*

„ iii. 29 *ὃς ἂν δέ τις βλασφημήσῃ τὸ πνεῦμα τὸ ἅγιον οὐκ ἔχει ἄφεσιν* ‸ *ἀλλὰ ἔνοχός ἐστιν αἰωνίου ἁμαρτίας.*

Lc. i. 67 *εἶπεν* (for *ἐπροφήτευσεν λέγων*).

„ ii. 26 *κεχρηματισμένος δὲ ἦν...*

„ iii. 22 *υἱός μου εἶ σύ· ἐγὼ σήμερον γεγέννηκά σε.*

„ iv. 33 *πνεῦμα δαιμόνιον ἀκάθαρτον.*

„ ix. 55 *καὶ εἶπεν Οὐκ οἴδατε ποίου πνεύματός ἐστε.*

„ x. 20 *δαιμόνια* (for *πνεύματα*).

„ xi. 13 *ἀγαθὸν δόμα* (for *πνεῦμα ἅγιον*).

„ xiii. 11 *γυνὴ ἐν ἀσθενείᾳ ἦν πνεύματος.*

„ xxiv. 37 *ἐδόκουν φάντασμα θεωρεῖν.*

„ „ 49 *καὶ ἐγὼ* ‸ *ἀποστέλλω τὴν ἐπαγγελίαν μου ἐφ' ὑμᾶς.*

Jo. iii. 34[1] *οὐ γὰρ ἐκ μέτρου δίδωσιν ὁ θεὸς τὸ πνεῦμα.*

„ vii. 39 *οὔπω γὰρ ἦν τὸ πνεῦμα* (+*τὸ* D^b) *ἅγιον ἐπ' αὐτοῖς* (D^b *αὐτούς*).

„ xi. 33 *ἐταράχθη τῷ πνεύματι ὡς ἐμβριμούμενος* (*sic*).

„ xiv. 16 *ἵνα μένῃ εἰς τὸν αἰῶνα μεθ' ὑμῶν.*

„ „ 26 *ὃ πέμψει ὁ πατήρ μου.*

[1] Cod. Bezae wants Jo. i. 6 to iii. 26.

Jo. xv. 26 ὃν ἐγὼ πέμπω ὑμῖν παρὰ τοῦ πατρός μου...ὃ παρὰ τοῦ πατρός μου ἐκπορεύεται.
„ xvi. 13 ὅσα ἀκούσει λαλήσει.
„ xx. 21 κἀγὼ ἀποστέλλω (D*) ὑμᾶς.
„ „ 22 ἐνεφύσησεν αὐτοῖς.
Acts i. 5 ὑμεῖς δὲ ἐν πνεύματι ἁγίῳ βαπτισθήσεσθε καὶ ὃ μέλλετε λαμβάνειν (D*) οὐ μετὰ πολλὰς ταύτας ἡμέρας ἕως τῆς πεντηκοστῆς (D*).
„ ii. 1 καὶ ἐγένετο ἐν ταῖς ἡμέραις ἐκείναις τοῦ συνπληροῦσθαι τὴν ἡμέραν τῆς πεντηκοστῆς, ὄντων αὐτῶν πάντων ἐπὶ τὸ αὐτό.
„ „ 47 πρὸς ὅλον τὸν κόσμον.
„ „ „ ἐπὶ τὸ αὐτὸ ἐν τῇ ἐκκλησίᾳ.
„ iv. 24 οἱ δὲ ἀκούσαντες καὶ ἐπιγνόντες τὴν τοῦ θεοῦ ἐνέργειαν.
„ v. 9 πειράσαι τὸ πνεῦμα τοῦ κυρίου.
„ vi. 10 οὐκ ἴσχυον ἀντιστῆναι τῇ σοφίᾳ καὶ τῷ πνεύματι τῶ ἁγίῳ ᾧ ἐλάλει· διὰ τὸ ἐλέγχεσθαι αὐτοὺς ὑπ' (ἐπ' D*) αὐτοῦ μετὰ πάσης παρρησίας.
„ „ 11 μὴ δυνάμενοι οὖν ἀντοφθαλμεῖν τῇ ἀληθείᾳ τότε ὑπέβαλον κτλ.
„ viii. 17 δίδοται τὸ πνεῦμα τὸ ἅγιον.
„ xi. 17 κωλῦσαι τὸν θεόν, τοῦ μὴ δοῦναι αὐτοῖς πνεῦμα ἅγιον πιστεύσασιν ἐπ' αὐτῷ.
„ xv. 29 εὖ πράξετε, φερόμενοι ἐν τῷ ἁγίῳ πνεύματι.
„ „ 32 προφῆται ὄντες πλήρεις πνεύματος ἁγίου.
„ xix. 1 θέλοντος δὲ τοῦ Παύλου κατὰ τὴν ἰδίαν βουλὴν πορεύεσθαι εἰς Ἱεροσόλυμα, εἶπεν αὐτῷ τὸ πνεῦμα ὑποστρέφειν εἰς τὴν Ἀσίαν. διελθὼν δὲ τὰ ἀνωτερικὰ μέρη ἔρχεται εἰς Ἔφεσον καὶ εὑρὼν κτλ.
„ xx. 23, 28 τὸ ἅγιον πνεῦμα (for τὸ πν. τὸ ἅγιον).

Codex Bezae wants viii. 29 Φιλίππου to x. 14, and fails us from Acts xxii. 29 to the end of the book.

Ueni Creator Spiritus,
mentes tuorum uisita,
imple superna gratia
quae tu creasti pectora.

qui Paraclitus diceris,
donum Dei altissimi,
fons uiuus, ignis, caritas,
et spiritalis unctio.

tu septiformis munere,
dextrae Dei tu digitus,
tu rite promissum Patris
sermone ditans guttura,

accende lumen sensibus,
infunde amorem cordibus
infirma nostri corporis
uirtute firmans perpetim.

hostem repellas longius,
pacemque dones protinus;
ductore sic te praeuio
uitemus omne noxium.

per te sciamus da Patrem
noscamus atque Filium,
te utriusque Spiritum
credamus omni tempore.

sit laus Patri cum Filio,
sancto simul Paraclito;
nobisque mittat Filius
charisma sancti Spiritus.

INDICES

In the first of these indices only the more important references are included, chiefly those to passages discussed in this book.

The third index is limited to matters incidentally mentioned. The reader will find that the titles of the chapters, the headlines of the right-hand pages, and the marginal references are a sufficient guide to the chief subjects of the book.

I.

II.

III.